John M. Belohlavek

University of Nebraska Press : Lincoln & London

The Foreign Policy

of Andrew Jackson

"Let the Eagle Soar!"

Material in the following chapters
has previously been published in
different form: Chapter 2 in
"Let the Eagle Soar!: Democratic
Constraints on the Foreign Policy
of Andrew Jackson," *Presidential
Studies Quarterly*, Winter 1980,
pp. 36–50; Chapter 6 in "Andrew
Jackson and the Malaysian Pirates,"
Tennessee Historical Quarterly,
Spring 1977, pp. 19–29; Chapter 8
in "The Philadelphian and the
Canal," *Pennsylvania Magazine
of History and Biography*, October
1980, pp. 450–61.

The paper in this book meets the
guidelines for permanence and
durability of the Committee on
Production Guidelines for Book
Longevity of the Council on
Library Resources.

Library of Congress Cataloging
in Publication Data

Belohlavek, John M.
Let the eagle soar!

Bibliography: p.
Includes index.
1. United States – Foreign rela-
tions – 1829-1837. 2. Jackson,
Andrew, 1767-1845.   I. Title.
E384.8.B44   1985
327.73   85-1007
ISBN 0-8032-1187-2

Publication of this book was
aided by a grant from the
Andrew W. Mellon Foundation.

For Susan

Contents

Acknowledgments

Too many years ago, in my boyhood, I had my first real exposure to Andrew Jackson in the unforgettable lyrics of a Johnny Horton song about the Battle of New Orleans. Of course I had heard of "Old Hickory" in junior high school: the teacher had painted a rather pedestrian portrait of a president who was the mystical hero of the "common people" and had instituted something called the "spoils system." Horton's lyric, however, was about frontiersmen roughing up the British—the kind of stuff that would drive a curious boy to a library in search of more information.

My interest in Jackson grew, despite the reality that the years have not been terribly kind to the General. Research in social, labor, Indian, and political history raised serious questions about his commitment to the plain folk (and their commitment to him). Not surprisingly, as an undergraduate and then graduate student, my regard for Jackson ebbed and flowed with each new wave of scholarship. But through it all, I have continually found him to be fascinating and elusive, complex in his simplicity or perhaps simple in his complexity.

Two men have played major roles in influencing my views of the old General and stimulating my interest in the era—Robert Remini and Edward Pessen. While I sometimes find myself in disagreement with them, each has left his mark. Both have pointed to the need for a study of Jacksonian foreign policy, a void I hope this book will fill.

In pursuing this goal, I have been ably assisted and encouraged by colleagues and friends who have added to the evolution of the manuscript at various stages of research, organization, and writing. Roger R.

Trask, Harvey Nelsen, George Mayer, and Ben Procter painstakingly read an entire draft and acted as (generally) friendly critics. Gary Mormino, Jim Swanson, David Powell, and Jim Ricci read particular chapters and delighted in pointing out my errors in grammar.

Special thanks are in order to the staffs of the manuscript room at the Library of Congress and the microfilm and reading rooms at the National Archives; their cooperation facilitated my research and reduced the number of headaches. At the University of South Florida, the staffs of the interlibrary loan office and Florida Historical Collections (especially Jay Dobkin and Paul Camp) generously provided materials, research space, and a readily available microfilm reader. Research assistants at the Maryland Historical Society, the New York Public Library, and the Historical Society of Pennsylvania have provided invaluable aid in examining special collections.

The project received strong sideline support from Nat Jobe (the legendary "Sage of St. Paul"), Ray Arsenault, David Carr, and Roy Van Neste. My sister, Judy, kindly provided comfortable accommodations and jelly doughnuts during my research trips to Washington, D.C.

It would have been impossible to spend those long hours with Old Hickory, however, without the patience, love, and understanding of my long-suffering wife, Susan, who kept the encouragement and the bourbon flowing. This is for her.

Introduction

As the rabble ran amuck, grinding mud deep into the carpets, shattering glasses, breaking furniture, and staining drapes with good Kentucky bourbon, the capital's dowager empresses and gentlemen of property and standing heaved a collective sigh of apprehension and disgust. Andrew Jackson's Democracy had entered the White House. In March 1829, in the chair earlier occupied by Washington, Jefferson, and Madison, sat a tough-talking westerner who was deadly with both word and weapon. This outsider brought with him little formal education, no diplomatic experience, minimal congressional service, and a promise to reform what he perceived as a corrupt system. Given the nation's domestic problems, the General's enthusiastic buckskin-clad supporters no doubt would have been astonished to learn that their hero would lavish a substantial amount of his attention on foreign affairs.

A crisis in government existed in the city on the Potomac long before Jackson's arrival. In fact, the eight years of Old Hickory's presidency witnessed the resuscitation of an executive office that had been almost comatose since the departure of Jefferson in 1809. Jackson's vigorous approach to his duties, his strong stand for the Constitution and "the people," have earned him high rankings from historians. Yet these scholars generally view the positive accomplishments of the Tennesseean from the perspective of his domestic programs: his aggressive Indian removal policy, crushing veto of the Second Bank of the United States, and outspoken defense of the Union in the nullification crisis with South Carolina. Rarely is Jackson's foreign policy prominently discussed or analyzed—in part, because it has been the traditional view of both political scientists and historians that domestic issues dominated the national scene in the post–Monroe Doctrine nineteenth century. Frequently, when a president exercised his prerogatives in foreign affairs, he was embarrassed by congressional opposition or defeat, often from within his own party. To many scholars, Jackson personifies this parochial executive pattern. According to this view, his myopic vision might clear long enough for him to bluster about American rights or American honor at a moment of crisis, but usually he exhibited little interest or, lacking a foreign policy, placed the responsibility for daily affairs in the hands of the Secretary of State.[1]

There are serious problems with this interpretation. It is certainly arguable that the advent of the Jacksonians portended a "restoration" of the agrarian values of the Jeffersonian republic. The General was a pragmatic man, however, not an ideologue. His nirvana could be found not on an eighteenth-century farm but in the accommodation of republican ideals with the dynamic growth that American agriculture and business experienced in the first half of the nineteenth century. As a moderate states' rights man, he saw no great conflict between promoting state prerogatives on issues such as Indian removal, banking, and internal improvements; railing nationalistically—to the point of threatening civil war—against nullification and disunion; and embarking on an aggressive, bold, and imaginative foreign policy. The Tennesseean eagerly pursued a policy of promoting commercial expansion, demanding worldwide respect for the American flag, restoring American prestige and national honor, and fostering territorial growth. Jackson believed in "Manifest Destiny" decades before the term was coined, and championed control of the continent to the Pacific Ocean. Accordingly, he was not the enemy of American business, as many contemporaries and some historians have portrayed him. Rather he engendered and nurtured the advancement of American commerce through his diplomatic missions, treaties with various foreign nations, and revitalization of the American navy.

The Jackson legend emerged from the fog-shrouded Louisiana morning of January 8, 1815, where neither the British nor American forces gathered outside New Orleans were aware that diplomats had ended the War of 1812 two weeks earlier at Ghent, Belgium. In the bloody battle that ensued, General Andrew Jackson's frontiersmen, pirates, blacks, Indians, and city folk hurled back the finest of Britain's military machine. It was cannon, not the legendary accuracy of American musketry, that won the day; but Americans, eager to trumpet the triumph of Western democratic republicanism over decadent European monarchism, did not allow the actual reasons for military success to compromise the illusion of victory by citizen soldiers led by a new Cincinnatus. The smoke had barely cleared and the refrain of the Scottish pipes still lingered in the marshes as Americans rushed to declare Andrew Jackson of Tennessee their newest hero. Balladeers were singing his glory even before Old Hickory embellished his reputation with a controversial invasion of Spanish Florida in 1818, ostensibly in pursuit of marauding Indians and defiant escaped slaves. Under fire from the administration of James Monroe, Jackson retired from the battlefield in 1821 to govern Florida briefly, before entering the United States Senate from Tennessee in 1823. By this time his presidential star was rapidly ascending.

Symbiotically, the American eagle—freed from the diplomatic and economic constraints of the Napoleonic Wars—also began to soar. Gone were the impressment of American sailors, the restrictive British Orders in Council, and the French Berlin and Milan Decrees that had compromised Yankee commerce and honor. A war of vindication had been fought between 1812 and 1815, and although the Americans had not defeated Great Britain, this "second war for independence" demonstrated that the former colonials would stand fast to defend their rights.

The War of 1812 did more than produce a new frontier hero. Americans became painfully aware of their economic dependence upon Europe and moved quickly to rectify that imbalance. In 1816, led by such former "War Hawks" as Speaker of the House Henry Clay of Kentucky and Congressman (soon to be Secretary of War) John C. Calhoun of Carolina, Congress endorsed a second Bank of the United States and a protective tariff to guard infant industries against foreign competition. While this "American System" smacked of Hamiltonian wine in Jeffersonian bottles, it reflected the progressive thinking of the young Democratic-Republicans who discovered that nationalistic programs might have a place in an expanding, developing country. A move toward economic self-sufficiency or independence could prevent the United States from becoming embroiled in another unwanted war.

American politicians and merchants adopted an opportunistic attitude toward European conflict. Yankee commerce in 1790 showed a modest $20 million in exports and $22 million in imports. As the Wars of the French Revolution became increasingly heated, American sail assumed a greater role in the neutral carrying trade, reaching $60 million in 1806. In addition, American flour, rice, wheat, corn, tobacco, and cotton exports reached $42 million prior to the War of 1812. Imports, largely of English and German textiles and manufactured goods, climbed to $37 million during the same period. But following the declaration of war in June 1812, the economy quickly collapsed. The charter of the first Bank of the United States had expired in 1811, providing no central resource for government financing during the conflict. Nascent American industry staggered; agriculture suffered; fishing foundered. In 1814, exports plummeted to $7 million and imports to $12 million. Not surprisingly, as the economic shock waves receded in 1815, government leaders sought to apply balm to festering wounds.

After the peace at Ghent and the final crushing of Napoleon at Waterloo, American ports became centers of frenzied activity. The Europeans, so long denied American cotton, grains, and lumber, imported these items at a record pace. By 1818 the total reached $74 million, including $31 million to England and $9 million to France. The German states, the Iberian peninsula, the Netherlands, the East and West Indies, China, and South America consumed the remainder of American exports. Although New York remained preeminent as the nation's major port, the dominance of cotton in the export trade ($31 million) was visible in the rise of New Orleans, Charleston, and Savannah as export centers, surpassing Boston and Philadelphia.

At the same time, the import trade also skyrocketed, reaching $102 million in 1818. Americans eagerly bought the foreign goods that had been absent so long from their markets, and the British were more than willing to flood the country with their stockpiles. The merchants of England—contemptuously called "a nation of shopkeepers" by Napoleon—once again demonstrated their business acumen: by attacking the American market they often took an immediate loss but succeeded in sharply reducing their inventories of India textiles, metal products, glass, and hats—and almost crushing competing American infant industries. Congress responded with a modest (20 percent) tariff in 1816, but European goods continued to glut the market. Duties, raised to 30 percent in 1824, grew to an oppressive 50 percent in 1828 in the almost desperate attempt to stop the surge.

The tariff, combined with the shattering Panic of 1819, cooled the overheated economy. High imports that drained American specie, erratic and inflationary policies of the Bank of the United States, excessive issues of paper money, and speculation and overextension in land all linked to produce economic collapse. The demand for American goods promoted a land boom, especially in the South and West. Fueled by easily available funds provided by the national and state banks, and hopeful of ever-increasing prices, farmers planted additional crops on mortgaged lands. The bubble burst in the fall of 1818 when the bottom dropped out of the cotton market. Anguished agrarians blamed the English and the bankers, but certainly not themselves, for the crisis.

American commerce stagnated through the decade of the 1820s. A variety of factors aggravated the malaise: increased demands on the domestic market, European tariffs in response to higher American duties, resumption of normal trade patterns after the explosion between 1815 and 1819, and lack of cheap and efficient internal transportation to facilitate the exchange of goods. This is not to suggest that trade receded to pre–War of 1812 levels, but commerce with the major markets in Europe, especially Great Britain, did suffer.

The advent to power of the Jacksonians in 1829 ushered in a resurgence in American commerce. Old Hickory reduced the tariff in 1832 but continued to provide protection for the vital cotton, woolen, and iron industries. Trade problems with Great Britain over the West Indies were resolved by treaty in 1830; partial shipping reciprocity, begun in 1815, was expanded to full reciprocity under Jackson. Surpluses in cotton and grains accompanied increased European demand for these products in the 1830s. Americans made the exchange easier by building an extensive canal system and maximizing the use of the rivers via the technology of steam.

By 1836, exports rose to $107 million and imports to $190 million. Cotton had already become king, constituting almost two-thirds of the exports. Great Britain remained America's major trading partner, while

France and other Continental nations made up the bulk of the remaining trade. Despite energetic efforts by the Jacksonians to develop new markets in the Middle East, the Far East, and Latin America, the dollar amount of this commerce formed only a small fraction of the European trade.

Then Jacksonian prosperity was swept away by the Panic of 1837. Abnormally high imports, land speculation, and unsound banking practices in the United States merged with the shifting patterns of specie shipment and international trade in Great Britain to initiate the depression. Yet in these ebb-and-flow cycles of the American economy, the Jackson presidency represented a high-water mark.

The extent to which the President and his economic and foreign policies were responsible for this prosperity is, of course, open to debate. Most historians would likely agree that the reduction of the tariff in 1832 was a wise move. There would be less concurrence, however, on the General's decision to veto the recharter of the Bank of the United States in 1832. The Bank's expiration in 1836 and the earlier placement of government funds in the pro-Jacksonian (and sometimes marginal) "pet banks" have been perceived by some scholars as contributing to the Panic of 1837. But in spite of Jackson's questionable banking policy, he made signal contributions in other areas. For example, in an age in which American economic well-being depended on international trade, Jackson promoted commerce through his steadfast pursuit of commercial treaties and ancillary development of the diplomatic and consular corps.

During the presidency of George Washington, American ministers were present in Great Britain, France, Spain, the Netherlands, and Portugal. During the succeeding administration of John Adams, ties were established with Russia and Sweden. The United States hesitated to move from this largely European base for almost a quarter-century. Following the War of 1812, however, the Americans sought to secure and expand their North American borders. James Monroe (with the steady hand of John Quincy Adams in the State Department) presided over the negotiated disarmament of the Great Lakes and a Canadian boundary with Great Britain, the acquisition of the Floridas from Spain, and the establishment of a claim to a latitude of 55 degrees in the Northwest from Russia.

At the same time, it became apparent that Latin America, in revolt against Spain, was turning to Great Britain for trade and political inspiration. Additional British influence in the Western Hemisphere was unacceptable to the United States and conflicted with American desires for commercial hegemony and the vision of a hemisphere comprising democratic republics based on the American model. The Monroe Doctrine in 1823 and the ill-fated attempt of John Quincy Adams administration to participate in a Pan-American conference (the Panama Congress) in 1826 offer examples of Washington's efforts to minimize European involvement in what Americans hoped would be a Yankee sphere of influence. Both Monroe and Adams courted the affections of the newly independent Latin nations. They granted recognition to Colombia, Mexico, Chile, Peru, Brazil, Buenos Aires, and the Central American Republic in the 1820s, dispatching representatives to extend the hand of Yankee friendship.

Concurrently, the evolution of the consular service provided a major enhancement to the American commercial presence. George Washington assumed the initiative with the appointment of over thirty consuls scattered about the globe. Congress assisted by providing for the formal organization and instruction of the consular service in 1792. Consuls aided in the protection of Americans and their property. Acting as arbiters, they settled disputes between seamen and their masters and took particular care of maritime interests. Consuls also served as active commercial agents, gathering information and examining opportunities for trade expansion. Their functions included collecting revenues and garnering duties on imports and tonnage; in fact, their compensation came from these fees and from private business ventures. This system proved financially inadequate for most agents, however; it was difficult for consuls to maintain their social standing and influence on such a limited income. As a result, some agents charged exorbitant fees; others falsified papers. By 1834 over 150 agents served in as many ports, but almost all had become commission merchants, motivated by greed and self-interest.

The Jacksonians sought to both expand and reform the consular service. The faults inherent in the system, the occupation of some outposts by adventurers and ne'er-do-wells, and the hazardous climates of many cities prompted a close scrutiny of the entire operation by the

State Department. Secretaries of State Martin Van Buren and Edward Livingston conducted lengthy investigations of the service during Jackson's first administration. In 1831, Livingston specifically urged a salary base for the agents as a mandatory reform. Unfortunately, an inert Congress never enacted his recommendations. The system would not be modified to provide for a salary structure until 1856.

Jackson effectively utilized the expanded consular service, special agents, and regularly appointed ministers and chargés to build commercial bridges with Latin America, as well as the Middle East and Far East. In many cases he discovered, as other presidents had before him, that His Majesty's navy and merchant marine posed the most serious obstacle to establishing harmonious relations and commercial ties with new markets. American trade in 1821 exceeded $80 million, but was only $4 million with Latin America and $8 million with the Far East. In both areas the Union Jack trimmed Yankee sails. Old Hickory sought to close this gap. His agents established bonds of good will (Venezuela, Peru-Bolivia, Turkey, Siam, and Muscat) and negotiated commercial treaties (Chile, Mexico, Great Britain, and France) around the globe. While some of these markets did not bear fruit rapidly, the pacts indicated the General's awareness and his willingness to seek out new partners to supplement or substitute for the sometimes unreliable Europeans.

The period 1815–29 saw dramatic changes in the course of American commerce and diplomacy. The United States emerged from the War of 1812 with a new-found confidence and self-respect, epitomized by Jackson. Americans realized the need for both greater self-sufficiency and additional markets for their agricultural goods. Simultaneously, a vision emerged suggesting that the United States was endowed with a democratic mission in the Western Hemisphere.

Whether the nation sought to extend these principles actively or passively remains open for debate. The territorial expansion, the negotiation of new commercial treaties, and the flirtation of the national government with entangling alliances in Latin America evidenced an emerging United States capable of exerting greater influence—through her agricultural wealth and naval might—than ever before. The missing ingredient had been a chief executive with the popular, political, and legislative support to embrace the worldwide destiny of a growing America. Andrew Jackson would prove to be that man.[2]

What motivated the President in his foreign policy decisions? The answers seem to be nationalism and economics. Jackson marched to the drumbeat of rhetoric that sounded like a combination of George Washington and John Jacob Astor. Old Hickory desperately wanted the United States to achieve equal status and respect among the first families of world powers. Perhaps his motives were personal—a search for glory and the vindication of his honor. More than likely they were a blend of individual ego and the raw patriotism derived from two wars against Great Britain, a provocative encounter with Spain (in Florida), and steady border conflict with the Indians. Ego and patriotism combined conveniently with economic *Real-politik*. Jackson viewed any slights to the American flag or attacks upon American honor as violations against himself—and acted accordingly. He repeatedly stated the maxim, "Ask nothing that is not clearly right and submit to nothing that is wrong."[3]

While his administration encouraged democracy within Latin America, the chief executive firmly believed that the United States should maintain a "no entangling alliances" posture and that a neutral stance would insure national growth. As he told Congress in December 1832, "[This policy] is daily producing its beneficial effect in the respect shown to our flag, the protection of our citizens and their property abroad, and in the increase of our navigation and the extension of our mercantile operations."[4] Jackson perceived that for the United States— a nation of twelve million—rich in commodities and teetering on the brink of an industrial revolution, an intimate link existed between agriculture, manufacturing, internal improvements, and foreign trade. Reflecting the frugality of republican economic philosophy, Jackson was determined to extinguish the national debt. Success hinged upon continued United States prosperity and international trade.

Old Hickory's annual messages to Congress provide special insight into his views on foreign affairs. Usually the segment devoted to foreign relations consumes fully a third and sometimes as much as half of his addresses. The President, by content and tone, made his priorities and views very clear. Europe, the Old World with which Jackson had an approach/avoidance conflict, consumed most American exports, and Jackson sought the respect (for himself and the nation) of the governments in London, Paris, and Madrid. Consequently, he devoted most of the space in his messages to discussions of European relations and problems. Jackson spoke in glowing terms of Great Britain (a nation "alike distinguished in war and peace"), and of old ally France. He expressed deep concern over the West Indian trade with England, the "lucrative" commerce with France, and the valuable exchange of goods with Spanish Cuba and Puerto Rico.[5]

With the possible exception of Mexico, Latin America became a secondary concern. Good relations south of the border were imperative, not only for trade purposes but also because of border disputes and Jackson's desire for Texas. But although drawn by the siren song of commerce, the President was repulsed by the constant political turmoil in Latin America that disrupted both trade and diplomatic ties, and his accompanying view of the Latin character bordered on disdain. Occasionally, however, he would wax eloquent on the potential of the Southern Hemisphere. In 1831 he exuberantly extolled the benefits of the contemplated "magnificent project," an Atlantic-to-Pacific ship canal in Central America, that would make trade with the region of "the greatest importance."[6]

Africa, Asia, and the remainder of the world concerned the Tennesseean only as additional trade opportunities opened in these areas, or some depredation or assault upon a United States ship or citizen had to be avenged.

The advance of commerce, the major thrust of Jacksonian foreign policy, was virtually inseparable from the promotion and defense of American nationalism. Seeking commercial advantages in the old markets of Europe and the newer markets of Latin America and the Middle and Far East often exposed Old Glory to abuse and attack. Old Hickory's strident advocacy of American nationalism appears in his views on merchant claims, violations of rights of American vessels, and territorial expansion. From the outset of his administration, Jackson sought to reassure farmers, businessmen, and shipowners of his commitment to American rights by insisting upon the payment of the many claims owed Americans from recurring maritime violations, particularly by European interests. Jackson pushed for a powerful navy as a necessity to convince nations large and small of his commitment to defend Yankee sail and threaten recalcitrant debtors.[7]

The President generally conducted foreign affairs with a patience that challenges his combative image. Sometimes, however, he yielded to his saber-rattling ardor. The clearest example occurred during the frustrating wait for the French to fulfill the provisions of their 1831 treaty with the United States by paying their claims; Old Hickory's expressions of "regret" and "disappointment" in 1833 soon changed to ringing charges of "injustice," discussion of a "stain on the national honor," and a call for reprisals. His nationalism was also reflected in an ardent desire for the annexation of Texas (as far as the Pacific coast) to secure United States borders and add to the nation's riches."[8] As the "symbol for an age," Jackson moved energetically to both proffer and accept challenges to the manhood of the young republic.

Chapter 1

The Jacksonian Vision: The Formative Years

The Jacksonian image of America has its roots deep in the soil of the frontier. As historian Robert Remini has emphasized, Old Hickory envisioned an expanding United States, a dream that melded with his own goals and presented him with opportunities for personal greatness. Born in the backcountry of Carolina in 1767, the teenage Jackson was severely wounded and imprisoned during his participation in the American Revolution. His father had died before his birth; the tragic loss of his mother and both his brothers during the war left Jackson virtually alone. Abandoning the plea of his departed mother to become a man of the cloth, the ambitious youth opted instead for the law. Admitted by the age of twenty-one to the bar in North Carolina, he quickly moved to the promising western district that would soon become the state of Tennessee. Tall, slim, with deep blue eyes and reddish hair that curled over his forehead to cover a British saber scar, Jackson displayed an unmistakable aura of energy. In little more than a decade he had become a force to be reckoned with on the turbulent frontier: planter, land speculator, militia officer, lawyer, and horseman par excellence. The perceptive young barrister had also made the right contacts, insuring himself a proper place in the social and political structure of the brawling new state. Notwithstanding his controversial marriage to the recently divorced and socially prominent Rachel Donelson, an alliance with powerful politico William Blount stabilized Jackson's position in the community. His mentor's notions of strong personal loyalty and desire for American expansion (often for personal or selfish motives) undoubtedly influenced the younger man.[1]

In Jackson's thought, however, idealism blended with and sometimes transcended the pragmatism of frontier politics. While he was hardly a philosopher of the Jeffersonian stripe, the Tennesseean was surrounded in his formative years by the thoughts of founding fathers Madison and Washington, and must surely have gleaned something from them. In 1788, Madison had conceptualized the link between commercial and landed empire in the *Federalist* No. 10: "Extend the sphere both commercially and territorially and you will make it less probable that a majority of the whole will have a common motive to invade the rights of other citizens." He postulated that growth of the American empire could save liberty and republicanism from destruction by factionalism.

While it is questionable that the youthful Jackson read the *Federalist Papers*, the adult Jackson did expand upon Madison's tenets. In a practical sense he was undoubtedly even more impressed with Madison's ideas about the West. At one point Madison likened the possible loss of the Mississippi River to treason on the part of the central government and told James Monroe, "The use of the Mississippi is given by nature to our western country, and no power on earth can take it from them." What Madison feared almost transpired in the Jay-Gardoqui Treaty of 1786 with Spain, in which the central government would have compromised the westerners' use of the vital river in exchange for commercial concessions to benefit eastern merchants and farmers. Although the southern states defeated this agreement in Congress, the perceived betrayal of the West promoted there a marked distrust of eastern capitalists.[2]

Washington's Farewell Address of September 1796 very likely influenced Jackson as well. This classic statement of empire suggested a future United States that would dominate the North American continent while its commerce reached out (without entangling alliances) to the entire globe. When Jackson became first a congressman (in 1796–97) and then a senator (in 1797–98, after the Senate dismissed Tennessee's William Blount over an alleged plot to bring the British into Spanish Florida), he perceived the need to combine western expansion with the advancement of eastern commercial interests. He now had the opportunity to observe the successes and frustrations of American diplomacy firsthand. Like many frontiersmen, Jackson distrusted the federal government, which always seemed to place eastern mercantile interests ahead of those of the frontier. While he approved the Farewell Address, the Tennesseean deeply resented Washington's pro-British foreign policy, inactivity in securing the frontier from Indian attack, and (amazingly) political patronage policies. In particular, the machinations of nascent party politics proved genuinely offensive to him. After witnessing the infighting over the Quasi-War with France and the Alien and Sedition Acts, the young senator resigned his seat in disgust to return to a judgeship in Nashville.[3]

Over the next quarter-century the ideas of the founding fathers regarding Amercan expansion and commerce seemed to be vindicated, and Andrew Jackson played an important role. Thomas Jefferson defended American commerce and honor (and extended the power of the presidency in foreign affairs) by battling the Barbary pirates. His purchase of Louisiana, unsuccessful attempts to obtain Florida, and dispatch of the Lewis and Clark expedition all reflected increased American interest in territorial expansion. The inability of the Madison administration to defend the nation's maritime interests, and thus its national honor, placed the United States in the embarrassing position of going to war against the British in 1812. Some historians claim that a compatible desire for the extension of United States territory into Canada and Florida prompted the conflict.

Although the War of 1812 produced no winners, it certainly enhanced the international position of the young republic. In the aftermath of the contest, the United States arranged a joint claim, with Great Britain, to the Oregon country; acquired Florida from Spain by the Transcontinental Treaty of 1819; and in 1823 pronounced the Monroe Doctrine, the cornerstone of United States policy in Western Hemispheric affairs.

Jackson participated, of course, as the leading military figure in the war with England, first as the victor over the Creek Indians in the Southwest and then as the "Hero of New Orleans" in January 1815. His bold, and questionable, invasion of Florida in the spring of 1818 in pursuit of Indian raiders further enhanced his reputation. In the course of that assault, Jackson destroyed Spanish property and executed two British subjects. When a proposal to censure him surfaced in James Monroe's cabinet, Secretary of State John Quincy Adams conducted a lively defense of the over-eager General; the perceptive Adams realized that Old Hickory's actions would open the door to a final resolution of the Florida question with an embarrassed and weakened Spain. Elected to the United States Senate a second time in the spring of 1823, Jackson served little more than two years before resigning to concentrate his efforts on capturing the presidency.

The conduct of foreign policy never emerged as a major public issue in the Adams-Jackson presidential contest of 1824–25. With the Democratic-Republican Party of Jefferson shattered and the caucus nomination meaningless, Jackson gained popular support in all areas except New England. As a national military hero, he delighted almost everyone; as a national political novice, he alienated almost no one; and the collapse of the established party system virtually precluded a genuine dialogue on issues. The nationalistic postures of both House Speaker Henry Clay and Secretary of State Adams after the War of 1812 marked them as candidates who could be expected to encourage an aggressive stance for the federal government in both domestic economic and foreign policy. Secretary of the Treasury William H. Crawford, though he had spent time as Minister to France, chose to emphasize economic affairs, particularly a return to the states' rights principles of Jefferson and opposition to national banks, protective tariffs, and federally funded internal improvements. The passage of the controversial Missouri Compromise in 1821 insured that the subject of slavery expansion would continue to bubble just beneath the surface of the national consciousness, but few people had any idea exactly where Jackson stood on such questions, and he made little effort to clarify his position.

In the November ballot, the General won a plurality of the popular and electoral vote. But lacking a majority decision, the contest went to the House of Representatives, where Adams, with Clay's support, won on the first ballot. Jackson took his defeat bitterly, viewing it as the result of a "corrupt bargain" of vote trading in the House between the forces of Adams and Clay. The fact that the new President soon named Clay as Secretary of State simply confirmed the hero's distrust of the system and convinced him of the need for reform in Washington.

While the Adams-Clay forces (soon referred to as National Republicans and by 1834 as Whigs) were able to claim the White House, they controlled the House only through 1827 and never dominated the Senate. The majority position held by the Jacksonian Democrats and their Crawfordite allies enabled them to batter any national domestic programs that met their disapproval. Time after time, the combination attacked and defeated imaginative Adams proposals such as a naval academy, a national university, lunar observatories, and public roads.[4]

In foreign affairs the Jacksonians could have been just as merciless, but they shared with the Adams-Clay forces a common vision of an imperial America in the tradition of Madison's *Federalist* No. 10, Washington's Farewell Address, and the Monroe Doctrine. A southern cotton planter and a midwestern grain farmer, a New Englander factory owner and a Baltimore merchant, all could recognize the advantages of a balance between territorial and commercial expansion. Subtle differences that emerged during the 1820s, however, helped define the direction the Jacksonians would take when they achieved power.

One major issue, which indicated a reluctance on the part of many future Jacksonians to stray from traditional ideals, was the question of the recognition of Greek independence from Turkey. A wide variety of Americans, including Jefferson, Monroe, Edward Everett, and William Henry Harrison, expressed support for the Greek revolution of the 1820s. By January 1824, American sympathy for the Greeks had become so aroused that Daniel Webster brought the issue to a floor fight in the House, urging recognition of their independence. Several Jacksonians immediately opposed the measure. Joel Poinsett of South Carolina argued that it would violate the premise of two spheres articulated in the Monroe Doctrine. The ever-combative John Randolph of Roanoke evoked the specter of slavery by noting that since the Greeks were in a condition of servitude, any condemnation of that institution outside the United States could be used as ammunition by the antislavery forces within. The Virginian also invoked the Farewell Address, claiming in a strict interpretation of that document that recognition of a revolutionary nation constituted a violation of the principle that American foreign involvement be limited to commercial intercourse.

Significantly, it was not only current and future Jacksonians who opposed recognition; so did the conservative Crawfordites, who viewed Greece as simply too remote for American involvement, and the Adams men who shared Poinsett's stand of firm noninvolvement in European affairs. Federalist Samuel Breck of Pennsylvania contended that recognition of Greece would alienate the Turks and likely put an end to the lucrative American trade with the port of Smyrna on the Aegean Sea. Only the Calhoun forces, probably motivated by the 1824 presidential contest, actively worked with Webster's cadre. Not surprisingly then, the New Englander's resolution died in a House vote in early 1824.[5] But the factional alliance on the question of Greek recognition suggests no hard-and-fast split on the issue of American involvement in European affairs. Rather it points to the relative unanimity of opinion that endorsed moral approval of the Greeks but stopped short of recognition or aid. The Jacksonians, at least, while concerned about advancing American commercial interests around the world, opposed involving the United States in alliances, wars, or revolutions unless such conflicts posed an ultimate threat to American security.

This was especially true when, during the Adams presidency, the chief executive moved to align the nation with Latin American republics in the Pan-American Conference. The inter-American gathering precipitated perhaps the most obvious clash between the Jackson and Adams forces. In his first annual message to Congress in December 1825, Adams announced that he had accepted an invitation to participate in such a meeting, to be held in Panama the following year. This prompted immediate outcries, led by Democratic Senator John Branch of North Carolina (later Jackson's Secretary of the Navy), that the President was usurping congressional power. These charges were the initial salvo in a battle that raged for fifteen months on the floors of Congress. Debate was heatedly partisan and unhesitatingly insulting. One duel resulted between the wildly excitable Randolph of Roanoke and Secretary Clay (with no damage done to either party), and another between House members Thomas Metcalfe of Kentucky and George McDuffie of South Carolina (with the combatants using rifles!) was narrowly averted.

The Jacksonians used several arguments in opposing the conference, in addition to stressing violation of Constitutional prerogative by the President: (1) embroiling the country in an entangling alliance with Latin American nations could jeopardize its freedom to expand independently, and perhaps place the United States in the uncomfortable position of defending the former Spanish colonies against attack from their former mother country; (2) discussion of such matters should not be held in remote Panama or Mexico but in Washington, where Americans could keep a watchful eye (and presumably control) over events; (3) since the newly independent and struggling Latin American nations were inferior to the United States in international rank, they should not be dealt with at a peer level; (4) the Latin Americans were racially inferior and, even worse, had generally abolished slavery, thus opening the possibility of racially mixed delegations negotiating as equals with the United States representatives (the southern pulse especially quickened at the mention of black Haitian delegates).

The leaders of the Jacksonian opposition to the Panama Congress reads like a roll call of prominent figures in Old Hickory's first administration. Martin Van Buren of New York, Thomas Hart Benton of Missouri, Littleton Tazewell of Virginia, Levi Woodbury of New Hampshire, and Robert Y. Hayne of South Carolina led the crusade in the Senate, while James K. Polk of Tennessee and James Buchanan of Pennsylvania fought the good fight in the House—all to no avail. The stalling tactics of the Jacksonians finally succumbed to the good sense of the Congress and the administration's stated argument that such a conference would foster Yankee commerce in Latin America, especially vis-à-vis the British. An undeclared concern, however, was that a combination of Latin American states might move to liberate Cuba from Spanish control, an action unacceptable to Adams and Clay, who wanted the island in the American sphere. On March 14, 1826, the Senate voted 24 to 19 to approve the mission (only one of the minority voters was a National Republican, John Holmes of Maine), and several days later, by a similar margin, the Senate confirmed the appointment of John Sergeant and Richard C. Anderson as the American representatives to the conference. The Jacksonian forces delayed the appropriations for two more months before the House granted final approval by a vote of 134 to 60. After this Herculean effort, it is particularly tragic to note that Anderson died en route to Panama, and Sergeant arrived after it had adjourned.

To what extent were the actions of Jackson's men in Congress a reflection of his own feelings about the conference? Old Hickory's correspondence reveals a deep-seated concern for the Latin Americans. Like Adams and Clay, Jackson felt a moral responsibility to promote the freedom of the former Spanish colonies; however, he was not willing to enter into a premature alliance. If the time came when "a combination of leagued powers" threatened the Latins, then some form of concerted action might be taken. "This [an invasion] must be prevented or our government will be jeopardized—and we will have a bloody contest with the combined despotism of Europe." The General particularly feared foreign incursion into Mexico, where strategic advantage could be taken of the American South and West.[6]

However, for Jackson, the Adams-Clay flirtation with South America was a premature rush to judgment on the principles of the Monroe Doctrine and potentially compromised Washington's premise of "no entangling alliances" and traditional neutrality. As Old Hickory told a correspondent, "The moment we engage in confederation or alliances with any nation we may from that time date the downfall of our republic." Thus Jackson's view of the Monroe Doctrine was conservative, limiting its application to foreign interference in Mexico or perhaps the transfer of Cuba—both areas of major security, territorial, and commercial concern to the administration. Typically, too, Jackson read politics into the scenario by suggesting that the Panama Congress was a scheme to enhance the power of the presidency and the reputation of White House heir-apparent Henry Clay.[7]

While the National Republicans and Jacksonian Democrats evinced substantial disagreement over the United States involvement in an inter-American conference, no quarrel existed over the active role the Yankees should play in vying for Latin American trade (against stiff British competition) and securing United States borders against potential European incursion through territorial expansion. Consequently, when President Adams dispatched South Carolinian Joel Poinsett as Minister to Mexico in 1825, the Jacksonians could not have been more pleased. Secretary Clay's instructions urged Poinsett to negotiate a commercial treaty based on the principles of reciprocity, and to work for the purchase of the province of Texas. Poinsett appeared to be the ideal choice for the post. As a well-traveled diplomat without portfolio, the Carolinian had been an observer of revolutionary Latin America for Presidents Jefferson and Madison, and the liberal credentials worn prominently on his sleeve should have endeared him to most revolutionary regimes. Unfortunately, Poinsett's tenure in Mexico City was a disaster. First, he did not like Mexicans or respect their government. Second, he took seriously the segment of his instructions that urged him to foster religious freedom and a liberal form of government in Mexico.

Poinsett, comfortable with a land and a language with which he had grown familiar, was welcomed in Mexico City in June 1825, but thunderclouds quickly formed on the political horizon. Although President Guadalupe Victoria was a liberal, his powerful Minister of Foreign Affairs, Lucas Alamán, was a pro-British conservative. Alamán was in league with the suave and clever English diplomat Minister Henry G. Ward. Ward sought with great success to insure Mexican markets for British goods, and Mexican industry and mines for British capital. He emphasized the theme that the United States was an imperial power seeking only to exploit Mexico commercially and territorially, and Poinsett's instructions to acquire Texas went far in giving Ward's schema singular credibility. Poinsett sought to balance this anti-Americanism through an organization of liberal forces based upon the order of York Rite Masonry, intended to reform Mexico using the American model. Ward countered with a similar organization of Scottish Rite Masons.

By the end of the Adams presidency, Ward had emerged victorious. The English gained a most-favored-nation commercial treaty, lent millions of dollars to the Mexican government, and invested similar amounts in industry. Poinsett, rebuked on a reciprocity treaty, signed a less than satisfactory commercial convention that still remained unratified in Mexico City in 1829. In self-righteous frustration, he lectured the Mexicans on their need to look to their northern neighbor for guidance and assistance. For his meddling in Mexican affairs and overbearing demeanor, the Latins requested Poinsett's recall in the fall of 1829. No matter that Jackson, who had taken office in March, increased the offer for Texas from $1 million to $5 million dollars; in an obvious attempt to emphasize their unwillingness to sell Texas, the Mexican government planned to abolish slavery in the province and dispatched a general to strengthen military and economic ties with the area.

The Jacksonians could hardly relish Poinsett's ouster. Although probably secretly delighted at another foreign policy failure of the Adams administration, the Democrats did want Texas. The South Carolinian's blunders had simply strengthened the British position and made the Mexicans all the more apprehensive about American goals. Jackson, in sharing his predecessor's desire for westward expansion, later appointed an even more mischievous representative, Chargé Andrew Butler, dooming the acquisition and ultimately leading to the Texas War for Independence in 1836.[8]

Although the Pan-American Conference and the Poinsett mission were the two low points of Adams's foreign policy, there were other controversial areas where the National Republicans also suffered reverses. The failure to resolve the West Indian trade issue with Great Britain constituted a major setback for American commerce. Since the American Revolution, the British had closed their Caribbean ports to foreign sail, denying the United States a very lucrative trade. In 1818 the frustrated Monroe administration closed American ports to British vessels sailing from the West Indies. Although the United States modified this restriction slightly in the early 1820s, the English struck the trade a death blow in 1825: they reopened their West Indian and North American colonies to foreign commerce but attached discriminatory provisions aimed particularly at the United States. A sharp increase in tariff duties and a quid pro quo that would oblige the Americans to exchange domestic port trade for British colonial port trade were unacceptable to Adams and Clay, and commerce collapsed. To the credit of the administration, it did not allow the ill will created by the West Indian problems to affect the resolution of other questions with Great Britain. Between 1826 and 1828 the able Albert Gallatin negotiated two treaties with the British crown: the first extended indefinitely the joint occupation of the Oregon country by Great Britain and the United States; the second provided for the submission of the long-disputed Maine—New Brunswick boundary to the King of the Netherlands for arbitration.

The administration scored some additional modest gains in Europe by negotiating treaties with Denmark, Norway and Sweden, the Hanseatic republics of northern Germany, and Prussia. In Latin America, in addition to the Mexican treaty, commercial agreements were struck with the Central American Republic (Clay had also seriously considered the construction of a transisthmian canal through either Mexico or Central America) and the Empire of Brazil.[9]

In part, the Jackson years represented a continuation of the goals and some of the policies of the Adams administration. Old Hickory's diplomacy, however, was characterized by a sharper, harder-hitting edge that produced greater success. Trade with Europe and Latin America would be broadened, and parts of the Middle East and the Orient brought under the American commercial umbrella. Unresolved merchant claims from the Napoleonic Wars would be settled, and the possibility of a canal further explored. "Pirates" in the Indian Ocean and the South Atlantic who dared threaten American commerce felt the swift retribution of the reconstituted United States navy under Old Hickory's command. Operating by traditional tenets of United States foreign policy, Jackson contributed significantly to the advancement of trade and growth of national respectability. His vision of a continental destiny for America and efforts in that direction paralleled those of the leading expansionists of the era, including John Quincy Adams.

Chapter 2

"King Andrew" and His Court: The Policy Makers

Many historians have seen the Jackson years as constituting a revolutionary era in American politics. Some, such as pioneer biographer James Parton, lament what they perceive as the leveling impact of frontier democracy upon the young nation. Throughout the nineteenth century the majority viewpoint contended that Old Hickory had brought a blustery arrogance to the presidency that hardly flattered that exalted office. His high-handed attitude toward both Congress and the courts earned him the sobriquet "King Andrew I" from the Whig opposition. His supposed institution of the "spoils system" of patronage won him the ongoing enmity of the champions of "good government." The issue then historically has been not whether the Tennesseean held sway over domestic politics, policies, and patronage but whether he used that power to the benefit or to the detriment of the American government and people.[1]

Jackson's extension of the power of the presidency did not function in an information vacuum, however. Emotional, caustic, outspoken, sure of his own direction, Old Hickory still needed the counsel of men he could trust, in both foreign and domestic affairs. The Cabinet has traditionally offered American presidents a sounding board for foreign policy views; the Monroe Doctrine, for example, was the product of a series of intense Cabinet meetings in which presidential aspirants John Quincy Adams and John C. Calhoun participated. But after floating presidential timber for decades, the Cabinet under Jackson lost its buoyancy in what appeared to many to be a sea of mediocrity. Perhaps not everyone agreed with the opinion expressed by South Carolina politico James Hamilton, Jr., to Martin Van Buren in 1829: "If I went into the cabinet, I would cut my throat." But it is clear that the group of advisors on foreign affairs surrounding Jackson differed markedly in intellect and influence from their predecessors. Journalist Holmes Alexander referred to this cadre as the "most unintellectual cabinet we ever had" and argued that their claim to fame was the comic relief they inserted into the solemn drama of history. Many prominent contemporaries—including future secretaries Martin Van Buren, Edward Livingston, and Louis McLane, as well as Richmond editor Thomas Ritchie—bemoaned the colorless band of men supposedly commanding the ship of state. Van Buren, the Red Fox of Kinderhook, lamented, "There was probably not one of these malcontents more disappointed than myself by the composition of the new administration." It was likely, however, that the New Yorker's disillusionment sprang from the fact that he was not invited to participate in Cabinet selection to any great extent, whereas the fortunes of his archrival, Vice-President John C. Calhoun, were numerically if not ably represented.[2]

These critics probably misunderstood Jackson's intent for the Cabinet. As a man conditioned by military command and imbued with a sense of both the strength and responsibility of the presidency and its role as a coequal branch of government, the General formulated his own domestic—and foreign—policies. Of course, he sought advice from friends, counselors, and the legendary "Kitchen Cabinet," as well as the official Cabinet, but Jackson insisted on making his own decisions. He knew only one of his Cabinet members intimately (Secretary of War John Eaton), but he defended his selections as a means to unite the factions of his emerging Democratic Party. While Jackson intended to listen to their ideas, his vision of President-Cabinet relations involved secretaries who functioned as lieutenants, carrying out policies they had little voice in deciding.

Besides Van Buren and Eaton, the first Cabinet included Calhoun supporters John Branch of North Carolina (Secretary of the Navy), John Berrien of Georgia (Attorney-General), and Samuel D. Ingham of Pennsylvania (Secretary of the Treasury). William Barry of Kentucky (Postmaster-General) was a lightweight westerner who leaned toward Van Buren's camp. Only the wily and capable Old Kinderhook, destined to succeed Jackson in the White House, and the controversial

Eaton, whose marriage became a *cause célèbre* in capital society, have earned an ongoing place in history.[3]

Jackson's Cabinets were a revolving door; every post but one was manned by at least three different secretaries (State had four and Treasury five). The exception was Postmaster-General Barry, who held his position until 1835, finally proving to be so incompetent that he was indicted by Congress for malfeasance and fraud, and forced to resign. Jackson promptly appointed him Minister to Spain. The President moved his subordinates around like chesspieces; today's secretary could be appointed as a diplomat, only to reappear as a Cabinet member at a later date. It mattered little, since their influence (except for Van Buren's) was as transitory as their tenure. Contemporary accounts reveal that the General met with his formal Cabinet only sixteen times in eight years, six of these to discuss foreign affairs. The Cabinet was not a democracy. As confidant and later Postmaster-General Amos Kendall explained, "He [Jackson] never took a vote. . . . Questions were submitted and discussed; but when it came to the decision, he took the responsibility." Jackson preferred to meet with his officials individually to discuss matters pertaining to their specific departments and, in some cases, beyond. Disagreement with "the Old Man" did not mean exile, but it was painfully clear who had the final word.[4]

What of the Kitchen Cabinet, that extraofficial body that supposedly had the closest bonds with the President? Historians Richard Longaker and Richard Latner have examined the influence of this group upon Old Hickory; their separate findings reveal that the role of the formal Cabinet did, in fact, decline as the Kitchen Cabinet rose to become a powerful force within the administration. The name itself struck terror into the hearts of the Whig opposition. A shifting, loose-knit group comprising largely trusted westerners, the Kitchen Cabinet did not meet formally. The dozen participants often held sinecures in obscure government posts (William B. Lewis was custodian for the renewal and repair of the White House furniture, for example), or, occasionally, were members of Congress or the formal cabinet. Though men moved in and out of the circle, the inner ring was composed of newspapermen Amos Kendall and Francis P. Blair of Kentucky, Andrew Jackson Donelson of Tennessee (the President's nephew), Roger B. Taney of Maryland (who served as Attorney-General, Secretary of the Treasury, and Chief Justice of the Supreme Court), and Secretary of State and Vice-President Martin Van Buren.

While Van Buren was the most potent of the familiar faces, Kendall and Blair also rose to the surface of this political brew. Both men were editors in the Blue Grass state—Blair would later edit the administration's Washington *Globe*—and their loyalty was first and foremost to the President. They agreed with Jackson on basic political principles, and sought to advance his cause and that of the Democratic Party rather than their own personal fortunes. In these goals they differed notably from Van Buren, who, as Vice-President in the second Jackson administration, particularly channeled his energies into avoiding any controversy that could jeopardize his nomination and election to the White House in 1836; and from Calhoun, who, as Vice-President in the first administration, struggled unsuccessfully to balance an evolving states' rights philosophy with his ambition to follow Jackson. But even those who argue for the preeminence of the Kentuckians as Jackson's leading advisors (rather than Van Buren) agree that while Kendall and Blair were very influential in the banking and nullification questions, they had little or no influence on the inception of other programs. Latner puts the situation in perspective: "However influential his western advisors were, Jackson controlled his administration and sought counsel from others."[5]

In other words, the President was not a puppet with a group of faceless, nameless men pulling the strings, as Whig cartoonists delighted in caricaturing him. The members of the Kitchen Cabinet, like those of the formal Cabinet, were often friends but nevertheless subordinates; advisors but not policy makers. Jackson was the driving force of his administration, and those around him frequently had to content themselves with counseling restraint.

"General Jackson dominated everything so completely," historian Eugene McCormac adjudged, "that it is not easy to determine the attitude or influence of any member of the cabinet." Contrary to the views of some others, Jackson allowed his staff little flexibility either in policy formation or in carrying out the daily affairs of their departments. He went to Washington with the idea of reform—of cleansing the Augean stables—and this included the State Department, where reforms, especially in organization, were enacted through the efforts of Van Buren and McLane. But the General as President was flawed by an inability to delegate authority. Despite his sixty-two years and fragile health, he insisted on monitoring everything from consular appointments to the location of privies. He felt responsible for policy made by his administration and, as a result, could allow very little discretion in judgment on the part of his subordinates. As he once told a cabinet head, "[you are] merely an executive agent, a subordinate, and you may say so in self defense."[6] Fortunately for Jackson and the nation, the size of the federal government (including the Department of State) was small, almost manageable.

The overpowering personality and style of the President affected his four Secretaries of State differently. But none of these men was as distinguished a secretary as Jefferson, Madison, Adams or Clay. The most influential was the former New York senator and governor, Martin Van Buren (1829–31). The slight, balding man with tufts of red hair protruding from the sides of his head disarmed both friend and foe with his bright blue eyes and engaging manner. He administered the department with credit and dignity, but his mind and his heart were in domestic policy, not diplomacy. Samuel Flag Bemis, however, overstates the case when he argues that "there is very little evidence he had much to do with foreign affairs." Biographer John Niven is closer to the mark in his praise of Matty Van's smooth style, noting that he was "direct, open and conciliatory." Niven emphasizes the strong role that Van Buren played in chalking up a string of successes that embarrassed the National Republicans during his two-year term. But the cagey Dutchman undoubtedly perceived his future role when he discovered, upon arriving in Washington in the spring of 1829, that Jackson had already committed the ministerial posts in England (Senator Littleton Tazewell of Virginia), France (Senator Edward Livingston of Louisiana), and Colombia (Representative Thomas Moore of Kentucky) without consulting him.[7]

The choices were not without merit. Tazewell was a Norfolk lawyer whose lengthy congressional career had culminated in the chairmanship of the Foreign Relations Committee; a politician whose loyalties moved toward Calhoun, he had been considered for Secretary of State. Livingston was an old crony of the President from their days in New Orleans during the War of 1812; a distinguished expert on the law, he also had the advantage of speaking fluent French. Moore, a youthful thirty-two, was a well-connected westerner who had been a loyal Jacksonian in Congress during the 1820s.

Luckily for Van Buren, Tazewell and Livingston declined the appointments. Tazewell, as a member of the Senate Foreign Relations Committee, had studied Anglo-American trade problems in depth and was pessimistic about their resolution; Livingston simply could not leave the country for at least four months. These facts gave the Fox an opportunity to pay off some political debts by selecting his own subordinates, with whom he could maintain a degree of cooperation and loyalty. While both Tazewell and Livingston were men of solid political and diplomatic reputations (perhaps too solid to suit an insecure Van Buren), he argued that pressing problems with both England and France required men of youth and vigor. The President, given his own age, was probably not concerned about the fifty-five-year-old Tazewell and the sixty-five-year-old Livingston. However, in later conversation with his new Secretary, Jackson admitted his "great mistake" in making the appointments and said that when the New Yorker named new selections, "it was more than probable that he would adopt them."[8]

Van Buren attempted a fast shuffle of the cabinet deck that would have resulted in sending Calhounite Berrien to London and moving Van Buren ally Senator Louis McLane of Delaware into the Cabinet. But Berrien refused, and McLane, who desperately wanted a Supreme Court appointment, agreed to pay his political dues at the Court of St. James. Van Buren found an old Virginia ally to travel to Paris in Representative William C. Rives. As an additional sop, the President allowed Van Buren to appoint a Minister to Spain, and the Secretary immediately suggested Senator Levi Woodbury of New Hampshire. Woodbury, however, was interested only in a limited mission for a specific purpose; when such assurances were not forthcoming, he, too, declined. The President then chose Governor Cornelius P. Van Ness of Vermont, another New Englander, about whose appointment Van Buren remarked, "My relations with his family had been for years of an unfriendly character, but I cheerfully acquiesed in his selection."[9]

The administration filled the two other major European posts, Russia and the Netherlands, with a combination of political pragmatism and logic. The President and his Secretary of State, as was their habit, were riding in Virginia one afternoon when the subject of the Russian mission came up in conversation. Since no burning issue presented itself at the Czar's court—although the advantage of a trade treaty would be welcomed by American merchants and shippers—Van Buren suggested quixotic John Randolph of Roanoke as a possible choice. Brilliant but quite mad, the volatile Virginian was a political favorite of the conservative Old Republicans of his state and a personal favorite of Van Buren from their days in the Senate. Randolph, quick of tongue and pistol, also had a duel with Henry Clay in 1826 to recommend him to the President. But Van Buren, probably recognizing the likelihood that sooner or later Randolph would turn on Jackson, thought it would be better to assign him out of the country—where he could do little harm and perhaps some good—and postpone the ultimate collision. Although the urbane Randolph had been to Europe three times before, in the 1830s "St. Petersburg, considering the means of transportation, was about as far from Washington as a man might get and still remain in this world."[10]

The mission to The Hague was significant at this point because of the extended Anglo-American debate over the Maine–New Brunswick boundary and the role of the King of the Netherlands as arbiter on the issue. William Pitt Preble of Maine, who had been actively involved in the controversy, was a logical choice for the post to watchdog the deliberations. But as John Niven indicates, Preble, "self-centered and self-righteous," proved to be a disaster.[11]

The Van Buren regency in the State Department lasted until April 1831. It was not without its successes, especially the resolution of the trade difficulties with Great Britain over the West Indies and the negotiation with France of a treaty to provide for payment of damages inflicted upon American commerce during the Napoleonic Wars. After negotiations the Danes agreed to similar payments, and the Turks accepted a commercial treaty opening the Black Sea to American sail. Van Buren was not brilliant but worked assiduously in a direct, businesslike manner. He kept the President constantly informed as events developed and appears to have executed Jackson's designs almost flawlessly. When political relationships frayed and split in the spring of 1831, obliging Van Buren to resign with the remainder of the Cabinet, Jackson felt a genuine loss of both his confidant and Secretary of State. For

Van Buren, however, the departure may have been politically timely; he could enjoy the splendor of success without the risk of tarnishing his image, which is sometimes the fate of those exposed in the public trust for long periods. The Fox contented himself with crediting others for his successes—the ministers, but especially the President. He moved on briefly to the Court of St. James's before returning to the United States and the vice-presidency in the second Jackson administration.[12]

The new Secretary was Edward Livingston, who had been the President's first choice as Minister to France in 1829. The affable Louisianan, really a transplanted New Yorker, was selected largely upon Van Buren's recommendation. Jackson, who considered his friend "illy qualified for the performance of executive duties," resisted the appointment, and he was not the only one to question Livingston's abilities. Correspondents of Jackson's secretary, Nicholas Trist, remarked that Livingston was too old and unable to conduct an important negotiation, and that he had "every qualification except tact and forecast." Another told Jackson that Livingston lacked the necessary "energy of decision." After Livingston had served little more than half a year, Jackson seemed inclined to agree. In December he penned Van Buren an evaluation: "You are aware of the friendship I have for Livingston, and the respect I have for his talents, that he is a polished scholar, an able writer, and a most excellent man, but he knows nothing of mankind . . . his memory is somewhat failing him and a change in due time would be pleasing to him and with your consent beneficial to me." Jackson knew that Livingston had disagreed with him on several key domestic policy issues, including the recharter of the Bank of the United States and the federal funding of internal improvements, but he had been willing to overlook this in the hope that the Secretary would confine his efforts to foreign affairs. Livingston did not prove so agreeable. He moved into the vanguard of the Cabinet, opposing the General on the Bank question and compounding his liability to the White House. By the summer of 1832, Jackson had decided to transfer the equally troublesome but more talented McLane from the Treasury to the State Department and dispatch Livingston to France to facilitate the enactment of the new French treaty. The shift occurred in May 1833.[13]

Livingston's biographer, William Hatcher, challenges those critics who have attacked the capacity of the Louisianan to carry out his executive duties, pointing out that "Jackson dominated foreign relations in the same manner that characterized his conduct of domestic affairs. . . . His vigorous method . . . allowed but little opportunity for initiative on the part of any of the four secretaries of state who served during his presidency." Livingston basically continued those policies begun in the Van Buren regime, but unlike Van Buren he had little impact on diplomatic appointments; he even found himself chastised by the President for hiring a clerk without executive approval. Between 1831 and 1833 there were diplomatic accomplishments: treaties with Russia and the Kingdom of the Two Sicilies, a mission to the Orient to open trade and garner port facilities, the arbitration of the boundary between Canada and Maine by the King of the Netherlands, and movement toward the acquisition of Texas. But Livingston was only tangentially involved in any of these actions. He was probably more delighted than the President at the lifting of the State Department mantle.[14]

Incoming Secretary Louis McLane was the Talleyrand of the Jackson administration. Although McLane was formerly a Federalist, Jackson recognized his many talents and appreciated his loyalty, regardless of past allegiance. McLane (whom the President constantly referred to as "McLean") joined James Buchanan and Roger B. Taney as prominent Federalists who had seen the Jacksonian light. Although he disagreed with the President on basic economic philosophy and the role of the Bank of the United States in particular, he had proved to be a most successful diplomat in his two-year stint in Great Britain. As a result, when the Cabinet underwent reformation in the spring of 1831, McLane had found himself in the powerful post of Secretary of the Treasury.

The new Secretary was, in fact, an ambitious man. The White House was his ultimate goal; unfortunately, his old friend Van Buren (with Calhoun now out of the picture) remained the chief stumbling block. McLane had attempted a palace coup prior to the Democratic Convention in 1832 whereby elderly and respected Senator Samuel Smith of Maryland would have received the nomination for Vice-President; McLane would have moved into the State Department, and Philadelphian William Duane into the Treasury; Van Buren would have been out in the cold. The scheme fell through, of course, and Van Buren received the second slot on the reelection ticket. But this did not deter McLane from continuing to press his case into 1833. When a new Cabinet shake-up occurred on the heels of the Bank Veto that summer, McLane did move into the State Department and his ally, Duane, into the Treasury. Unhappily for McLane, Duane proved at first obstinate and then hostile to the President's plans for removal of federal funds from the Bank of the United States. When the angry General quickly dismissed Duane in September, McLane's days, too, were numbered. He endured until mid-June 1834 before finally submitting his resignation.

McLane's brief one-year tenure as Secretary of State is especially disappointing in view of the natural intelligence, congressional service, and diplomatic experience that made him probably the best qualified of the four men who served in the State Department under Jackson. But his political position, marginal from the outset, evaporated in the heat of the Bank controversy, and his skill as an administrator and a diplomat could not compensate for his political weakness. During his thirteen months McLane was more a witness to than a prosecutor of foreign policy. The Maine boundary controversy dragged on, as did dealings with Mexico over the purchase of Texas, with McLane for the most part watching quietly on the sidelines. The United States ratified treaties with Chile, Muscat, and Siam, but he had little to do with these successes. The President did encourage the Secretary's bold reform of the State Department into eight better-organized and more efficient bureaus, but success in this endeavor failed to compensate for his other liabilities. McLane's resignation in June 1834 was his exit visa from politics. He spent the better part of the next ten years as a railroad president.[15]

McLane's successor, and the man who served not only Old Hickory but Van Buren in the State Department, was the venerable warhorse from Georgia, John Forsyth. As a veteran senator and former Minister to Spain, he had frequently been mentioned since 1831 for various cabinet posts and diplomatic missions. Doggedly loyal and patiently ambitious, Forsyth was an excellent choice, given the President's style and the Vice-President's goals. Like McLane before him, he moved with energy to reform his department, much to the delight of the President. The highlight of the Georgian's reorganization, which lasted until 1870, was a reduction to four bureaus.

Forsyth was a man of talent, both administrative and diplomatic, but like his predecessors he was allowed little freedom of movement. After his first year in office, rumors were rife of his impending resignation. One newspaper, alluding to the influence of Kitchen Cabinet member and later Postmaster-General Amos Kendall, reported, "It must be mortifying to a man like Forsyth to find himself a cypher when in contact with a man like Kendall." But Forsyth remained, perhaps in anticipation of the day when his old friend Van Buren would become chief executive and the harness would be loosened. Biographer Alvin Duckett elaborates: "Forsyth acted in the role of faithful subordinate. He was overshadowed by the President, of course, but he succeeded in placing a restraint upon the rash tendencies of Jackson. While he did not determine policy, his moderate views undoubtedly had some effect." With purpose and usually tact, the able Georgian dealt with the pressing problems of the French claims and the disintegration of Mexican-American relations over Texas as a trusted lieutenant at the side of his General.[16]

In spite of the revolving door in the State Department, the President and all four of his secretaries agreed on one substantive matter: the need for internal reform. In his first annual message to Congress, Old Hickory pointed to the stresses and overburdening of the State Department and called for changes. The Department consisted of the Secretary, the Chief Clerk, and thirteen underclerks, plus the Patent Office, which fell under its jurisdiction. The total salaries of the employees barely exceeded $20,000. Yet this handful of public servants supervised fifteen diplomatic posts (eight in Europe and seven in Latin America) and more than 140 consular posts; and over the course of the next decade, the Jackson administration would add six diplomatic assignments (Naples, Turkey, Brussels, Prussia, Venezuela, and Texas) and a dozen new consular slots. As Secretary of State Edward Livingston suggested in 1833, the nation was receiving an incredible bargain: its foreign affairs, including commerce exceeding $170 million, were being conducted with a budget averaging $200,000 annually. Ministers received $9,500 per year, and chargés d'affaires were paid $4,500; consuls earned only the fees they charged on incoming American cargoes. Both the organization of the department and the restructuring of the salary schedule became high-priority items for each of the four secretaries.[17]

The frequent abuse of the fee structure and the presence of incompetent or corrupt consuls produced scores of complaints from American merchants and ship captains. Secretary Van Buren moved to investigate and remedy the problems. He requested that Daniel Stroebel, who had consular experience in Bordeaux, prepare a statement on possible improvements in the consular system. Stroebel's report of February 1831 urged the creation of a salaried service with a prohibition on the conduct of personal business—an ongoing source of potential conflict of interest. Congress never acted on the consul's recommendations, however, and the problems continued into Livingston's tenure in the State Department.

The Louisianan echoed Van Buren's concern over the consular and diplomatic corps. In 1833, after careful study, Livingston presented his analysis of the problems and suggestions for change. In a lengthy document to the President, he outlined the need for a strict codification of the consular service, a salary structure (with prohibitions about entering into commerce), and a fee scale. The Secretary sought, fairly, to compensate the consuls adequately ($2,000 per man) so they would not be obliged to seek added income in commerce. Such ventures were creating conflicts between themselves and the merchants and captains they were intended to be promoting. Under a salary system, better men could be brought into the service and, with them, integrity and impartiality.[18]

Livingston made similar recommendations regarding the diplomatic corps. He pointed to the expense of entertainment and residence at many European courts, congressional failure to appropriate salaries for secretaries of legations, and the lack of an official filing system for correspondence (in many cases the minister in charge considered official correspondence to be his own, and took it with him when he departed a post; in some legations no official archives remained). Livingston urged that allowances be provided for housing, clerks, and office supplies. Unfortunately, the parsimonious Congress acted on neither Livingston's consular nor his diplomatic recommendations. Instead, the House of Representatives moved in 1832 to request its Committee on Foreign Relations to look into the expediency of reducing the number of ministers abroad to three! The committee reported back that it could not endorse such a measure, not because it would disrupt the nation's foreign affairs but because it might be interpreted as an unconstitutional interference with the President's power of appointment. Livingston's only success in the matter was the enactment of his newly revised code of general instructions to all consuls, in which the Secretary brought together for the first time in an organized fashion all the legislation and the administrative regulations pertinent to the consular service.[19]

The task of reorganizing the department itself fell to his successor, Louis McLane. McLane's order of June 30, 1833, provided for the first wholesale reorganization since the department had been established in 1789. Under the administration of the Chief Clerk, who became, in essence, the Undersecretary of State, eight bureaus were set up: (1) Diplomatic, (2) Consular, (3) Home, (4) Archives, Laws, and Commissions, (5) Pardons and Copyrights, (6) Disbursing and Superintending, (7) Translating and Miscellaneous, and (8) the Patent Office. Since no formal organization had existed before 1833, the changes seemed deep and far reaching. In reality, neither duties nor procedures were drastically changed, but because they were specifically prescribed, the functioning of the staff was made more efficient. The department even set firm hours (10:00 A.M. to 3:00 P.M.) during which all clerks were expected to be in their offices.[20]

When John Forsyth took over the State Department in 1834, he eliminated three of the new bureaus (Pardons, Archives, and Disbursing) and gave their tasks to others. The Home Bureau, with four clerks, was made the largest and most responsible. Further fine-tuning was accomplished in 1836, but the department maintained its essential McLane-Forsyth organization until 1870. In spite of widespread changes, however, the number of personnel and their salaries did not significantly increase in the period.[21]

The proposals and reforms of the four Secretaries of State reflected basic and justifiable concerns held by themselves and the President. The rewriting of the consular code by Livingston and the reorganization of the department by McLane and Forsyth were major steps toward improved efficiency in conducting United States foreign policy; however, the failure to persuade Congress to increase the staff (especially the overworked diplomatic and consular bureaus) and raise the salaries of department employees at home and abroad served as a constant irritant in both acquiring and keeping qualified personnel.

In other matters, however, the President achieved greater influence with the legislative branch, against which he guarded the prerogatives of his office as jealously as against his cabinet. Fortunately for the Tennesseean, with the brief exception of the years 1833–35, the Democrats controlled both houses; as a result, Congress frequently complied with his wishes, allowing Jackson to take the lead in foreign affairs. In the two years that the Whigs (former National Republicans and their allies) controlled the Senate, with archfoe Henry Clay as chairman of the powerful Foreign Relations Committee, Jackson discovered how meddlesome Congress could become. While the French claims issue was reaching a boiling point, Clay sought with some success to wreak havoc on Jacksonian policy. But the Whigs did not oppose Old Hickory solely on partisan grounds; many saw the Senate as the single safeguard against an irresponsible executive. Because of the President's mastery of the lower house, only the upper chamber stood in the path of tyranny. As Henry Clay warned the Senate in 1834:

We are in the midst of revolution, hitherto bloodless, but rapidly tending towards a total change of the pure republican character of government, and to the concentration of all power in the hands of one man . . . the government (in eight years) will have been transformed into an elective monarchy—the worst of all forms of government. The preliminary symptoms of despotism are upon us, and if Congress does not apply an instantaneous and effective remedy the fatal collapse will soon come on and we shall die—ignobly die, base, mean and abject slaves.[22]

Clay's colleague and rival for the White House, Massachusetts Senator Daniel Webster, railed against the President's high-handed treatment of his Cabinet members: "The first functionaries in the departments [are reduced] to a subserviency as slavish and indefinite and dependence as degrading and complete as any which ever existed at the footstool of Asiatic despots." And Congressman Richard Fletcher complained about the presidential abuse of the House, where "Representatives had become machines for the use of the executive. . . . Executive power has become a very colossus, which bestrides the land from one end to the other; and . . . if we do not overthrow it . . . it will crush liberty . . . the Constitution." Sage and cynical observer John Quincy Adams, elected to the House following his White House years, commented on the "tone of insolence and insult in his [Jackson's] intercourse with both Houses of Congress, especially since his re-election which never was witnessed between the executive and the legislature before. The domineering has heretofore been usually on the side of the legislative bodies to the executive . . . and Clay has not been sparing in his use of it. He is now paid in his own coin."[23]

Jackson's bold executive style frightened and puzzled the Whigs, most of whom believed in strong congressional government. The problem was how to recapture the initiative or restrain the President. Since the Whigs were a loose-knit, anti-Jacksonian North/South coalition, they tended to shy away from concrete measures and well-defined theories. Clay considered utilizing the impeachment provision in response to Jackson's vetoes and Cabinet dismissals, but several men knowledgeable in such matters, including James Madison, advised him against it. The Senate did censure Jackson in the spring of 1834 for his removal of the federal deposits from the Bank of the United States without congressional sanction. The unrepentant General fired back a response decrying the encroachment of congressional powers on his office and warning that the "corrupt and venal Senate" had overthrown the liberties of Rome long before Caesar reached her gates.

The wailing and gnashing of teeth on the part of the Whigs did little to deter the President in either foreign or domestic affairs. He believed in and recognized the function of Congress—especially the Senate's role in foreign policy—but legislators could not constitutionally abridge, stipulate, or increase certain presidential powers. Foreign policy belonged to the executive branch and could not be initiated by Congress. Jackson recognized this facet of the modern presidency and acted upon it. As Clinton Rossiter emphasized, Clay and the Whigs went astray initially in their assumption that executive power was inherently antipopular. Jackson's insistence that he, rather than Congress, represented the will of the people, seemed to them "the babbling of a fool or the blustering of a tyrant." But Jackson was the first President elected by the popular vote of the people—not the congressional caucus or the state legislatures—and he intended to maximize this advantage.

As long as the United States held itself aloof from the world, Congress could maintain its dominance. But the President began to outstrip Congress and the courts in the race for power and prestige because of the nation's increasing role in world affairs. In the 1830s the United

States was on the brink of continental dominance, and Old Hickory was ready to step over the edge. French traveler Alexis de Tocqueville wrote that "it is chiefly in its foreign relations that the executive power of a nation finds occasion to exert its skill and its strength." Jackson was willing to accept the responsibility for the flexing of American muscle. Congress, upon occasion, might make the first move in foreign policy; but generally, for constitutional and political reasons, its role was to advise the President.[24]

Jackson's control of foreign policy exceeded his dominance of the Cabinet and mastery of Congress. The President so wove his thread into the fabric of everyday affairs of the State Department that literally no appointment, regardless of level, could be made without his approval. Office seekers regularly wrote to leading administration members inquiring about consular or diplomatic posts: one aspirant told Nicholas Trist that his older brother had served with Jackson at New Orleans; a New York businessman who desired to get his agent a consular appointment in Central America sent Van Buren a wheel of bucktail cheese from his father's farm as an inducement; and when a consular vacancy appeared in Chile, a knowledgeable Empire Stater attempted to work through powerful Treasury Secretary Levi Woodbury, helpfully suggesting that the two leading candidates for the post were not party men.[25] Such efforts generally produced few results, however. The recipient of the missive would often inform the inquirer that "the President must decide."

Even Van Buren found that despite the General's confidence in him, Old Hickory shadowed his appointments. It was probably a combination of genuine concern and deep-seated frustration that prompted the Fox, soon after his resignation in 1831, to advise the ailing President to find a way to relieve himself of the pressure of small matters. And later, as Vice-President, Van Buren told a correspondent, "You know that strictly speaking I have no right to meddle in the matter of appointments, but you do not know to its true extent how little I do so."[26]

Poor Edward Livingston, though a long-standing personal friend of Jackson, found himself unable to make the most piddling of appointments. The Secretary once foolishly named a clerk in the patent office without consulting the President. When the man was revealed to be an enemy of the administration and "of fraudulent character," Jackson instructed Livingston to recall the appointment and chastised him for contributing to filling "our departments with spies and traitors."[27]

Louis McLane, whose own political position was often precarious, advised his friends not to count on his influence with the President. McLane's biographer, John Munroe, is obliged to point to the selection of a substitute member on the Neapolitan claims commission as a reflection of his power. Levi Woodbury, no doubt weary of office seekers by 1836, told one diplomatic aspirant in stressful tones that the Secretary of State and the President made such appointments without the knowledge of the other heads of departments. He confessed that he had made some recommendations, "but it has been my misfortune to urge the appointment of several personal and political friends very strongly and repeatedly without success. But knowing that all my requests can not be gratified I do not complain. For every opening there are fifty or sometimes hundreds of applicants sustained by positive recommendations." Clearly, such recommendations had to emanate from loyal Democrats, and final approval must come from the White House.[28]

The men chosen to carry out the policies emerging from 1600 Pennsylvania Avenue had to remain flexible in their attitudes and approaches to their missions. Sometimes the chief executive was the apotheosis of calm and reason, the quintessential diplomat, but just as often he was the tough-talking frontier general from the Waxhaws who ordered the Mediterranean Squadron to prepare for action. This unique combination of reason and saber rattling left America's rivals and enemies generally off balance and sometimes perplexed. But the President's ultimate goals of defending the national honor and fostering American maritime interests could not be mistaken.

His support of the nation's front line of defense—the navy—provides particular insights. A report to Secretary of the Navy John Branch in 1829 by the Board of Navy Commissioners, a body of naval commanders authorized by Congress to provide assistance to the Secretary, contained a scathing and cynical denunciation of the naval establishment. The board criticized the exaggerated size of the navy and the marginal character of many of its officers; it recommended "a judicious pruning" of some of the "useless suckers" who had reposed under the naval banner for too many years. The board reminded Branch that the Naval Pension Fund and the Navy Asylum on the Schuykill existed for those dismissed from the service.

While the Secretary rejected such brash advice, he was obliged to turn his attention to the condition and size of the navy and its budget. In the last year of the Adams administration, the navy had in commission one ship of the line (74 guns), four frigates (36 to 44 guns), twelve sloops (18 guns), and four schooners (12 guns). The budget was approximately $4 million. Events of the next several years, especially in the Indian Ocean and the Mediterranean Sea, would prompt the President and Congress to press for a stronger naval establishment.[29]

Navy Secretary Mahlon Dickerson praised Congress in 1834 for its "liberal policy" and the "ample means" it had provided for the gradual increase and improvement of the navy. While approximately the same number and types of vessels were still in commission, vast strides had been made, including the construction of three new schooners (the *Enterprise*, the *Experiment*, and the *Boxer*). Other ships that had been on the stocks for years moved closer to completion, and those that had been under repair approached seaworthiness.

By 1836, with the French claims situation developing into an international crisis and the Democrats in control of both Houses of Congress, the naval budget increased to almost $6 million. At the same time two additional frigates (the *Columbia* and the *Macedonian*) and a new ship of the line (the *North Carolina*) were finished and launched. Five frigates were already in commission, plus the numerous smaller ships. A year later the navy had added the ship of the line *Pennsylvania*; repairs on the *Columbus*, the *Ohio*, and the *Delaware* were complete; and the razee *Independence* was ready to sail. The naval appropriation escalated to almost $7 million, and the American flotilla was the strongest it had been since the War of 1812.[30]

But the President wanted more. In his farewell address in March 1837, Jackson urged Congress to increase funding for the maritime, arguing that "your Navy will not only protect your rich and flourishing commerce in distant seas, but will enable you to reach and annoy the enemy and will give to defense its greatest efficiency by meeting danger at a distance from home. . . . We shall more certainly preserve the peace when it is well understood that we are prepared for war."[31]

The frustration felt by those who failed to fall into the mainstream of the naval power movement was reflected in the debate over a bill introduced by Whig Representative John Reed of Massachusetts in February 1837. When Reed proposed to build six small brigs (at a total cost of $400,000) to protect American commerce in the West Indies and off the coast of Brazil, an angry William Dunlap, a Tennessee Democrat, sought to add an amendment granting $10,000 for the construction of a hospital for the "poor, honest, industrious laboring classes" of Memphis. Dunlap choked on the insistence of the eastern seaboard for additional ships, harbors, and forts while the west received nothing: "You say to the world that you will appropriate hundreds of thousands of dollars for the protection of the property of the wealthy, while you refuse to appropriate anything for the protection of the lives of the poor." Although he spoke like a true legendary Jacksonian, Dunlap's amendment was defeated, and so was he in his reelection bid. His denouncement contained a ring of truth, but he was a voice in the wilderness, even within his own party.[32]

The procommerce attitudes of the President, his Cabinet, the diplomatic agents of the government, and many members of Congress can be seen in both the daily conduct of administration affairs and specific diplomatic problems. In attempting to establish the legitimacy of the claims of American shipowners and merchants against the French and the manner in which the negotiations should proceed, the administration solicited advice from those with a vested interest. Secretary Van Buren received numerous suggestions from Charles O. Clapp, the son of millionaire shipowner-merchant Asa Clapp of Maine. The elder Clapp was not only one of the leading voices of Maine mercantile interests (only Massachusetts and New York exceeded Maine in registered tonnage) but also the father-in-law of Levi Woodbury, soon to be Secretary of the Navy and then Secretary of the Treasury. Sage counsel also arrived from Democratic Senator Samuel Smith of Maryland, a very wealthy and prestigious Baltimore merchant as well as a politico. Smith's advice received both the serious consideration of Van Buren and the personal attention of the President. While Smith approved highly of the selection of William Rives as Minister to France, he believed that negotiations on the claims could best be handled by a confidential agent. Naturally, he had in his employ just such a man—fresh from the opium trade at Smyrna in the Middle East. Van Buren politely refused the proffered assistance.[33] A second group of claimants proceeded nonetheless to operate independently until their scheme, which likely involved the bribery of members of the French Chamber of Deputies, was uncovered and squelched in 1831.[34]

Chicanery, bribery, and a hand-in-glove relationship between public and private interest did not seem out of order in the minds of many, since the stakes reached into the millions of dollars. When the ink dried on the various treaties, Old Hickory's agents had succeeded in garnering $4.5 million from France, $2 million from Naples, and approximately $600,000 each from Denmark and Spain. Not only had the President salvaged the national honor in obtaining justice in these twenty-five-year-old claims, but he had filled the pockets of American merchants with unexpected wealth. Secretaries of State Van Buren and Livingston made extensive efforts to maintain communication with interested merchants, insurance company presidents, claims agents, and politicians. Livingston thoughtfully advised Maryland entrepreneur Robert Oliver that he was "very desirous of including your claim, if it can be done with advantage and propriety."[35]

Many businessmen were ecstatic over the General's successes. A Salem correspondent told Levi Woodbury that merchant Joseph Peabody was "highly gratified" over receiving $100,000, and "the general sentiment is that no man but General Jackson could have accomplished this business." In sharp contrast, Jackson would have been angered by the remarks of Samuel Smith but likewise appreciative of their irony. The Maryland senator lamented that "the men who reap the greatest advantage from the success in all our foreign relations—I mean the merchants—are generally hostile to the President, although he has obtained for them payment from Denmark and France to almost $6 million . . . and yet [he] has been and is daily abused and attacked in the most unqualified language applicable only to the vilest miscreant."[36]

The "daily abuse" that the President endured, however, only served to heighten his awareness of the political nature of the claims. Some of the beneficiaries, after all, were Democratic businessmen. Maryland Congressman Isaac McKim, for example, was a claimant and the scion of an old and powerful Baltimore house. He, along with Senator Smith, provided an excellent conduit for advice and information between the State Department and the mercantile community. Anti-Jacksonians approached the situation cautiously. In New England they wisely selected a wealthy Democratic claimant ($150,000) and ship captain, Nathaniel West of Salem, to present their claim petition before the President.[37]

At the same time, Jackson chose commissioners who would award the claims on a somewhat less than bipartisan basis. The three-member Danish commission included George Winchester, William J. Duane, and Jesse Hoyt. Winchester, a Jackson elector in 1824, was the brother of the president of the Baltimore Insurance Company, a claimant against Denmark. Duane, a Philadelphia lawyer who championed Old Hickory in 1828 and would be named Secretary of the Treasury in 1833, was an intimate friend of millionaire merchant banker and claimant Stephen Girard. Hoyt was a Democratic spearbearer and retainer from New York City, a crony of Van Buren and C. C. Cambreleng.

The Neapolitan commission consisted of Democratic partisans Wyllis Silliman of Ohio, Peter V. Daniel of Virginia, and John R. Livingston of New York. Silliman had the political good fortune to be the brother-in-law of Secretary of War Lewis Cass, while Livingston was the brother of former Secretary of State Edward Livingston. Daniel, a member of an old Commonwealth family, was a Jacksonian lawyer of modest reputation. (He would refuse the post of Attorney-General in 1834; later, Van Buren would appoint him to the Supreme Court.) The Virginian resigned from the commission prior to the final 1835 session and was replaced by Joseph Cabot of Massachusetts. Cabot was related to the Philadelphia wholesale merchant firm of Perit and Cabot, and joined Silliman in encouraging Woodbury to seek the Vice-Presidency in 1836.[38]

The membership of the powerful French commission was perhaps the most controversial. The President sought to appoint Philadelphia editor and former New Orleans comrade-in-arms Stephen Simpson. Simpson was not only an ardent Jacksonian but had worked for the Bank of the United States as a clerk and had written scathing attacks upon the institution, which delighted the President. He had been considered for the Danish commission in 1830, but the General nominated him for the more important French trio in 1832. His rejection by the Senate infuriated Old Hickory, who told Van Buren, "We shall never have peace with these men until they are made to understand the character of Andrew Jackson better than they now do." Only the Little Magician's smoothing of the President's ruffled feathers prevented the chief from throwing the nomination defiantly back into the Senate. A second commission member, former Democratic Senator Thomas Williams of Mississippi, resigned after serving from the fall of 1832 to the spring of 1833. Thus the final commission included George Washington Campbell of Tennessee, distinguished former Senator, Secretary of the Treasury, Minister to Russia, and longtime personal friend of Andrew Jackson; John K. Kane of Pennsylvania, a former Federalist reborn in the Jacksonian faith in 1828 and enemy of the Bank of the United States; and Romulus Saunders of North Carolina, a loyal Democratic Congressman and state attorney-general in the 1820s.

Since Jackson perceived the commission patronage as a function of the chief executive and nominated exclusively Democrats, it would be naive to assume that politics did not play a role in the awarding of the claims. It should be reasserted, as Samuel Smith noted, that National Republican/Whig businessmen were the major beneficiaries of the claims rewards because they had often been the Federalist merchants and shipowners during the Napoleonic Wars. However, a number of these businessmen were Jacksonians, and the President intended to insure that while American business in general would benefit from the treaties and the commissions, his supporters in particular would not be neglected.[39]

Unquestionably, Jackson utilized executive patronage policy in foreign affairs to foster the growth of and solidify the Democratic Party. Historian Robert Remini has observed, "Probably Jackson's principal failure as President centered mainly on his many wretched appointments. A few of them nearly destroyed him." While this statement has merit, for every Anthony Butler alienating the Mexicans, there was a William Rives pacifying the French.[40]

Since presidential diplomacy was conducted through the use of consuls (whose major function was, of course, commercial), ministers/chargés, and special executive agents, Old Hickory did not hesitate to use his appointment powers by selecting men for each post with an eye toward their political loyalty. (This is not to suggest that he would not maintain a capable National Republican in office: Henry Wheaton as Chargé to Denmark, for example.) Understandably, the President dispatched his most talented, intelligent diplomats to Europe, since the bulk of American trade and the most outstanding problems were with those nations. Less distinguished individuals, especially westerners, appeared to be his choice for Latin America; he was paying political debts in an area where the United States, although often a distant second, was attempting to be commercially competitive with Great Britain. Several brief examples, however, will illustrate the difficulties Jackson encountered with political appointees in the foreign service.

Jackson's energetic steps in resolving claims and negotiating commercial treaties in Europe, Latin America, the Middle East, and the Orient paved the way for Livingston's revisions of the consular code in 1833 and a sharp expansion of the consular service between 1829 and 1837. The agents, often acting as representatives for large mercantile houses, expected to profit from their appointments, but those who hoped to grow wealthy from the fees paid by American vessels landing at their ports were generally sorely disappointed. Nevertheless, the competition for consular posts during Jackson's presidency is indicative of the optimism of the business community about the potential for American commerce under the Tennesseean's leadership.

Nicholas Trist is one of the shadowy figures on the stage of American politics and diplomacy. Best known perhaps for his role in negotiating the Treaty of Guadalupe Hidalgo, which ended the Mexican-American War of 1846–48, Trist had entered the State Department as a clerk in 1828. He was a proper Virginian who learned to speak French, studied law with Thomas Jefferson, and then married into the Monticello family. Taking up the political standard of Andrew Jackson, Trist became a favorite of the President, who named him his private secretary in 1829. But after four years of loyal service to Old Hickory, Trist became concerned over his health (he had begun to spit blood and feared consumption) and his marginal economic situation. Accordingly, he asked the President for a diplomatic post that would be both healthful and lucrative. Havana seemed to be the answer. A close friend of Trist's was surprised by his decision to leave Washington, but when he "duly reflected upon the barren nature of the field of politics and the poor harvest it yields to its most successful cultivator, I no longer hesitate to approve your choice."[41]

The perceived financial potential of the Cuban post is reflected in the heated competition for the appointment when incumbent consul William Shaler died in 1833. A group of New York insurance executives, supported by powerful Jacksonians such as Congressman C. C. Cambreleng and Collector of the Port of New York Samuel Swartwout, had urged the selection of businessman John Hefferman. In May 1833,

Trist received several letters from Hefferman and his supporters delicately offering "pecuniary compensation to you if a relinquishment of your claim in my favour could be accomplished." The duly concerned merchant emphasized that the tropical nature of the climate would be ill-suited to Trist's health problems, that the cost of living in Havana was exorbitant, that he (Hefferman) spoke Spanish fluently and Trist did not, that Vice-President Van Buren was a friend of Hefferman's, and (the *coup de grâce*) that the post was not really financially rewarding. All of this communication and intrigue served only to irritate Trist, who promptly fired back a letter telling Hefferman that "in the fall, perhaps sooner, I shall go to Havana, which will probably be my residence for some years, should I live so long."[42] While Jackson's confidence no doubt gratified Trist, the President, who was probably aware of the pressures being applied, angered some of his Empire State political and business supporters by his decision.

Within a week of his appointment, Trist began to establish contacts with merchants in New York, Boston, and Philadelphia who might wish to work with him on a consignment basis. As a former member of the White House staff, Trist had little difficulty gaining the cooperation of the mercantile community, especially those who were Democrats.[43] But he may have had second thoughts about his rapid rejection of the insurance industry's offer when he began receiving correspondence from Vice-Consul Richard Cleveland in Havana. Cleveland warned his new chief that the revenues had averaged only $6,575 for the previous three years and that Havana was, in fact, an expensive city. He also cautioned Trist not to carry on the risky business of consignment merchant because of the high capital investment. Even worse, Cleveland described Havana as "a dreary sojourn for a lady educated in the United States. It is a destestable place to rear a family of children and it can only be under peculiar circumstances that such a residence can be endured." A disappointed Trist responded that he had expected the revenues to be at least $2,000 higher and that everyone he had spoken with had assured him of the profitability of the consignment trade. He quickly decided that he would leave his family in Virginia and simply try to return home as often as possible.[44]

Trist spent the next two years attempting to convert a consular appointment into a means of financial independence for himself and his family. He lobbied the administration for additional pressure upon Madrid for a reduction in the tariff on American vessels, and engaged in the cigar and sugar trade in an effort to supplement his income. But the Spanish continued to refuse to lower the duties, and few people wanted to buy the overpriced and inferior cigars. Loneliness also caught up with the Consul, who traveled to Virginia each summer and did not return to Havana until after the Christmas holidays.[45]

Trist's experiences were in many ways typical of the high expectations and low rewards encountered by American consular officials all over the globe. Since consuls were generally businessmen affiliated with large mercantile houses, Trist's political appointment was unique. His difficulties, however, were not the result of his inexperience so much as of the diplomatic and political climate in Madrid. His brief flirtation with business diplomacy ended in 1836, when he returned to a post in the State Department, where he ultimately became Chief Clerk under James K. Polk.[46]

While commercial involvement was the duty of a consul, such activity was questionable—if not a conflict of interest—among ministers or chargés. Neither Thomas P. Moore nor Robert McAfee could be considered a "wretched appointment," but the activities of both as ministers to Colombia were controversial, demonstrating the problem of placing an inexperienced western politico in a situation where he could be tempted by influential mercantile interests.

Moore was a favorite of the President because of his loyal support in the 1828 election in Henry Clay's home state. His appointment had the endorsement of such Democratic stalwarts as William Rives, John Bell, James Hamilton, Jr., and C. C. Cambreleng. Moore had been a congressman but had no diplomatic experience prior to traveling to Bogotá. He quickly found himself in trouble—both with certain revolutionary movements in Colombia for his support of President Simon Bolivar, and with some Americans over the rival claims of two families, the Karricks and the Holdings. In the latter situation, the Minister promptly lent his sympathies to the Karricks. This proved to be a wise decision on his part, since the Karricks were related to the wealthy and powerful merchant Elisha Riggs of Washington, D.C. Moore told Riggs in January 1830 that if the Secretary of State ordered his noninterference in the matter, "I will do indirectly that which I can not do directly." Naturally, Moore assured Riggs that he would accept no compensation for his efforts. Not surprisingly, Captain Holding, who lived in Cartagena, complained to the State Department, and the Secretary reminded Moore that a letter dated 1827 was on file in Bogotá, ordering noninterference.[47]

As good as his word, the Minister spent the next several years working quietly to further the Karrick claim. He continued to protest indignantly when Holding attacked his bias, while telling Riggs, "I need not assure you that at all hazards I will maintain your interests." While the slippery Moore was not being directly remunerated for his efforts on Riggs's behalf, there was consideration given. In the summer of 1831, Moore dispatched his black "major domo," Shannon Taylor, to New York with $3,000 to buy goods for the Colombian market. Taylor received the aid of Riggs's agents, and in February 1832 the Minister reported that a sizable profit had been made in the venture. When Moore decided to depart Colombia in 1833, he wistfully told Riggs that he would give him a final report on his business holdings and urged the merchant to contact Moore's successor so that the game might continue. Fortunately for all parties concerned—except Captain Holding—Robert B. McAfee, also of Kentucky, was named as the new Chargé to Bogotá.[48]

Sounding much like his predecessor, McAfee wrote Riggs in September 1833, informing him of the activities of the "sanguine and obstinate" Holding and telling him "I will attend to it [your claims] most faithfully, altho as a chargé d'affaires I cannot attend to it—as an individual I can serve you . . . you may rely upon my whole attention to this business for you." Over the next several years the efficient diplomat managed to obtain a compromise with Holding on the claim and to present it repeatedly to the Colombian government—but to no avail. As he prepared to return to the United States in the fall of 1836, a frustrated McAfee explained that only a petition to Jackson and Congress might move the South Americans off dead center, and even then it would take seven years to get results.[49]

It would not be an exaggeration to suggest that the two American diplomats were "in the pocket" of Elisha Riggs, serving virtually as his agents. In return they received certain commercial and financial considerations from his associated mercantile houses. While such activity might not have been illegal or even necessarily a conflict of interest by the nineteenth-century definition of the term, it represented a compromise with their traditional duties. Their advocacy role and the profits that they made because of it also demonstrate that these westerners, like their old chief, evidenced no animus toward business when the proper personal or political incentives were present.

The President relied not only upon constitutionally designated diplomatic officers to carry out his wishes but also upon sometimes controversial special agents. Depending on the political makeup of the Congress and the explosiveness of the object of the mission, the role of the special agent could be significant. Jackson, who believed in executive energy in foreign policy, did not hesitate to name such officers when he thought the situation required it.

The Rhind commission serves perhaps best to illustrate Jackson's problems with such agents. During a Senate recess the President named three commissioners—merchants Charles Rhind and David Offley, and Commodore James Biddle—as representatives to negotiate a treaty with Turkey in 1829. Although their efforts were fruitful the following year, an angry Senate rebuked the chief executive for his disdain of their role in policy making. Focusing upon the question of an appropriation for the recently completed mission, a lengthy debate began in February 1831 over the President's flexibility in appointing agents. Conservative states' rights Virginia Democrats Littleton Tazewell and John Tyler led the assault upon executive privilege. Two future Secretaries of State, Edward Livingston and John Forsyth, managed the defense. When the smoke cleared, even though the Jacksonians held a slim majority in the chamber, enough disgruntled Democrats had joined with the National Republican minority to disapprove the President's actions. The better disciplined House of Representatives softened the slap, however, engineering the removal of the offensive proviso in conference committee.

Whether the motives were political or constitutional, the Senate had made its point, but—perhaps typically—there was little alteration in Old Hickory's behavior. Even though agent Rhind added to the President's headaches after the completion of the Turkish treaty, Jackson still dispatched Edmund Roberts on a similar mission to Southeast Asia in 1832 and Charles Biddle to Central America in 1835 to examine a transisthmian route. Jackson was clearly sensitive to criticism by the Senate and aware of their constitutional advise-and-consent role, but he rarely let them interfere with what he considered as his major function as the formulator and executor of foreign policy.[50]

Nowhere was Jackson as active in pursuing his goals as in Europe. Here the supposedly parochial Tennesseean revealed himself to be a complex man, capable of adapting his diplomatic style and mood to the nation and situation. Here, too, he achieved some of his greatest successes and suffered some of his most embarrassing moments.

Chapter 3

The European Scene: Commerce, Claims, and Conflict

Almost a quarter of a century ago, historian David Brion Davis discussed the theme of the rise of countersubversive groups during the Age of Jackson. Davis recounted the feverish activity of these xenophobic organizations and how they rushed to crush those elements that threatened to destroy traditional American society and values from within. Most prominent among their targets were the Mormons, the Masonic Order, and Catholic immigrants. While these "anti" organizations succeeded in driving the Mormons to the Great Salt Lake and the Masons underground, they could never stem the floodtide of German and Irish immigrants. What was perhaps most ironic, Davis conjectured, was that the danger of foreign invasion was probably more remote in this period than in preceding decades. If Davis is correct, and many Americans were concerned about European subversion of traditional values, the question arises whether this concern translated into a more isolationist foreign policy for the United States. It did not.[1]

Certainly Andrew Jackson never veered sharply from the doctrines of Washington and Monroe, but he did pursue positive and aggressive relations with Europe that stimulated American commerce, travel, and interest. The Europeans remained preoccupied with reform, revolution, and major power struggles between the parliamentary democracies of the west (England and France) and the autocratic monarchies of the east (Russia, Austria, and Prussia). While friction in Europe rarely broke out into armed conflict during this period, tensions ran high. Not unlike the earlier Federalist Era, the possibility existed diplomatically of "America's success from Europe's distress."

The key clearly was Great Britain, undisputed mistress of the seas with her powerful navy and extensive merchant marine. Since American goals under Jackson were (1) the settlement of claims against various nations for violations of American shipping during the Napoleonic Wars and (2) the encouragement of commercial relations, the English would prove the major stumbling block. In smaller countries—Portugal, Spain, the Netherlands, and Belgium—British political influence and commercial domination made the negotiation of treaties difficult, if not impossible. Agreements often had to be cleared through London, where the Ministry did not welcome the additional competition or influence of the upstart Yankee Republic.

Still, Jackson registered an amazing string of victories, among them spoliations claims treaties with Denmark, France, Portugal, and Spain and trade revisions or new agreements with Great Britain, France, Russia, and Spain. By 1836, United States exports had increased by more than 75 percent and imports 250 percent over those of Jackson's first year in the White House. Critically, two-thirds of the exports and imports involved the Continental trade. Jackson and his agents combined the ability to threaten, cajole, and intimidate with patience, flattery, and understanding, depending upon the nation and the circumstance. This is not to suggest that all of Old Hickory's diplomatic representatives were ideal choices, or their missions successful. But more often than not, the diplomatic efforts of the Jacksonians meant increased profits for American businessmen and a new-found respect for the United States and her President.[2]

GREAT BRITAIN

The saga of Anglo-American relations prior to the advent of Andrew Jackson to the White House had been a tale of empire and commerce. The savvy British had for decades been aware of the Yankee expansionist impulse, having experienced it themselves in the invasion of Canada in 1812. They also observed with more than casual interest the U.S. purchase of Louisiana from the French in 1803 and the acquisition of Florida from Spain in 1819. Within the decade of the 1820s, United States interest in Latin America accelerated, as demonstrated by the Monroe Doctrine, and the recognition of and commercial treaties negotiated with the new southern republics. The English, for whom such commercial and perhaps territorial designs were both an economic and a strategic threat, viewed with suspicion the American energy channeled in this direction. Foreign Secretary George Canning, witnessing this movement, envisioned a United States–led confederacy in the Western Hemisphere that would be inherently anti-European. While Canning was likely engaging in hyperbole, the Duke of Wellington, then Prime Minister, was not when in 1828 he expressed the fear that England's greatest danger for war was with the United States. His colleague, Sir Robert Peel, ventured the suggestion that the Americans might use the excuse of putting down piracy or a slave insurrection to gain possession of Cuba. The British supposition that the Americans also wanted to conquer Canada made a strong defense necessary for that province.

The counterpoint of this concern for an expansionist United States was a general lack of respect for America and her political institutions. A casual reflection upon federal mismanagement of the War of 1812 was enough to convince an Englishman of inherent systematic ineptitude. Moreover, Jackson's ascendancy as leader of the "mobocracy" and the tinderbox issue of state sovereignty could only further weaken the fragile union.

Across the Atlantic Ocean, Andrew Jackson made Anglo-American relations a high diplomatic priority. In doing so, and with the successes that would follow from this decision, Jackson fostered one of the greater ironies in early American diplomatic history. His perception of Great Britain has gone largely unchallenged in American historiography. From his Revolutionary boyhood, when a British saber left him bleeding but uncowed, to the cotton-bale defenses outside New Orleans in January 1815, where he rallied his men against those forces that sought to crush the spirit of the infant republic, Jackson had been the quintessential Anglophobe. Within the past decade, historian Michael Rogin has gone so far as to suggest that Old Hickory's knee-jerk emotional responses to Mother England were reflections of deeply rooted psychological problems. It would perhaps then be logical to assume that the hot-tempered General would be eminently unsuccessful in his conduct of diplomacy toward Great Britain. Perhaps he would appoint as his representatives men of like mind, who would exacerbate the marginal status of the relationship between the two nations and personally offend the British crown through self-righteous pronouncements. Fear that this would occur likely existed in both Washington and London.

Instead, the opposite came to pass. After the failure of the Adams administration to resolve the pressing questions of the West Indian trade and the Canadian boundary, Jackson moved forthrightly and without animosity to settle them. His agents included the talented Delaware Federalist Louis McLane, the trusted Martin Van Buren, and finally the loyal and capable former Speaker of the House, Virginian Andrew Stevenson. Each of these men was a fine choice. While Jackson realized that Great Britain was the major American rival for commercial empire throughout the world and a prime obstacle to territorial expansion in North America and the Caribbean, he also knew that he could not intimidate the English as he would the Neapolitans or threaten them as he would the French. His attitude toward the English remained calm and dispassionate throughout, reaching the point of co-operation and understanding in the case of the Falkland Islands in 1831–32, when he accepted the British occupation of the recently vacated islands in what appeared to be a violation of the Monroe Doctrine.[3]

Clearly, the first priority of the new Jackson administration was a restoration of the lucrative direct trade with the British West Indies. This trade, a critical component of American economic prosperity in the colonial era, had been sharply limited by the Jay Treaty of 1794. After the War of 1812, American diplomats tried earnestly to reopen the trade but found the English less than receptive. By 1825 the situation had worsened to the point that when London attached a series of restrictive measures, the Adams administration refused to comply. The British accordingly closed their West Indian ports to ships departing American ports, and Adams promptly reciprocated. Imaginative Yankee shippers and merchants skirted the burdensome laws through indirect trade via Canada and Danish or Swedish islands in the Caribbean. But the issue was a marked embarrassment to the White House, which tried unsuccessfully to resolve the matter by treaty in 1827. The highly protective tariff of 1828, even though supported by many Jacksonians, was endorsed by the administration and interpreted by the English as a slap in the face. Not surprisingly, then, Adams's failure to resolve the West Indian imbroglio became an issue in the 1828 presidential race.

When Jackson emerged triumphant, it was incumbent upon him to deal with this issue as quickly as possible. The President, Secretary Van Buren, and Minister McLane developed a strategy that involved the repudiation of the Adams position and the adoption of a more conciliatory posture. McLane was to inform the British that the American people in 1828 had voted out of concern not only for domestic issues but for foreign policy as well. Thus the new team in Washington felt empowered to offer new solutions, such as accepting the British restrictions of 1825, and settling the question by statutory law rather than by convention or treaty. In a partisan fury, the National Republicans railed against Jackson's olive branch and the political betrayal of their failed diplomacy. Gaining the respect and recognition of Great Britain, however, was a signal priority for Andrew Jackson, a man who had fought that country's dominance most of his life. As Van Buren told McLane, "I am persuaded that there has been no event in his [Jackson's] public life that has caused him as much regret as he would experience in failing to be instrumental in the establishment of the very best understanding between the United States and Great Britain."[4]

McLane was not oblivious to the pressure-cooker situation in which he would be placed. The Minister noted that he had unwisely built Old Hickory's "cherished hopes and expectations beyond any reasonable calculation and it will be difficult to bring his mind down to . . . a level of talents one could be able to expect." When McLane arrived in London in September, he conferred with outgoing Minister James Barbour and other informed sources, and was encouraged by the rumored favorable disposition of the Ministry of Earl Grey. His optimism quickly faded, however, after his initial meeting with Foreign Secretary Lord Aberdeen in mid-October. They discussed the West Indian trade and the equally protectionist British Corn Laws and American Tariff of 1828. Aberdeen was not encouraging about restoration of the colonial trade, citing the tariff as a prime obstacle: would it be reduced within the next session of Congress? McLane replied that he could not comment with any certainty. The upshot was that there was little prospect of alteration in the West Indian situation. Even the American's suggestion that Congress would pass laws conforming with the British statutes of 1825 made little impact. Aberdeen informed him that he would have to consult the Board of Trade. Apparently, the Ministry preferred to wait and watch through the winter session of Congress in anticipation of some modification of the tariff.[5]

Months passed with little progress. McLane busied himself gathering information, lobbying officials, and identifying his obstacles. A number of vested interests had serious capital investments riding on the West Indian trade—bankers, planters, shipowners, and merchants in England, Canada, and the West Indies. As talks languished in the winter of 1829–30, Jackson sparked renewed hope with his December annual message to Congress. Sounding very much unlike the Anglophobic warrior he had been in his youth, the President noted, "With Great Britain, distinguished alike in peace and war, we may look forward to years of peaceful, honorable, and elevated competition. Everything in the condition and history of the two nations is calculated to inspire sentiments of mutual respect and to carry conviction to the minds of both that it is their policy to preserve the most cordial relations. Such are my own views, and it is not to be doubted that such are also the prevailing sentiments of our constituents." The London *Times* effused that "never since Washington's day, had a message included so much that was valuable and so little that was offensive."[6]

Despite the warm words of the President, and the equally positive response within the British press and official circles, McLane was unable to get a response to his proposals. The Minister was also well aware that his chief had given him ample time—more than six months—to reach an accord and that his patience was rapidly declining. In fact, Jackson would urge Van Buren in April to begin drafting a recommendation for nonintercourse between the United States and Canada if the British response was negative. McLane, who must have felt the situation slipping away, dispatched a forty-page memo to Aberdeen on March 16, outlining his position again and asking for an answer. None was forthcoming.[7]

At this point the Minister demonstrated a stroke of genius by encouraging American legislative initiative on the issue. Chosen for the task were powerful New York City merchant, congressman, and Van Buren intimate C. C. Cambreleng, and Baltimore merchant Senator Samuel Smith, who had been advising the executive on this subject for months. Cambreleng had already submitted a report, which McLane circulated widely in England, assailing the tariff and promoting free trade. The positive response that the paper received coincided with a warming of the British attitude. By the end of March, McLane was confidently telling Cambreleng, "We shall recover the direct trade."

Jackson prodded the Congress with an encouraging message on May 26, suggesting that positive dispatches were due daily from McLane. The final obstacle collapsed with the Senate's passage of a Smith-sponsored measure on May 29 authorizing the President to issue a proclamation of reciprocity when he had satisfactory evidence that the British would resume trade based upon the Act of 1825.[8]

The winds of trade were now shifting because of American action. Prior to May, resumption of commerce was based upon the British pledge to revoke orders closing the West Indian ports if Congress repealed the acts that had prompted the closings. The American initiative now empowered the President to open the trade at his discretion. He would issue the proclamation opening American ports on October 5, and the English would follow suit on November 5. But through the summer, McLane continued to apply pressure to Aberdeen. In July he informed him of the recently passed law in Congress that reduced the duties on West Indian produce (especially molasses, but also salt, cocoa, and coffee). Now that it was apparent that the American President and Congress were willing to compromise, McLane insisted that Parliament do the same. Finally, on August 17, the Foreign Secretary informed McLane that American trade would be restored on the basis of the Act of 1825. (The accord came not a day too soon. King George IV had died and been replaced by his brother, William IV. A new ministry would also be formed in October with the collapse of the Wellington-Aberdeen coalition. Earl Gray would move to direct the new government as Lord of the Treasury, while Lord Palmerston, with his questionable friendship for the United States and conservative commercial policies, would become Foreign Secretary.) The reciprocity agreement of 1830 was a triumph of common sense. The British would revoke their Orders in Council of 1826 and admit American vessels to colonial (Canadian and West Indian) American ports. The United States agreed that their vessels must trade only in American goods, and directly to the ports. The Crown reserved the privilege of tariffing colonial products that competed with American goods, while Washington admitted English ships carrying their colonial products on a most-favored-nation basis.[9]

Jackson was delighted and relieved when he learned of the compromise. As he confided proudly to Anthony Butler, it was "an indication of the disposition of Great Britain to meet us half way in establishing relations between the two countries on a fair and reciprocal basis which is the only sure guarantee for their future peace and the steady advancement of their prosperity and fame." Most Democrats, including southern Senator Robert Y. Hayne of South Carolina and Richmond editor Thomas Ritchie, were equally pleased with the outcome. They were all well aware that the accord could be advantageous in the upcoming congressional contests, especially in the Northeast.[10]

Not surprisingly, the National Republican opposition was furious over the course of events in the summer and fall of 1830. Jackson offered nothing more than Adams had, but the diplomatic style and approach proved critical. McLane was given cooperation, time, and the flexibility to offer an American initiative based upon executive and congressional action. This token of Washington's cordiality and good faith enabled negotiations to turn the corner. But the opposition press bitterly challenged the procedure, claiming that McLane was about to barter away the Tariff of 1828 or, worse still, United States honor and dignity. On the floor of the Senate, Daniel Webster of Massachusetts and Peleg Sprague and John Holmes of Maine vilified the President and attacked the value of the trade. Holmes's resolution to press for an inquiry into the entire matter, however, never came to a vote. When word arrived that a compromise solution had been agreed to by the British, the anti-Jacksonians were obliged to change their tactics: Jackson and McLane had been taken in by the crafty English, the editors now contended, and agreed to terms that the sage Adams never would have conceded. While they continued to raise the dubious argument about the value of the trade, the opposition did strike home in arguing that it had actually never been lost—only redirected. But their voices of protest were soon drowned in the overall swell of rejoicing. As historian Lee Benns so succinctly claims:

Whatever advantages British shipping reaped following the arrangement were not due to the arrangement itself but to the advantages which Great Britain held in the geographical location of her colonies and in her right to impose discriminating duties to protect the products of those colonies against foreign competition. Against the former it was useless for the United States to protest; against the latter it had no legal right to protest. For four years Adams had vainly striven to force Great Britain to surrender these advantages in respect to the United States and had eventually completely failed in his effort. Jackson had faced the situation as it was, had sought to secure all that might reasonably be expected, and had eventually gained all that he had sought.[11]

With the West Indian trade issue—the primary goal of his mission—now settled, an exhausted but triumphant McLane petitioned to return to the United States. The President, however, denied his request. He had one further delicate issue for his representative to help guide toward a successful conclusion.

Since the Peace of Paris in 1783, which ended the American Revolution, the northeastern boundary between the United States and Canada had been unresolved. By 1822 a commission established under the Treaty of Ghent (1814) had produced only contradictory claims. The 100-mile-long disputed area, involving primarily Maine and New Brunswick, interested the British largely as a route for a much-desired military road between Quebec and St. Johns. For the expansion-minded Americans, while the region was better for timber than farmland, it came wonderfully close to the St. Lawrence River. The King had offered to compromise and even grant navigation of the St. Lawrence in exchange for the road in 1824, but Secretary of State Adams had refused. American stubbornness was based on the legitimate hope that the boundary line would be drawn down the highlands separating the rivers that emptied into the St. Lawrence from those that fell into the Atlantic Ocean (except the St. Johns).

Maine became a state in 1820, placing added pressure on Washington to determine a definite line. Accordingly, in 1827 the Adams administration had signed a pact with Great Britain that provided for the gathering of evidence and the submission of the results to the King of the Netherlands, who would act as arbiter. The United States position was defined by veteran diplomat Albert Gallatin, Minister to Great Britain in 1826–27, and William Pitt Preble of Maine. After two years of research, the agents defended the United States claim on the basis of the documents used in the 1783 negotiations, especially seventeenth- and eighteenth-century England land grants. The British based their argument upon geographic discrepancies—or, as historian James Callahan deems it, "an ingenious quibble"—regarding where the Atlantic Ocean stopped and the Bay of Fundy began, and the fact that the Americans in 1783 had never claimed any territory north of the St. Johns River.[12]

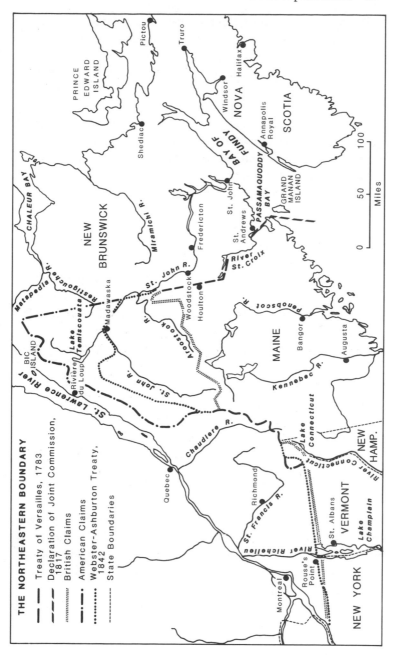

THE NORTHEASTERN BOUNDARY

— — — Treaty of Versailles, 1783
– – – Declaration of Joint Commission, 1817
·········· British Claims
—··—··— American Claims
••••••••• Webster-Ashburton Treaty, 1842
——————— State Boundaries

When Jackson assumed office in the spring of 1829, the position statements had not yet been submitted to the King, but it was already apparent that resolution would not come easily. Secretary of State Van Buren nervously discussed the matter with British Minister Sir Charles Vaughan and told him of the critical importance of keeping Maine informed on all matters. Cornelius Van Ness, the former governor of Vermont and commissioner under the Ghent agreement, wrote Van Buren regarding the deliberations of the commission established to determine the boundary. Their findings revealed that the American position—at least as it affected a portion of the claim—was weak, and therefore the United States had understandably not pushed for a final solution.[13]

Jackson and Van Buren were undoubtedly well aware of both these points, especially the political sensitivity of the issue. They used questionable judgment in dispatching the emotional Preble in November 1829 to serve as Minister to the Netherlands. Soon after his arrival, the American position was sent to him for delivery to the King prior to the April 1, 1830, deadline. Preble received instructions to remain at The Hague and await the monarch's expected decision in January 1831. It is clear, however, from the Minister's correspondence in 1830, that the American claims were in jeopardy. Preble's initial impressions of the King had been most positive, and he was optimistic that the monarch would be fair in his decision. However, as the summer passed, a revolution that resulted in Belgian independence shook the Netherlands. This splintering of the nation was blamed on the liberal forces running rampant throughout western Europe, and unfortunately, the image of the Jackson administration epitomized liberalism in the Western Hemisphere. Preble also became aware of the power of Great Britain in influencing the politics and policies of foreign courts. Weeks before the King rendered his decision, Preble's frustration reached its boiling point; he complained to Van Buren that the "court is full of jealousy, intrigue, bad faith and venality." Not adept at such games, the American could only watch events swirl around him and caustically observe to a Maine colleague "that the United States will not be satisfied with an improper decision."[14]

On January 10 the anticipated bad news reached Preble: The King had decided against identifying the "highlands" that formed the basis of the 1783 treaty claims, deeming such a line "inexplicable and impractical." Instead, he utilized the more convenient river system, drawing a compromise line that gave the United States almost 8,000 of the 12,000 square miles in dispute. Since most of the lost territory would be sacrificed by Maine, the reaction of the American Minister was swift and predictable. A furious Preble immediately protested formally (without his government's authorization) and fired off a letter to Van Buren complaining, "The truth seems to be that the King has bartered away a large portion of our territory to his good friend and ally for the purpose of obtaining a generous slice of Belgium." He exercised less restraint in telling William Rives, Minister to France, that "this government is distinguished for a crooked, double dealing policy."[15]

Auguste Davezac, Secretary of Legation at The Hague, reinforced Preble's claims, although without the accompanying emotionalism. He informed Jackson that the Minister had done all that was humanly possible against the almost insurmountable odds of European politics. The Belgian, French, and Polish Revolutions had disrupted the commerce and political stability of the Continent. The Netherlands was simply a pawn in a chess game conducted by the major powers, and she had little choice but to be thrown into the arms of the British crown— "England had become the arbiter of their destinies." As Cornelius Van Ness metaphorically observed, "It was an unfortunate moment for us to have this decision take place, when the old King of Holland has his nose just above water and is looking to England as a drowning man would look at a plank floating near him."[16]

The American reaction to the decision was one of almost universal disapproval. The objections took two major courses: (1) that the King was under the undue political influence of Great Britain and should have disqualified himself from making the award in such tumultuous times; (2) that the King had violated his proper role as arbiter and, instead of deciding the issue on the conflicting claims of the 1783 treaty, had acted as mediator, thus exceeding his authority. McLane called the award "capricious and arbitrary." James Hamilton of New York argued that the decision was not binding, because the monarch who made the award was the King of Holland, not the King of the Netherlands. The matter was also a threat to domestic tranquillity and a constitutional problem: the reaction of Maine would undoubtedly be negative, and as Hamilton argued, the federal government could not surrender part of a state without that state's approval. A more level-headed Van Ness confided to Van Buren that in substance the award was not damaging to

American security or agricultural interests. Maine would certainly sacrifice a sizable area of real estate, and New Hampshire and Vermont would also lose small strips of land, but the Americans would, after all, receive two-thirds of the disputed property.[17]

That the question was one of principle did not escape the President's notice. He told Old Kinderhook in March that "we must step with care, but I can see no difficulty in the case." While he seemed inclined to accept the award, Jackson was well aware that the sovereign power of the states could not constitutionally be impaired and that Maine would have to be cajoled into acceptance, which would require maximum patience and diplomacy. By the summer of 1831, both Preble and McLane had returned to the United States to share their advice on the issue with the White House. There were hard questions to be answered. What public posture should Jackson adopt? What course of action should he recommend to the Senate? How should he deal with Governor Samuel Smith and the Maine legislature?[18]

By August 1, Jackson had decided to accept the award. After weighing the benefits and losses, the President agreed largely with the position earlier taken by Van Ness, the Minister to Spain. The loss of a million acres of bad land in Maine and New Hampshire was not critical to American agricultural or security interests. The greater danger was that if the question dragged on, it might evolve into a border war and then explode into an unwanted general war. Such a risk was hardly worth the potential reward of delaying resolution further. Jackson instructed Van Buren, newly appointed but unconfirmed Minister to England, to inform His Majesty's government that if Britain approved the award, he would refer it (even though the United States was not legally bound to accept it) to the Senate for advice and consent; for the present, however, he would not move until he learned what the British response would be. By August 10 he had his answer in an interview with Preble, and the positive English response set the diplomatic wheels in motion. Jackson instructed Van Buren to convince Palmerston that the situation was most delicate. The President's position with the Senate and the citizens of Maine would be strengthened if the British would move first in publicly acknowledging their acceptance of the decision.[19]

By late September, Van Buren happily informed his chief that an informal discussion with the Foreign Secretary had produced the desired results: Palmerston had assured the Minister that Jackson would have his confirmation of British intentions before the next session of Congress. Two weeks later the Ministry demonstrated further good will by suggesting to Van Buren that London was willing to establish a commission to readjust the boundary line where it might be necessary. Clearly, the English were eager to cooperate in reaching a final determination. But problems quickly erupted for the President in both Maine and Washington. In November of 1831 an election in the border town of Madawaska resulted in violence and the arrest of four Americans by Canadian authorities. Simultaneously, Jackson was preparing his recommendations to the Senate on the question. Throughout the summer the Old Warrior had taken no public position on the award, but he began to have second thoughts about his reticence. Confiding to Van Buren that he feared his administration might be charged with "want of good faith" if the Americans rejected the arbitration, he reconsidered the value of making a public statement. However, his advisors convinced him that the Senate would likely approve the decision in an effort to harmonize relations between the two countries. The President was aware of the broadsides that would be fired in the path of resolution, especially those laid down for political effect, but he was optimistic that he could handle them "pretty well." In this judgment he would prove incorrect.[20]

The Jackson administration adopted a twofold strategy in its attempt to gain acceptance of the King's decision. Secretary Livingston would act as liaison with Governor Smith, the Maine legislature, and any representatives they might choose. It would be Livingston's task to gain the consent of the state to surrender its claim to the disputed territory to the federal government, clearing the way for a presidential acceptance of the award. It became increasingly more apparent that to gain this concession, Maine must be compensated for its losses, probably in the form of federal territory. Meanwhile, reluctant acceptance of the decision would be guided through the Jacksonian-controlled Senate by Littleton Tazewell of Virginia, chairman of the Foreign Relations Committee. The President, of course, particularly in an election year, remained above the fray, lest he tear additional holes in his political coat with this rather thorny issue.[21]

The strategy encountered expected opposition. Senator Peleg Sprague of Maine led the assault on the new line, arguing that the federal government lacked the constitutional authority to give away land belonging to a sovereign state and claiming that the United States was not obliged to accept the ruling of King William as arbiter. He urged that the Senate reject the ruling and that the administration reopen negotiations. As expected, the matter was referred to the Foreign Relations Committee. Reporting on March 21, Tazewell's group contended that while the President was not bound by the decision, expediency dictated that he should accept it to finally resolve a troublesome question. As the report headed into the full Senate for debate, Livingston was also making significant progress. On February 3, William Preble, now the agent for the state of Maine, informed the President that his legislature had just passed a series of resolutions opposing The Hague's decision and denying the right of the federal government to transfer its property to a foreign power. Almost immediately, Preble began to feel the pressure from Washington. The President met with him and intimated that the Senate would endorse the award. Tazewell bluntly said that the offer was expedient and Maine should accept it. Livingston soft-talked the agent with a lecture on how the President was concerned about national honor and the rights of Maine—and then he suggested the compensation.[22]

Preble dutifully communicated the proposal to Governor Smith, who in turn placed it in the hands of the legislature. That body, meeting in secret session, voted on February 22 to accept the President's offer on the condition that the final agreement between the United States and Great Britain must be approved by the legislature. Jackson was pleased with the progress of events thus far but troubled by the unconstitutional stranglehold Maine wished to place around the neck of any Anglo-American agreement. He urged Livingston to meet with representatives of Maine and resolve the residual details. In April 1832 the Governor appointed Preble, Nicholas Emery of Portsmouth, and Revel Williams of Augusta to meet with Livingston, Secretary of the Treasury McLane, and Secretary of the Navy Woodbury. In their meetings during the last two weeks of May, Preble and his associates made it apparent to their counterparts that Maine insisted on new negotiations based upon the 1783 treaty. If those should prove unsuccessful, then the state would approve compensation for lost territory. Livingston agreed; Washington would initiate additional efforts on a new line, but that failing, the President would then feel compelled to endorse the King's line. He would also follow an earlier suggestion by Van Buren and urge

Congress to compensate Maine with the proceeds of the sale of one million acres of land in the Michigan territory. This offer had understandable appeal to the state agents, who conditionally accepted and pledged to recommend it to their legislature.[23]

Since the entire operation hinged upon the Senate's approval of the line and agreement to offer compensation in the West, all was held in abeyance until their decision—but with the election only five months away, the National Republicans were not about to add to Jackson's foreign policy accomplishments. With presidential candidate Henry Clay leading the way, followed by Daniel Webster and the indefatigable Sprague, opponents of the report of the Foreign Relations Committee ripped it apart by amendments. On June 16 the Senate voted 35 to 8 that King William's decision was not binding; the critical vote came one week later when the chamber recommended 23 to 22 to reopen negotiations with Great Britain based on the Peace of Paris.

Old Hickory suppressed his frustration and disappointment at the months of wasted effort and immediately authorized the new talks. Livingston explained the Senate's objections to British Chargé Charles Bankhead and attempted to be optimistic that renegotiation would prove fruitful. After all, even if the 1783 "highlands line" remained elusive, Maine had tentatively agreed to compensation, which would remove a major constitutional stumbling block to resolution. Jackson also suggested that the new talks might most profitably be carried on in Washington, not only because it was closer to Maine but because the United States presently had no Minister at the Court of Saint James's. This embarrassing situation resulted from the Senate's rejection of Van Buren's nomination in January 1832. A handful of disgruntled southern Democrats, most of whom preferred Vice-President John C. Calhoun as the heir apparent to General Jackson, had joined the National Republicans to create a tie vote, and the South Carolinian had no doubt delighted in using the power of the chair to break the deadlock by casting his nay vote. Calhoun's actions simply confirmed in Jackson's mind the rightness in making Van Buren the vice-presidential nominee. As the angry chief scribbled defiantly to one of his lieutenants, "This is the only way that the indignity offered to the Executive and the nation, and the insult to Europe can be repelled and confidence restored in our foreign relations."[24]

The renegotiation proceeded at a snail's pace. The President desired to move quickly, but he encountered a series of problems that delayed the appointment of a new emissary until May 1834. Chargé Aaron Vail in London attempted to carry on as best he could, but the British were noticeably piqued. The British Undersecretary of Foreign Affairs told Vail that new talks were "out of the question." Palmerston was less adamant but perplexed at the American refusal of a line he considered more than generous to the United States. As for the Treaty of 1783, continued insistence on using it as a basis for discussion was likely to "embarrass the negotiations." Vail continued to press for the reopening through the fall of 1832 but found the Ministry more concerned with European problems, such as the ongoing turbulence over Belgium and the civil war in Portugal. For the Americans the boundary question remained of signal import in their foreign policy; for the foremost power in the world, however, it was only one (and a minor one at that) of a number of crises.

Vail was able to talk with British Minister Sir Charles Vaughan, who would soon depart for Washington and was apparently not looking forward to negotiating in the United States if he would be obliged to deal with representatives of Maine—especially William Preble, whose views he considered "narrow and mincing." Finally, in mid-October, Vail had an extended conversation with Palmerston that produced results. The Foreign Secretary was firm, without being hostile, that the English were not going to begin new talks until American views were clearly and formally declared. Vail could only "suppose" what the administration might desire, and his suppositions were insufficient reason for Palmerston and the cabinet to spend lengthy hours in discussion. The Foreign Secretary did, however, express his concern for the return "of so favorable an administration to the talks" in the November elections.[25]

Jackson, solidly reelected, pressed Livingston for a settlement of the boundary line. He wanted the talks to commence as soon as possible, whether in London or Washington, and had the Secretary confidentially offer the post of American Minister to former House Speaker Andrew Stevenson of Virginia. Stevenson would not be confirmed until 1836, but Jackson's intentions to proceed with the negotiations were clear.

Unfortunately, by March 1833, when Vaughan arrived in Washington to begin discussions, the slim edge the administration held in dealing with Maine had evaporated. On March 4 the state legislature reasserted that all international agreements regarding its boundary would lack binding force unless submitted to the residents of Maine in town meeting for their approval. This unrealistic proposal, combined with demands to locate the highlands line and guarantee joint navigational rights on the St. Johns River, hamstrung Livingston in his talks with Vaughan. The British viewed the American federal-state relationship as maddening and the utilization of the 1783 treaty as "utterly hopeless." While Vaughan perceived Jackson as a strong-willed President and one well disposed toward England, he found him "feeble and temporizing"[26] on the possible collision with a state government.

The Minister's perceptions differ markedly not only with Jackson's challenge of South Carolina over the tariff and nullification in 1832–33 but also with a story related by the President's secretary, Nicholas Trist, in May 1833. Trist recalled that the General, Secretary of State Edward Livingston, Secretary of the Treasury Louis McLane, and Secretary of War Lewis Cass had gathered at the White House around a map of the Northeast. Livingston, drawing a proposed boundary on the map, pointed out that the line was likely to raise a clamor. The President exploded, "I care nothing about clamors sir, Mark me! I do precisely what I think just and right." And for emphasis, Trist noted, "as he uttered the last, his forefinger came down perpendicularly on the map."[27]

Vaughan may have misjudged the President's willingness to challenge a state, but he was painfully aware of the problems that Jackson now had to face with both Maine and the Senate. The New Englanders had rejected the King's award chiefly because it ignored free navigation of the St. Johns River. The British perception was that the St. Johns was only a first step toward the ultimate goal—control of the St. Lawrence—and to Vaughan's mind, Jackson had neither the power nor the political inclination to challenge the frontier ambitions of the New England states. Since the prospect of an increased American presence on the Canadian frontier was unacceptable to His Majesty's government, they must firmly reject the Senate's demand for the St. Johns and urge a return to King William's decision of 1831.[28]

By the spring of 1833, Livingston had stepped down from the State Department, to be succeeded by Louis McLane. McLane had been a federal commissioner in the May 1832 discussions with Maine's agents and was well aware of the problems. His one year as Secretary of State was filled with frustration regarding the boundary line. Hoping to win the support of Maine, McLane sought to consider afresh Livingston's proposal for a joint survey commission. This group would explore the disputed northeastern region and locate the elusive highlands line once and for all; their recommendation would be binding. To placate Maine, the highlands would be connected with the source of the St. Croix River as prescribed by the Treaty of 1783. To the British, the Secretary seemed to be mouthing repetitive platitudes; they responded with silence. McLane's successor, John Forsyth, continued the correspondence through 1834, trying to find "the true line" in the highlands.[29]

Late in the year, Vaughan agreed to accede to Jackson's request and establish a joint commission to determine a border, if the Americans would drop their demands for the St. Johns River access. This, of course, the President could not do. Nevertheless, on December 28, 1835, the British formally withdrew their acceptance of the King's award of 1831 and recommended a simple division of the property in half, utilizing the upper branch of the St. Johns as a dividing line. On February 29, 1836, Jackson—with Maine and the Senate looking over his shoulder—was obliged to decline. The General repeated his request for a joint commission but alternatively offered a mouth-to-source boundary of the St. Johns River if he could get Maine's approval. Within a week British Chargé Charles Bankhead replied that he was not sanguine about the crown's acceptance of Jackson's proposal, but Forsyth urged that it be submitted for cabinet approval nevertheless.[30]

There the issue remained frozen through the remainder of the year. It was apparent that the British deeply resented the intrusion of Maine in matters between two sovereign governments and that Palmerston was not about to surrender the St. Johns River. The administration, as long as the state remained adamant about the river and a highlands settlement, had little flexibility in negotiating. With time running out on Jackson's presidency, the anxiety level increased proportionately in Washington. The Old Warrior badly wanted this ongoing issue and several minor problems concluded before he departed the White House in March 1837.

To resolve these matters, it became imperative to dispatch a representative to London immediately. The post had been vacant since the

Senate failed to confirm Van Buren in January 1832. Old Hickory had intended to nominate Andrew Stevenson in 1833, but the arrival of Vaughan to conduct the parlays in Washington and internal political considerations had postponed the process until the spring of 1834. Sadly, by then the opposition had gained control of the Senate, where a coalition of Whigs and dissident Democrats led by Clay, Webster, and Calhoun defeated the nomination by one vote. An irate Jackson refused to select a substitute for the loyal Stevenson. The following year he sounded out Senator Hugh Lawson White about majority support for Stevenson in the upper chamber. White was not encouraging, so the President withheld nomination until the composition of the Senate had changed in 1836. On February 18 he once again presented the Virginian's name to that august body, which two weeks later confirmed the nomination by a 26–19 margin.[31]

Stevenson arrived in London on June 30, 1836, but received no special instructions on the boundary issue until the end of the year, when Forsyth encouraged him to solicit a response to the still-unanswered February proposal. A February 1837 meeting between Stevenson and Palmerston changed neither's position; the Foreign Secretary explained once again that the 1783 treaty was an unacceptable basis for talks, that a highlands line was almost impossible to agree upon, and that the crucial issue of control of the St. Johns could only be resolved by a conventional boundary line. Stevenson could only painfully fall back upon the American insistence on the highlands and remind Palmerston that Maine's vested interest must be considered in all their discussions. The issue remained unresolved for the next five years.[32] (Ironically, when the boundary was settled in the Webster-Ashburton Treaty of 1842, the United States, although gaining the St. Johns access, received almost 1,000 fewer square miles than specified in King William's award of 1831. Moreover, while Maine and Massachusetts received cash compensation of $250,000 each for property sacrificed, this amount was hardly equivalent to what Maine would have realized from the sale of the million acres of Michigan land.)

The other points of contention with Great Britain in the period focused upon the delicate slavery question and therefore generated sparks of controversy. Stevenson demanded payment for the slave cargoes of three American ships that had been confiscated and liberated in the British islands of Bermuda and the Bahamas between 1831 and 1835. In October 1839, after almost three years of negotiation, His Majesty's Exchequer agreed to pay $115,000 for the 210 slaves on two of the vessels. The third claim was not settled to the general satisfaction of the Americans until 1853.

The African slave trade and the insistence of the British on the right of search and seizure posed a particularly prickly problem for Stevenson. He was well aware that the energetic Palmerston had concluded a dozen bilateral treaties with European powers to outlaw the slave trade and allow English cruisers to stop, search, and seize suspected slavers. By the conclusion of the Jackson administration, only the United States remained reluctant to cooperate in ending this despicable traffic in human cargo. After the conclusion of an Anglo-French pact on the slave trade in 1833, Sir Charles Vaughan had spoken with Secretary of State McLane about participating in the venture. He was promptly informed that the administration was not interested; in fact, the Senate had just rejected a treaty with Colombia because it contained a mutual search provision. The slaveowning sympathies of the executive and Congress combined with the indignant rejection of the British practice of intruding upon the American flag on the high seas to doom any serious talks on the subject.[33]

The election of Andrew Jackson in 1828 had not been well received in Great Britain. Van Buren comments in his autobiography that the Bank of the United States, through its friends in the newspaper and financial communities, tried to prejudice the British Ministry and the public mind against the General, suggesting that his victory possibly meant war. McLane encountered some of the fruits of their efforts when he arrived in London in 1829. To Levi Woodbury he noted the manifestation of anti-American feeling in England; to William Rives, the apprehensions created by Jackson's "ferocity."[34]

Fortunately, Charles Vaughan, although a National Republican sympathizer, was responsible enough to help ameliorate his government's fears about this quarrelsome frontier Democrat. Moreover, the dominance of Lord Palmerston as Foreign Secretary from 1830 to 1837 (with a brief interval from the fall of 1834 to the spring of 1835) turned out to be a boon to positive relations. Palmerston was naturally more interested in events in Europe, the Middle East, and the Orient than in

America. His policy of friendship and accommodation toward the Americans, as evidenced by his quick acceptance of the King's Maine boundary decision and his offer of mediation in the claims crisis with France in 1835–36, are obvious examples of a conciliatory spirit founded upon pragmatism: a conflict with the Americans would drain energy and resources and require a shift in focus away from more critical areas. Despite the gloomy predictions that had greeted the advent of a Jackson presidency, Palmerston and Vaughan could fairly say that they had received better treatment from Jackson than from any of his predecessors. The Americans returned the fond "hands across the sea" accolades when Van Buren and Vail emphasized that Palmerston was a diplomat of "the most fair, liberal and friendly character." The efforts of McLane, Van Buren, and Vail also helped. Old Kinderhook discovered that the British military could even joke about his chief's victory at New Orleans. Vail reported in 1835 that "Jackson is decidedly the most popular President in England we ever had."[35]

Certainly, much of the credit for that must go to the President himself. He was cooperative, not confrontational. He sought compromise while allowing for competition. His goal was to establish mutual respect with the major world power. The failure to resolve the northeastern boundary should be blamed upon the obstinacy of Maine and the political opposition within the Senate; Jacksonian policy was sound but frustrated. While the West Indian agreement was his most visible diplomatic triumph, the level of accord and awareness achieved with Great Britain in the Falklands dispute with Argentina, in the imbroglio over spoliations claims with France, and in the Texas Revolution suggest that Jackson ushered in a new era of Anglo-American understanding.

Unfortunately, that understanding did not extend southward into the Iberian peninsula. Neither Spain nor Portugal, wracked by chaotic economic and political situations, were in any mood to repay the claims or negotiate the commercial advantages that Jackson believed were due the United States.

IBERIA

After the American Revolution, the United States maintained a tenuous relationship with the Spanish Empire, whose government had given lip service (but little else) in aid of the rebels. Even in the 1770s and 1780s, Madrid was well aware that Spanish territory lay directly in the path of the ambitious young republic. The Spanish, pressed by the Wars of the French Revolution and Napoleon, made concessions grudgingly: first the Pinckney Treaty in 1795, which granted the Americans use of the Mississippi River; then the ill-fated transfer of Louisiana to the French, who quickly sold it to Thomas Jefferson in 1803; and finally, the loss of the Floridas in 1819 following Jackson's invasion in pursuit of renegade Indians. Between American imperial designs and the revolutionary wars in Latin America, the Spanish empire was simply melting away. The King realized that having lost nearly all his North American possessions, he must stoutly defend his one remaining jewel, Cuba.

The Spanish were not uninformed about American designs upon the island, but Washington was caught in a diplomatic bind. How could it endorse republican revolution throughout the remainder of Latin America and support the continuance of colonialism in Cuba? Yet if the island were someday to fall under United States control, it would serve Yankee interests in the meantime for the island to remain dominated by a severely weakened Spain. Possession or protectorship by either a stronger European power (England or France) or an ambitious Mexico or Colombia would defeat American designs. The possibility of a race war on the island, perhaps instigated by Haiti, also brought shudders of terror to the White House. This would not only end a dream held by some of extending American slavery to Cuba but would place an antislavery dagger at the throat of the South. Thus American policy reflected the status quo: a reinforcement of the no-transfer principle of the Monroe Doctrine. In 1825, Minister to Spain Edward Everett had pledged his government's ongoing support of Spanish rule in Cuba. In return, the Spanish were to open their ports to American shipping. Unfortunately, Madrid failed to live up to its part of the bargain, and discriminatory duties continued to vex American policy makers into the 1840s. Behind the conciliatory facade of American toleration of Spanish rule in Cuba, however, was the veiled threat that Spanish commercial policy must be reformed to allow for more open trade and the penetration of Yankee capital. Madrid's failure to modify its policy might jeopardize Spain's very possession of the island.

The political convulsions that wracked the Iberian peninsula in the early nineteenth century had a marked effect on diplomatic relations with the United States. The Americans nervously eyed the intrigues of Spain and Portugal for three reasons. First, the administration of James Monroe had endorsed the notion of a republican Latin America. While most of the Spanish empire (with the notable exception of Cuba) had seized the moment of turmoil of the Napoleonic Wars to revolt successfully against the mother country, there was no pledge from Madrid that attempts would not be made to reconquer the wayward colonies. It was to the Americans' interest, both ideologically and commercially, to convince the Spaniards of the folly of military conquest. Second, reparations claims had been made by American business against both the Spanish government (for over $1 million) and the Portuguese government (for $150,000) for damages done to shipping in the recent revolutions. Third, favorable commercial treaties, especially with Spain, were a high priority of the Jackson administration. The United States averaged slightly over $1 million in imports from and approximately $400,000 in exports to Spain during the first Jackson administration. Much more important, the Americans imported more than $8 million annually in Cuban sugar, coffee, and tobacco and exported over $5 million to Cuba, largely in agricultural produce. Of all ships entering and leaving the island's ports, almost 50 percent were American; indeed, the dollar value of Yankee trade with Cuba was second only to that of Spain herself. To protect that vital commerce, the President stationed four consuls in Cuba and four more on the lucrative island of Puerto Rico. The necessity of such energies is apparent when the trade is placed in the context of the total value of American imports (ca. $100 million) and exports (ca. $80 million) in 1831–32. Although the United States had negotiated a commercial treaty with Spain, the tonnage duties and tariff rates sharply discriminated against Yankee sail.[36]

With such problems facing the incoming Jackson administration in 1829, it is not surprising that the President considered Madrid the second most important diplomatic appointment (after St. James's). When Secretary of State Van Buren suggested the nomination of Senator Levi Woodbury of New Hampshire for the post, he chose wisely. Woodbury possessed the strong commercial ties through marriage necessary to understand the Spanish situation and had served as the chairman of the

Senate Committee on Commerce. Although the prospect of losing another valuable ally in the upper house pained Old Hickory, the resolution of the Iberian questions took precedence. The impatient chief executive made it clear, however, that he would countenance no delays in departure and likewise would not respond positively to a request for return to the United States until the goals of the mission were accomplished. Such stringent requirements did not sit well with Woodbury, a dedicated family man whose wife and children were not eager to cross the Atlantic for an indefinite period of time (at least four years). Unfortunately for the President (and Van Buren), Woodbury, after deep reflection, declined the nomination.[37]

The President soon thereafter offered the mission to another New Englander, Governor Cornelius P. Van Ness of Vermont, a man as devoutly Jacksonian as Woodbury but less sympathetic to Van Buren. Van Ness accepted the important and lucrative post ($9,000 annually) and departed for Madrid in the fall of 1829. Jackson, evincing his usual candor, gave the minister his instructions: Van Ness was to obtain a new commercial treaty based on the principle of reciprocity, and to resolve the six-year-old claims question upon which Madrid had been procrastinating. These tasks might be facilitated by reminding the Spanish that the United States was a loyal friend of the King and had recently interposed when a combined Mexican-Colombian expedition threatened Cuba. Van Ness was to assure the Spanish that the American navy would remain vigilant to stop any similar move in the future. Jackson was aware that events in Europe placed Spain in "an embarrassed and dependent situation" and feared that a transfer of the island to France or England might result. While not referring specifically to the Monroe Doctrine, the General made it clear that such a move must be opposed and that the geography, market, and slavery questions all gave Cuba a special significance for the United States. Further elaborating on American involvement with the former Spanish colonies, Jackson offered to act as mediator to facilitate recognition of the Latin American republics by the former mother country.[38]

The new minister had not been in Madrid a year when good fortune crossed his path in the form of a coup in France. The French Revolution of July 1830, which overthrew Charles X, sent shock waves through Spain. Charles was related to Ferdinand of Spain and had constituted a vital prop to his regime. The lack of French support, combined with internecine feuding over the succession to the throne, placed Ferdinand in a weakened foreign policy posture. He was in no position to challenge any power militarily, even the United States. Seizing the moment, Van Ness urged the President to recommend measures to Congress that would coerce a settlement from the Spanish crown. "The stronger the language used the better as long as it doesn't amount to a threat," he suggested. "There is no other way of obtaining justice from them."[39]

Much to the diplomat's disappointment, however, the President simply chose to report that "the subjects of difference with Spain have been brought to the view of that Government by our minister there with much force and propriety, and the strongest assurances have been received of their early and favorable consideration." Unfortunately, Jackson's optimism was misplaced. Van Ness was obliged to report in January 1831 that the Spanish government would neither deal with the claims issue nor negotiate a new commercial treaty. The disconsolate diplomat admitted failure and requested a new assignment within the year. In his despondency, Van Ness angrily criticized a presidential consular appointee in Spain, describing him as "a despicable vagabond" and pointing out that Old Hickory must have been "entirely ignorant" when he nominated him. His apology the following week likely did little to ingratiate him with the President.[40]

The successful completion of the French claims treaty by Minister William Rives in July 1831 rekindled Jackson's hopes for a settlement with Spain. The dam had been broken, he felt, and the issues could be resolved. The President decided that the commercial treaty was the first priority and that if Spain did not back off on its harsh regulations, he would be obliged to recommend retaliatory measures to Congress. The Spanish claims, on the other hand, did not merit an international conflict, and Jackson informed Secretary Livingston that if negotiation failed, the government would abandon them rather than institute reprisals. Soon thereafter he went before Congress with his annual message, criticizing the Spanish denial of responsibility for the ship seizures and hinting at executive recommendations if a new effort by Van Ness fell upon deaf ears.[41]

The President's words left their mark. Early in 1832, Van Ness reported that the Spanish government had reopened the talks on both the claims question and the commercial treaty. By midsummer Van Ness succeeded in exacting a conditional reduction of tonnage duties on American vessels arriving at Spanish continental ports. While this was a significant step forward, the tonnage differential in the Caribbean continued, and the claims issue remained.[42]

By the spring of 1833, Jackson's patience became exhausted. Livingston informed Van Ness that the tariff duties in Cuba and Puerto Rico had become so offensive "that some retaliatory measures are indispensable" without rapid changes in Spanish policy. The President had not yet made such recommendations to the Congress, hoping for a solution. But the matter could not be delayed beyond the December meeting of the legislature, "unwilling as we are to enter into a warfare of restrictions." Van Ness, whose mission had been a series of disappointments, simply wanted to come home. His request was denied—until he had settled the issues or had "lost all hope of succeeding." Instead, the Minister was given new marching orders, instructing him to warn the Spanish about the "onerous duties" in the Caribbean and the possibility of a disastrous trade war. At the same time, Van Ness was reminded that the President was still concerned about the claims of American merchants but willing to compromise on that issue. Old Hickory had suggested in his annual message to Congress in 1832 that some of the American claims—which reached $1.2 million—might be exaggerated. He also correctly recognized the exhausted state of the Spanish treasury. These two factors caused him to tell Van Ness to ask for $800,000 but to compromise on $600,000 if necessary. Jackson was even willing to accept the sum in Spanish stock and spread the amount over a ten- to fifteen-year period. In this critical situation the President wisely recognized the unstable nature of the Spanish crown and ministry, and sought to obtain modest concessions to salvage American honor and close the issue.[43]

In December 1832, Van Ness had reasserted the ridiculous American claim of $2.5 million. This was almost embarrassing, since Jackson at the same time was giving Congress an admittedly exaggerated figure of half that amount. Following the President's lead, the Minister in February reduced the demand substantially to the $800,000 the administration had allowed. After several months of deliberation, His Majesty's representative, Don José de Heredia, told Van Ness that the government was willing to pay $500,000. Since this sum would be paid in Spanish stock worth, by Van Ness's calculations, only $380,000 in the Paris or London market, he refused. By early June, Secretary of State Don Francisco Zea Bermudez agreed to increase the amount to $600,000. Through the remainder of the year the American futilely continued to press for $800,000, hoping the Spanish would come up to $700,000. By December 1833 the situation was rapidly degenerating in Madrid. The King had died, giving power to the Queen regent, and civil war threatened. The impoverished Spanish treasury was likely to suffer even greater strains in the coming months. Therefore, on February 17, 1834, Van Ness signed the claims treaty and removed an annoying, if not critical, obstacle in the path of Spanish-American harmony.[44]

Thus, by the beginning of 1834, Jackson could inform Congress of the settlement of one outstanding issue, but the Caribbean duties remained a thorn in the side of harmonious relations. With calm resolution rather than anger, the President asked Congress for discriminatory duties against Spain.[45] That body replied positively in the 1834 session, and on June 30 Jackson signed into law a measure that would not go into effect until March 1836—which allowed the Spanish almost two years to repeal (or at least lower) the repugnant tariffs. But the Madrid government, in the midst of a civil war, was not in the mood to compromise. Instead, it increased the duty on flour, a vital commodity in the American trade, to the point where its importation into Cuba became prohibitive.[46]

As the months dragged on and relations worsened, it became more apparent that Van Ness's marginal diplomatic skills—in addition to his temper and patience—were collapsing under the pressure. Finally, in May 1835 the Minister received notice that he had been succeeded by Postmaster-General William T. Barry of Kentucky, who had recently been investigated by Congress for misdeeds in office and had resigned amidst a storm of controversy. Such a man was a poor choice for the resolution of delicate diplomatic matters in a heated political climate, but that fact turned out to be irrelevant: the fifty-one-year-old Barry died suddenly in Liverpool, en route to Spain, in August.

Van Ness, who earlier had pleaded for another appointment or a ticket home, now passionately wanted to remain. But the New Englander's failures were too many and his irascible behavior too widely known; Secretary Forsyth told him bluntly that he had become an "embarrassment to the department." In spite of his instructions to step down, however, Van Ness continued to perform his ministerial duties, and a troubled Jackson (perhaps too quickly) selected controversial cabinet member John Eaton, former Secretary of War and most recently territorial governor of Florida, to succeed Barry. But Eaton, whose assignments included reopening the tariff talks and encouraging Spanish recognition of the Latin American republics (an effort that had thus far gotten nowhere), proved as difficult for the State Department to manage as Van Ness had been. The diplomat left New York with his wife, Peggy, in August 1836, but six months later still had not arrived at his post. A rebuke from Forsyth had little effect, and Eaton's behavior was a harbinger of his four-year tenure in Spain.[47]

The reduction of the tonnage duties between continental Spain and the United States in 1832 and the settlement of the claims issue in 1834 both represented significant accomplishments in the Jackson administration's Iberian goals. The success was due largely to the energies of the President and the timing of his statements and recommendations to Congress, as well as the perseverance of the cantankerous Van Ness. Yankee businessmen still faced high duties in the Cuban trade, but negotiation for reduction of those tariffs bordered on the impossible amidst the Carlist Wars of succession that raged throughout the 1830s.

Problems with the other monarchy nestled on the Iberian peninsula were as confused but never as critical as those with Spain. The Napoleonic Wars had disrupted the Portuguese monarchy and thrown the English into a critical decision-making position. The British had successfully urged Dom Juan to take refuge in the colony of Brazil and allow Great Britain to defend Portugal. He stayed in Rio de Janeiro after 1815 as King of Portugal and Brazil, and British troops remained in occupation upon Portuguese soil. By 1820 the Portuguese were on the verge of revolt, demanding the return of their King. He obliged them in 1821, leaving behind his son Dom Pedro as regent in Brazil. Although Dom Juan intended Brazil to remain a colonial possession, his son declared independence in 1822. Dom Juan could do little about this situation, since his own hold upon the Portuguese crown was tenuous and dependent upon British arms. When Dom Juan died in 1826, civil strife ensued between the liberal parliamentarians and the monarchists, who supported Dom Miguel, the youngest son of the late King. Dom Miguel triumphed in 1828, much to the disgust of many European governments, including Great Britain, which refused to recognize his legitimacy. This set the stage for a power struggle between Dom Miguel and his older brother, Dom Pedro of Brazil, who claimed to be entitled also to the throne in Lisbon.[48]

Andrew Jackson entered the White House as the rival Portuguese factions began to press their claims with foreign governments. The President carefully weighed the information that he received from both sides, including obvious hints from the Brazilian government that his recognition of Dom Miguel would jeopardize American relations with that government. Nevertheless, Jackson moved in October 1829 to grant recognition to Dom Miguel and also decided to allow Chargé d'Affaires Thomas L. L. Brent of Virginia to remain at his post to resolve the outstanding problems between Portugal and the United States. While several minor claims by American shipowners were a nagging issue, the President was most anxious for a commercial treaty. American rice, flour, fish, and lumber were discriminated against, generally in favor of the omnipresent British commercial and political presence in the kingdom. While Brent was unsuccessful in gaining the treaty, he was able (under some pressure from Jackson) to negotiate a claims settlement in January 1832. The pact involved just four vessels and totaled only $150,000, but the agreement fit another piece into the successful completion of the claims puzzle—an ongoing foreign policy goal of the administration. The fact that the payments would be delayed over five years caused no ill feeling (unlike the similar failure of France to pay promptly), since the administration was aware of the embarrassed state of the Portuguese treasury.[49]

Brent's success was timed perfectly. By the summer of 1832, the forces of Dom Pedro (with English assistance) had invaded Portugal, and the nation was embroiled in civil war. The situation became additionally complicated by the threats of both Spain (on the side of Dom Miguel) and England (on behalf of Dom Pedro) to send troops in support of their favorites; as 1832 progressed, the family feud threatened to spark a general European war. Reason prevailed, however, and the combination of British-sanctioned intervention by Spain and the stupidity of his generals obliged Dom Miguel to capitulate in 1834. The crown was placed upon the head of young Dona Maria, the daughter of Dom Pedro, causing a temporary suspension in relations between the United States and Portugal. The President chose this opportunity to select a new chargé to attempt the negotiation of a commercial treaty.[50]

Edward Kavanagh of Maine, a loyal Jacksonian who had served two terms in Congress before he was defeated in the Whig backlash from the Bank War, could have been the first Catholic senator from New England. Instead, in 1835, he chose to accept the President's offer to serve as the American representative in Lisbon. (No doubt his relationship with Secretary of the Treasury Levi Woodbury was a factor in his appointment.)[51]

Kavanagh proved himself a bright and talented diplomat operating in a Byzantine maze of European politics where constant cabinet changes, court intrigues, and foreign influences all spelled frustration for American goals. A political liberal, Kavanagh was not the most popular diplomat at court, and his advocacy of a commercial treaty also affected the quasi-colonial status of Portugal with England. Despite these obstacles, on several occasions the Chargé felt that negotiations were moving in a positive direction for a commercial treaty, but each time some calamity would occur or some objection would be made that stalled the talks. By the time Jackson left the White House in March 1837, Kavanagh was not yet successful. His perseverance paid off, however, with the signing of an agreement in 1840.[52]

The resolution of the Spanish and Portuguese claims were minor victories for the Jackson administration, as was the commercial treaty with Madrid. The major goal, reduction of duties with Cuba, remained elusive—not for want of American energy or commitment, but as an indication of Spain's determination to protect what remained of its fragile empire.

RUSSIA

As the Jacksonians scanned the European horizon in hope of improving American mercantile opportunities, Russia glimmered far off in the distance. Even though the Czar's armies had proved themselves a force to be reckoned with in the Napoleonic Wars and his shadow loomed increasingly large over eastern Europe, Russia's goals only tangentially came into contact with those of the United States. In 1824 a Russo-American pact had been concluded, securing a ten-year Yankee claim to the North American coast from Oregon to Alaska. Occasionally, a Russian sailor would defect in an American port or arguments would arise over fishing rights between the two nations, but such issues were not critical. Thus, when the President made his initial appointments of European ministers prior to Secretary of State Van Buren's arrival in Washington in the spring of 1829, it is not surprising that the seat at St. Petersburg was still vacant. In an effort to placate and reassure his lieutenant of his confidence, Jackson encouraged Van Buren to select someone proper for the post. With some misgivings, the Secretary decided upon congressional veteran and conservative Jeffersonian John Randolph of Roanoke. Van Buren chose the volatile Virginian not for his diplomatic skills but rather because he had a fondness for him and also perceived him as a potentially uncontrollable opponent of the administration who might best be stationed at a distance. The Secretary felt that if the diplomat succeeded, the accomplishment could be lauded; if he failed, little would be forfeited by the experiment.

Randolph was by all accounts a poor choice. Although regarded by many as brilliant, witty, and articulate, he was emotionally unstable and tubercular. His outspoken republicanism—he later referred to the Czar as "a genuine Cossack, implacable, remorseless and blood-thirsty"—almost insured that he would not be favored at court. But to the administration's way of thinking, the major purpose of the Russian mission should be the negotiation of a commercial treaty to expand American trade with the Black Sea. Observant merchants were aware of Russia's imperial goals, which would likely thrust her into the forefront of European commercial powers. While this had not yet occurred, now was the time to negotiate with the Czar a favorable agreement automatically applicable to lands comquered in the future.[53]

After some delay, Randolph arrived in St. Petersburg in August 1830. Within a few days he decided that the climate was unsuitable for his health and soon reboarded a ship, bound for London. Before his departure, he had begun the inquiry into a commercial treaty but had been obliged to treat with acting Foreign Secretary Prince Lieven.

Lieven was then Ambassador to England; he was visiting St. Petersburg when asked to take over temporarily the duties of the ill Count Nesselrode. Randolph recognized the slim possibilities of negotiating with the Anglophile Lieven and perceived that the recent July Revolution in France had heightened Russian fears regarding republican governments—including that of the United States. In such an unreceptive environment, little could be accomplished, and Randolph exercised the option extended to him by the President to return to England if the situation warranted it. Randolph's health deteriorated in 1831 however, and instead of returning to St. Petersburg, he sailed for New York in August.[54]

The departure of the Minister created a vacuum that Secretary of Legation John Randolph Clay found impossible to fill. Clay, one of four Americans in St. Petersburg, existed in less than splendid isolation. The chaos of European revolution and the cholera pushed any discussion with the Americans into the background. While the talks foundered, rumors flew in Washington over Randolph's successor. The embarrassment over the Virginian's mission combined with a growing awareness of the importance of Russian trade to remove this post from the farcical category. The President now considered prominent New York politico James A. Hamilton and former Federalist Congressman James Buchanan of Pennsylvania for the position. Buchanan, anxious to prove his loyalty to the President, had coveted the post of Attorney-General when the cabinet resigned in 1831, but another ex-Federalist— Roger B. Taney of Maryland—had received that appointment, leaving the Pennsylvanian with few options. Although his French was weak, his widowed mother objected, and the move would damage his law practice and hinder his efforts to control the Keystone Democracy, Buchanan accepted the mission in June 1831.[55]

Since Randolph had not yet returned to the United States, the administration cautiously delayed announcing Buchanan's appointment and allowed him the luxury of waiting almost a year before departure. When he did sail in April 1832, his goal was to complete his negotiations rapidly and return from this rather "genteel exile" as soon as possible. Quickly, the urbane and entertaining American diplomat became a favorite of the Emperor and Empress. He countered anti-Czarist reports in the American press by describing Nicholas I as "a very popular sovereign . . . all classes of people with whom I have conversed . . . entertain the most exalted opinion of his ability, integrity and justice. I would consider his loss as the greatest misfortune that could befall Russia." Certainly Nicholas was a tyrant who eschewed civil liberties, but Buchanan personally respected the Czar, whom he regarded as "one of the best despots in Europe." The American was able to differentiate between the cumbersome and often corrupt bureaucracy that burdened the nation and the Czar himself, who created "a calm of despotism."

Undoubtedly, Nicholas relished this rare esteem from a foreigner. For his part, the engaging Buchanan utilized his parlor skills as a storyteller and dancer to amaze and delight the court. His imaginatively vivid tales of America apparently found their mark in a society whose mythology included a patron saint (Alexander Nevsky) who had sailed up the Neva River on a grindstone. The Pennsylvanian judiciously viewed Russian society as a strange blend of barbarism and civilization—although he never adjusted to the food: he once described a sour soup as possessing a taste "that would have repulsed a Delaware Indian."[56]

Discussion regarding a commercial treaty had begun soon after Buchanan's arrival at St. Petersburg in June. The Minister perceptively realized that recent European events could have a dramatic impact upon his negotiations. The bloody crushing by Czarist armies of a liberal uprising in Poland had made Nicholas even more wary of Western democracies; the French and British had been openly sympathetic with the Poles, and only the moderation of Earl Grey and Lord Palmerston had staved off actual democratic intervention in the crisis. At the same time, the Czar was concerned about the separation of revolutionary Belgium from the Netherlands and anxious to break the budding entente between England and France in support of the Belgians. Finally, the integrity of Turkey was critical to the Russians, since any foreign intrusion there would jeopardize the Black Sea trade. While the Russians had joined with the British and French to crush the Turkish fleet at the Battle of Navarino in 1827, the Czar was justifiably concerned about the stability of the Ottoman Empire and felt obliged to secure it against either internal or external enemies. Buchanan did not agree with the often heavy-handed tactics the Czar utilized to achieve his imperial goals, but the Minister's ability to recognize the fears and weaknesses of the court strengthened his hand in negotiation.

The Russians were very interested in a reduction of the oppressive duties of the American "Tariff of Abominations" of 1828, which affected their sales of hemp and iron. Buchanan could assure them that the President was pressing for a lowering of the tariff; in turn, the United States wanted advantages in moving sugar and other raw materials into Russia via the Black Sea. As the discussions progressed into August, Buchanan with delight informed Count Nesselrode that the tariff of 1832 would reduce the duties by 50 percent on hemp and similarly on iron. But to his disappointment, this revelation brought the Minister no immediate word of concessions; on the contrary, he heard nothing from the Foreign Secretary for six weeks. Finally, in early October the Count relayed the word that the Czar had rejected the treaty. Apparently a major stumbling block had been the American insistence on a joint pledge on maritime rights for neutrals, including free ships, free goods, a definition of contraband, and the legality of a blockade. The Russians were understandably hesitant to approve such an agreement without serious consideration of the English reaction, especially at a time when they were seeking her favor. The rejection was conditional however; if Buchanan would make some modifications in the offensive passages, Nesselrode would present it once again to the Czar. He did so, but heard nothing in reply.

Two events then occurred to insure the successful completion of the pact. The British and French concluded an agreement on October 22 guaranteeing the independence of Belgium and sharply reducing the Czar's need to court the English further. Additionally, Buchanan conceived the brilliant plan of urging Nesselrode to hold the signing of the treaty at a gala celebration on the Czar's birthday in December. The idea was a stroke of genius.[57]

Buchanan and Count Nesselrode signed the commercial treaty on December 18, 1832. The wily Pennsylvanian had opened a new era in Russian diplomacy by achieving an arrangement that many European nations had sought for decades. The principles of reciprocity were insured, along with most-favored-nation status, which would serve the Americans well in the Black Sea trade. True, Buchanan had failed to obtain the desired provisions for the guarantee of neutral rights, but this sacrifice seemed to him only minor. The next American diplomat could solve that puzzle.

How had Buchanan succeeded where others before him had failed? Certainly, events in Europe had assisted in encouraging the Russians to improve their southern trade and insure themselves of a dependable, neutral commercial partner. But credit must be given to Buchanan, who (although a much maligned President in the 1850s) demonstrated considerable diplomatic skill and patience. His lighthearted behavior at court masked a keen perception of Russian attitudes and the impact of the events he observed firsthand. The Minister understood that Russia's fear of the West was a reflection of weakness. The Russians were battered ideologically and physically in the first half of the nineteenth century. Everywhere they looked, liberalism reared its ugly head— sometimes, as with the Polish uprising of 1831, much too close to home. Buchanan recognized, without sympathizing, that the Czar was obliged to secure his own borders with Poland. The Minister went so far as to defend the Czar against the charges of cruelty to the Poles that were leveled in the American press. He felt Russian brutality had been exaggerated by Congress. This was an old and bitter feud, fueled by revolutionary ideology but buried in ethnicity and time.[58]

Buchanan's views, however, were out of the mainstream of American public feeling. Russian Chargé Dimitri von der Osten-Sacken had been battling a floodtide of editorials and tavern chatter in Washington since 1830. His public efforts made little impact, so the Russian government ordered him to confine his energies to assuring a neutral position on the part of the Jackson administration. While Buchanan busied himself flattering and cajoling the Russian aristocracy in the fall of 1832 in an attempt to get approval of his treaty, Osten-Sacken was greeted with *Globe* editorials praising the virtue of the freedom-seeking Poles. The Chargé protested to Secretary of State Livingston, suggesting that an insincere Jackson was proffering a commercial relationship with one hand and sanctioning anti-Czarist editorials with the other.

The President, usually a maelstrom of righteous indignation in such circumstances, wisely held his temper, recognizing the critical timing involved. Livingston waited two months, until December 1832, before he asked for a withdrawal of the offensive remarks. Osten-Sacken refused to comply, and Buchanan was informed of his reticence. By this time, however, the commercial treaty had been signed, and Nesselrode was not about to disturb the euphoria of the moment. The Count supposed that Osten-Sacken surely could not have meant to impugn the honor of the President, but in any case he would be recalled.

The Russians also assumed, erroneously, that Buchanan would become the Czar's "spokesman to the west." Nicholas was sensitive about the attacks on his Polish policy in the American, French, and British press, and he envisioned the understanding Pennsylvanian as someone who could help rectify his poor image; surely Buchanan could influence Jackson to encourage positive articles about the Czar as a balance to the liberal press. When the Minister tried to explain that the government had no control over the press in the United States, the mystified and disbelieving Czar then wondered why the Democratic Party had "official" organs.[59]

His major task completed, the weary diplomat requested a return to the United States. Buchanan was tired of the food, the weather, the constant surveillance by the police, and the opening of his mail by authorities. It took months for letters to arrive; the salary was insufficient for the lifestyle at court; and his political career at home was beginning to suffer. But Buchanan was obliged to eat the bitter fruit of success. The administration rejected his petition for recall, encouraging him to stay on and complete the negotiations on the neutral rights provisions.

An angry Buchanan unfairly blamed Livingston for his continued penance, claiming the Secretary was "either too old, or too much engrossed with other affairs and therefore unfit to perform his duties." Nevertheless, the Minister dutifully spent the first half of 1833 attempting to obtain agreement from Nesselrode on neutral rights. Not only was he unsuccessful, but the Count held out little hope for an altered state. The Russians had conceded as much as possible in the commercial treaty of December 1832. They must still reckon with the English fleet. While it was now unlikely that Great Britain could be wooed to join the conservative monarchical Holy Alliance, it would not advance the Russian cause to deliberately agitate the English.

When Livingston departed the office of Secretary of State in May to be replaced by Louis McLane, therefore, Buchanan took the opportunity of the transition to return to America in August 1833. Although several men were considered to succeed him, including Georgia Sena-

tor John Forsyth (soon to be Secretary of State), the appointment ultimately went to a Pittsburgh judge, Senator William Wilkins. Wilkins
attempted to separate the Russians from the British fleet but encountered the same obstacles that had finally defeated Buchanan. In November 1835, Nesselrode sent Wilkins a finely worded note that curtailed
discussion of the subject until it came up again during the Crimean
War of the 1850s.

The new minister's second assignment was to negotiate an extension of American trading and fishing rights above latitude 54°40' in
Western North America, as granted in the Treaty of 1824. The ten-year
trial period was about to expire, and the Russo-American Company
intended to reclaim its monopoly in the area. In the summer of 1834 the
Russians arrested several Americans in violation of the law. Count
Nesselrode openly admitted that the obstacles to an extension were the
company and the extensive capital invested in North America.[60]

Wilkins left Russia in December 1835 without scoring a victory on
either the maritime rights or the trading-fishing extension. These issues, irritating but not critical in nature, would be left for resolution to
Van Buren appointee George M. Dallas of Pennsylvania. Jacksonian
efforts to bring the United States into closer commercial concert with
Czarist Russia must be adjudged a qualified success. Such minor victories would not individually spin the economy around but were pieces
of the European trade puzzle; the President had made another move
towards its completion and the resulting revitalization of the American
commercial empire.

Without question, however, the major problem for the Jacksonians in
Europe was the restored Bourbon monarchy of France. Not only were
the French major trading partners with the United States, but their reluctance to pay the millions of dollars owed American shipowners and
captains for violations of neutral rights during the Napoleonic Wars
sullied the honor of the Yankee republic and was a constant irritant to
businessmen and politicians alike.

Jackson hoped to resolve the issue without disrupting the harmony
and lucrative commerce between the two nations. A rude awakening
awaited him.

Chapter 4

France: Commerce, Claims, and Conflict

By 1829, although the great Lafayette was still alive in Paris, the spirit that had made him the embodiment of cooperative Franco-American relations during the Revolutionary era had long since died. First, the close bonds that existed during the War for Independence snapped in an undeclared naval war between the United States and France in the 1790s. Then, although relations improved slightly during Jefferson's first administration, highlighted by the Louisiana Purchase, they collapsed amidst the violations of American rights on the high seas that accompanied the renewal of the Napoleonic Wars. French harassment became so great, in fact, that extensive debate occurred about whether to declare war on France, as well as England, in 1812. The stifling of the French Revolution by the establishment of Napoleon's empire and the restoration of the Bourbon monarchs in 1815 further separated the former allies.

One bond that continued to command the attention of the two governments, regardless of politics, was a very valuable commercial intercourse. The United States was the largest importer of French merchandise in 1831 (at a total value of 134 million francs) and second largest exporter to France (51 million francs). The exchange was conducted largely in commodities: American hides, flour, rice, sugar, coffee, indigo, cotton, and naval stores for French silks, wines, brandies, and finished goods. Although the two nations had completed a commercial convention in 1822, serious inequities remained, especially on cotton and tobacco.[1]

While the Jackson administration no doubt sought to rectify these commercial injustices with a major trading partner, a more pressing and emotional issue remained from the Napoleonic Wars—the spoliations claims. When England and France moved to renew their bloody conflict in 1806–07, both sides attempted to gain economic advantage through the restriction of neutral commerce. The British in their Orders in Council and the French in the Berlin and Milan Decrees prohibited American vessels from visiting ports controlled by their enemies before reaching a friendlier destination. Thomas Jefferson's 1807 embargo, which forbade American ships to leave port, further complicated the situation; it prompted an additional French decree in 1808 ordering all Yankee vessels seized in French ports, since they could not be American—Jefferson's law had prohibited them from sailing. Napoleon followed with the Rambouillet Decree in March 1810, allowing the French to seize all American sail in port since May 1809. This was theoretically to retaliate against the American Non-Intercourse Act of 1809, which barred French ships from American ports on penalty of confiscation. By the time the United States declared war on Great Britain in June 1812, Napoleon had seized more than 300 ships and cargo valued at over $7 million. Although the Madison administration protested vehemently, the Emperor refused to agree to the legality of the American claims.[2]

After peace returned to Europe, Madison dispatched the venerable Albert Gallatin in 1816 to resolve the claims issue and restore commercial ties on the basis of reciprocity. Six years of negotiation produced but scant results. The Bourbons would not accept responsibility for the depredations of the demonic Corsican, nor could Gallatin make progress in achieving commercial reciprocity. Instead, the French claimed that the United States was in violation of Article 8 of the 1803 Louisiana Treaty, which granted most-favored-nation status to France in the ceded port (New Orleans). Paris contended that in the various treaties negotiated following the War of 1812, the United States had provided for tariff reductions that negatively affected French trade. They naturally expected compensation for their losses. The French complicated matters further with the introduction of the half-century-old Beaumarchais claim, an ancient debt—which Beaumarchais's heirs claimed never had been paid—pertaining to goods delivered to the supply-short Americans during the Revolution. Both Gallatin and his successor, James Brown (Henry Clay's brother-in-law), were cautioned not to allow the French to link the settlement of the spoliations claims with the Louisiana Treaty and Beaumarchais. As a result, negotiations remained at a stalemate throughout the 1820s.

Andrew Jackson decided that Edward Livingston was the ideal choice to settle these outstanding matters with France. Mature, sophisticated, fluent in French and an expert in the law, the Louisianan had the added advantage of having been a personal friend of the President since the War of 1812. But personal problems prohibited Livingston from accepting the appointment at this time. Thus the choice of a new minister fell to incoming Secretary of State Van Buren, who upon the recommendation of James Hamilton, quickly decided upon Virginia's William Rives.[3]

Rives was only thirty-six years old, an age that caused such veteran politicos as William Crawford to question his ability to cope with heavy responsibility. But Van Buren, the Red Fox of Kinderhook, was alert to the politics of patronage. Rives was a trusted party man who had worked hard for Jackson's election. The Virginia Commonwealth had been ignored in cabinet appointments, so lost ground must be made up elsewhere. The choice proved to be a fortunate one. Rives, a planter and southern gentleman, spoke French and possessed the essential natural charm, yet was intelligent, tough, and persevering; he would not be bluffed or worn down by his more experienced Continental adversaries.

The unresolved question, however, was how much the novice diplomat should try to obtain. Both Hamilton and Gallatin had supposed that $4 to $5 million would suffice to placate the claimants, but the administration was unsure. Van Buren decided that the wisest course would simply be to allow the French to make the first offer, which Rives would relay to the United States for consideration. Like their predecessors, the Jacksonians urged their agent to keep the spoliations claims separate from other issues if possible, but in a sharp departure from past policy, they did agree to permit joint discussion rather than allowing the talks to collapse. Jackson was also willing to admit responsibility for the Beaumarchais debt and to deduct one million livres (approximately $125,000) from the American claims to pay the heirs; however, the White House was not prepared to admit that France had special privileges at New Orleans or legitimate claims to reimbursement duty fees. Clearly, Rives had the support of an administration that was optimistic about solutions and ready to compromise to achieve them. Furthermore, the administration was convinced of the fundamental correctness of its position on the claims and confident that they would be resolved.[4]

Although Rives was well aware of the importance of the claims issue, vested interests began applying pressure on him even before he left Virginia. The Minister received correspondence and visitations from agents of various businessmen who assured him that they possessed the necessary influential contacts in Paris to assist in his negotiations. One such individual, a Mr. Jaussard, was the friend of Baltimore merchant and Democratic Senator Samuel Smith. Rives met with Jaussard in New York in August 1829 and, although finding him to be "a contriving sort of man," believed that he could be useful in facilitating the talks. With millions of dollars at stake, the American claimants lacked the administration's confidence in the inexperienced Virginian's ability to accomplish a settlement alone.[5]

Rives, his wife Judith, and Minister to England Louis McLane left the United States for their new assignments in late August 1829 aboard the *Constellation*. Unfortunately for the Virginian, his arrival coincided with yet another change in the French government. Although there had been only two Bourbon monarchs since the fall of Napoleon—Louis XVIII (1814–24) and Charles X—the Revolution had left a residue of party factions, ranging from the ultraroyalist right, which wished to do away with a parliamentary charter and establish an absolutist monarchy, to the liberal left, which sought to do away with not only the charter but the monarch as well. Moderate groups hoped to preserve both the monarchy and the charter, and to reestablish France economically and politically in the European community, and they had enjoyed some success in accomplishing these goals under Louis. However, the advent of Charles to power opened the way for the ultras and resulted in a sharp polarization of politics.

Rives arrived at a most inopportune time. A new ministry under the leadership of Prince Jules de Polignac as Minister of Foreign Affairs had just been formed. Polignac was an ultraroyalist, an Anglophile married to an Englishwoman; he was stubborn, egotistical, and unpopular with his peers. Rives immediately perceived that the Prince faced strong opposition in the Chamber of Deputies (the French parliament) and that he would likely approach the question of the American claims "with timidity."[6]

The American Minister arrived in Paris on October 1 and met with the Minister of Foreign Affairs two days later. It was not until November 2, however, that the first serious discussion of the claims issues occurred. Rives's argument was almost immediately discounted by Polignac, who "feared" that the Bourbons could not be responsible for the acts of Napoleon. The American countered by noting that the Emperor had ruled for over a decade and that his government had been recognized around the world. In addition, France had already paid indemnities to the British (over $12 million) and Germans, thus admitting the principle. Not surprisingly, Polignac argued that the cases were different but that he was really as yet not fully informed on the substance of the issues. He assured Rives that further discussions would occur when he became more familiar with the available information. While the Minister was pleased with the "frank and cordial" nature of the discussions, he remained concerned that the new government, with its weak political base, would have little time to deal with the American claims. And even if it did, Rives wondered, would its representatives have the courage to confront the discontented French people with added responsibilities?[7]

Almost six weeks passed before Rives had another opportunity to discuss the claims with Polignac. The American's fears had become reality: the Prince had not taken the time to examine the materials and was unprepared to deal with the subject. Rives attempted to impress upon him the seriousness of the matter in the American consciousness. This was not merely a matter of individual claims but of national honor and rights. In an effort to avoid total embarrassment, Polignac feigned casual knowledge of the American position and commented that he was not impressed by it. Seizing this opening, Rives pressed the argument that past French governments had allowed that the Yankees did have some legitimate claims. The key was to determine which were justifiable.

When the two ministers met again, it was apparent that this time the Prince had at least superficially examined the cases. Polignac was willing to admit that those American vessels that had been seized and burned at sea had been destroyed by virtual "acts of piracy"; however, he was reluctant to agree that the shipowners whose property was seized under the Berlin and Milan Decrees should be compensated. Since the decrees were the law of the land and the Americans argued that Napoleon's government was legitimate, then those ships seized were in violation of those laws and liable to seizure. Polignac cleverly argued that if the Americans wished to set aside the Napoleonic decrees, then the Louisiana cession should also be declared invalid. Rives contended that the decrees violated international law and treaties between the United States and France. Although the negotiators were unable to arrive at a general agreement, in a January 13 letter Rives grasped the concession on the burning of the ships at sea to ask the Prince to declare a specific amount of remuneration. His inquiry brought no reply.[8]

When they met again two weeks later, Rives was disappointed that Polignac was still not prepared to discuss the issue in any depth. Instead, the Frenchman insisted upon expressing indignation over Jackson's annual message to Congress in which he had used the phrase "possible collision" to describe Franco-American relations. Rives, perceiving this outrage as a stalling tactic, explained that the President was expressing sorrow rather than anger at the state of affairs. He reminded Polignac that the United States government was taking the negotiations very seriously. Either Old Hickory's words or Rives's perseverance apparently made an impact on the Minister: by mid-February he conceded that the French were liable for all property not legally condemned and for those ships burned at sea—but not for the ships and cargoes confiscated under the Berlin and Milan Decrees. Despite these concessions, Rives was not optimistic. He knew that the Chamber of Deputies, about to meet in March, contained an antiministerial majority; worse still, the talk on the street and in the press was not favorable to the American claims. To combat the anti-Americanism, Rives called upon the legendary Lafayette, persuading him in the interests of Franco-American harmony to use his influence to soften the militancy of the fourth estate and the Chamber.[9]

Lafayette had little opportunity to work his persuasive magic; recognizing the sentiments of the Chamber, the King simply prorogued the body until September. While this was only a temporary respite from a legislative onslaught, it did clear the way for Polignac and Rives to deal with more substantive issues in their negotiations. Rives advanced as far as drafting a preliminary treaty urging the establishment of a joint commission to determine the legitimacy of the various claims. Polignac devoted his time to studying French concerns, such as Article 8 of the Louisiana Treaty, which he introduced into the discussion with Rives in mid-March. This surprise move placed the Virginian in a difficult position. When he told the Prince that the United States was unwilling to admit any French claims of indemnity, Rives feared that Polignac might use the excuse to break off the negotiations. Happily, this did not occur; the talks continued into April but with few concrete gains. Almost in desperation and certainly without authorization from Washington, Rives took the bold step of suggesting to Polignac (at a cocktail party) a quid pro quo: the Americans would reduce duties on French wines and silks if Paris would abandon claims based on the Louisiana Treaty. Polignac, clearly interested in the proposal, remained noncommital but did his part for international cooperation by moving to name a French committee to examine the American claims in detail.[10]

Unfortunately for the Virginian, the talks remained stagnant for the next two months. Polignac was distracted by the French expedition that resulted in the occupation of Algiers, while the commission debated the American claims. Rives did, however, receive some encouraging news from Copenhagen: Chargé Henry Wheaton had settled the Danish claims. Might the French now be induced to end their Fabian tactics of delay and come to an accord? The flame of hope burned brighter in Rives's mind.

The claims against Denmark, associated with those against France, dated back to the Napoleonic Wars when Danish cruisers set upon neutral American vessels. As early as 1811, President James Madison had dispatched an agent, George W. Erving, to resolve the matter, but he had made little progress. Although Washington had no formal diplomatic station in Copenhagen, succeeding presidents pressured the Danes for a settlement. The Danish government, however, shaky and impoverished from the recent conflicts, was in no condition to pay the Yankees. Minister John Randolph of Roanoke, as he passed through

Copenhagen on his way to St. Petersburg in 1830, perhaps was not far off the contemporary mark when he noted that "the History of Denmark is already written. It is finished. Her career is ended. The jealousy of the four great powers may preserve to her a nominal independence." But the monarch would be better off, Randolph conjectured, reducing his army to a base garrison to repair the forts and care for the munitions.[11]

The Jacksonians wisely recognized the precarious geopolitical and financial situation of the Danes. Consequently, the President applied only gentle pressure to the resolution of the situation. The tensions, temper, and collapse of patience later discernible in French negotiations were absent from the Danish talks. It was important to obtain a precedent-setting treaty from Copenhagen: if the Danes would settle, a domino effect might result in discussions with Paris and Naples, where the dollar amounts and national pride were interwoven at a higher level. John Quincy Adams had been successful in obtaining a commercial agreement with Denmark in April 1826. Trade between the two countries, especially as it affected the Danish West Indies, was significant, and the agreement was a harbinger of the resolution to the claims dilemma. Adams had immediately seized the moment and dispatched talented international lawyer Henry Wheaton to Copenhagen as chargé d'affaires, with liberal instructions that allowed him great flexibility in arranging the terms of settlement. The Americans preferred a commission to determine amounts due to individual citizens but would accept lump sum payment. Additionally, the Danes would not have to pay cash; periodically redeemable stocks would be sufficient.

While Wheaton spent the next several years in a frustrated quest for settlement, private agent John Connell—a Philadelphia lawyer who represented many of the claimants—met with Foreign Minister Count Schimmelmann, agreed upon a $76,000 payment for several of his clients, and returned briefly to the United States in March 1828 to report his triumph.[12] After witnessing Connell's success, Wheaton became convinced that the only way the issue could be settled was by a single payment. He also felt a sense of urgency at this point: if the Foreign Office felt comfortable negotiating with a private agent, what did this say about its view of the American government's depth of commitment to redress those grievances? For that matter, why should the financially embarrassed Danes eagerly pay the claims when their fellow offenders in Paris and Naples showed no inclination to do so?

Wheaton labored tirelessly through 1828 to convince King Frederick VI and Count Schimmelmann that the Americans had a defensible legal position. The King attempted to argue that most of the claims were nonnegotiable because they had been unfavorably ruled upon earlier by Danish courts. Wheaton, in turn, contended that such decisions had affected only private litigation, whereas now the United States was moving to seek justice on a nation-to-nation basis. Wheaton's arguments, combined with a decision for reparations by the Russian Czar in a similar case, vindicated his position and prompted a compromise mood in Copenhagen.[13]

It is to Jackson's credit that despite Wheaton's avowed support for John Quincy Adams, the Chargé was allowed to remain at his post at this critical juncture. Even more significantly, the President and Secretary Van Buren relied heavily upon the informed judgment of Wheaton and private agent Connell as to the terms of a settlement. Clearly, Old Hickory was concerned with a prompt resolution of the matter consistent with national honor and incorporating reasonable financial remuneration, but he was also hoping to use it as a model for France and the Two Sicilies.

In August 1829 the Danish commissioners offered a paltry $230,000 to settle the claims. Wheaton, after conferring with Connell, countered with a request for $1.7 million. The stunned Danes held a second conference with the Chargé in September, in which they challenged the neutrality of the American vessels and the alleged arbitrary nature of the Danish court rulings. Wheaton responded with his solid command of international law. There the matter rested as the American forwarded the Danish offer and information on the conferences to Van Buren. The year 1829 ended with no progress made, Jackson disgruntled over the dollar amount offered by the Danes, and a disappointed Connell reporting the turn of events to his claimants and the government.[14]

In early 1830, Jackson instructed his Secretary of State to convey to Wheaton his keen disappointment at Danish intransigence. If nothing could be done to alter their position, the President said in a "friendly but firm" note, "the present Executive would not be wanting in all suitable exertions" to back up his demand for the indemnity. This thinly veiled threat suggested a trade war, which would cause the Danish economy much greater suffering than would paying the claims. Seeing a new crisis approaching, King Frederick VI stepped in on March 23 and ordered his commissioners to increase the indemnity. Once the logjam had broken, the negotiators quickly agreed upon and signed on March 28 a treaty releasing the Danes from further obligation after a three-installment payment of $650,000—a sum considerably higher than the $500,000 many merchants had expected to obtain. Again, the administration had scored an enviable triumph. American honor had been upheld, a generous amount paid to the claimants, and a diplomatic cornerstone laid. As a euphoric Wheaton advised colleague William Rives in Paris, "the French will no doubt be angry at this precedent of a nation paying their honest debts."[15]

Credit for this accomplishment largely belongs to the erudite and persevering Wheaton, whose even and unrelenting logic and diplomatic skills outweighed his domestic political preferences. (His success led to an appointment in 1835 as chargé to Prussia, where he was instructed to open commercial talks with the newly federated German states.) But recognition must also be given to the President, whose patient policy and timely pressure assisted in producing the long-sought-after results.

While Rives delighted in Wheaton's success, he brooded over the minimal impact it made upon the progress of French negotiations. The troubled Ministry was not eager to deal with international precedents that might jeopardize its own political existence. The slowness of Polignac's claims committee troubled Rives and compelled him to seek information from inside sources about its deliberations. His contact was Alexandre Mechin, a member of the Chamber from the Liberal Party who was favorably disposed to settling the claims. Mechin's son Lucien, a lawyer in the United States, acted as the agent for Thomas Kittera, one of the claimants.[16]

As the negotiations dragged on, Rives also received unsolicited aid from America. In early April, Van Buren informed him that several individuals wished to hire agents to assist Rives by lobbying the French government. Nervous claimants, including wealthy Baltimore merchants William Patterson and Robert Oliver, sought to employ John

Connell to help in facilitating the settlement. Connell, fresh from his triumphs in aiding Wheaton in Copenhagen, had frequently been called upon for his expertise by the administration.

However, the plan to utilize Connell to assist claimant agent George Gibbs in Paris met with the sharp disapproval of the Jacksonians. Samuel Smith, reporting to Van Buren that Gibbs had offered to place 100,000 francs at the disposal of a certain person in Paris, cautioned, "I am afraid Mr. G. will do some mischief." James Hamilton informed Rives that Gibbs contemplated "a very unworthy attempt" that would disgrace both the government and the claimants—a clear hint that Gibbs planned to bribe the deputies. Hamilton thought Rives should tell Gibbs that he knew of the scheme and that the police would be informed if Gibbs proceeded. Van Buren hinted that several of the claimants wished to assist the process by the use of bribes—"means which this government could never sanction"—and was more forceful on this point in a private letter to Rives several days later. The dangerous nature of Gibbs's scheme caused consternation in the State Department, and a wave of concern apparently swept the White House that the Virginian might become involved in this "intrigue," which the French could then use to terminate negotiations. The administration sought to fend off the advances of the merchants by offering Rives the option of an assistant, even though, Van Buren warned, the claimants could not agree on any one representative. Rives settled the issue by telling Van Buren on May 29 that he had trouble enough with "strange and capricious people" and did not need the additional headache of a meddling agent.[17]

Rives waited patiently through May, hoping that his offer of reduced duties on French wines would influence Polignac and that the commission would render a favorable report. His hopes were shattered in the first week of June when the Prince penned Rives a tough note, expressing his disappointment at American intransigence on the Louisiana Treaty. There quickly followed an announcement from the commission that $1 million would be fair payment to the United States, and even this amount should be subject to the reduction of claims from Article 8. Since the President had just suggested a sum of $6 million as reasonable, the French offer was little more than an embarrassment.[18]

Moreover, Rives was rapidly losing respect for both Polignac and his policies. While the Prince possessed courage and devotion, he was a man of modest intellectual talents; the Virginian conceded that he was "as honest as a Frenchman under the corrupting tendencies of their mock religion and the incurable defects of their national character can be," but his policies were filled with inconsistencies and contradictions. Rives bitterly noted that "nothing is certain but what is past and irrevocable."[19]

The ploy of exchanging wine reductions for an abandonment of French claims seemed to have fallen flat amidst the political pressure on the ministry related to the upcoming elections. Rives feared for the future of the public peace if those elections returned an antiministerial majority to the Chamber. He realistically understood what the Royalists would do to stay in power. Rives found himself observing from the sidelines as other events dominated the field. Polignac had been in charge of the successful expedition that had seized Algiers for France, but he now faced determined diplomatic opposition from England and Russia. The forthcoming elections were both a referendum on Polignac's ministry and a threat to the very existence of the Bourbon dynasty.[20]

Thus politics forced the American claims aside, but the French did promise Rives that they were working on a treaty draft that would be finished by the end of July. By mid-month word had leaked out that the finished document would insist upon reciprocal claims of payments or concessions in the wine trade "in perpetuity." Since the United States was willing to provide such commercial advantages for only a limited time, a crestfallen Rives perceived this as "a virtual and final refusal of our just demands." At this most dismal juncture, good fortune took the form of revolution.[21]

The elections had returned a sufficient number of antiministerial deputies to displease Charles X. Accordingly, on July 26, 1830, he dissolved the new Chamber, called for new elections, and limited the freedom of the press. The response in Paris was almost instantaneous: the city seethed with revolution as Lafayette returned from the country to take command of the National Guard. With its cooperation, the monarch was forced from power and a provisional government was formed, consisting of a number of deputies. Quickly, the Chamber met and on August 7 offered the title of King of the French to Louis Philippe, the

Duke of Orleans. An ecstatic Rives reported "one of the most wonderful revolutions which have ever occurred in the history of the world." Although representatives of other European nations hesitated to attend Louis's coronation, Rives was highly visible, thus giving tacit American recognition to the revolutionary regime.[22]

There was good cause for the perceptible change in Rives's mood. Lafayette, who had been his friend and confidant for months, was now in a position of military authority. And the Minister himself found an affection for the new King and his wife that had always been lacking with Charles. Over the next year Rives and his wife became favorites at court, to the extent that the Queen was selected as the godmother of their newborn daughter in July 1832. The new French government proclaimed a liberal constitution and named Count Louis Mole, a man Rives respected, as Foreign Minister.

All these positive factors gave the American reason for optimism. It was, unfortunately, misplaced. Conversation with various French leaders revealed their position that while American claims might be just, to pay them would both strain the treasury and be politically very unpopular. Rives had been warned of the former problem when the government unexpectedly moved in 1830 to channel American tobacco imports through one agent to the French Regie. Since the Regie itself was a monopoly established by the government to control the price and flow of tobacco, this became a monopoly upon a monopoly, which would cut sharply (25 percent) into American profits.[23]

With this parsimonious attitude now plain, Rives urged Jackson to act. It was increasingly clear that France was not willing to pay scarce funds to satisfy ancient debts, now was the French Ministry convinced that this was a national issue in the United States; surely the American people would not consider it worth the risk of war and the loss of the lucrative Franco-American trade. Rives consequently urged the President to escalate the pressure upon the French by joining Congress in a chorus of outrage, demonstrating that the claims were a matter of broad-based concern and not simply the whimpering of a few unhappy merchants. Direct threats should not be used, Rives advised, but a mention in the executive message to Congress of a strengthening of the navy and possible commercial retaliation would not fall upon deaf ears in Paris.

While Rives awaited a response to his suggestion of tightening the vise, he continued his discussions with Mole in September. The Foreign Minister sought additional delays by declaring for a new committee to examine the claims. Rives suggested either a mixed commission to determine the amount and legitimacy of the claims, or a fixed amount settlement to be dispersed by an American commission. On October 15, Rives learned that a new five-man French commission would be appointed to study the issues. But two breakthroughs were achieved in Mole's admission of the justice of the American claims and the possible tradeoff of Article 8 claims for a reduction in wine duties.[24]

The new committee debated the merits of the American claims over the next five months as Rives watched, waited, and listened to the bits of information he could garner from conversations with two of the more sympathetic members. A shake-up in the Ministry in November resulted in the replacement of Mole with Marshal Maison, followed rapidly by Count Horace Sebastiani, thus further complicating the negotiations. The information Rives gathered from his committee contacts and the new Foreign Minister indicated that finances, not principles, posed the chief obstacle to resolution. Jackson, aware of Rives's problems, attempted to smooth the way. In November the administration approved an earlier French proposal to institute reciprocal duties on French wines and American cottons. The next month the Secretary of State informed the Minister that the President was cognizant of limited French financial resources and recent political problems and thus was patiently willing to listen to any "fair proposal" the French might offer.[25]

The new year began without any proposals or definite word from the commission. The situation seemed to brighten with the appointment of the talented Louis Serurier as the new Minister to the United States. This especially pleased Rives, since he believed that an ongoing problem had been the lighthearted manner in which previous French diplomats in Washington had considered the American claims. Receipt of Jackson's message to Congress also inspired Rives; its firm but not threatening tone was exactly what he had hoped for. As he told Van Buren in February, progress was being made in the talks because of the groundwork laid during the ministry of Count Polignac and "the new system of action introduced by the administration of General Jackson, which substituted for the coaxing, begging and hoping diplomacy of former administrations, a firm and energetic language, worthy of a nation whose rights had been violated and determined, at all events, to have an answer to its demands of redress." Rives became steadily aware that although Lafayette was well-meaning, his opinions were without weight in the Chamber, and he had fallen from favor with the court. Louis Philippe was "too feeble, too undecided and too anxious to compromise" to resolve the crisis in French politics. In a flight of spread-eagle adoration, Rives suggested that only one man has "the energy, the promptitude, the tact and the spirit of command to govern the French and that is Andrew Jackson," but the Minister emphasized that he was confident the American people would not give him up to be "King of the French."[26]

As spring approached, Rives remained on an emotional rollercoaster. Conflicting rumors about the final report of the commission frustrated the Virginian, and no doubt his frustration turned to anger in April when he learned that there were both majority and minority reports. The former was a vindication of the legality of the Napoleonic decrees and consequently a denial of the claims based upon them; however, it did allow for certain classes of claims—such as those ships burned at sea—and a payment of between $2 and $3 million. The latter accepted the decrees as a violation of international law and recommended remuneration of up to $6 million. Both majority and minority stood fast on the French interpretation of the Louisiana Treaty and regarded a reduction in the duty on wines as of little value to France. Even though the trusted Lafayette had communicated the progress of the discussions to him, Rives was still clearly stunned by the outcome. The Virginian lamented to William Preble, "Affairs are not good here. I have met with a backwardness and repugnance in relations . . . which is entirely contrary from what I expected."[27]

In his meetings with Sebastiani in late April, Rives adopted a new hard line. He hinted at commercial retaliation if matters were not solved to the satisfaction of the United States, refused to link Article 8 to the American claims, and referred to the French offer of 15 million francs (about $3 million) as "a mockery." Two days later, on April 28, Sebastiani increased the sum to $4 million, but Rives again refused. In ensuing discussion the American asserted the legitimacy of his position, prompting the attentive Sebastiani to add another half-million dollars in what he termed an ultimatum and his final offer. But the momentum had shifted in Rives's direction, and he pressed his advantage: arguing that the Americans could rightfully claim over $6 million, he hoped to entice the Frenchman to further concessions. On May 1, the Count explained that only he and Casimir Perier, president of the Council of Ministers, supported even the $4.5 million amount, which was double the majority recommendation of the commission. Rives also realized that the French were not eager for arbitration of the issue, so he continued to push for a mixed commission to settle the legitimacy of the claims. The cagey Sebastiani knew, in turn, that Rives wished to keep the issue out of the political chaos of the Chamber of Deputies. When Perier suggested freezing the question until the Chamber met in two months, a standoff resulted, then a compromise as Perier agreed to present the matter to the council again in May.[28]

On June 1 the council, with audible grumbling, agreed to their president's plea to add another million francs for a total of 25 million ($4.6 million), to be paid in six equal yearly installments at 4 percent interest, bringing the final amount to 28.5 million francs. Rives warily hesitated before providing a definite response to this new final proposal. Wisely, he talked first with Lafayette, who assured him that, in fact, this would be the financially pressed Ministry's highest offer. Rives also checked the Gallatin-based report of 1822, which suggested that $5 million would be a generous figure, given the dubious nature of some of the claims. Rives was therefore convinced that the $4.6 million would satisfy the claimants. Perhaps even more important for the Virginian's political future, he received word from a Washington correspondent that the sum also met with the approval of the President.

Once Rives had agreed to the French offer, all that remained was to hammer out the other matters in conference with Sebastiani. This was accomplished in mid-June with minor irritation. The Beaumarchais heirs would be paid 1.5 million francs (about $270,000) of the 3.7 million they claimed; both bottled and casked wines would receive varied rate reductions for a ten-year period; the Americans would get a reduced duty on long-staple cotton and the abandonment of French claims under Article 8 of the Louisiana Treaty.[29] Rives had won a hard-fought victory over personality, bureaucratic, political, and special interest obstacles. It was only appropriate that the treaty be signed on July 4.

Rives's euphoria over the successful conclusions of his negotiations was tempered by the realization that he had not been officially authorized to accept a specific dollar amount; in fact, he was supposed to submit a sum to the White House for approval prior to a treaty arrangement. Additionally, he had bordered upon usurpation of the legislative function by committing the Congress to tariff reductions without their authorization. Under the circumstances, the Minister decided to take his family to the French countryside for the summer and wait for the shock waves to reverberate back across the Atlantic.[30]

The waves from the White House hardly rose above a ripple. For the long-suffering President, who had pressured but never threatened, Rives's success more than compensated for his unauthorized aggressiveness. Martin Van Buren, preparing to become Minister to Great Britain, reassured the President of the fairness of the amount and expressed confidence that the Senate would approve the treaty. However, new Secretary of State Edward Livingston, respected in the law, aroused the President's apprehensions about whether the Beaumarchais claims would be deducted from the total claims due American merchants (they would be) and whether it would not be wise to submit the wine reduction to Congress as a recommendation rather than a mandate. With an election approaching in 1832, Old Hickory was particularly sensitive to the political windfall from the treaty but understandably worried about potential charges of executive usurpation of legislative powers.[31]

Back in Paris in September, Rives was well aware of the criticism of the treaty among the French politicos, the public, and the press, who viewed it as an abuse and a giveaway. When he learned that Livingston desired him to reopen the issues of the Beaumarchais deductions and the obligatory reduction in the wine duties, a disheartened Rives— knowing that such actions would give a reticent French government the opportunity to withdraw from the treaty—dismissed these matters "as light and frail as cobwebs," and sought to ally the President's fears by utilizing Van Buren as an intermediary. The Red Fox later wrote to Rives assuring him that neither Livingston nor the Senate would amend his treaty into oblivion. The knowing New Yorker cynically pointed out that "there is too much money at stake and too great a portion of it belonging to the opposition . . . to allow the indulgence in their factious and unprincipled propensities."[32]

Rives took no chances, however; he assumed the initiative with Congress by writing letters to Virginia Senators Tyler and Tazewell (chairman of the Foreign Relations Committee), Jacksonian lieutenant Thomas Hart Benton of Missouri, and opposition power Daniel Webster of Massachusetts to help pave the way. His efforts were rewarded. The treaty was introduced in the Senate on December 7 and referred to committee, where Tazewell guided its passage. As Samuel Smith pointed out to Rives, it would be impossible to get two-thirds support in the Senate without some votes from the National Republicans. But Smith knew, as Van Buren did, that the influence of powerful constituents who would profit greatly from the claims outweighed the inclination to discredit the administration. Even so, Henry Clay attempted to get the wine provision eliminated, and failing in that, he moved to postpone approval; that, too, was unsuccessful. In late January the Senate approved the treaty unanimously and on February 2 the United States and France exchanged ratifications. Congress rounded off any rough constitutional edges by passing a tariff reduction on wines at its next session.[33]

The reaction of Americans was justifiably joyful. Reuben Beasely, consul in Le Havre, praised Rives, suggesting that "the claimants ought to erect a statue to you." Van Buren referred to the document as a "great treaty" and hinted to Rives that rewards would come his way for such meritorious service. The Jacksonian press was, not surprisingly, unrestrained in its praise. The Richmond *Enquirer* called Rives's handiwork "as good a treaty, by all counts, as could possibly have been expected." The Philadelphia *Sentinel* deemed it "more satisfactory than was anticipated." Papers throughout the nation echoed the same theme—except, of course, for the opposition press. The *National Intelligencer* sniped that the Revolution of 1830, not the efforts of Rives, Van Buren, or Jackson, had made the treaty possible. But only the most partisan of papers, such as the Salem *Gazette*, could object to the amount of the settlement.[34]

William Rives, basking in the glory of his triumph, asked for and received permission to return to the United States in the spring of 1832.

He was tiring of France after three years; even the summer sojourn in the countryside in 1831 had bored him. "It is monotonous and dull to the last degree," he told Van Buren. "The country is a vast and dreary solitude broken only now and then by dirty villages in which the population congregate." Rives had briefly been considered for the mission to Naples to resolve the claims there and flirted with thoughts of the vacant London ministry after the Senate rejected Van Buren. Instead, he decided to return to Virginia, perhaps to a Cabinet post in the second Jackson administration. However, he had to be temporarily satisfied with a Senate seat, which he filled when Littleton Tazewell resigned in the summer of 1832.[35]

Rives departed for the United States in October 1832, leaving the legation in the hands of the secretary, Nathaniel Niles. Jackson wished to dispatch Edward Livingston to the post as part of a new Cabinet shuffle but thought it wise to wait until after the November election. The election was followed by a four-month encounter with South Carolina over the tariff and nullification, a crisis that commanded the President's attention until a compromise was worked out in March 1833; consequently, the Cabinet maneuvers were not made until May, and Livingston did not depart from New York until August 14.

In France in the interim, Niles was obliged to deal with the new Foreign Minister, the Duke Achille de Broglie. Relations between the two men proceeded pleasantly into 1833 as Niles requested the documentation necessary for the American claims commission to begin its deliberations. Although the French refused to surrender the papers without payment for reproduction, this appeared to be only a minor squabble. Problems arose in February, however, when the first installment of four million francs fell due. Since no specific method of payment had been arranged, the Secretary of the Treasury wrote a draft to be presented to the French Minister of Finance. The bill would be handled by the Bank of the United States, whose agent in Paris would collect the funds. Although the French Minister to the United States, Louis Serurier, had been notified of the procedure, he ignored it because the information came from the Treasury, not the more appropriate State Department. Likewise, Niles had informed the French government of American intentions. But when the bill was presented to the Minister of Finance, he refused to pay it, claiming that the funds had not been appropriated by the Chamber of Deputies.[36]

Jackson was furious. He and the Congress had abided by the treaty provisions and reduced the duties on French wines. Now, the French were not only refusing to pay but exhibiting no real regret, instead appearing miffed that the Americans had proceeed with collecting the bill without having prior authorization. De Broglie seemed exasperated as he explained to Niles that the French government, like the American, required legislative approval of treaties before they could take effect. The Minister assured Niles that the issue was only pro forma; the treaty would be submitted and the money appropriated by the Chamber in its next session. Jackson was not convinced and replaced Niles with the more experienced Levett Harris as acting chargé.

The President, becoming increasingly impatient with Livingston, had wanted the sixty-seven-year-old diplomat to leave in June. But the new difficulties seemed to bother the Louisianan, who told Rives that "should they make any serious demands you must go over and complete your work. . . . I shall certainly be unequal to the task." Livingston may have been serious or simply flattering Rives, but in any case he tarried while Jackson fumed and the Chamber debated. Meanwhile, Harris did his best in a steadily worsening atmosphere. His discussions with de Broglie brought explanations of pressing financial problems and further assurances of payment. But even though Minister of Finance Jean Georges Humann presented the treaty in early April and spoke strongly of its commercial benefits, the Chamber ignored the issue for more pressing matters—especially aid to Greece—until June. The Chargé recognized that the treaty was in serious trouble. The Chamber was reluctant to pay an amount that many deputies considered exorbitant. Many also believed that the French had granted concessions too willingly to the United States, making the issue also a political liability that jeopardized the very survival of the Ministry.[37]

By June it was apparent to Harris that the Chamber would not approve the treaty, despite an impassioned plea by Lafayette. Sensing disaster, Council of Ministers President Andre Dupin and de Broglie urged Harris to "tranquilize" Jackson by explaining that political and financial realities, as well as critical Continental obligations, would force postponement of the issue until the next session in December. Old Hickory was not impressed by French excuses. He requested Secretary of the Treasury Louis McLane to defend the American position on the method of payment to Serurier. In his instructions to Livingston, Jackson insisted that the right of the United States to present another bill of exchange should not be challenged under any circumstances. For added emphasis, Livingston arrived on the powerful 74-gun ship of the line *Delaware*, a fact not lost upon the French press or public.[38]

The King, the court, and the Ministry most cordially received Livingston in September. Guests of honor also included Thomas P. Barton, Livingston's son-in-law (who replaced Niles as Secretary of Legation), and Captain Ballard of the *Delaware*, who estimated for interested listeners that if required, the United States could put fifty ships to sea in rapid order. The new Minister's first duty was to assess the government's attitude and determine the possibility of payment the following February. Before he departed from the United States, Livingston had supposed that the Chamber would not risk the lucrative wine and silk trade for so small a sum as the claims. Although the summer postponement brought second thoughts, frequent fall meetings with the King and his leading Ministers assuaged his fears. The congenial, French-speaking diplomat became convinced that the claims issue would be made a priority in the December session of the Chamber.[39]

He revealed his deeper insecurity about ultimate passage in his October 13 advice to McLane, however, suggesting that Congress might wish to suspend the trade provisions of the treaty until resolution occurred. In a note two weeks later he must have confused the Secretary of State by telling him of the strong English influence at Court, and that the United States should do nothing to upset the French, such as retreating on American treaty responsibilities. This would be seized upon by the Ministry, he argued, as an excuse for not executing its obligations. By November, Livingston demonstrated a growing anxiety, worrying about the heavy deficits of the French treasury and telling McLane, "I am by no means sanguine in the expectation of an easy or speedy issue to the question." The Minister wanted the President to be firm but moderate in his annual message to Congress, to convince the French "that we will not be trifled with." But Jackson, rejecting his agent's advice, was patient and reassuring in his address, clearly agreeable to allowing the Chamber another opportunity to appropriate the funds.[40]

As the new year approached, a wary Livingston came to a fuller ap-

preciation of the priorities of the French Ministry for the coming legislative session. Civil war continued in Portugal, and internal problems
in Spain threatened to justify French intervention. There was ongoing
concern about the increased role the Russians were playing in the Ottoman Empire, a region in which the French were attempting to maximize their influence. Although he was officially optimistic, Livingston's
vacillation about a desirable White House posture revealed his recognition that the unpopular American claims were a sideshow on the stage
of European politics.

Understandably, the harmonious tone of the President's message
was well received in Paris. A dispatch reached Livingston soon thereafter, explaining that the President had already sent his message to
Congress by the time Livingston's note urging a more aggressive stance
arrived, "should the United States unfortunately be driven to coercive
measures to enforce the treaty, it is not probable that they will be of as
mild a character as that you have suggested."[41]

With Jackson's patience about to expire, the bill to appropriate was
introduced into the Chamber in January 1834. Referred to committee,
the measure remained there for two months, while Livingston became
increasingly fearful. On March 12 he joyfully reported its recommendation by the committee and cautiously predicted passage in the Chamber by a large majority. His attitude promptly changed after listening
to several days of debate. Attacks on the treaty came from all political
corners, and the required ministerial support was weak. De Broglie
spoke for the treaty, but the Minister of Finance was silent when asked
about the potential impact on Franco-American trade. The Chamber
defeated the bill, regarded by a majority as too great a concession, by a
narrow vote of 176 to 168. Although de Broglie resigned that night, to
be replaced by Count Henri de Rigny, this issue was not a ministerial
question. Later conferences with de Broglie revealed that his strategy
had been to adopt a low profile on the controversial measure in the
hope that it would pass. Livingston believed it failed because the Ministry had simply not exerted enough energy in its behalf. The situation
would remain in status quo until the new Chamber met in December.
Livingston, realizing the impact the rejection would have upon Old
Hickory, pleaded with de Rigny to advance the date of the next session, but to no avail. As an old friend, the Louisianan knew an embar-

rassed Jackson could not face Congress in the fall without a new course of action. Consequently, he recommended a suspension of French imports (except for the wine covered in the treaty).[42]

In Washington word of the failure of the treaty coincided with a domestic political debacle that humiliated and infuriated the President. Almost two years earlier Jackson had vetoed the recharter of the Bank of the United States, a quasi-public agency approved by Congress but managed largely through a private board of directors. The Bank, which housed federal revenues, appeared to Old Hickory to be abusing its extensive power, and he sought to decentralize the banking system by removing the government's deposits from the national bank and placing them in selected "pet banks." This action prompted a "Bank War" between Jackson and the Bank president, Nicholas Biddle, who began to manipulate the economy with his institution's funds. These maneuvers convinced Jackson of the correctness of his course. Without the authorization of Congress, the President appointed a new Secretary of the Treasury, Roger B. Taney, and ordered him to remove the deposits—again without legislative approval. Partisan politics clouded the issue, since the National Republicans who dominated the Senate had generally championed the Bank. The resultant uproar ultimately brought about the rejection of Taney (and incidentally, Minister to England Andrew Stevenson) and the censure of the President by the Senate in late March 1834 for usurpation of legislative power.

Not surprisingly, then, the already depressed chief executive received the word from France with "painful surprise." Navy Secretary Woodbury labeled the Chamber's action "unexpected and mortifying," telling a correspondent, "I have never known in him [Jackson] or others a more decided disappointment—or a more firm resolve to vindicate our rights and honor." Secretary of State McLane shared the General's view of the seriousness of the Chamber's rejection. Ambitious for the White House and with an eye toward pleasing the President, McLane argued that the French were procrastinating and that letters of marque and reprisal should be instituted. But such a policy could have meant the capture or seizure of French ships or property as an indemnity fund for the claimants, and Secretary Taney registered his strong opposition, fearful that reprisals might lead to war and undermine the President's credibility with Congress in the midst of the Bank crisis.

Veteran observers of French politics added their advice as to the wisest course of action. George Gibbs, still the leading agent for the claimants in Paris, urged that a mission be sent to France under Van Buren's leadership to write a new treaty. Former Chargé Nathaniel Niles suggested a nonintercourse bill and a $10–$20 million appropriation for the navy. William Rives believed that the Chamber legitimately viewed the issue as a constitutional matter in which it had been slighted. The pressure of heavy duties on silks, he ventured, would convince them of the seriousness of the White House.[43]

Slowly but surely the voices of moderation began to take effect on the President. Taney and, especially, Vice-President Van Buren labored diligently to restrain Jackson and obtain time for Minister Serurier to present an official explanation to the administration. The Red Fox certainly did not want his election hopes dashed by an unnecessary war with France. By the first week of June, Jackson had abandoned McLane's proposal of recommending reprisals in a special message to Congress. Serurier had promised on June 5 that his government would treat the matter in a more careful manner at the next session; these firm assurances, combined with the calm counsel of his advisors, convinced the President to give the French Chamber still another chance. Economic warfare was not Jackson's style; as he wrote to Livingston in late June, "I cannot recommend a war thro' the Customs House." But if the French failed to accommodate the United States in December, the President promised, "you will find me speaking to Congress as I ought." Secretary McLane, outmaneuvered on a major policy issue by Van Buren, resigned on June 16.[44]

Disappointingly, Livingston reported that the French saw American patience as a sign of weakness, and a movement was afoot for renegotiation at a smaller amount. The Minister, lacking instructions, felt embarrassed, nervous, and apprehensive about the proper course to take. Since the American claims seemed to be ignored by the press and politicians in Paris, Livingston believed the momentum for passage could not be initiated without a push from the United States. There was further frustration when a preparatory calling of the Chamber took place in late summer of 1834. An excited Livingston urged de Rigny to take this opportunity to introduce the American claims, thus permitting Jackson to present Congress with a *fait accompli* in December. De

Rigny refused, explaining that no laws would be voted on at this session but that the Ministry was hard at work preparing a case for January. Such reluctance elicited steely resolve in Washington. An October encounter between Louis Serurier and former Georgia Senator and new Secretary of State John Forsyth resulted in a barbed discussion. Forsyth, "cool and polite," explained the President's concern over the delay in payments and stated that appropriate recommendations might have to be made to Congress. An angry Serurier defensively inquired whether the Secretary thought that his government was evading its responsibilities and suggested that the United States seemed unclear whether it wanted the treaty executed or a war with France.[45]

As the shadows of conflict loomed larger in the fall of 1834, Livingston began to feel still more pressure. An extended late summer vacation to Switzerland prompted a flurry of rumors about his health. A prejudiced Nathaniel Niles, who had been dismissed by Jackson, told Rives that Livingston was "in his dotage" and that he and his wife cut a very sorry figure around Paris: he was convinced that no one would speak to him; she dressed in black, and the ladies ignored her. Consul Beasely reported a tale that the Minister had lost his mind; while this was not true, Beasely opined, Livingston's poor health dictated the prompt dispatch of a special mission.[46] In actuality, Livingston's course mattered little; he awaited the action of the Chamber in January and, more important, the President's message to Congress in December.

The failure of the special session of the Chamber of Deputies in the late summer to deal with the claims sealed a policy in Old Hickory's mind. A fearful Rives peppered the administration with letters, hoping to preserve the peace and his hard-won treaty. Although Van Buren agreed with him that temperance and firmness constituted the proper course, he could not say as much for the President. Jackson relied heavily upon the advice of the trusted New Yorker, yet he had decided to take strong measures. The sage Vice-President might try to cajole the Tennesseean to moderation, but as the moment of decision drew nigh, Van Buren assured him, "We shall not differ."[47]

As the weeks passed, Jackson became more irritated with the French Ministry. De Rigny claimed that his government was disposed to pay the claims, but did not necessarily intend to do so. The President accused him of playing word games that resolved nothing. The Ministry was stalling, shuffling members in and out weekly, and as Livingston suggested, this political insecurity made the American treaty even more tenuous. In Washington, Serurier feared the worst. He attempted in November to get Forsyth to define exactly what Jackson would say in his annual message. The Secretary was noncommittal, pointing out that the Constitution demanded that the President make some recommendations to Congress. Jackson would probably urge that no definite action be taken until the Chamber met once again. The Frenchman took little comfort in Forsyth's words. He prophetically advised his government to expect a message that would be "very painful."[48]

Forsyth attempted to numb the pain by applying verbal balm to the President's draft message; however, when the Secretary met with Jackson, presidential secretary Andrew Jackson Donelson, and Washington *Globe* printer John Rives, his handiwork was quickly discovered. Donelson was reading the draft aloud, unhesitatingly and distinctly, until he came to the passage relating to the $5 million debt, which Forsyth had made "but a shade different." Jackson was pacing the room, puffing on his pipe, until he heard the altered paragraph. The President paused, stopped, and said, "Read that again, sir." This time Donelson read the words clearly, and Jackson, instantly aroused, exclaimed, "That Sir, is not my language, it has been changed, and I will have no other expression of my meaning than my own words." Phrasing more strongly importing a threat was immediately inserted, and the President instructed John Rives to let the document pass from his hands only "at his peril." The story was often repeated that prior to delivering the address, the President told his advisors, "No, gentlemen, I know them French. They won't pay unless they're made to." (Historian William Hatcher claims that Jackson had disliked the French since the numerous conflicts with them during his martial law reign of New Orleans in 1815.)[49]

The December 1 message ignored the pleas of his more conservative advisors, such as Rives and Van Buren, for economic legislation. Jackson had six months earlier told Livingston he would not make war through the Customs Houses, and his Minister continued to prophesy a bleak Chamber session unless the General adopted a strong position. Thus the President, roundly condemning the French government for failing in its obligations, moved directly to the matter of reprisals: if the Chamber did not authorize the appropriation of funds during its next session, Jackson wanted the power to confiscate ships and property. Then, having emerged with his diplomatic guns blazing, Old Hickory settled back "in rampant spirits" to observe the impact of the message. He did not have long to wait. The press immediately divided along partisan lines. The Whig *National Intelligencer,* Niles *Register,* and New York *Courier* did not deny the legitimacy of the American claims but urged greater restraint in their pursuit. Repelled by the un-American attitude of the opposition editors, the administration's Washington *Globe* claimed that criticism of the President's policies played into the hands of the French.[50]

In the Senate, the Whig-controlled majority on the Foreign Relations Committee sought to both embarrass and constrain the President. Led by Clay, Mangum, and Sprague, the committee reported on January 14, 1835, that "it was inexpedient at this time" to grant authority for reprisals to the executive. While the *Globe* correctly postulated that there were not three men in the French Chamber more anxious than these three Whigs to thwart Jackson, they were not alone; the vote to endorse the committee's recommendation was unanimous. Historian Hatcher sees Clay as "reprehensible" and "bordering on disloyalty" for suggesting that the French might observe Congress's stance on the message before acting and postulating that the Chamber might seek an explanation from the President about his message before they voted an appropriation. Even Clay's biographer, Glyndon Van Deusen, allows that congressional actions were "an unwarrantable intrusion upon the Executive conduct of foreign affairs."[51]

While it is true that Clay postured politically for the upcoming congressional and presidential elections, his actions also called attention to the Senate's constitutional role in foreign policy—and most Democrats ageed with him, including Foreign Relations Committee members Nathaniel Tallmadge of New York and John P. King of Georgia. In December, Tallmadge told Rives, "We must now maintain national honor or be disgraced," but he did not speak on behalf of the President's request for reprisal power. Senator King confessed he was "looking for a way out": he did not want a war with France, but neither did he wish to give the French the impression that the United States was weak. Before the Senate vote, King confided to Rives, "The truth is that I soon found that it would be extremely impolitic to push the recommendation of the President as a party measure, as one could not unite our friends upon it."[52]

The attitude in the Democrat-dominated House of Representatives was somewhat more militant. The Foreign Affairs Committee chairman, C. C. Cambreleng, rejected Clay's "supplicating spirit" and urged admitting that "it is time to look a little to our own dignity and treat her [France] as a nation with whom we may be compelled to go to war." Cambreleng conceded that there was no spirit for conflict in either House at that moment but implied that the United States might be obliged to declare war if nothing had changed by the next session of Congress.[53]

The President had not been supported by the Congress, even the members of his own party, in what was considered a premature request authorizing reprisals. The Vice-President seemed philosophical about the turn of events in late January when he noted that "it terminated about as well as could be expected." The Washington *Globe*, managed by Kitchen Cabinet member Francis P. Blair, attacked the opposition for lack of patriotism but cautiously avoided endorsement of Jackson's proposals. While the President was undoubtedly serious in his request for reprisal authorization, perhaps the fundamental intent was simply to obtain the serious attention of the French government. Prior to December 1834, few informed observers in either Paris or Washington seemed optimistic about the passage of the appropriation in the Chamber. Could Old Hickory's tougher stance, one sure to be tempered by the Congress, harm the American cause?[54]

The message reached Paris on January 8, where, as banker John Welles reported, "this able document created a great sensation"; the issue would now be viewed not simply as a financial matter but as a serious international political issue. Livingston concurred that the reprisal threats had ignited a storm, offending French honor and wounding French pride. The King recalled Serurier from Washington so that his Minister would "no longer be exposed to hear language so offensive to France."[55]

In Paris the initial French response was so overwhelmingly negative that for a brief time Livingston thought it perhaps even dangerous. But although the French offered the Minister his passports, he decided to remain until ordered home by Jackson. As the "American question" heated up in the Chamber, a constitutional struggle developed over the role of that body in a treaty-making process. At the same time, merchants in Lyons, Bordeaux, and other cities vulnerable to reprisals or, especially, war exerted commercial pressures on the deputies. In mid-January the Ministry presented the treaty to the Chamber at the same time that it recalled Scrurier. Deputy P. T. Guestier, a merchant and a relative of Consul Reuben Beasely, pointed out this contradiction in policy, bemoaned the confusing politics of the issue, and commented, "The more I see of my countrymen, especially here, what stiffnecked, self-willed and prejudiced natives they are." Still, he believed that reason would prevail amidst the chaos and the bill would pass.[56]

The following two months were painful for Livingston. His health continued to decline, and he found himself *persona non grata* with the King and the Ministry. Increasingly uncomfortable, almost uninterested at this point, the Louisianan seemed eager for a letter of recall. He was obliged to watch as the treaty was referred to committee, where it languished for weeks. In the meantime, the political turmoil increased as the de Rigny government fell and de Broglie returned to power. Even so, Livingston predicted that the treaty would win in the Chamber by a fifty-vote margin.[57]

The Jacksonians taking no chances, in February 1835 increased the pressure upon the French. Serurier had already departed for Paris, leaving the delegation in the hands of Chargé Alphonse Pageot. Forsyth informed Livingston that a man-of-war would be awaiting him, and he should request his passports should the Chamber fail to pass the appropriation. The House of Representatives sought to strengthen the President's hand with a special fortifications bill: with traditional foe John Quincy Adams leading the way, the Jacksonian-dominated House easily passed (by 107 to 75) a measure supporting the maintenance of the 1831 treaty and granting the chief executive $3 million to prepare for the nation's defense in case France should declare war during a congressional recess.[58]

Not surprisingly, the bill stalled in the Senate, where it encountered a storm of protest. The two veteran Whig spokesmen, Henry Clay and Daniel Webster, marshalled the assault. Clay branded the measure a "blank check" that gave the President unnecessary powers. Under the Constitution, he said, Congress possessed the power to raise armies and create a navy; to support such a provision would be to surrender all governmental power to the executive. If war should be declared, the nation (that is, Congress), not the President, should declare it. This measure was dangerous, Webster warned, emphasizing its vagueness and the necessity for Congress to maintain control of its warmaking powers. "It is the excuse of everyone who desires more power than the Constitution or the laws give him, that if he had more power he could do more good. Power is always claimed for the good of the people; and dictators are always made, when made at all, for the good of the people." Samuel Southard of New Jersey stated that he would not give such broad authority to any one man—not even George Washington. Benjamin Leigh of Virginia (who had recently defeated William Rives for the Senate) waxed eloquent in his description of how this law would turn the nation into a military monarchy: "They might as well say that the President should be made consul for life or Emperor of the American people."[59]

The arguments in behalf of the bill, based on the need for readiness in a potential conflict with France, held little weight in such a heated partisan atmosphere. The measure went down to defeat in early March by a vote of 29 to 17, with the Senate carefully timing its balloting so that a House adjournment prevented a compromise. The Whig press, led by the *National Intelligencer*, could barely control its animosity toward the President, noting "The country is not yet ready for a dictatorship."[60] Yet the opposition found itself in an unenviable position. While their motives in opposing the fortifications bill were both constitutional and political, the Senate had allowed the country to be placed in a possibly precarious position in the event of conflict. As historian Richard McLemore has noted, support for the President's more aggressive stance can be inferred from (a) the efforts the Senate made in the fall of 1835 to throw the blame for the bill's defeat upon the House; (b) the opposition press, which, while criticizing the measure, promised that Congress would act if the French failed to endorse the treaty; and (c) the intimacy between Adams and Jackson, suggesting the growth of bipartisanship on the execution of the treaty.

While McLemore overstates his case in saying that "the administration appeared to have practically the unanimous support of the country in its program to force the payment of the indemnity," certainly the momentum was moving in the President's direction. This trend was not lost upon the French. It was no longer possible to argue, as some correspondents had done in January, that Jackson spoke only for himself and not for the nation. The President was in a rage over the "disgraceful course of the faction of the Senate," but the ever-vigilant chief—although in declining health—advised Livingston not to worry about the unprotected seaports and towns in America, vowing, "I will defend them."[61]

The French Chamber responded to internal commercial and political pressures as well as to the marked stubbornness of the Jackson administration. Debate on the appropriation for the claims payment began on April 9 and lasted little more than a week before it passed by a majority of more than 150 votes. Unfortunately for Franco-American relations, however, an amendment demanded that the President explain his remarks of December 1834 before the money would be paid. Livingston, frustrated beyond the breaking point, could not believe it. He had already explained to de Rigny on January 29 that the President was constitutionally obliged to report the status of the issue to Congress; his message had been purely an internal communiqué between branches of government and was not intended as a threat to France. By attaching the amendment to the appropriation bill, the Chamber was forcing upon the President a humiliation that in Livingston's mind was tantamount to rejection of the treaty. The Minister determined to leave immediately and asked for his passports, but not before lecturing the French ministers on their failure to understand the nature of the American government. By the end of April, Livingston had departed leaving the mission in the hands of Thomas P. Barton, and a new level of crisis appeared to be at hand.[62]

Barton's dispatches throughout the summer of 1835 reveal a growing rigidity in the French position. The Ministry perceived its request of the President as "a trifling concession," hardly the stuff of international conflict. Paris would simply wait for the next executive message or, if need be, the next presidential election before taking further action. The Chargé noted that the Ministry, with information provided by Pageot in Washington, was aware that the issue was much more serious. The bankers and merchants also feared the outcome; the Rothschilds, who labored long and hard for a settlement, had been awarded the expedition of the claims, but they realized nothing could be done until Jackson apologized. Although many, such as William Rives, regarded the French demand as "a silly condition," few who knew the President believed he would yield. Major Lewis confided to Rives, "I have good reason to believe that the President will not advance another inch in the matter." As Levi Woodbury told Secretary of War Lewis Cass in June, it would ultimately be in the power of the Ministry to determine the question. Many of these politicos pointed to the small matter of the concession, that it had been urged for political reasons, and that the French would settle for next to nothing as an explanation. But Jackson would not yield. If the French did not remit the amount due before the next session of Congress, Old Hickory promised to recommend a trade embargo and letters of reprisal until the debt was paid. Still, as he told Amos Kendall, he believed France would pay, and "without apology or explanation; from me she will get neither."[63]

In mid-June, de Broglie attempted to obtain a statement of American intention. He wrote to Pageot, asking him to inform the Secretary of State of the actions of the Chamber and the position of the King and Ministry. The French would comply with the appropriation when the President expressed his regret at his prior message; until that time His Majesty would be obliged to think that instead of a misunderstanding, Jackson's intent was calculatedly provocative. Pageot approached Forsyth with the letter and urged that it be forwarded to the President. The Secretary instead discussed the matter with Jackson, who irately told Forsyth that it was not an official communication to the American government, and if it became official, Pageot should be chastised for the arrogance of supposing to tell the President of the United States what he could or could not communicate to the Congress. This intrusion upon domestic political institutions became a dominant theme in Jackson's mind. He railed about French interference, asserting that it would be disgraceful for him to explain or apologize. The Chamber had insulted the United States, and no American would submit to such treatment.[64]

The State Department promptly conveyed this sentiment in September to Barton, who was told to ask for his passports if the Ministry proved unwilling to commit to an appropriation. When, after a late October conversation with de Broglie, Barton realized that the French were not about to convey the funds, he did request his passports. He believed the French were stalling until after the next presidential election and had no intention of paying unless Jackson apologized.[65]

In his December 7 message to Congress, Jackson stunned almost everyone, including his own supporters, with his moderation. The President discarded an earlier draft in which he berated the French government for bad faith, attacked the Senate for its failure to support his military defense measures, and affirmed that though war was not imminent, the authority to grant letters of marque and reprisal would be requested from Congress. In that draft he had defiantly written, "She [France] has already heard the voice from Maine to Louisiana; no apology, no explanation. My heart cordially responds to that voice, no explanation, no apology." But in place of these words (which were likely an accurate reflection of his true feelings), what the chief actually presented was a mellow-toned explanation of the claims issue. The President did chide the French for their conditional amendment and their reluctance to accept Livingston's disavowal of presidential threats, and the Hero of New Orleans was apparent in his declaration, "The honor of my country shall never be stained by an apology from me for the statement of truth and the performance of duty." There would be no surrender. But buried amidst the recapitulation were these words: "The conception that it was my intention to menace or insult the Government of France is . . . unfounded." Livingston, Van Buren, and Forsyth had done their work well. A compromise had been reached.[66]

Jackson's message was eagerly awaited in Paris, where the winds of war were beginning to blow stronger. A rising level of anxiety had become clearly noticeable in the letters of several American observers in France, predicting that war was likely. In the United States, merchants talked openly of a ruinous war over "a matter of mere etiquette," but by 1836 many Americans likely shared the sentiments of a Massachusetts correspondent who told Levi Woodbury, "Let the worst come."[67]

The British Ambassador in France, Lord Granville, and Foreign Secretary Lord Palmerston had carefully followed the seriousness of the situation, Great Britain growing steadily more troubled as her valuable continental ally seemed to be slipping into an unnecessary conflict with the United States. Such an event would disrupt the French economy and enact untold havoc upon the French merchant marine and navy. While Louis Philippe probably possessed the maritime might to defeat the Americans, a war would drain limited resources and side-track him from the more vital arena of the European balance of power with the autocratic eastern monarchies. A Franco-American War would also mean a blockade of United States ports and the disruption of the valuable cotton exports to English textile mills. Thus, in the fall of 1835, the British had begun to involve themselves actively in the process of mediation.

Palmerston spoke with Chargé Aaron Vail in early November about French anxieties on the matter and took the liberty of having British diplomatic agents in the United States forward correspondence that suggested French eagerness to reach an accord. When Thomas Barton left Paris in November, severing diplomatic ties with France, Palmerston quickly informed Vail that the British government did not wish to see the situation "carried to extremities." But December brought the mobilization of the French navy, ostensibly to protect the West Indian colonies in event of war but perhaps for more offensive purposes. In London, insurance rates on French merchant vessels rose sharply, and some goods were transferred away from ships flying the tricolor. The situation seemed to be disintegrating rapidly, as the English fired letters urging mediation to both Paris and Washington. By the beginning of February, British diplomats had received confirmation from both capitals, and Jackson informed Congress of the British offer on February 8. While the positive reception of Jackson's December message in Paris made the British effort unnecessary, the Foreign Secretary instructed Granville to keep the pressure on and to advise the French government to accept the President's disclaimers. Despite the caterwauling of the opposition press, de Broglie required little inducement to bring this troublesome issue to a close.[68]

Unfortunately, the time lag in communication produced vexing last-minute tensions. Barton's return to the United States had prompted a similar recall from Washington of Chargé Pageot, who, offended by Jackson's message and without knowing that his government had accepted it as sufficient explanation, took it upon himself to stir the diplomatic waters further. He sought to embarrass the administration by publishing de Broglie's letter of June 17, 1835 (which clarified the apology-for-payment quid pro quo) in the New York *Star* and New York *Journal of Commerce*. One opposition newspaper seized on this missive, which Pageot had attempted unsuccessfully to submit to Forsyth, as a "friendly gesture" on the part of the French government that had been ignored by Jackson and his Secretary of State. The *National Intelligencer* condemned the administration for its "blundering diplomacy" and attacked Forsyth for "confounding dignity and superciliousness, self-respect and false pride."

While fending off the petty intrigues of Pageot and the whining of the Whig press, the President felt that because there had been no official word yet of French willingness to pay the claims, a special message should be delivered to Congress reaffirming his position. This time, however, the words would reflect a characteristically tougher stance. The President invited Barton (who had just arrived in Washington), Forsyth, Livingston, and Van Buren to the White House on January 14 to discuss the note. Barton, noticing the apprehension of all three diplomatic veterans, inquired, "'Gentlemen, do you want oil poured upon the flames, or water?' 'Oh, water, by all means,' exclaimed the company in chorus." Barton adjusted his approach accordingly. He explained to the agitated President how incensed the French populace had become over the claims; the issue, now a matter of French honor, could easily topple a ministry and perhaps a monarchy. This effort seemed to defuse the General, and the quartet proceeded to spend the afternoon softening the tone of the document.[69]

The message that reached Congress on January 18 was firm but not threatening. Jackson reiterated his demand for payment according to the treaty and recommended commercial exclusion of French ships and goods from American ports should it not be promptly forthcoming. Because of the rumored assemblage of the French navy, he also urged rapid appropriations for the American navy and for coastal defenses. Democrats generally applauded the President's forthrightness, perhaps sensing that the Old Warrior had done his best to resolve the crisis and preserve American (and his own) honor. But the British found this follow-up statement regrettable in its potential for agitation, and the opposition papers continued to carp and criticize: Jackson had acted irresponsibly by not responding to the de Broglie letter of June 17; the President had moved toward mediation without consulting the Senate; and, of course, the January message indicated that the President was "averse to a temperate course."[70]

The debate over the second statement to Congress proved to be superfluous, since the French had responded positively to the December message. The absence of normal diplomatic channels obliged Paris's acceptance to be forwarded through Charles Bankhead, the British chargé in Washington, on February 15. One week later the President advised Congress that the matter had been settled (although Palmerston continued into March to discuss mediation and offer his diplomatic agents as conduits), and on May 10, Jackson could joyfully inform the Congress that the four installments due had been paid.[71]

American pride at the outcome was exceeded only by the widespread sense of relief. Veteran diplomat Richard Rush rejoiced, "The issue cannot fail to raise the American name in the most solid attributes of character abroad, albeit it must redound to the credit of the administration at home." A more euphoric correspondent exulted to William Rives, "How well everything moves on! The French war which seemed likely to arise is over, the treasury is full to overflowing, not one of the opposition candidates will obtain a single electoral vote. So much for war, pestilence and famine."[72]

The spoliations claims dominated Franco-American relations for a quarter-century. The crisis that followed the failure of the French to appropriate funds reveals perhaps most clearly the hand of Andrew Jackson in foreign affairs. Emotional and iron-willed, Old Hickory attempted to apply his headstrong frontier style with France in the same manner as he might treat a recalcitrant Indian nation. The French had insulted American honor and interfered with his constitutional right to communicate with the Congress. After strengthening the American navy to vanquish Malaysian pirates and Argentine interlopers, Jackson was not about to back down at the French challenge. The peace could be preserved, but only if honor were vindicated.

The French crisis passed, and a comparatively unimportant issue fortunately was resolved without war. But in the process several significant elements of the American system revealed themselves: (1) Congress could be and was an all-important restraint upon executive warmaking power. Even though often revealing an inability to overcome the heated partisan climate of the period and generally lacking a constructive alternative, Congress refused the President reprisal authority and denied him carte blanche to prepare the nation for war (the latter restraint could have been particularly embarrassing if the French had attacked American shipping and coastlines). (2) Members of the cabinet acted on two occasions to restrain Jackson from harsh words that would have fanned the flames of patriotic passion. By urging delay in April–May 1834 and moderation in December 1835–January 1836, Forsyth, Livingston, and especially the crafty Van Buren contributed to preserving the peace. Certainly, Jackson did not want war, but without the advice of men he had faith in, he might not have altered his course in the direction of conciliation. As Secretaries of State, these men realized better than the President the frustration of trans-Atlantic communication and the need for patient diplomacy. Turn-of-the-century political scientist John Fiske perhaps best summarized the impact of the spoliations claims controversy: "The effect of Jackson's attitude was not lost upon European governments, while at home the hurrahs for Old Hickory were louder than ever. The days when foreign powers could safely insult us were evidently gone by."[73]

The treaty of July 1831 was the crowning glory of the foreign policy of the first Jackson administration. A primary objective of the Tennesseean had been the settlement of the spoliations claims with European nations that had refused to pay claims now twenty years old. The President had informed Congress that he would operate under the maxim, "Ask nothing but what is right, permit nothing that is wrong." Now, his success with Denmark and France would open the way to settlement with Naples, Spain, and Portugal. Each would be handled in a different manner with various diplomatic, economic, political, or military pressures applied.

As a result, Old Hickory not only gained over $7 million in claims (in contrast to the previous administration, which had achieved nothing) but began to alter the atttitude of the Europeans toward the United States. The President, his Secretaries of State, and his diplomats generally displayed a determination and forthrightness that erased the smug foreign condescension of earlier years toward the weak, divided, and ineffectual national leadership and replaced it with a newfound respect for the General and his brash young republic.

As the President moved to open new markets and settle additional claims disputes, his two major weapons continued to be an aggressive policy and a strong navy. In dealing with the Mediterranean, however, Jackson demonstrated a patience and a flexibility that reflected the complexity of both the man and his diplomacy.

Chapter 5

The Mediterranean World: A Sea of Opportunity

For two generations before Jackson, the Mediterranean Sea held a special concern for American politicians and merchants. Expanding commerce had brought on a major foreign policy crisis with the Barbary pirates of North Africa and the Kingdom of the Two Sicilies (which included Naples and the island of Sicily). The Moslem princedoms of Morocco, Algiers, Tripoli, and Tunis, nominally under the suzerainty of the Turkish sultan, gained considerable income from the tribute paid by European nations to protect their commerce from attack. The newly independent United States decided it could not—or would not—pay, and the American government built a navy to deal with these marauders. While the fleet was under construction in the 1790s, however, treaty arrangements were completed that temporarily forestalled the employment of the squadron.

Nevertheless, the existence of these vessels (including the *United States*, the *Constellation* and the *Constitution*) proved fortunate, since the John Adams administration soon found itself in an undeclared naval war with France between 1797 and 1800. Then, during the first year of Jefferson's presidency, the Bashaw of Tripoli—disgruntled over treaty payments—moved against American sail in the Mediterranean. The President responded with his fleet in a four-year war that subdued, if it did not defeat, the pirates.

James Madison considered the trade in that region, especially to southern European ports, important enough at the conclusion of the War of 1812 to dispatch Stephen Decatur to the area with a squadron to teach the restless buccaneers respect for the American flag. Madison had also been obliged to deal with the crisis that followed the capture of American vessels in Neapolitan ports between 1809 and 1811. Because of the onset of the war with Britain, Madison was unable to devote full attention to this violation of American neutrality, but it became a stumbling block to establishing positive relations with the Kingdom of the Two Sicilies after 1815.

The general European peace that followed the Napoleonic Wars stimulated merchant interest in expanding trade into the Adriatic and Black Seas and the eastern Mediterranean. John Quincy Adams was successful in negotiating with Austria a treaty that opened commerce with Trieste on the Adriatic in 1829. Jackson, however, saw correctly that much more could be done to harmonize relations with the Mediterranean states and to improve commercial ties with Turkey and Naples.

THE OTTOMAN EMPIRE

Geography was the cruel master of the Ottoman Empire in its declining history. As the imperially minded European nations expanded in the eighteenth century, the Turks found themselves at an uncomfortable crossroad. The English, desirous of a link to India through the Middle East, insisted upon the stability and political integrity of the tottering dynasty. The French, recognizing the inability of the Sultan to defend his provinces, hungrily eyed Egypt. From the north the Russians, ever eager to influence events in southeastern Europe and the Black Sea, sought to gain hegemony in Constantinople.

The situation reached crisis proportions in the 1820s. A revolution in Greece that captured the imagination of the Western world confronted Sultan Mahmud II: the Greeks, brandishing their ancient culture, democratic traditions, and Christianity, arose against the Moslem Turk, inspiring the romantic soul of many Europeans and Americans who sought to aid their cause. Lord Byron died there, and a British admiral and British general lent their able leadership to the fight for independence. The French and Russians were likewise sympathetic. This unlikely trio allied in 1827 and dispatched a joint fleet under British Admiral Edward Codrington to resolve the crisis. When the Turks attempted to land reinforcements in October, the Admiral urged an armistice. Confusion reigned, however, and a naval battle ensued at

Navarino, where the fleets of the Sultan and his principal lieutenant, Mehemet Ali of Egypt, were virtually destroyed.

The victory of the allies at Navarino signaled the end of the Greek War for Independence, but Hellenic success was purchased at a high price. As historian James A. Field, Jr., has observed, Turkey needed a strong army to resist Russian intrusion, and a powerful navy to hold the far-flung empire together. Instead, the Sultan found himself with a weakened army and a shadow navy with which to control Asia Minor, Arabia, Syria, Lebanon, Egypt, the Sudan, Crete, and a host of eastern Mediterranean islands—and the problem would become particularly acute if another province sought to win its independence.[1]

It was within this context of crisis that the United States moved to open relations with the Ottoman Empire. Americans had been trading with Turkey, largely through the port of Smyrna, since 1785. But since no treaty existed, the Yankees were obliged to deal through the English Levant Company, which held a monopoly on British trade in the area: the Americans paid the English tariff and then a gratuity to the company for the privilege and protection of its services. Fortunately, merchant David Offley, who arrived in 1811, made a separate and more lucrative arrangement with the Porte that gave the Americans the right to use the French tariff.

After the War of 1812, Washington cautiously explored the possibilities of a trade agreement. In 1820, James Monroe dispatched Luther Bradish, who reported that the United States was losing over $1 million per year because of the absence of a treaty. It was Bradish who cautioned Secretary of State Adams that if the administration intended to open negotiations with the Sultan, it must be done with the utmost secrecy; Great Britain especially, but the other European nations generally, would intrigue against an unwelcome trade rival. On the basis of the envoy's report, small steps were taken in the decade to improve relations. The United States officially named Offley as consul at Smyrna in 1824, and during Adams's term as president—in 1825 and 1828—Offley made tentative efforts that were ultimately unsuccessful. The Americans were understandably torn between the desire to improve their trade posture and the reluctance to violate traditional foreign policy tenets by involving themselves in the existing turmoil.[2]

Inspired perhaps by Adams's failure in yet another sphere, Jackson made the achievement of a Turkish treaty a high-priority assignment. The President recognized that the trade at that time was confined largely to the exchange at Smyrna of rum and cotton cloth for opium, fruits, and nuts, but he anticipated the potential for exporting American manufactures not only to Turkey but to the Russian Black Sea ports as well. Aware that the Europeans were intensely jealous of the trade and that earlier talks had foundered partially because the Americans insisted on a most-favored-nation provision, Jackson urged concession. To make the initial inroads, the United States would accept a slight discrimination in duties, perhaps 1 or 2 percent over what the British or French paid. Obviously, Jackson anticipated that this discrepancy would soon be rectified. The President named Offley, Commodore James Biddle of the Mediterranean Squadron, and New York businessman Charles Rhind as agents in September 1829. Their instructions emphasized that Rhind should lead the negotiating team, since Biddle was a naval officer and Offley slightly tainted by past discussions. To insure that the British would not have advance warning of the mission, the cautious Van Buren kept all the relevant papers in his private rooms.[3]

Rhind sailed from New York on September 14 and joined Biddle and Offley at Port Mahon, Minorca. The three men proceeded to Smyrna, but the merchant went on alone to Constantinople. The talks began in February 1830, and although plagued by British intrigue, Rhind was quickly successful; by the time the other commissioners arrived in May, the pact already had been signed. The New Yorker was granted more than he could have expected—most-favored-nation status and a provision for extraterritoriality.

The real reason for the Sultan's capitulation to American interests at this juncture, however, was a secret provision: the American representative in Constantinople would assist in obtaining shipbuilding agreements and timber in the United States to reconstitute the Turkish navy. The Sultan was aware that the American carrying trade was the second largest in the world, surpassed only by the British, and that the United States navy was a well-constructed force to be reckoned with. While it was evident that Yankee commerce with Smyrna was now exceeded only by that of the English, it was American fir—not cottons—that increased the Porte's pulse rate. The secret provision was probably imperative in order to gain the commercial concessions Rhind desired, but it deeply disturbed his fellow commissioners. While they were likely piqued at not having taken part in the negotiations, their complaints about a violation of the American principle of noninvolvement rang true.[4]

The Ottoman treaty had a rippling negative effect on the major participants. The Senate approved it in February 1831 but first threw out the offensive article on shipbuilding. In the course of the debate, Jackson was mercilessly attacked by a cadre of senators who believed that he had usurped the constitutional powers of the Senate by appointing the commissioners without its consent. The Secretary of State also incurred some residual scars. As a Virginia correspondent told Nicholas Trist, "The Turkish mission has injured Van Buren greatly. . . . Before that he stood exceedingly high in this state."[5]

Rhind had hoped to be appointed Minister to Turkey and return with the ratified treaty. However, his impetuosity in agreeing to the shipbuilding provision combined with an additional error in judgment to doom his chances. As part of the treaty-signing process, an exchange of gifts had occurred, the Sultan generously presenting the American agent with four Arabian horses. Although it was unconstitutional for an official to accept gifts for government service, the inexperienced New Yorker both desired the horses and did not wish to offend the monarch, so he brought them with him on his return to the United States. Rhind's insistence on his right to retain the horses further embarrassed the administration. The President threw the matter into the lap of Congress, but its members declined to take the responsibility. While lamenting to James Hamilton that Rhind had caused him "much pain," the troubled President was still considering sending him to Turkey with the ratified treaty. Hamilton, the New York district attorney, who had witnessed the legal fiasco, urged instead that the President dispatch the talented linguist and State Department veteran William B. Hodgson.[6]

While Hodgson, who spoke fluent Arabic and some Turkish, would be ideal for the purpose of treaty exchange, Jackson sought someone more prestigious for the permanent mission as chargé. His first choice was Boston-born merchant and virtual career diplomat, George Erving. Erving, a bachelor who had served Jefferson in London, Madison in Copenhagen, and Jefferson, Madison, and Monroe in Madrid, seemed the grizzled veteran necessary for the task ahead. The fact that he had not gotten along well with Secretary of State John Quincy Adams only recommended him further. The well-traveled Bostonian had been to Constantinople previously, however, and the thought of returning repulsed him. He told Van Buren that it mattered little whether the United States was represented by a minister, chargé, or consul, since they were all viewed the same by the Turks. As for Ottoman government, it was "rife with corruption and cupidity."[7]

Erving's prompt refusal opened the way for Jackson to repay a political debt. In the spring of 1831, Commodore David Porter, late of the United States navy, was languishing in North Africa as Consul-General to the Barbary States. An officer with a long and distinguished career fighting the British and pirates in the Caribbean, Porter had recently fallen on hard times. His overeagerness in battling the buccaneers had led to a landing on Spanish-held Puerto Rico and a court-martial for "hostile acts to a friendly power." He resigned, rather than stand trial, and gained employment in the Mexican navy, a step that proved to be professionally and financially disastrous. When Jackson moved into the White House in March 1829, he promised his old comrade-in-arms, a loyal Democrat, that he would find a suitable position for him. Over the next twelve months Porter refused offers to become naval agent at Gibraltar, United States marshal for the District of Columbia, and governor of the Navy Asylum—the commodore deemed each of these positions either below his status or lacking in pecuniary reward—before accepting the North African post in 1830.

It is likely that the President appointed Porter to Turkey for both personal and diplomatic reasons. Although the career navy man possessed what one historian referred to as "a quarterdeck attitude" when it came to dealing with his subordinates, Old Hickory was also cognizant of the Sultan's priorities as manifest in the rejected secret article of the treaty. If the United States government would not directly participate in the construction of a Turkish navy, would it not benefit the Porte (and Turkish-American relations) to have a man of Porter's skills and knowledge in residence for consultation?[8]

In April 1831, the 24-gun sloop *John Adams*, with William Hodgson and the Turkish treaty aboard, sailed from Norfolk, Virginia, bound for the Mediterranean and a rendezvous with the Commodore. Porter, of course, eagerly accepted the appointment, and the two men arrived in Constantinople in August. The assignment was delicate, since the Chargé was obliged to explain to the offended Turks why the Senate had rejected the shipbuilding provision of the treaty. Van Buren urged him to tell the Sultan that he was, of course, welcome to build ships in American ports, but that the government could not be committed to take part. Just in case logic failed, Congress had appropriated $25,000 to purchase gifts for His Highness.[9]

Upon arrival the diplomat's problems were compounded by the attitude of his chief interpreter, or dragoman, an Italian of questionable character named Nicholas Navoni, who had hoped for the diplomatic post himself; the presence of Porter and Hodgson agitated him. Since Hodgson's Turkish was still weak, the Italian's delaying tactics further complicated negotiations. But Porter persevered. After weeks of discussion, plus a $9,000 snuffbox and a $5,000 fan, the Sultan signed the agreement on October 5. But to demonstrate that he was miffed by the Senate's action, the Turk increased the duty on American shipping from 3 percent to 15 percent. Porter's protests, but more particularly his cooperation with the Sultan's naval efforts, resulted in a lowering of the duties by the summer of 1832.[10]

While Hodgson sailed for the United States with the ratified treaty, Porter remained to assuage wounded feelings. He quickly impressed the Porte with his knowledge of naval affairs, becoming an informal advisor on reform in the Turkish navy. At the same time he recommended that the Sultan employ the talented American shipbuilder Henry Eckford to reconstruct his fleet. Eckford, who had worked with Porter in building ships for the Mexican navy, had engaged in earlier discussions about a Turkish project with the discredited Charles Rhind. Even though Rhind was not appointed, he sailed with Eckford in the latter's vessel, the *United States*, with the idea of convincing the Sultan to hire him. The fine lines of the *United States* and the *John Adams* were enough to persuade the monarch of the quality of American craftsmanship. By October 1832, Eckford had obtained a crew of carpenters from New York, started construction on one frigate, and ordered a live oak frame from America for a second.

Tragically, work had hardly begun when Eckford died of an intestinal disorder, and his body was shipped home in a cask of wine. But his able foreman, Foster Rhodes, inherited the project and saw it through to completion. Although other warships were built in the intervening years, the most triumphant moment occurred in the summer of 1837, when Rhodes launched a frigate, two cutters, and a brig within one hour. What had been a shell of a navy after Navarino had been rebuilt in a decade to include eleven ships of the line and a dozen frigates—a force that rivaled the Russian Black Sea fleet and would give a rebellious prince cause for second thought. Not only was the American presence strong in the rebuilding program, but under Porter's guidance, Turkish officers received instruction from their counterparts in the American Mediterranean Squadron. The Sultan's request of the loan of Yankee officers for his fleet was denied, but a former American captain took command of a Turkish frigate. Needless to say, this increased American influence was the source of some discomfort in London, and Washington was not unaware of the link between American standing at the Turkish court and the growth of commerce. The United States duly rewarded Porter in 1839 by upgrading his rank from chargé to minister.[11]

Porter's stiff-necked attitude and posture of command, which served him well as Commodore and even as advisor to the Sultan's navy, was a liability when dealing with his staff. Biographer David Long portrays him as a man of pride, arrogance, formality, and abrasiveness; a man accustomed to giving orders and to receiving the deference accorded to naval officers. Porter was vindictive and discriminatory, an Anglophobe who also disliked Mexicans and Jews. Perhaps this unique blend of strengths and weaknesses could have been utilized in a diplomatic capacity only in the Ottoman Empire of the 1830s. The liabilities were made apparent when Hodgson returned from the United States in 1832 to assume the posts of dragoman and Secretary of Legation. Navoni had infuriated the Chargé to the point of dismissal, and Porter wished the talented linguist to return and take his position. Hodgson soon discovered, however, that the officer-turned-diplomat expected unswerving obedience and loyalty. Even more annoying, he brought his two nephews into the office staff, supplanting many of the duties and some of the prestige Hodgson had expected to come his way. By December the interpreter was writing to Secretary Livingston to complain of "abuse of office" (nepotism) and the poor organization of the legation.

To Porter, such protest bordered on insubordination; he proceeded to relieve Hodgson of his secretarial post and consult another dragoman, sever his pay allowance, and refuse to receive either him or his dispatches. Hodgson was rapidly becoming a nonperson and had little leverage with which to combat the influential Porter.[12]

The President, however, was not unaware of Hodgson's considerable talents and the Commodore's equally large ego. Although Hodgson requested a transfer to the Barbary States, Jackson had a much more important mission in mind.

For several years Mehemet Ali, the Viceroy of Egypt, had grown increasingly restless under the constraints placed upon him by the Sultan. The Egyptian leader had sublimated his own imperial desires in the 1820s to become Mahmud's most able, if not trusted, lieutenant and had suffered as much as his master at the Navarino debacle of 1827. For his loyal service over the years, Mehemet had been promised the Syrian provinces, but the Sultan never delivered them. Angry and contemptuous, the Viceroy assigned his son Ibrahim to lead an army of conquest in 1831. Victory came quickly and easily; by December 1832 the provincial forces had approached the gates of Constantinople itself.

The European powers watched the progress of events carefully, since the independence of Egypt and the splintering of the Ottoman Empire would produce serious commercial and strategic consequences. The French were less than covert in their involvement and support of the Egyptian Pasha as they sought a foothold in the Middle East. The British, troubled by events that threatened their Red Sea–India link, nevertheless hesitated to act. Only the Russians moved to the commitment of forces. The signing of a highly unusual pact between the Czar and the Sultan in 1833 likely saved Constantinople from Ibrahim's army, but at the cost of maximizing Russian influence with the Porte. Although the Ottoman Empire still theoretically remained intact, Mehemet Ali's triumphs suggested an independent Egypt—possibly extending onto the Arabian peninsula—in the not far distant future. It was within this political and diplomatic context that Andrew Jackson decided to explore the possibility of opening relations with the Viceroy.[13]

Although the establishment of an Egyptian mission provided a convenient safety valve to relieve the pressure building between William Hodgson and Commodore Porter, the idea had been explored even earlier in the year in Washington when Francis Leiber, an emigré intellectual and political gadfly, had communicated with Navy Secretary Woodbury in February 1833 about the advantages of developing commercial ties with both Greece and Egypt. The winter of 1832–33, however, highlighted by the tariff and nullification controversy with South Carolina, was a particularly trying time for the administration. When the compromise tariff resolved the crisis in March, an apologetic Woodbury brushed the Professor off by telling him that the region would be hard to deal with until the existing problems between Turkey and Egypt were resolved. Leiber continued for the next eighteen months to press the Secretary about an expedition, but at the same time that cabinet officials were reading his letters and conferring with him, Hodgson was already in Cairo.[14]

William Hodgson was an excellent choice for this potentially profitable mission. His years of experience as chargé at Algiers had given him a knowledge of Arabic, exposure to Moslem culture, and a mentor in Consul-General William Shaler; the merchant had taught the young diplomat how to survive the political patronage wars that might have terminated his career. Hodgson had received the support of John Quincy Adams and former Adams Postmaster-General (and recently appointed Supreme Court Justice) John McLean. Shaler, an old friend of Van Buren's, showed Hodgson how he could subtly move into the Jackson camp. It was, after all, the Red Fox's lieutenant James Hamilton who had propitiously recommended Hodgson's appointment to the President.

Hodgson's instructions were to travel to Alexandria and spend no longer than three months determining the political and economic condition of Egypt. Was Mehemet Ali in a position to negotiate a separate commercial treaty? If so, what benefits would such an agreement hold for American merchants? Because of the ever-present intrigue of the Europeans, in addition to the likely objection of the Sultan to such a mission, the venture was to be kept secret, and Hodgson was to report back to Washington at its conclusion.[15]

An eager reception awaited the American agent when he arrived in Egypt in September 1834. Mehemet Ali and his Foreign Minister visited with Hodgson twice and demonstrated an avid interest in a commercial bond with the United States. The two countries produced similar agricultural goods (cotton, rice, grains, and tobacco), but there were other mutually advantageous items to be exchanged: the Pasha was attracted especially to American naval stores for his growing fleet, while Hodgson expressed interest in the 100,000 pounds of opium annually produced in Egypt. After concluding his talks, the American toured Cairo and traveled up the Nile before returning to the United States in the spring of 1835. His recommendations were tentative: although trade potential with Egypt was limited, Mehemet Ali threatened to expand his empire beyond its already extensive bounds and would probably soon achieve independence from Constantinople; until that time actually arrived, it was inadvisable to consider a treaty, but the likelihood warranted the establishment of a consul-general in Alexandria. Jackson declined to take this step, but he did upgrade John Gliddon's post from consular agent to consul and established consuls also at Beruit, Damascas, Aleppo, and Cyprus.[16]

Since Porter seemed reticent to travel throughout the Empire and his influence was needed at the Sultan's court, the President investigated further commercial possibilities through an additional mission. Old Hickory appointed Lewis Cass, former Michigan territorial governor and Secretary of War, as the new Minister of France in the fall of 1836. Cass had irritated the General with his inefficiency in managing his Cabinet post and with the basic "timidity and weakness of [his] character." With the French crisis under control and relative harmony restored, the timing was sound to exile this troublesome lieutenant, even though Jackson's administration was drawing to a close; moreover, since responsibilities in Paris at this juncture were far from onerous, Cass could be sent on a commercial reconnaissance of the eastern Mediterranean.[17]

Nicholas Trist reported a White House conversation in which an associate teased the President about a rumor that the new Minister to France had saved $25,000 in order to visit Europe, Asia, and Africa for the purpose of writing a history or travelogue of those continents. Jackson, ever secretive about such missions, vaguely commented that "if I knew it to be so, I would recall him on the spot, for he had no permission of the kind except that which it is usual to grant, in the confidence, of course, that it is not to be abused. He wished to have an unusual latitude in this respect and got something of the sort inserted in his instructions, but I had them altered." Cass only wintered in Paris before embarking on a six-month (April–October 1837) cruise on board the *Constitution*. His travels took him through Italy, Greece, Turkey, Syria, and the Holy Land and finally to Egypt to visit with Mehemet Ali. While the wandering Minister immensely enjoyed his pilgrimage, no substantial recommendations and certainly no treaty emerged from it. Within the next few years a new Egyptian-Turkish War would erupt, prompting European intervention and severely limiting the foreign policy flexibility of the Pasha.[18]

It was perhaps most disappointing for the Americans that the expected commerce with the Ottoman Empire did not materialize during the Jacksonian era. Only Smyrna with its drug traffic prospered. But opium, which Consul William Churchill referred to as "our grand article," consumed precious little space in the hold of a ship, obliging the captain to seek additional cargo at other ports. The obvious economic problem was the similarity in agricultural goods, but additional factors hindered the trade. The Tariff of 1828 levied prohibitively high duties against raw wool, a major Turkish export. Various diseases, especially the plague, ravaged the Near East, isolating some areas for months. The Black Sea trade languished because the ports had too little to offer to make the hazardous journey through the Straits worth the effort for an American pilot; by 1837 various consuls dejectedly reported that American trade with their ports had slowed to a trickle.[19]

THE BARBARY STATES

Yankee sail faired even worse in the ports of the Barbary States. American consuls functioned in both a diplomatic and a commercial capacity in Tunisia, Morocco, and Tripoli (Algiers became a French territory in 1830) at a scant $2,000 per year. Their major role, however, was not commercial. The State Department's Chief Clerk told the new consul to Tangiers that United States trade was "very inconsiderable" and the appointee to Tripoli that the trade is "very inconsiderable now, as it has always been"; in lieu of transacting business, they could assist in aiding shipwrecked sailors or freeing those captured and held for ransom by wandering desert tribes.[20]

Luckily, few such problems appeared to confront the Jackson White House; those that did occur stemmed from the activities of the consuls themselves, sometimes to the great embarrassment of the President. A case in point was that of consul Samuel Carr, the agent at Tangiers. Before he left Maryland in the fall of 1831, he was in serious financial trouble and constantly hounded by his creditors. It was increasingly apparent that Morocco might be a haven from his pursuers but would provide no relief for his empty wallet. Consequently, the imaginative diplomat-turned-entrepreneur stopped in Paris and contracted with an engraver to complete a medal commemorating the Hero's victory at New Orleans on one side, backed by a scene from the Jackson electoral triumph of 1828. Carr supposed that at ten francs in bronze and twenty-five in silver, the medal should sell well in Europe, and perhaps also in the United States. Unfortunately, funding the venture required the "unorthodox drafting" of his consular funds from bankers for the United States in London. Carr had hoped to remain in Paris long enough to obtain additional funds from the visiting Martin Van Buren, but when collectors began not only to pressure him but to harass Minister Rives for payment of Carr's debts, the moment was auspicious to depart for Morocco. The State Department did not approve the Consul's financial legerdemain or his reticence to leave the French capital, but by the time his letter of recall arrived, Carr had already departed for Tangiers.[21]

The situation declined, if possible, from bad to worse. On September 15, Carr found himself in a street brawl with two Moroccans who were "anxious to trace a few Saracen hieroglyphs on my belly." Amazingly, Carr got the best of the contest and wounded one of his attackers. Irate, he viewed the assault as an attack upon the American flag and demanded that several naval vessels appear to impress the local population. Much to the consternation of the State Department, the Consul also became heavily in debt in Tangiers. He quickly squandered $1,500 borrowed at Gibraltar and $2,500 more at Tangiers. Carr had discovered in just a few weeks that not only were the Moors "a savage and barbarous" people but, just as important, "this is the last place in the world to sell anything."

On October 1, 1832, James Leib of Pennsylvania arrived in Tangiers to rescue the United States from further embarrassment. The displaced Consul—angry, debt-ridden, and furious at the administration for removing him without a hearing—did not initially take his frustration out on his replacement, commenting that "he seems well bred enough considering the state that he is from" (Carr was a southerner). But the tranquility lasted only a matter of weeks before Carr attempted to kill Leib. This news compounded the President's impression (reinforced by Leib's correspondence) that the former agent was a criminal, a maniac, or both. To save the United States further humiliation, Leib was empowered to draw $4,000 to pay Carr's debts and ship him back home promptly, with a responsible person to look after him if necessary.[22]

No doubt Jackson was much relieved to conclude this disastrous minor episode in his foreign policy, but then the reliable Leib placed him in another annoying situation. As the treaty with Morocco approached renewal, the Emperor presented Leib with gifts: two horses and a lion. Having recently confronted a similar situation with the Sultan, the President ordered that all three animals be sold for the best price possible—unless the horses were of quality stock, in which case they should be sent to the United States "by the first suitable opportunity." This time the President, a racehorse connoisseur, wanted an opportunity to examine the unconstitutional gifts.[23]

Leib apparently knew little about horses and less about lions. He sold the horses to a ship captain, James Riley, and shipped the lion back to the United States. When Riley arrived in New York, the State Department informed him that an error had been made and that his understanding would be appreciated. Secretary of State John Forsyth and Collector of the Port of New York Samuel Swartwout were involved in paying the Captain, out of government funds, for the passage, care, and keep of the animals. Riley received over $500 for the horses and $300 for the lion, and all three were shipped to Washington, where the President generously gave the lion to the joint ownership of the St. Vincent's (Georgetown) and Washington orphan asylums. The horses' final destination appears unknown. By 1837, as the ratification of the Moroccan treaty was imminent, the wary Jackson specifically told Leib not to accept any more presents from the Emperor.[24]

NAPLES

American relations with the Kingdom of the Two Sicilies during the first quarter of the nineteenth century were tenuous at best. No commercial treaty existed; in fact, ill will over the failure of the Neapolitans to pay spoliation claims from the Napoleonic Wars frayed potential ties. In 1809, Joachim Murat, the Bonapartist ruler of Naples, granted by special decree an invitation to American merchants to import goods into the city. This exemption to the restrictive Berlin and Milan Decrees of Napoleon, who had placed rigid limitations on American sail trading with Europe, was eagerly seized upon by hungry New England merchants. Within months some forty-nine ships had gathered in the harbor, whereupon Murat simply seized them and their cargoes. Hundreds of sailors were sent home on a vessel chartered by the American consul. American protests went unanswered, and the onset of the War of 1812 precluded aggressive action by the Madison administration. In 1816, however, the President dispatched the able William Pinkney of Maryland to attain satisfaction from the restored Bourbon monarchy of Ferdinand I. The emissary's lack of success was matched by that of John Appleton, who served the John Quincy Adams administration in the fruitless quest for a resolution of the claims.[25]

When Jackson took office in March 1829, he understood that France was the key to the claims issue: if the French would agree to accept responsibility for the claims against their country, then the Neapolitans would be obliged to do so as well. Minister William Rives labored through revolution and accompanying changes in monarchs and ministries to formulate an acceptable treaty with France in the summer of 1831. Jackson, ecstatic over Rives's effort, pressed new Secretary of State Edward Livingston to move quickly on the Neapolitan situation. A new monarch, young Ferdinand II, had recently assumed the throne, and the Americans hoped that he would be more receptive to their entreaties for settlement.[26]

Unfortunately, official Washington had become rather jaded about the morality of the Neapolitans. European expatriate Francis Leiber told Navy Secretary Woodbury that "all Italian governments are bad and greatly corrupted . . . the lowest depth of wretchedness is reached in the Neapolitan government. I should not fear to exaggerate very much when I call the Neapolitan government a conglomeration of greedy corruption. . . . Every Italian minister can be bought. You can obtain anything." The well-traveled author James Fenimore Cooper doubted that honesty could succeed with the Neapolitans, since they were "habitually corrupt." With such information from respected sources influencing the decision-making process, the strength of the negotiator and the strategy to be utilized took on greater significance.[27]

Probably the man most deserving of the appointment to the Kingdom of the Two Sicilies (if one excuses the exhausted William Rives, who desired to return to the United States) was Minister to Denmark Henry Wheaton, a brilliant international lawyer fresh from his settlement of the Danish claims question, who was sitting bored in Copenhagen. But valued as Wheaton's services were, he was an unrepentant Adams man. While Old Hickory would call upon him again in the future, for the present the challenges and rewards must be given to loyal Jacksonians. Therefore, in October 1831, the President selected a thirty-nine-year-old former congressman, John Nelson of Maryland. Nelson, a talented lawyer and conservative Democrat, also happened to have been a Georgetown messmate of Martin Van Buren a decade before.[28]

Nelson's instructions were a marvelous blend of the carrot and the stick. Once the claims issue was resolved, the United States would be eager to discuss a commercial convention that would markedly benefit Neapolitan wines, silks, and art goods. Moreover, for the financially strapped Neapolitans, total payment could be spread over a four- to six-year period. If, however, the Italians continued to deny their responsibilities, then the President would urge Congress "to take such measures as to insure full compensation." Not wishing to waste time, the President wanted an answer by March 1, 1832. Since Nelson arrived in Naples on January 19, accompanied by four warships, it was clear that Jackson's veiled threat was very real and his patience limited.[29]

Nelson moved aggressively with the Minister of Foreign Affairs, Prince Cassaro. The fundamental American argument relied heavily upon international law, which suggested that an actual government is the legitimate government of a nation. The American barrister dismissed the Neapolitan argument that Murat had been a usurper, not the legitimate ruler of Naples, and that Napoleon forced confiscations upon him. It seemed implorable, too, that all the proceeds of the sale of Yankee merchandise had gone into Murat's pocket alone and none into the public treasury. French willingness to pay the claims clearly compromised the Neapolitan argument, and the strength of the American position blunted Cassaro's response. Instead of dealing with the questions head on, he preferred to send the claims issue to the King and the legislative Council of State for their deliberation, while he dealt with the commercial treaty. Nelson held firm: no claims, no commerce. The month of March arrived without a reply from Cassaro, who had departed for Sicily, and it was rapidly becoming apparent that the Italians would slyly delay until Congress adjourned, thus rendering any sanctioned operation against them unlikely until the following year. On March 12, the angry diplomat penned a strong letter to Secretary Livingston in which he emphasized the ability of the Kingdom to pay the claims and ridiculed the power of the Neapolitan army and navy. A show of American naval force might be a convincing demonstration of United States determination to resolve the issue. The dispatch left on the following day aboard the U.S.S. *Ontario*.[30]

While Nelson waited for a reply from Washington, he continued to play a cat-and-mouse game with Cassaro. The Prince pleaded poverty, denied responsibility for Murat's acts, and urged negotiation of the commercial treaty. Even more disconcerting, the King formally rejected Nelson's interpretation of international law regarding the legitimacy of Murat's rule. This was particularly frustrating for a lawyer of Nelson's skill, and he felt obliged to respond in what amounted to a ninety-three-page legal brief on the subject. Probably the only reason he remained in Naples was the hope that there were either firm orders or a fleet on the way from the United States.

On July 25 the frigates *Brandywine* and *Constellation* arrived from Port Mahon, throwing the city into a temporary panic. The King was called back from Abruzzi, and the government rapidly planned defenses against the anticipated assault by this massive array of firepower. But the situation quickly cooled when it was discovered that the vessels were on a routine visit, not a special mission of destruction from President Jackson.

Fully six weeks later, newly appointed Mediterranean Squadron Commander Daniel T. Patterson sailed into Naples harbor with the long-awaited presidential response for Nelson. The diplomat, who was expecting a fiery epistle from the Old Soldier, marveled at its moderation. Demonstrating surprising patience and understanding for the Neapolitan government, the President had refrained from recommending harsh measures to Congress; he was inclined to give the Italians another chance. It was, after all, an election year, and Jackson probably saw no reason to give his congressional critics additional ammunition. The frigate *United States*, now supplementing American firepower in the area, was to remain twenty days. If no positive response was forthcoming from Cassaro within that time, Nelson was instructed to ask for his passports. The President would then take whatever action he felt constitutionally necessary.[31]

On September 21, Cassaro, weary and depressed by the recent death of his wife, met with the American Minister once again. This time the Prince admitted the justice of the claims and attempted to settle on a miniscule amount. He also pressed again for a commercial treaty, but Nelson remained inflexible. The Neapolitan position became increasingly untenable. The *John Adams* and the *Concord* arrived to make the American naval forces in the harbor even more formidable. At the same time, the Italians could not ignore the rumors rampant in the American press that the 74-gun *Delaware* had set sail for ports unknown. Yankee editors who argued that the President could not or would not institute military action against Italian ports or commerce without congressional approval probably provided little solace to the worried Neapolitans.[32]

The presence of the American fleet in Naples likewise troubled the English. In London, American Chargé Aaron Vail reported to Livingston that the diplomatic community there believed it was hardly coincidental that the Mediterranean Squadron maintained such a high profile throughout Nelson's negotiations. A rumor was also circulating widely regarding United States interest in the small island of Lampedosa, between Sicily and the Barbary Coast, as a potential naval station. Vail attempted in August to investigate the base-in-lieu-of-claims suggestion and found it verified by an "informed colleague." A major stumbling block to such a transfer, of course, would be the English reaction to a new power in a region the British crown jealously guarded. British Foreign Secretary Lord Palmerston candidly told the Chargé that the Neapolitans had asked the advice of the King's ministers on the legitimacy of their obligations and whether the granting of the island would damage Anglo-Neapolitan relations. Palmerston assured Vail that while His Majesty's government had no intention of interfering actively in a matter between the United States and the Two Sicilies, he had honestly told the Italians that London would prefer a cash settlement to a property transfer. At the same time, the London *Globe* reported that Jackson desired the Sicilian port of Syracuse, where the American fleet planned to winter, and that the Neapolitan counter offer of Lampedosa had been "rejected with disdain."[33]

The Italians took the opportunity to consult with the French, who a year before had agreed to a claims treaty; in June their Chargé in Paris spoke with Foreign Minister Horace Sebastiani. Because of the antiquity of the issue and the tendency of the Americans to exaggerate the amount due them, Sebastiani recommended settling upon one-third the sum demanded—which he declared the French had done.[34]

As the rumors flew, Nelson furiously threw himself into the task of arriving at a reasonable dollar figure for the claims. Earlier in the summer, Cassaro had again pleaded poverty and inquired about payment in works of art, a suggestion that stunned the Minister. Nelson believed he was acting fairly in submitting a sum of 3,150,000 ducats (approximately $2.6 million) as the principal payment (he decided to forgo requesting a like amount in interest, which would represent 5 percent accrued over the previous twenty years). When Cassaro and Nelson met on September 25 to haggle over the figures, they argued at length about the sum Murat had realized from the sale of the American vessels and their cargoes. The Prince suggested that His Majesty might pay one-third the amount requested, but no more—dire financial straits prohibited it. The American felt obliged to counsel Cassaro unequivocally that the sum must exceed one-third or he would demand his passports. Backing further into a corner, the Italian stated that a convention could not be drawn up before the twenty-day deadline expired. Then he posited that a commercial convention should be part of the agreement. Nelson simply shook his head, reemphasizing that the claims could be resolved in a few simple articles in a matter of hours, and he would absolutely not discuss commerce until the spoliations pact had been signed.

On September 30, Nelson visited the foreign office to hear the Neapolitan counter offer. By King Ferdinand's calculations the American merchants were due approximately 800,000 ducats—coincidentally the sum Sebastiani had suggested! The pained diplomat felt uncertain exactly what response to make; both laughter and anger probably crossed his mind. Cassaro urged Nelson not to reject the amount hastily, but to reconsider his own demand and let the game continue. After some soul searching, the American reduced his figure to 2.5 million ducats. The following day, upon learning that the King would not budge from the 800,000 figure, a disappointed Nelson returned to his apartment, packed his clothes, asked for his passports, and alerted Commodore Patterson to prepare the *Concord* for imminent departure.

Over the next several days, Austrian and Sicilian representatives of the King called upon Nelson and urged him to stay a few weeks longer, assuring him that the situation would be resolved. Nelson refused. Then, on October 5, as he prepared for his final audience with Ferdinand, a note arrived from the Foreign Office. Would the American agree to meet one final time with Cassaro? He yielded. On October 6 the two men discussed the possible and the impossible for two hours, each pleading that he could go no higher or lower. The sum finally agreed upon—2,115,000 ducats (about $1.7 million)—came close to covering the amount of principal the American merchants had demanded. Additionally, the United States would receive 4 percent interest on the claims over the nine-year period of payment. Washington was empowered to distribute the money by whatever means the government deemed appropriate. While some National Republican businessmen may have grumbled partisanly because Jackson had accomplished what Adams could not, they were overjoyed at the amount.[35]

Although the treaty was signed on October 14, Nelson did not arrive in America until the first week of December 1832. Jackson had undoubtedly hoped to add the Neapolitan settlement to the already impressive foreign policy accomplishments of his first administration, but that proved unnecessary, as the President won reelection by a resounding 55 percent of the popular vote. In January 1833 he proudly presented the pact to the Senate, which readily approved it on the 19th; even such usual skeptics as Henry Clay and John Tyler were grudgingly obliged to vote aye.[36]

Once again, Jacksonian diplomacy had emerged triumphant. The American consul in Le Havre, France, suggested that "the battle of Naples was won in Paris." Likely he was correct; the triumph of William Rives in 1831 had opened the door for the successful conclusion of the twenty-year claims dispute with the Neapolitans. But the final resolution also involved the proper amount of pressure and finesse in word and action from Jackson, Livingston, and Nelson. The perceptive Minister, recognizing the moderate course his chief chose to pursue, thus wound his way through the frustrating series of delays and discussions in September and October of 1832. The presence of Patterson's Mediterranean Squadron lacked subtlety, but combined with the promise of commercial rewards to follow an agreement, it produced the desired results.

The President moved immediately to negotiate a commercial treaty. Even before the Senate had formally accepted the claims agreement, Livingston asked Nelson if he wished to return to Naples. When the weary Marylander politely refused, the Secretary suggested dispatching Auguste Davezac, then Chargé to the Netherlands.[37] The Hague presented few challenges for an American diplomat at this juncture, and his presence would not be seriously missed. In addition, Davezac was eminently qualified for the post. Born in Santo Domingo, he had studied in Paris and become a well-regarded criminal lawyer in New Orleans. He had taken part in the Battle of New Orleans, where Old Hickory cited him for bravery. His marriage to the sister of Secretary Livingston further complemented his career. With his brother-in-law in the cabinet, in 1831 Davezac was appointed to the legation in the Netherlands, where he developed a reputation for insight into social, political, and economic conditions on the Continent.

Livingston wished the negotiations for the commercial treaty with Naples to be carried on in secret. Therefore, he instructed Davezac to inform all concerned parties that he was simply traveling to Naples to exchange conventions and not to mention the commercial aspect of his mission. To continue the secrecy, Davezac was ordered to correspond with Washington in cipher. No doubt, the Secretary of State wisely realized not only that communication leaks abounded in Italy, but that once other Europeans became aware of the American goals, they would do everything possible to thwart the mission.[38]

Davezac left Holland on May 1 and three weeks later arrived in Naples. Unfortunately, no business could be transacted for the next fortnight because of the festivities surrounding the marriage of the King's sister to the Grand Duke of Tuscany, and the added excitement of the discovery of a plot to murder the twenty-one-year-old monarch. Thus, it was not until June 8 that ratifications could be exchanged and the process of commercial negotiation begun.

Davezac had been instructed to offer free importation of Neapolitan silks, fruits, statuary, and paintings (but not wine) for ten years in exchange for the admission of American rice, cotton, and fish on the same terms. Through initial conversations with Prince Cassaro and with consul Alexander Hammett, who had lived in Naples for a quarter-century, Davezac quickly discovered a number of roadblocks to success. Among other Europeans, the English were a particular problem: Naples had granted 10 percent reductions on the duties of imported British goods, and they were understandably not anxious to share this bounty with their Yankee rivals. Livingston had even targeted English cottons in his March instructions as a prime subject for Davezac's consideration. But a second obstacle presented itself in the form of local Neapolitan industries and producers of agricultural goods (including cottons) who were receiving government protection and were therefore equally opposed to American competition. A third problem was the American interest in guaranteeing the rights of neutral vessels in time of war. While this had little practical impact upon the Neapolitans, it meant a good deal to the English, whom the King was reluctant to offend.[39]

In spite of the hurdles, through the hot Neapolitan summer Davezac was emminently successful in courting the friendship of powerful European banker Karl Rothschild and in charming Prince Cassaro, his daughters, and the impressionable Ferdinand II. The negotiations appeared to promise ultimate triumph (so Davezac informed his government), although Cassaro had warned that the Commission of Commerce, which would meet in September, must approve. But soon information began to wend its way to Davezac of British and French efforts among the commissioners to scuttle his proposed treaty. The American worked frantically with the King, Cassaro, and the Minister of Finance to combat this opposition. By October he was again optimistic and wrote Washington that a quid pro quo of Neapolitan wines, brandies, and sewing silks might be exchanged for American tobacco, cottons, and rice.[40]

But each time resolution appeared certain, new delays occurred, and Davezac's frustration was matched only by that of his government. After six months of negotiation and too many premature promises of success, he was still emptyhanded. On December 26, Secretary of State McLane wrote him that the President was giving him ten days after the receipt of the letter to complete the treaty. If this should prove impossible, the Minister was to inform the Neapolitans, without anger, that his return to his duties at The Hague was imperative. He should assure them that Jackson still remained hopeful of reaching an agreement in the future. On January 21, Davezac wrote McLane again that he was on the verge of success, although he complained bitterly about the obstructionism of the English and bureaucratic delays inherent in the Italian system. Soon thereafter, he received the Secretary's December missive and was obliged to convey his orders to Cassaro. The Prince, in the unenviable position of attempting to balance a desirable arrangement with the Amercians against the powerful opposition of his European neighbors, urged Davezac to remain a while longer. But the promise of a treaty days or weeks in the future could not hold the American, who suggested sarcastically that negotiations be held in Washington, out of the sphere of Continental intrigue.[41]

Davezac left Naples in March 1834, and while Jackson felt no ill will toward the Kingdom, he also made no further efforts to gain a commercial treaty. Between a cholera epidemic that ravaged America and struck fear into the hearts of the Italians (obliging them to quarantine Yankee vessels) and the lack of a treaty, American trade with the Kingdom of the Two Sicilies collapsed in 1835. Martin Van Buren dispatched a new minister to Naples in 1838, but not until 1845 was the long-sought-after commercial agreement signed.

Jacksonian policy in the Mediterranean proved to be a qualified success. The Turkish Treaty of 1830 granted the United States generous trading privileges, and the presence of Commodore Porter, martinet though he may have been, gave the Americans a personal advantage with the Sultan that was the envy of the European community. The disappointing commercial intercourse with Asia Minor, the Black Sea ports, and Mehemet Ali's Egyptian domains had far less to do with politics and policy than with the quality and type of goods to be traded. The positive relations developed with the Barbary States reflect the importance of the American merchant marine in the Mediterranean and the need to provide for the protection and care of its sailors. The presence of a formidable Mediterranean Squadron in the fall of 1836 (months after the crisis with France had evaporated), consisting of two 44-gun frigates, a sloop, and a schooner, shows the importance that the Jackson administration placed upon the area for existing and potential commerce.

As for the Neapolitans, Davezac's failure to obtain a commercial convention only slightly tarnishes the luster of Nelson's success in settling the claims. Jacksonian diplomacy was a timely blend of patience, understanding, and a show of power. The President, even when negotiations appeared to be crumbling, never demonstrated the anger he revealed to the French. Perhaps he understood the tenuous position of the Neapolitans, buffeted by the winds of the great powers. Even though Davezac failed, the spadework had been done, and Jackson left the door open for additional negotiations at a more favorable time. As in the Danish claims, Old Hickory had procured a respectable sum from an impoverished nation, American honor had been upheld, American merchants were gratified (if not always grateful), and international recognition of the chief executive as a man to be reckoned with continued to strengthen.

The Jacksonian vision went far beyond the Mediterranean's new markets. If those proved disappointing, why not explore possibilities in the Far East or Latin America? Accordingly, urged on by members of his Cabinet and Congress, Jackson moved to unfurl the Stars and Stripes around the globe. Of course, as in the Mediterranean, a strong naval presence would be needed to protect American honor, as well as American sail. The missions of Edmund Roberts and his efforts to develop ties with Japan and Southeast Asia provided insight into the worldwide horizon of Jacksonian America.

Chapter 6

The Asian Challenge: Pirates, Opiates, and New Frontiers

Since the days of Marco Polo, the teas, spices, and silks of the Orient had enticed and enriched the European merchant. As trade with the Far East increased in the seventeenth and eighteenth centuries, so did the pressure for colonies, and the governments of Great Britain and the Netherlands raised their imperial standards in the region. But as other countries moved to dominate the Indian Ocean, the newly independent United States did not hesitate to carve out her own commercial empire. While the Americans, unlike their European counterparts, were not seeking colonies, Yankee sail threatened the carrying trade of rivals worldwide and came to control the African coast, Arabia, and Persia. A seafarer from Salem earned a 700 percent profit on the first large cargo of pepper from Sumatra in 1790, while the *Recovery*, of that same port, opened the coffee trade with Mocha in 1798. Within the next half-century Americans came to dominate commerce in ivory from Zanzibar and opium from Smyrna.[1]

The Americans had also developed a lucrative trade, beginning in the 1780s, with China. While the Chinese restricted foreign market access to Canton and recognized no foreign diplomatic agents, these limitations seemed only a minor impediment to commerce. In the age of Jefferson some of the most eminent Yankee traders, including John J. Astor of New York, Stephen Girard of Philadelphia, Joseph Peabody of Salem, John Donnell of Baltimore, and James and Thomas Perkins of Boston were active in the opium traffic. Unfortunately, they found themselves at a sharp disadvantage in competition with their English counterparts because of the lack of specie in the United States. The

American trade with China had been conducted as a hard metal business, often utilizing Spanish silver bullion. However, as this item was difficult to obtain and the source undependable, especially in the volume the Americans needed, some other means of exchange became imperative. The Turkish port of Smyrna, 175 miles east of Constantinople, provided the solution. From Smyrna, United States traders placed Turkish opium in direct competition in China with its British rival from India. Leading American firms such as Russell and Co. made substantial fortunes in the 1820s and 1830s. In 1832, American companies imported almost 100,000 pounds of opium into China.[2]

The need for capital also sharply affected American trade with India. Almost every port east of the Cape of Good Hope (including British India) would accept only Spanish coin or specie, and it also cost approximately $50,000 to outfit a merchantman for the Oriental trade, a sum few American businessmen could risk. In spite of these difficulties, the United States had a profitable carrying trade with India prior to the War of 1812, particularly while the English were bogged down with the menace of Napoleon.

By 1816 the Europeans had begun to reassert themselves economically, and the Americans had passed a protective tariff that crippled the trade in Indian coarse cottons. Among a population that rarely drank alcohol or ate meat, the Yankees discovered only a limited market for New England rum, beer, pork, and beef. This, combined with the reassertion of British commercial hegemony, caused the dollar amount of the trade to collapse from $4.5 million in 1816 to $1.2 million in 1824. Commerce languished into the 1830s. Only the introduction of the ice trade from New England to Calcutta in exchange for rhinos, lions, tigers, and elephants provided a modicum of relief. But the market for exotic animals was rather limited, and by 1841 only five ships a year were visiting Calcutta.[3]

QUALLAH BATTOO

Except for the pepper trade, the Americans had given cursory attention to the East Indies prior to Jackson's presidency, attempting rather to gain concessions from the British in the West Indies. But Americans had taken control of the commerce of Sumatra, with hundreds of ships making Batavia a port of call between 1795 and 1831, and the world pepper price was set in the Salem, Massachusetts market. Political control of the island, however, was confused and troubled. The British and Dutch maintained joint claim until after the Napoleonic Wars, when the British abandoned interest in lieu of more lucrative possibilities at Singapore. The Dutch, although jealous of their prerogatives on the island, lacked the resources either to shut down the American trade or to control the titular leader of the natives, the King of Acheen, and his nominally subservient rajahs. As a result, for decades the Americans and Sumatrans profited greatly from the pepper trade at the expense of the uninterested British and impotent Dutch. Unfortunately, the bottom dropped out of the pepper market in 1830, leaving both ship captains and natives scrambling for what little profit remained.

Into this tense situation in 1831 sailed the *Friendship* of Salem on a routine voyage. The resulting events would capture the attention of the President, the Congress, the press, and the nation, and act as a stimulus and a harbinger of a new aspect of Jacksonian foreign policy.[4]

The sun had just risen on Monday, February 7, 1831, when the crew of the 316-ton *Friendship*, seventeen officers and men, began loading pepper into her hold at the west Sumatran port of Quallah Battoo. Captain Charles Endicott, two of his officers, and four crewmen went ashore to supervise the weighing of the freight (the Captain's presence was necessary, since both the natives and the Americans habitually tried to cheat each other at the scales); the remainder of the crew observed the cargo placement on board. Late in the afternoon, as First Officer Charles Knight was busily engaged in taking an account of the loaded pepper, the native Malays suddenly attacked him and his shipmates. Knight and two seamen were stabbed to death, and three others were wounded. Four men narrowly escaped by diving overboard, swimming two miles to shore, and hiding in the underbrush.

From his position on the beach, Captain Endicott noticed the increasingly disorderly movement aboard the ship. When he and his officers observed crewmen jumping into the sea, they immediately leaped into their launches and paddled for the *Friendship*. Chased by three Malay boats carrying forty to fifty men each, Endicott realized that it was too late to save his besieged comrades, so he quickly set his course for Muckie, a port twenty-five miles down the coast from Quallah Battoo. The Captain knew that three American vessels—the *James Monroe* of New York, the *Governor Endicott* of Salem, and the *Palmer* of Boston—were anchored there and might be called upon to help recapture his ship.

The men of the other ships did agree to aid him, and on February 9, after the local rajah rejected their demand for the release of the *Friendship*, they attacked. No match for the superior American firepower, the natives abandoned the captured ship. When Endicott jumped aboard, he discovered angrily that his vessel had been stripped of everything save the pepper in her hold. The Malays had plundered over $12,000 in specie and $8,000 in opium, plus various stores, provisions, instruments, and everything else of value. The ship secured, Endicott sailed for South Tallapow, where the exuberant Malays added insult to injury by stalking him through the streets and taunting, "Who is greater now, Malays or Americans?" and "How many Americans dead? How many Malays dead?"[5]

News of the outrage traveled quickly, and a variety of irate protests followed. In Sumatra, Robert Ibbertson, chief United States commercial agent, complained directly to the King of Acheen, Sultan Mahomed Shab, the titular head of the loose-knit confederation of tribes on the island. The Sultan would not take responsibility for the actions of his rajahs, but he did offer to sell the American merchantmen a "pass" through the treacherous Quallah Battoo area. Most American captains rejected such bribery, unconvinced that the Sultan really could enforce the agreement.[6]

Meanwhile, frustrated American shipowners began to buttonhole their Congressmen in Washington. Led by Massachusetts Senator Nathaniel Silsbee, a part owner of the *Friendship* who had lost $41,000 in the affair, politicians from the maritime states demanded government intervention. The petitions received a sympathetic hearing from Secretary of the Navy Levi Woodbury and President Jackson, who were already moving to deal with the assault. Until his movement, Jackson had no policy that applied to the Indian Ocean and Southeast Asia. While it was debatable whether the President could even identify Sumatra on a globe, the *Friendship* incident struck a responsive chord. Old Hickory considered the incident a blow to the national honor, signaling the need for a firm stand in that part of the world.[7]

Over the course of several weeks in midsummer of 1831, Jackson's administration investigated the case of the *Friendship*, and the President decided to take aggressive action against the Malays. The mighty frigate *Potomac*, over 1,700 tons, carrying 50 guns and a crew of 500, was given the assignment. Originally, the vessel had been slated to escort Minister-designate Martin Van Buren to England. Jackson, who would not tolerate such an insult to the American flag by these "pirates," hastily changed this plan. His enforcer was Captain John Downes of Massachusetts, a forty-seven-year-old veteran of the Barbary Wars and the War of 1812. Downes received orders to "proceed to demand of the rajah . . . restitutions . . . and the immediate punishment of those concerned in the murder of American citizens." If the natives did not comply within a reasonable period of time, the Commander was to seize the murderers, retake the stolen property, and destroy the ships and forts of the pirates. And, the chief executive sternly added, if such attacks did not cease, Downes was to promise the rajahs that he would dispatch additional warships "to inflict more ample punishment."[8]

Downes promptly sailed for the Pacific, leaving Rio de Janeiro on November 5, 1831, and arriving off Quallah Battoo on February 5, 1832. The *Potomac* hoisted Danish colors and attempted to disguise herself as a merchantman to avoid arousing the suspicions of the natives. Those Malays who sailed out to her, assuming she was a commercial vessel, were detained while preparations for the invasion were carried out. At four o'clock in the afternoon, Downes dispatched his lieutenants and several of the crew, dressed as merchant seamen, to reconnoiter the coast in a lifeboat. As the sailors approached the shoreline, they observed a band of well-armed natives standing on the sand, making menacing gestures with their weapons. The officers decided it was unsafe to proceed ashore and were unsuccessful in trying to persuade several of the natives to swim out to the boat. Their masquerade as pepper traders apparently over, the men returned to the *Potomac*, where plans were rapidly concluded for an attack on the Malays.

The intention was to capture the rajah and hold him hostage, demanding the cargo and the murderers as ransom. Swiftly and silently, despite the darkness and high surf, 250 sailors and marines disembarked at four o'clock in the morning on February 6, 1832. Landing on the beach one mile north of Quallah Battoo, they marched hastily toward the town's three small forts, constructed of dirt clods two feet thick and defended by six-pound cannon as well as men with muskets, and javelins. After several hours of bloody fighting, the marines over-ran each fortification and entered the town, driving the Malays into the jungle. Finally, by dawn's early light, the Stars and Stripes was dramatically hoisted on the parapets of Quallah Battoo. After the invaders determined that there was no cargo from the *Friendship* in the village, they plundered the town and set it ablaze. Unable to discover the money, opium, and murderers, or even the rajah, at least the force had taken revenge before they reembarked that morning. Two Americans were killed and seven wounded in the assault, while native casualties were in excess of one hundred dead and many more wounded.

The following afternoon Downes used the full force of his cannon to bombard the scarred shell of the hapless village for an hour and a half until the white flag was raised. In the morning the rajah's emissaries delivered a message to the Captain requesting peace, to which Downes would only agree after the property was returned and the murderers surrendered. To this end, he urged the rajah himself to come on board and negotiate. The Malay, fearing his own capture, instead sent several additional underlings to convince the Americans that they had already inflicted enough damage to lives and property in Quallah Battoo. Eventually, the Captain relented and agreed to peace, but he reiterated the strong presidential command that further attacks by the pirates would prompt rapid American reprisals. Downes remained in adjacent waters till midmonth, entertaining other rajahs and receiving their assurances of undying friendship for the United States. His mission accomplished to the best of his ability, he sailed for Batavia on February 18.[9]

Perhaps only a handful of Americans were aware of the drama unfolding in the Pacific. The seizure of the *Friendship*, though exciting to various shipowners and politicians, had not captured the attention of the press and public, and the mission of the *Potomac* to avenge the lost ship received little more coverage. One of the exceptions, understandably, was the Salem (Massachusetts) *Gazette*, which demanded protection of American commerce in the Pacific and Indian Ocean and "severe chastisement" to "put a stop to the increasing treachery and arrogance of these semi-barbarians."[10]

Jackson alluded to the incident briefly in his annual message to Congress on December 6, 1831:

A daring outrage having been committed in those seas by the plunder of one of our merchantmen engaged in the pepper trade at a port in Sumatra, and the piratical perpetrator belonging to tribes in such a state of society that the usual course of proceedings between civilized nations could not be persued [sic]. I forthwith dispatched a frigate with orders to require immediate satisfaction for the injury and indemnity to the sufferers.[11]

It was early in the summer of 1832 that word of Downes's actions reached Washington. The capital was already in a chaotic state: an impatient Congress was debating the explosive tariff issue, and the presidential veto of the Second Bank of the United States was expected imminently. Worse yet for the Jacksonians, 1832 was an election year. The National Republicans had already selected the "Sage of Ashland," Henry Clay, as their candidate, and the Anti-Masonic Party had chosen William Wirt of Maryland to battle Old Hickory's second term. Clay in particular opposed Jackson's policy on the bank and the tariff, and he welcomed the addition of further political fuel for the election fires. Perhaps the attack on Quallah Battoo could provide such kindling.

Andrew Jackson dispatched his monumental veto of the Bank on Tuesday, July 10, 1832. That same day, the editors of the opposition daily, the *National Intelligencer*, reported the attack on the Malays. They carefully set the tone for the charges against the President by first applauding Downes for his gallantry in launching the murderous assault, and emphasizing how the United States was justified in punishing those who had violated the rights of American citizens on the high seas. However, the journalists contended, it was shameful that the attack had been executed without first negotiating with the Malays in an attempt to obtain redress before resorting to violence resulting in the deaths of noncombatants. Perhaps more seriously, the editors lashed out at Jackson's abuse of executive power. Surely the government had the prerogative to initiate a reprisal, they declared, but "to Congress belongs the right to declare war." The President was making war without waiting for a declaration from the legislative branch, or even its consent. "If," the *Intelligencer* cautioned, "the President can direct expeditions with fire and sword against the Malays, we do not see why he may not have the power to do the same in reference to any other power or people." Thus, the paper viewed the Malayan affair not merely as an exercise in presidential brashness but as a crisis over the separation of constitutional powers.[12]

The following day the official Democratic Party organ, the *Globe*, rushed to the General's defense. Patiently explaining the circumstances surrounding the barbarous and piratical outrage by the savage natives, the editors chided the *Intelligencer* for its criticism of Jackson's prompt response in defense of American commerce. "These learned Puffendorffs," they fumed, "put forward the new and extraordinary doctrine that pirates can not be attacked, or their establishments broken up, without special act of Congress. . . . Shame upon such unmanly and disingenuous subterfuges for party effect. To what a desperate straight [*sic*] must an opposition be driven to resort to them." The *Globe* was steady, too, in its defense of Downes and his actions, asserting that if the Captain did deviate from his orders by waging the bloody assault, he probably had just cause and could answer to the people for it upon his return.[13]

The *Intelligencer* wasted no time in responding to the charge of being "soft on piracy." The "Puffendorffs" repeated that they were opposed in principle not to the President's quick response, but rather to the use of force to obtain satisfaction. They were also shocked that women apparently had been killed in the attack; another report noted the loyalty of "these Amazons" to their husbands and their willingness to fight to the death, blocking the marines from adopting traditional American chivalrous behavior when dealing with them. All this slaughter and nothing to show for it—not even the much-sought-after indemnity. The *Intelligencer* then presented an able defense of the Malays as a "civilized people." Pointing out their historic governmental structure and progress in the arts and literature, the paper challenged the image of the "half-naked savage." Should a village be destroyed and hundreds of people killed and wounded for the acts of a few criminals, the editors asked? After all, China had pirates along its coast, and it was unlikely that an American captain would raze a Chinese city if a similar incident occurred. Furthermore, the *Intelligencer* sharply criticized the *Globe*'s innuendos that Downes might have exceeded his instructions by attacking before negotiating, because he was "too old a sailor and too good an officer to have done that."[14]

The issue was too explosive to be limited to the Washington papers, and others quickly entered the fray. The New York *Commercial Advertiser* defended Jackson's actions and the American attack upon those "bloodthirsty savages," who, the paper noted, should not be confused with the "poor, innocent, unoffensive, harmless Tahitians." And although the New York *Journal of Commerce* cautioned that the "American government is carrying its summary process a little too far," most newspapers—even several generally hostile to Jackson—praised the President. "These savages have now been properly punished for the massacre of the crew of the *Friendship* and they will for the future, having felt our power, respect the American flag," editorialized one. Another noted that "the Malays can be seen in no other light than a treacherous, deceitful and piratical race. . . . It seemed necessary for the future benefit of our commerce, that an impression of prowess should be made upon this coast." Papers in Baltimore and Philadelphia also picked up the story and chose sides. The issue, now public in interest and national in scope, would force Congress and the President to act.[15]

On Thursday morning, July 12, Representative Henry Dearborn of Massachusetts, who had once practiced law in Salem and collected customs duties in Boston, proposed a resolution calling on the President to turn over to the House his instructions to Captain Downes and that officer's reports. The motion was supported by Democrat Michael Hoffman of New York, who felt that "it was due Captain Downes as well as the Executive after the remarks publicly made, that the facts be laid before the House." The resolution passed quickly, with the provision that Jackson could omit "such points as may, in his judgment, require secrecy." The following day, the President complied with the request and sent his instructions, plus Downes's report, withholding nothing. The General urged, however, that the House not publish them until the Captain had returned and been given the opportunity to clarify his actions further.

Jackson had a good reason for making this request. Downes had, in fact, exceeded his orders. The Presidential instructions of August 9 were to determine first whether or not the attack had been launched by pirates, and the Captain was definitely not authorized to make a clandestine assault upon the town; only if negotiation for restitution and indemnity failed was he to take punitive action. Secretary Woodbury

scolded the Captain: The President regrets that you were not able before attacking the Malays . . . to obtain . . . fuller information of the
particulars of their outrage on the *Friendship*. . . . On every circumstance influencing your judgment to dispense with these, he wishes the
fullest information since it may hereafter become material.

Jackson's anger and the thinly veiled threat of a court-martial were
not lost upon Downes. He explained to the President.

No demand of satisfaction was made previous to my attack, because I was satisfied, from what knowledge I already had of the character of the people, that no
such demand would be answered, except by refusal, and that such refusal would
proceed from want of ability, as well as of inclination, it being a habit generally
among this people to spend their money as soon as it is obtained.

Actually, the "knowledge" Downes possessed of the Malays was sketchy
at best, and there was little reason to assume that the natives had already disposed of the specie. Worse still, rumors were rife in the press
that children as well as women had been killed in the assault and bombardment, and the number of deaths was now estimated to be close to
two hundred.[16]

Despite these revelations, the *Globe* still gloated over Jackson's
prompt response to the House and challenged the opposition as to
whether "our excellent chief magistrate has been guilty of all the san-
guinary wantonness imparted to him. . . . They can now see whether
an 'unoffending people' has been maltreated by his directions." Jackson
probably did not share the confidence of the *Globe*. Although he was
not guilty of giving orders that resulted in the slaughter, certainly his
administration in an election year would be blamed for Downes's apparent overzealousness. Since the initial response to the action had
generally been favorable, however, the key at this point was to stall any
potentially embarrassing inquiry into the attack until after November,
and perhaps indefinitely.[17]

Not surprisingly, then, after some "desultory conversation" when
the documents reached the House floor on July 13, 1832, Jacksonian
Henry Hubbard of New Hampshire moved to send the material to the
Committee on Foreign Affairs. The seven-man body was stacked with
new Jacksonians (Thomas Crawford of Pennsylvania, Robert Barnwell
of South Carolina, James Wayne of Georgia) and veterans (James K.

Polk of Tennessee, and chairman William Archer of Virginia); only Edward Everett of Massachusetts and John W. Taylor of New York could be considered solidly in the National Republican camp. Acting with unusual speed, the committee recommended the next day that the correspondence not be published. The division within the committee became obvious, however, when floor debate began. Polk and others appeared indifferent, arguing that neither Old Hickory nor Downes would be damaged by the publication. But Everett, who represented the Captain's district, probably spoke for the majority of the committee when he noted, "From the papers communicated, it might be inferred that Captain Downes had transcended his instructions." He therefore opposed publication before Downes had had full opportunity to defend himself. Jacksonian Michael Hoffman, however, challenged the committee, asking his fellow Congressmen to "set the country right" about the calumnious accusations regarding presidential abuse of warmaking power. After a flurry of debate, his motion to print was solidly rejected.[18]

Operating from differing motives, the two parties in the House cooperated to remove a thorny problem from the President's side. The *Globe* conjectured that the General's enemies sought the official documents in order to sustain against him charges of abuse of power and slaughter of human life. But when they discovered that the pacific and rightful orders were apparently violated by an officer they admired and had rigorously defended, they attempted to stall the investigation.[19]

The defeat of the motion to publish did not end the controversy in the press, but the retreat of the *Intelligencer* became obvious. Of course, the editors had not seen Jackson's instructions, but reliable sources informed them that the orders did not violate the law. On the other hand, Downes's report did not seem satisfactory, though they expressed confidence that he would be exonerated when additional evidence came to light. Taking a final slap at the President, the *Intelligencer* still condemned the entire action, which resulted in the death of women and children by surprise assault, and the plundering and destruction of Quallah Battoo.[20]

On July 24 the President left Washington for the Hermitage, and the following day Congress adjourned. The *Globe* fired a preliminary salvo for the impending election:

The tariff is settled. The Bank vetoed. The Indians by this time we hope quieted. And all that remains for us this summer is to guard against Mr. Clay and the cholera—the preventative to the first is to be found in the intelligence, purity and independence of the people—the remedy against the second is their cleanliness, temperance and care. Let us look to these matters.

Understandably, the writer made no mention of the explosive Sumatran incident.[21]

The *Potomac* returned in the spring of 1834, bringing with her Captain Downes and the commander of the assault force, Lieutenant Irvine Shubrick. For the next three years (until the end of Jackson's administration) Shubrick remained on "waiting orders." Downes did not stand a court-martial, perhaps because the President simply did not wish to reopen the matter, but he never received a letter of thanks from the Navy Department for a job well done, nor did he command another vessel. He ended his career supervising naval yards and inspecting lighthouses. Jackson, of course, had gone on to another smashing victory at the polls in November 1832, despite the Bank veto, the tariff imbroglio, and Quallah Battoo.[22]

No knee-jerk response, the President's orders and actions regarding Sumatra were deliberate and thoughtful. By aggressively asserting the rights of the United States and the use of American military power, he also risked bringing the wrath of Congress down upon himself (even if that Congress was dominated by Democrats) for abuse of his office. But he survived and grew. By his boldness Andrew Jackson, nationalist, had demonstrated his desire to expand and protect American trade in the Pacific. Unfortunately for the natives of Sumatra, the protection had cost many of them their lives. But the American people, led by their President, caught up in the racism and expansionism of the nineteenth century, could without embarrassment glance backward and dismiss the tragedy at Quallah Battoo as a necessary lesson to be taught ignorant savages who would violate the rights of a young republic with a world destiny to fulfill.

EDMUND ROBERTS

Jackson's willingness to use the stick to gain respect for the American flag and the commerce that sailed under it was forcefully argued in the chastisement of the Sumatran pirates. In opening and securing the trade of the Far East, however, Old Hickory was not averse to using the carrot. The underrated missions of Edmund Roberts in 1832–34 and 1835–36 reflect the administration's commitment to widen economic horizons in such remote locales as Southeast Asia and Japan.

For the Jacksonians, the concept of exploring the trade potential of the exotic East began innocently enough in the winter of 1828, the twilight of the Adams presidency. Captain Edmund Roberts, a God-fearing veteran seafarer from New Hampshire, penned a letter of inquiry to his Senator and fellow Portsmouth native, Levi Woodbury, describing the untapped trade potential of the East African and Persian Gulf lands controlled by the Sultan of Muscat. Woodbury likely read the missive with some interest, since his father-in-law, Asa Clapp, was one of the wealthiest and most successful men of commerce in New England. Clearly, the Senator would close no doors to opportunity for his nation or his relatives without due consideration. Roberts, despite a rather checkered career, deserved such attention.[23]

Edmund Roberts had wished to follow in his father's footsteps by becoming a naval officer. He entered the service as a teenager but resigned within a few years to accommodate his widowed mother's desire that he remain at home with her. She soon died, however, enabling the aspiring young tar to sail off to Buenos Aires to join his Uncle Joshua in the mercantile and shipping business. Joshua soon expired, too, leaving his twenty-four-year-old nephew with a prospering business. Seizing the moment to increase his position, Edmund returned to Portsmouth, where he married into the powerful and prestigious Langdon family. At this juncture Lady Luck turned her back on Roberts, and he suffered severe losses in ship and cargo seizures during the Napoleonic Wars. Ten years later he was still struggling to recoup his losses. A briefly held consulship at Demarara, British Guiana, did little to enhance his fortunes. Nor did a joint venture in 1827 with Fish, Grinnell and Company of New York, in which Roberts personally sailed to Zanzibar; the New Englander encountered sharp trade barriers that virtually negated profit potential. Roberts's failure was partially compensated, however, by the development of a friendship with the Sultan of Muscat, who urged him to return to America and persuade his government to negotiate a treaty that would place American commerce upon an equal footing with that of other powers, especially Great Britain.

But the wheels of government turned slowly. Maybe the potential rewards did not seem worth the cost of a special mission. Or perhaps Woodbury's career, which was in transition because of the turmoil of New Hampshire Democratic politics, forbade attention to the matter. For whatever reason, the idea lay fallow for the next several years, during which time Roberts busied himself with another trip for Fish, Grinnell and suffered the personal tragedy of the loss of his wife and young son. The forty-six-year-old Captain now bore sole responsibility for eight daughters.[24]

Almost desperately, Roberts spoke again with Woodbury in August 1831 about the East Indian trade. His timing was propitious. The seizure of the *Friendship* had awakened the comatose concern that not only Woodbury but the President and other members of the Cabinet and Congress may have felt for the Eastern world. A clear need was evident to juxtapose the mission of the *Potomac* as enforcer with the dispatch of a special agent to open formal relations that might stave off pirates and enhance American commerce. Fortunately for Roberts, his "particular friend and old acquaintance" Woodbury had just moved into the Cabinet as Secretary of the Navy.[25]

By December 1831, Woodbury had spoken with the President and Secretary of State Livingston about an agent to the Orient and received a positive response. Roberts was instructed to visit Cochin China (Vietnam), Siam, Muscat, and Japan and to obtain whatever political and commercial information was available. Roberts confidentially told Woodbury that "the presence of our vessels and a few slight presents" would gain the desired concessions from the potentates. It was critical that the mission be kept a "profound secret," however, as Roberts told his daughters, "on account of its getting to the ears of the British government who would assuredly thwart me if possible." The devoted father was not at liberty to tell even his family the destinations of his two-year hegira. As part of his cover, Roberts was appointed secretary (at an annual salary of $1,500) to Captain David Geisinger of the 18-gun sloop *Peacock*. The vessel's ostensible mission was to board the new Chargé to Buenos Aires, Francis Baylies, in Massachusetts and carry him to the Argentine to resolve the prickly situation that had grown there over the Falkland Islands. Anyone who looked may have wondered at the presence of an old salt serving as the Captain's secretary.[26]

Before departure in the first week of March 1832, Roberts attempted to resolve the knotty problem of presents for the rulers. Jackson, ever the republican, adamantly opposed such gifts as compromising the dignity of the nation. Roberts, now a veteran of the East, knew that the monarchs considered such items their due; he urged that several thousand dollars invested in cut glass, watches, firearms, cutlasses, and music boxes would be money well spent. The neophyte diplomat finally won the day—and the promise of $3,000 worth of gifts—but with the admonition from Livingston to "husband your presents as much as possible, giving only what you find essential." Seemingly basing policy on dealings with the American Indians, the Secretary advised Roberts to give the gifts of no great value to the lesser officials when he first landed and reserve the rifles and muskets for the kings. Roberts, undoubtedly ecstatic to have been granted the presents, appears to have simply ignored the patronizing counsel.[27]

The *Peacock* arrived in Brazil in May and the following month reached Montevideo. Roberts, always the careful observer, eagerly submitted his suggestions to Secretary Woodbury about strengthening the power of the Brazilian Squadron to provide adequate protection for American merchants in case of war with Buenos Aires. His concern for the mercantile community extended from the Baltimore coffee merchants to the Salem pepper traders.[28] As the *Peacock* prepared to hoist anchor in late June, Roberts confided to his family that they were about to sail for Sumatra, and "if Captain Downes has not obtained redress for the murders and robbery of the ship we shall have the pleasure of destroying that infamous place." When they arrived in September, Roberts could report with some relief that the efficient *Potomac* had done its job by destroying the village and killing many of the "villainous inhabitants." Until this time the diplomat had enjoyed the adventure. He especially approved of the ship, captain, and crew, noting with obvious pride that not one man had yet been flogged.[29]

Then new orders arrived from the United States and events began to sour. Roberts was instructed to gauge the impact of the "*Friendship* Affair" and determine the possibility of negotiating a treaty with the

King of Acheen to secure American commerce in the Indies. In addition to commercial guarantees, Livingston wanted Roberts to investigate potential port sites at which American ships might be received and protected. The Jackson administration realized that the success of Roberts's mission would mean additional trade, which would require increased naval protection and the need for noncolonial stations. While not yet ready to embrace the theories that Admiral A. T. Mahan postulated some fifty years later regarding the relationship between sea power, colonies, and commerce, the Jacksonians were willing to take a step in that direction by throwing themselves directly into competition with the Europeans in that part of the world and seeking asylum for American vessels by treaty.[30]

Unfortunately for Roberts, this task was not easily accomplished. The *Potomac*'s bombardment may have won the respect of the islanders, but it placed them in no mood to grant the Americans concessions. Additionally, trade with Sumatra had plummeted from a peak of 1.4 million florins in 1823 to only 135,000 in 1832. This decline largely resulted from the illiberal trading policy of the Dutch, who owned the islands and increasingly enforced a state monopoly on the shipment of staple crops such as coffee, sugar, and indigo. A treaty with the Dutch for port and commercial privileges would have been far more appropriate than one with the native rajahs.[31]

Roberts looked at the second segment of his additional instructions with mixed feelings. Japan had moved sharply up the priority list in the administration's eyes, and Livingston told his agent in October that while a special mission was planned for Japan, Roberts would have to act as a stopgap. The anxiety attack on the Secretary's part seems to have originated in the rumor that both the Russians and the English were proceeding to open Japan to Western trade. The British East India Company had a ship ready to depart for Japan, while it was reported that a British naval vessel had shelled and burned a village on the northeast coast of the island. Roberts would offset the English maneuvers by sailing in a commercial vessel. This would solve a dual problem by avoiding the disgrace of disarmament (which the Japanese insisted upon for all visiting military ships) and relieving Japanese fears of gunboat diplomacy. Roberts was urged to promote the distinctions between the British and the Americans.[32]

Even at this juncture, Roberts was likely aware that both time and money were stumbling blocks to a Japanese mission. It was one thing to encourage him to engage a commercial vessel to take him to the island, but who would pay for it? And the promised presents for the dignitaries had yet to arrive. He had also been at sea for almost six months and had accomplished no goal of his mission. Burdened but undaunted, Roberts sailed for Canton in the fall of 1832.

In December, while the apostles of nullification railed against Jackson, federal power, and the tariff, Roberts reposed in splendid isolation in China, oblivious to threats to the Union. His concerns were more mundane—such as locating an interpreter and determining, still, where the presents might be. It was impossible to continue the journey without them. Finally, in frustration, Roberts proceeded to buy $3,000 worth of silks, watches, silver goods, and sweetmeats on credit through the merchant House of Olyphant (at 10 percent interest).[33] He also received valuable instructions from an old China hand, British clergyman Robert Morrison, who compassionately took the Captain under his wing and tutored him in the customs and habits of the strange lands he was about to visit. Morrison's first maxim was "Adhere to the truth." Perhaps as important as his advice was the loan of his son to serve as interpreter for the voyage.[34]

Armed with sage counsel, gifts, and a knowledge of Chinese, the diplomat left Lintin on December 29, 1832, bound for Cochin China. This was truly *terra incognita* for Americans: only two or three United States vessels had ever visited there. On January 5, 1833, when the *Peacock* touched at the port of Vunglum on the Vietnamese coast, the difficulties were immediately apparent. The Catholic priest in the town of 3,000 had heard of England, Spain, and France but never of the United States. Local officials severely restricted the movements of the foreigners while they sent word to their King in Hue about the strange visitors from an unknown land. After several weeks in which the Americans were treated with scant hospitality, several representatives from the Minister of Commerce and Navigation appeared, mirroring the priest's ignorance by inquiring about the king of the United States.

Robert explained his mission and his desire to travel to Hue and meet with the Emperor. The response to his request was a series of delays. Roberts found the Vietnamese to be arrogant, pompous, and

insistent upon degrading the American government and its representative. If Roberts wished to see the Emperor, he would be obliged to
perform the humiliating ceremony of "kowtowing" before him. In addition, the minions insisted that the letter from the President must be
delivered to the Emperor "in silent awe" and "with uplifted hands."

A furious Roberts later wrote his children that he would not tarnish
the honor of his country or debase himself to any nation under the sun,
"far less to a semi-barbarous people." He described Vietnam as one of
the most beautiful and picturesque places in the world, but also a country "lying under the depressing influence of one of the vilest despo-
tisms that disgraces the earth." The hard earnings of the people were
taken from them by a king and nobility even before the harvest was
ripe for the sickle. The inhabitants were wretched, poor, and filthy,
groaning under the weight of their chains.

Outraged and out of patience after a month of immobility, Roberts
issued an ultimatum that if approval for his trek to Hue was not received by February 5, he would depart. On the 7th, word had not arrived, and he again threatened to leave. Two days later, still unwilling
to compromise his own or the nation's honor, he told Captain Geisin-
ger to weigh anchor, and the *Peacock* sailed for Siam.[35]

In little more than a week, Roberts arrived at the Menam River,
where the winds of diplomacy took on a much warmer air: within several days he had received a response for his request to proceed to
Bangkok. Unlike the Vietnamese, the Siamese had had experience with
Westerners, having negotiated a treaty with British in 1826. Talks began
with the Phra-Klang (the diplomatic minister) soon after Roberts's arrival in the capital. But the Siamese, who placed little value on goods
that were Chinese and not Western, spurned the hastily purchased
American gifts of silver baskets and gold watches. Despite his unavoid-
able faux pas, the King's representatives treated Roberts well, providing
him with a house and excellent food. Within two weeks an agreement
modeled on the British treaty had been negotiated, granting the United
States most-favored-nation status and modest tariff duties. Roberts
tried (just as the English had) to incorporate "the valuable and highly
profitable" opium trade as a provision, but it was placed on the list of
contraband items at the last minute. Nevertheless, he was pleased with
the agreement, since he calculated that the available trade to American

ships approached almost two million Spanish dollars yearly, principally in rice, salt, and sugar.

As he prepared to depart, Roberts was granted an audience with the King, a privilege rarely extended to Westerners. The proud New Englander had impressed the Siamese by his refusal, which he emphatically declared at the outset of the negotiations, to kowtow and by the mighty vessel that had borne him to their shores. As a token of his appreciation, King Nang Klao allowed Roberts to enter the royal chamber standing up and with shoes on, requiring him only to bow his head. The scene was a spectacular one. As the diplomat walked into the hall of the "Lord of the White Elephant," he passed through double lines of soldiers, some armed with muskets, others with spears and shields. Hundreds of musicians clothed in red made a deafening racket as his party approached the gates and proceeded into the room, where they were greeted by dozens of elephants commanded by turbaned masters. The King, fanned by retainers to relieve the 94-degree heat, was guarded by a sword-brandishing retinue. After a brief twenty-minute interview, the treaty (with copies in Siamese, English, Chinese, and Portuguese) was signed, and presents were given to the Americans. Roberts received some marginal tokens of favor: elephant's teeth, sugar, pepper, and tin, "all of inferior quality and little worth." The disappointed diplomat blamed the Siamese officer in charge, who, he claimed, pocketed the difference between the good presents and the ones he received. To add insult to injury, the King requested additional gifts from the United States to be brought with the exchange of ratifications. This veritable shopping list included glass lamps, swords, and (strangely) stone statues of men and women dressed in various costumes worn in America. Still, after almost seven weeks in Siam, Roberts was a man vindicated in his principles; with a completed treaty in hand, he could depart on the third leg of his journey with great hope of success.[36]

Before sailing for African waters and an expected triumph with his old friend the Sultan, Roberts returned to Batavia, via Singapore, to reconsider his orders. Even though the *Boxer* had finally appeared in Sumatra with the twenty-three boxes of gifts, the New Englander felt that he lacked both the financial resources and the quality of offerings that would be required for the Emperor of Japan. Having been away more than a year already, and with Muscat ahead, the devoted father undoubtedly did not anticipate with pleasure a four- to six-month sojourn to Japan. Perhaps sensing a second mission, Roberts teased Livingston with information about the potential riches of the island, and described how archrival Britain was presently discredited. "By judicious management all the principal ports in Japan would be thrown open to American trade," he suggested. Roberts had also come to loathe steamy, swampy Sumatra, and his second voyage there simply confirmed his scant regard for the island and its inhabitants. He decided not even to attempt to negotiate a treaty with the King of Acheen, a ruler he considered powerless to control his subjects and a man he branded as "a savage."[37]

With his duty now firmly resolved in his mind, Roberts and the *Peacock* sailed from Batavia in the summer of 1832, arriving at the coffee port of Mocha on the Red Sea on August 31. This region was nominally under the control of Muscat but had fallen into the hands of a rebel Turkish prince and his 3,000-man army. Disappointed at this unexpected turn of events, Roberts quickly ordered the ship on to Muscat, where his friend Sultan Seyed Syeed ruled his troublesome domains. Three days after the American's arrival, the provisions of a trade agreement had been outlined, and the next two weeks were occupied in exacting the details in both Arabic and English (including a ridiculously low 5 percent tariff).

The thankful diplomat spent the next three days in revelry, dining on a roasted sheep stuffed with pistachio nuts. Presents were dutifully exchanged, with the American offering the same silver baskets and gold watches that had been viewed askance in Siam, plus Chinese tea and several yards of velvet. The Sultan wished to give Roberts a pair of Arabian horses for the President, but the emissary had to explain patiently that the United States Constitution prohibited their acceptance—in this instance surely a painful regret for a horse lover such as Jackson. On October 7, the Americans departed Muscat for Mozambique, the Cape of Good Hope, Rio, and then Boston on April 24, 1834—a voyage of two years and 45,000 miles.[38]

The Captain felt well satisfied with his mission, and he prepared lengthy reports on Siam and Muscat for the President and Secretary of State Louis McLane. Roberts extolled the virtues of agricultural Siam, expounding upon its fertility, the breadth of the empire (which ex-

tended into Laos, Cambodia, and the Malay peninsula), and the avail-
ability of its trade, which was now heavily carried by the Chinese. As
for Muscat, he combined praise of the commercial advantages with
some information that was sure to interest the President: the Sultan
had the largest navy between the Cape of Good Hope and Japan, including a 74-gun ship of the line and several frigates.[39]

Still, as Roberts journeyed to Washington in May, he felt apprehensive. He had declined to go to Japan, refused to treat with the Sumatrans, and been ignored in his dealings with the Vietnamese. How
would the administration balance his successes with his failures? On
May 10 a genuinely relieved and justifiably elated Roberts wrote his
daughter that Old Hickory had been "highly gratified at what he was
pleased to term the great success of my mission. The whole course of
my conduct is approved by the whole cabinet. So far so good and
highly flattering—there are but few toads in the puddle I flatter myself
at this moment in Washington [no one] quite so big as I am excepting
always Davy Crockett and Jim Crow."[40]

While the domestic political scene was rocked by the salvos fired in
the war over the removal of the deposits from the Bank of the United
States, Roberts, nonpolitical and having been long in self-imposed
exile, sought to reorder his financial house. He developed four strate-
gies for success: lobbying the Congress for additional compensation
for his recent mission, urging the administration to launch a second
effort in the Orient, strengthening his business ties in America as they
related to Far Eastern trade, and writing a publishable memoir of his
travels.

The effort to obtain added funds proceeded slowly. Although he
found a sponsor for a remuneration bill in Congress, Roberts grumbled
about the snail's pace of legislation and how he had served as an ambassador on a clerk's wages. Both McLane and incoming Secretary John
Forsyth endorsed his pay at the scale of a chargé, but little was done.
He had survived cholera in Manila, 112-degree heat in Arabia, and fe-
vers in Sumatra, only to encounter an unsympathetic Congress. Roberts also shifted the blame for the failure to reach an accord in Cochin
China. His emphasis was no longer upon national honor and self-
debasement but rather the lack of presents (which he could not afford)
and the exhaustion of provisions aboard the *Peacock*. Nevertheless, de-

spite deprivations and diseases that Roberts had encountered and endured, he somehow wished to return a second time.[41]

In discussing the recent mission with McLane, Roberts primed the diplomatic pump by hinting that if a treaty with Japan could be concluded, the road would also be open to trade with Korea and northern China. Unfortunately, his efforts were wasted with the Secretary, who was replaced by John Forsyth the following month. Roberts lost no time attempting to convince his new chief that another mission was in order, and Forsyth dutifully brought up the subject with the President in August. But Jackson remained uncertain, apparently pondering whether to instruct the naval commander who was to deliver the ratified treaties to Siam and Muscat to initiate the additional discussions (especially with Japan), or to dispatch Roberts once again. Forsyth cautioned his erstwhile diplomat to accept another offer of employment if it came his way.[42]

While waiting for the President's decision, Roberts occupied himself in exploring various business contacts in the East. The agent had taken with him on his voyage letters of introduction from several large houses and undoubtedly had gained valuable information. The China trade seemed the most lucrative, in tea and silks, but especially opium. For years, Perkins and Company of Boston had held a virtual monopoly on the Turkish drug imported into China, but it appears clear that the ambitious Roberts sought links with other powerful merchants, such as John Latimer of New York, in an attempt to break that vise grip or, perhaps, to negotiate an avenue into another nation in Southeast Asia.[43]

The summer of 1834 gave the energetic Roberts an opportunity to pursue his fourth financially promising project, publishing a popular account of his journey to the mystical lands of the East. He had kept copious notes on the voyage, and the editing could be done even if he should depart on a second mission; indeed, that event would likely strengthen the sales of the volume. While Roberts may have sensed a need to tell his fellow Americans about his adventure, the primary motive for publication was pecuniary. Roberts received a few admonitions from Secretary Forsyth to be judicious in his comments about Cochin China and Japan, in case a new effort would soon be made, but beyond that he was free to sell his impressions to the highest bidder.

Before the volume appeared, however, Roberts received word from the State Department that the President once again required his services.[44]

Edmund Roberts's first mission had whetted the commercial appetites of the Jackson administration. The President had his new advisors (Forsyth was now in the State Department and Mahlon Dickerson of New Jersey in the naval office) were so impressed by Roberts's initial efforts and the potential of the Oriental trade that the second expedition was granted generous financial and naval support. Just as important, Jackson demonstrated a willingness to learn from the difficulties of the first mission and attempted to show a spirit of cooperation without sacrificing the national honor. Roberts's primary diplomatic targets were Cochin China and Japan. This time, however, he carried a letter to the Emperor at Hue on which (in acceding to an earlier Vietnamese demand) His Majesty's name appeared at the top of the page and the President's below. The instructions urged the agent "to accommodate yourself to the peculiar notions and customs of the country, however absurd they may be . . . without compromising the dignity of your government." A shaky Roberts perhaps now feared that a kowtow might be deemed acceptable if it facilitated negotiations.[45]

Japan had engendered the strongest appeal, and a great deal of attention was given to preparation for that mission. Roberts was advised to avoid landing at Nagasaki, since the Dutch already operated a factory there and would likely attempt to thwart his efforts. Careful planning entered into the selection of presents for the Japanese ruler, as well. The administration had learned that the Emperor had requested sheep from the Dutch, but they had evaded him, reporting that sheep were hairy and it was impossible to make cloth from their wool. Therefore, the agent was to purchase the best ten merino sheep available and present them, along with gold watches, music boxes, sabers, rifles, coins, a map of the United States and—not so subtly—a set of prints of American naval victories. While Roberts had been allowed only $3,000 in presents for the initial journey (and those arrived much too late to serve him well), the government now spent $5,000 for gifts and empowered him to promise an additional $10,000 worth upon ratification of a treaty with either nation.[46]

The diplomat himself continued to be personally frustrated by the administration's insistence that his task remain secret, thus prohibiting the assignment of diplomatic rank above "special agent." Still, since his object on the second mission, as Roberts confided to his daughters, was to make his family "independent and comfortable," no doubt the tripling of his salary to $4,400 per year (plus expenses) provided a soothing balm for his wounded pride.[47]

The priority assigned to Roberts's journey by the President was reflected in the change of orders given to Captain E. P. Kennedy of the *Peacock*. Initially, Secretary Dickerson had instructed him to visit the settlements of freed American blacks established in Liberia, on the west coast of Africa, before sailing on to the Pacific (with a special stop at Quallah Battoo) and then on to the ports of western South America. These orders were scrapped; instead, Dickerson emphasized the importance of the Roberts mission and the responsibility of Kennedy to follow whatever orders the special agent should issue.[48]

As Roberts prepared to depart in April 1835 for another two-year sojourn, he wistfully told his daughter that when he returned this time, he would "settle down like an old sailor." By September the *Peacock* and the schooner *Enterprise* had touched at Rio and reached Zanzibar, off the east coast of Africa. The governor of the island was the son of the Sultan of Muscat, and the treatment accorded Roberts was little short of decadent; the agent described in great detail the dates, cloves, and coffee, the smells of the food and swirls of color at the bazaar, and the elegant dinners from silver dishes. After a week's stay, the *Peacock* weighed anchor for Muscat, where Roberts discussed religion and the world with his Arab hosts, read the Koran, and was introduced to a group of Bedouins and their camels. It is difficult to tell who was more impressed: the Bedouins made Roberts an honorary chieftain, while the New Englander reached for superlatives to describe "the fine manners and gentlemanly deportment" of the Arab gentlemen he met, and offered the conduct of the Sultan, a man of great virtue and piety, as a model for Christian European monarchs to follow.[49]

Having exchanged ratifications, renewed old acquaintances, and partaken of Muslim hospitality for several weeks, Roberts was obliged to return to the business at hand. In late September the Americans set sail for Bombay. But disaster struck quickly: four hundred miles from Muscat, near the island of Mazeira, the *Peacock* ran aground on a coral reef in the dead of night. While the ship was in no danger of sinking, pirates from the nearby coast soon discovered its plight and plundered the rafts on which the *Peacock*'s crew had staked their provisions. The awful possibility existed that unless help came, the ship itself might fall into the hands of the brigands.

At this juncture the boldness and courage of Roberts manifested itself. At next daylight, the old seafarer and seven sailors climbed into a twenty-foot boat and rowed wildly in the direction of Muscat and the aid of the Sultan. Their effort was discovered by the pirates, who chased them for some five hours, but darkness provided the Americans a path of escape. Subsisting only on bread and water, the sun-baked little band reached Muscat more than one hundred hours later.

While the "shipwrecked" Roberts recovered from his ordeal in lavish quarters, given coffee, sherbet, candies, fruit, and handkerchiefs perfumed with attar of roses and burning ambergris, the *Peacock* was still foundering. The imperial vessel *Sultani*, ordered out to the rescue, found the Yankee ship still afloat but leaking and missing eleven guns, which had been jettisoned in the effort to free the hull from the coral. Captain Kennedy had held off the pirates with cannon and musket fire, and fortunately, no lives were lost. The *Peacock* was able to limp into Muscat, where it was temporarily cemented by Arab pearl divers. The Sultan's immediate relief efforts and hospitality demonstrated once again his friendship for Roberts, and thus for the United States.[50]

Proffering profound thanks, the Americans sailed on for Bombay and then Ceylon, finally reaching Batavia in January 1836. Roberts clearly enjoyed this voyage, despite the near-tragedy off Muscat. Receiving what was a far cry from his reception in 1832–34, he told his daughters jokingly, "I am so accustomed to dining with emperors, kings, sultans, governors, etc., that I certainly ought to hold my head so high as finally to break my neck over all the small fry in the world."[51]

Although he had been gone for eight months, the agent had thus far only delivered the ratified treaty to Muscat, hardly the primary goal of his mission. As he planned to leave for Siam, Cochin China, and finally China by June, Roberts seemed optimistic, but his outlook faded when he discussed Japan. "I am afraid we shall fail in . . . Japan . . . but there is nothing like trying, we are suspected by the Dutch, but they know nothing." Several American missionaries in Batavia had spread a rumor that he was embarking for Japan, Roberts reported, and since that time he had been unable to purchase valuable charts of the coastline. Without the charts and an interpreter, the voyage would be perilous, if not futile.[52]

Most of the crew of the *Peacock* became ill with jungle fever shortly after leaving Bombay, forcing the delay of the remainder of the mission until mid-February. Roberts escaped the fever and made preparations for the exchange of treaties in Siam. Arriving there on March 27, the diplomat returned to Bangkok and a warm welcome from the King. An American brig was already unloading cotton goods and weighing sugar, tin, and pepper for export. The agent departed Siam after three weeks, likely pleased with his handiwork and the possibilities for American trade with the kingdom.[53]

At this point, after three years in Asia and having survived shipwrecks and pirates, swamps and deserts, Roberts contracted cholera. The ship's doctor urged him to return to the United States, but Roberts insisted on completing his mission. So the *Peacock* sailed on to Cochin China in May, where nothing substantial could be accomplished because of the diplomat's poor health and the lack of an interpreter. At Canton, his final stop, Roberts rested quietly in early June, wrote to his children, and listened impatiently to the reports that his impending voyage to Japan was common knowledge because the American missionaries had freely discussed the matter. Whether Roberts would have opened Japan almost twenty years before Commodore Matthew Perry and diplomat Townshend Harris accomplished that feat is, of course, a moot point. On June 11 he became delirious, gradually sank, and quietly died the next day.[54]

American foreign concerns in 1837 were fixed upon Texas, and domestic attentions mired in the Panic of 1837, so the news of the demise of special agent Roberts halfway around the world caused barely a ripple in the press. After all, he had succeeded only in exchanging the ratifications of existing treaties with Siam and Muscat, something any naval officer could have done. The historically low profile the Roberts missions have maintained is principally due to his failure to open Japan and the paucity of trade with Siam and Muscat.

In largely ignoring the voyages, however, historians have overlooked the critical inroads made by an American presence in the Orient. Following Roberts's journey, United States consuls were stationed at Singapore, Capetown, Zanzibar, and Muscat. Whalers, which constituted a substantial percentage of American vessels in the Pacific and Indian Oceans at the time, had additional stations available for rest, relief, and resupply. Most important, the Europeans, principally the Dutch and the English, became increasingly conscious of the trade rivalry portended by the Americans in the Far East. The first Roberts mission signaled an interest on the part of the Jackson administration in exploring the commercial potential of the Orient, the second a strong commitment to develop that potential.

The dispatch of the *Potomac*, the attack on Quallah Battoo, and the resulting vindication of the President and Captain Downes showed that the United States would use its increased naval might to punish pirates not only in the Caribbean but in the Indian Ocean as well. While it is clear that U.S. trade had existed in the Orient before 1829 and that previous administrations had been provided with information about the area, the fact is that Jackson acted while others debated. His administration scored no great gains in the Far East, but its pioneering efforts were a "foot in the door" that pleased politicians and the military, as well as the men of commerce. It was a keystone in building to the Far East a bridge that Presidents Tyler (China) and Fillmore (Japan) could cross.[55]

The construction of economic bridges within their own hemisphere also occupied the minds of the Jacksonians. The Monroe Doctrine of 1823 emphasized United States hopes for a republican Latin America. The President, not without reason, feared the territorial and commercial penetration of European powers in the area, especially Great Britain. Since Jackson had his own designs upon Texas and desired to increase the competitiveness of Yankee merchant sail in South America, the region received early and energetic attention from his administration.

Chapter 7

South America: Trade, Revolution, and British Rivalry

The siren song of Latin America had been heard in American cities and on American farms decades before Jackson entered the White House. Beginning with the presidency of Thomas Jefferson, the United States evidenced an active interest in expanding the young republic into the Caribbean and, perhaps, Central America. Continental South America remained too distant to be considered for territorial acquisition. When republican revolutions erupted during the Napoleonic Wars—led by "liberators" such as Simón Bolívar, José de San Martín, and Bernardo O'Higgins—the North Americans politely applauded their efforts but gave no practical assistance. The Yankees did eagerly pursue commerce in the region, but the economic warfare between Great Britain and the United States between 1806 and 1811, culminating in the War of 1812, embargoed the American merchant marine and allowed the English to make serious inroads into the commerce and politics of Latin America.

By the time James Monroe attempted to reassert United States leadership in the Western Hemisphere with his 1823 doctrine, the critical moment had passed: British influence in South American politics was almost insurmountable, and a constant source of frustration for American diplomats. The United States and Britain both viewed the fragile republics as a global power fulcrum; since they were incapable of taking care of themselves, a major nation would be obliged to step in and guide their political and commercial destinies. Continued revolution wracked many of the clearly unstable new nations, leading—for example—to the collapse of Gran Colombia and its splintering into Ecuador, Venezuela, and Colombia in 1830. Even where civil war was absent, international conflicts prevailed. Argentina challenged Brazil over control of Uruguay, and the Chileans moved to destroy a Peruvian-Bolivian confederation in 1836. A final factor in the Anglo-American rivalry, generally unspoken, was the growing antislavery sentiment of Great Britain, which collided with the goals of the slaveowning aristocracy that dominated the various branches of the U.S. federal government until the Civil War.

In 1808 the United States held a slight edge in the Latin American trade, but a quarter-century later English commercial hegemony was maddening to Yankee consuls. By 1830, British investments in Latin America totaled over 40 million pounds, her loans to the new countries more than $110 million, and her trade over $32 million. The Americans, in sharp contrast, had no money to invest and little to lend. Discounting the very lucrative trade with Cuba, American commerce with South America did not exceed $10 million.

There was little similarity in British and American trade goods (the former exchanging industrial items, the latter dealing in agricultural produce), but historian J. F. Rippy has suggested that the only items the Americans had to sell that competed with English merchandise were saltfish and household furniture. This did not prohibit a healthy rivalry for the carrying trade, however, even though the English outweighed the Americans almost three to one in tonnage. To facilitate this commerce, the Americans in the 1820s had negotiated treaties with Great Colombia and Brazil. The British had almost simultaneously concluded advantageous agreements with Buenos Aires, Colombia, and Brazil. Since these three nations commanded almost half of the total South American trade with the United States, it was imperative to nurture them. The collapse of American political and economic relations with the Argentines, the breakdown of the Gran Colombian union, the intriguing of American diplomats, and petty squabbling with Brazil all played a part in the failure of United States policy during this period. Economically aggressive but politically tentative, the Jacksonians allowed repeated opportunities to slip away. Their timidity, born of traditional political isolation and a limited interpretation of the Monroe Doctrine, combined with British resources to allow the English crown to remain the predominant foreign influence on the continent.[1]

ARGENTINA

Argentina was essential to the advancement of United States interests in the "southern cone" of Latin republics. American Chargé John Murray Forbes was appointed in 1825, the same year the British negotiated their commercial treaty with Buenos Aires. The Americans might have completed a treaty simultaneously had not Henry Clay preferred "mutual regulations" by the respective national legislatures. Hardly an adequate substitute for a formal bond, these placed American commerce (already only 25 percent that of Great Britain) at a marked disadvantage. Trade problems contributed to Forbes's generally foul mood. One scholar described him as the diplomat "of the gouty foot, the extraordinary memory, and the intense Anglophobia." The adjective "skillful" was rarely used to describe his diplomatic style. A wily diplomat, Forbes had spent twenty years in Europe and had been in Buenos Aires since 1820—sufficient time to hone both his attitudes and his prejudices.[2]

When Jackson assumed power in 1829, he decided to retain the veteran in office. For the President, Argentina was not a critical post; while a commercial treaty might be desirable, it held a lower priority in Jackson's mind than the resolution of several minor merchant claims. Aware of Old Hickory's singlemindedness on the subject of claims, Forbes also knew that an empty Argentine treasury hindered any settlement. The Chargé's position had not been enhanced by the Adams administration's refusal to mediate the Argentine-Brazilian War. When the British stepped in and did so successfully, American prestige suffered another setback.

The situation degenerated further with the eruption of an Argentine civil war in 1828. This contest between the Unitarians (those who desired a strong central government) and the Federalists (those who wished greater provincial authority) resulted in the triumph of Federalist General Juan Rosas by December 1829. Rosas, a dashing and ruthless gaucho leader, held the reins of power as a virtual dictator in Argentina almost uninterrupted for the next thirty years. Utilizing the army/militia and the church brilliantly, the *caudillo* argued that the alternative to his iron-fisted rule was chaos. He did, however, allow provincial self-governance in exchange for control over foreign affairs.[3]

Forbes was intrigued by the new leader of Argentina. Although not well educated, Rosas seemed to possess both knowledge and common sense; he appeared noble, patriotic, and magnanimous, reminding the Chargé of some great American Indian chief. Forbes wanted the opportunity to negotiate a commercial treaty with the governor, but by May 1830 the aging diplomat was in ill health and asked to be relieved of his post. Instead of granting his request, the administration continued to bombard him with instructions urging resolution of the claims issue. An angry and dying Forbes informed Van Buren in November that the Argentine government simply had no money, and he would move at an opportune time. This response infuriated Jackson, who did not envision auspicious times in the near future and whipped his Chargé on to "more strenuous exertions." Forbes died on June 11, 1831, after a painful and lingering illness, undoubtedly having ignored the President's pressures.[4]

At approximately the time of the Chargé's death, mail began arriving from Washington inquiring about Argentine claims to the Falkland Islands. The government at Buenos Aires had issued a decree dated June 10, 1829, asserting a claim to the Falklands, Tierra del Fuego, and other islands near Cape Horn. These lands had been previously held by Spain and became the possession of Buenos Aires when she won her independence in 1810. A second document, written by Louis Vernet, the governor of the Falklands, warned American sealing and whaling captains that they were no longer permitted to operate in Argentine waters, nor were they allowed to shoot cattle on the islands for food. Naturally, Jackson wanted an official explanation of the decree from the Rosas government, while the White House immediately reaffirmed the American right to use the fisheries and questioned that of the Argentines to claim the Falklands.[5]

The question of rightful claim to the Falklands is murky and complex. The French first attempted to colonize the islands in 1764, but the British occupied them the following year. Although the English established a settlement, they withdrew in favor of the Spanish in 1774. In the last quarter of the eighteenth century, sailors, especially American and British, used the islands as a "watering hole." There appeared to be little else to do with the windswept territory, dominated by two 2,000-square-mile islands. Since they were unoccupied by the early 1800s, the Spanish claim remained more theoretical than practical. In 1820 an Argentine naval officer sailed out and claimed the islands for his nation, but again, nothing else was done. Finally, in 1823, Buenos Aires appointed a governor for the islands and granted concessions for grazing land and fishing rights. Louis Vernet, a Frenchman who had only arrived in Argentina in 1820, received a grant and in 1829 was named governor. Vernet had a vision of colonizing the islands, and growing vegetables and raising cattle for profit. By 1831 there were perhaps some 50 to 75 colonists, including several indentured Negro servants.

When Vernet issued his restrictive decree, it was taken to Buenos Aires by his lieutenant, Matthew Brisbane. Brisbane, an Englishman, met with British Consul Woodbine Parish, who advised him that His Majesty claimed the Falklands and that Vernet should not interfere with British commerce. Accordingly, no English vessel or crew suffered harassment under the Vernet decree.

Apparently, the Governor's fears did not include American fishermen or the wrath of Andrew Jackson. In July and August of 1831, he seized three American schooners, the *Harriet*, the *Superior*, and the *Breakwater*. The *Harriet* was dispatched to Buenos Aires for "trial"; the *Superior*'s skipper negotiated a deal in which he would fish and share the profits with Vernet, and the *Breakwater* escaped.[6]

Word of the seizures reached Buenos Aires in the fall of 1831, where Consul George Slacum had assumed command of the American legation. Slacum, who had had a spiteful relationship with the late Forbes, has been described by American historian Harold Peterson as "a tactless diplomatic novice . . . particularly suited to inflame Argentine officials. His arbitrary and militant attitude, supported in Washington by a suspicious and impolitic administration, quickly sharpened a vexing issue." British scholar H. S. Ferns concurs, noting that Slacum was "an inexperienced patriot . . . [who] believed that the essential element in diplomacy was to assert, in the most intemperate language at his command, the self-evident and natural rights of the people of the United States to shoot and fish where they pleased."[7]

Slacum immediately protested the violation of American rights to Argentine Foreign Minister Nicolas Anchorena, a member of one of Buenos Aires's wealthiest and most powerful families, who was not intimidated by an American merchant. His response was to point out that as a consul, Slacum had no diplomatic status and could not protest. The Argentine's tact only infuriated Slacum, who continued to deny the right of the government to seize American vessels. His inquiry as to whether the Ministry officially sanctioned Vernet's decree was met with the reply that the Minister of War was investigating the capture and detention of the *Harriet*. While Argentine officials remained calm, waiting for the courts to act and for an official response from Washington, Slacum became increasingly incensed. It was apparent that the Ministry would not go beyond a statement reasserting Argentine prerogatives and denying American rights in the islands.[8]

Good fortune played into the hands of Slacum at this juncture with the arrival of Silas Duncan and the 18-gun sloop *Lexington*. Tragically for Argentine-American relations, the personality of the "aggressive, fiery and highspirited" commander matched that of the consul. Between November 29 and December 1, 1831, Duncan and Slacum planned a strategy for the rescue of the *Harriet*'s seven-man crew and the punishment of Vernet.[9] In a December 6 letter to Anchorena, Slacum threatened the dispatch of the *Lexington* to the Falklands unless the Argentines immediately suspended Vernet's powers to capture American vessels and restored the *Harriet* to her owners. Slacum undoubtedly felt his hand strengthened when Consul Parrish reminded him of the British claim to the islands. Nevertheless, his provocative strategy was as yet unauthorized by Washington and met with the strong protest of United States Consul Joshua Bond in Montevideo; indeed, a duel between the two consuls was narrowly avoided. On December 9, Anchorena responded to Slacum's note, reminding him once again that a consul did not possess the power to protest. The Minister warned that sending out the *Lexington* would be premature and unnecessary, since this issue could be handled through the courts and by official representatives of the two governments.[10]

Slacum viewed this reply as a stalling tactic and an inadequate response, so Duncan sailed, accompanied by the sloop *Warren*. Informing Secretary of State Livingston of his actions, Slacum with characteristic bravado declared, "It is indeed time, Sir, that this government should be made sensible of their obligations to respect our rights and to render justice to our citizens." Slacum described Vernet as "a bankrupt German" and "a private adventurer" who sought to monopolize the commerce of the islands and use them as a base for piratical attacks upon American sail. Naturally, he added, the Argentines were upset over the impending naval action, so a buildup of American forces in the area would be appropriate. The consul less than subtly suggested that only American occupation of the islands would insure uninterrupted flow of United States commerce.[11]

Duncan arrived off the Falklands on December 28, 1831, anchoring under the French flag. Three days later, using various ruses, the *Lexington* lured Brisbane and other officials aboard the vessel, while marines were landing at Port Louis. The marines spiked the guns, blew up the powder magazine, and sacked the houses. Some colonists fled into the interior, but the marines captured six leaders, placed them in irons, and took them aboard the *Lexington*. The warships remained about three weeks while Captain Gilbert Davison of the *Harriet* reclaimed his skins and other possessions from the warehouse. By February 3, Duncan had returned to Montevideo, where the prisoners were to be held pending their transfer to Argentine custody as "pirates."[12]

The reaction to the seizures of the fishing vessels and the subsequent attack by the *Lexington* was highly emotional in both Buenos Aires and Washington. The Argentines, with popular sentiment and the press aroused, became resolute in their defense of Vernet and their condemnation of Duncan. Not surprisingly, the Argentine government suspended Slacum from his consular duties.[13]

In Washington, Jackson, who had likely heard of the incidents in press reports of the sailors from the escaped *Breakwater*, mentioned the *Harriet*'s capture in his annual December message to Congress. He argued that the United States maintained the right to fish in Falklands waters, a right violated by men pretending to operate under the authority of the Buenos Aires government. He had sent a naval force to investigate the situation and protect American commerce in the South Atlantic. A chargé would soon be dispatched to replace Forbes and resolve the matter; meanwhile, the President asked the Congress "to clothe the executive with such authority and means as they may deem necessary for providing a force adequate to the complete protection of American fishing and trading in those seas." Having only recently dispatched the *Potomac* to chastise the pirates of Quallah Battoo, Jackson must have imagined a similar situation off the coast of South America. With American rights violated, her honor sullied, and an election year approaching, naval force seemed the most appropriate response.

The American press expressed interest but little passion over the sequence of events. Rather typically, the New York *Enquirer* noted that since Vernet had been appointed and recognized by the Buenos Aires government, he was not a pirate. Nevertheless, Port Louis had been destroyed; the question must therefore be asked what Duncan's orders were and whether he was aware of Vernet's authority. Was the Captain bound to respect that authority if it violated inherent American fishing rights? In contrast, the Stonington (Connecticut) *Phenix* reacted with unusual militancy. Since the *Breakwater* was a sealer out of Stonington, the newspaper's description of Vernet as "ferocious and lawless" and his colonists as "a gang of renegades" is not surprising. While discussion of Vernet's legitimacy and alleged "piracy" swirled in the American press, the President dispatched a diplomat to Buenos Aires to obtain some firm answers.[14]

His choice was Francis Baylies, a loyal but unrewarded lawyer and hack Democratic politician from Massachusetts. A three-term congressman in the 1820s, he had cast his electoral vote for Jackson in 1825, in the election won by favorite son John Quincy Adams. Failing at reelection, Baylies had gone on to serve in the state legislature. But he was not solidly aligned with the party leadership, who embittered him by their failure to support his congressional bid in 1831. Jackson had tried to console him with an appointment as Collector of New Bedford, but Baylies refused. The chargé slot at Buenos Aires seemed appropriate, even though Baylies's major qualification for foreign service appeared to be an abiding suspicion of Great Britain. He told a correspondent that the British were "reaching out around the world to control trade. They have colonies everywhere and are advancing slow but certain to the Sea of China." Their movement into the Caribbean and the Pacific, he suggested, jeopardized American trading and fishing interests. Former President Adams opined that Baylies was "one of the most talented and worthless men in New England"—a prejudiced view, no doubt, but it was true that Baylies—like Slacum—evinced a high-strung temperament, seemingly ill-suited to easing the tensions that filled Argentine-American relations in 1832.[15]

Baylies received his instructions from Livingston in January 1832, ordering him to depart for South America as rapidly as possible. The Secretary advised the Chargé that the President could not believe that, given the historically friendly relations between Argentina and the

United States, the government would authorize Vernet's aggressive policies. Instead, Jackson suggested that Vernet was abusing his authority and illegally using the Falklands as a base for piratical acts. Under the President's instructions, naval commanders in the area were to protect American vessels and free those that had been captured by Vernet. Livingston perceived this as the moderate course; the Governor's acts might have justified retaliatory hostilities, but Washington was willing to allow Buenos Aires the opportunity to disavow Vernet and reassure the Americans of their rights in the Falklands. In any case, the Americans doubted the legality of the Argentines' claim to inheriting Spanish sovereignty. Baylies was instructed to point out that the United States had fished in the area for over fifty years without challenge; therefore, Livingston contended, the Argentines had acted without properly informing Forbes or the State Department of the planned seizures. Unaware that Duncan had already destroyed Port Louis, the Secretary authorized Baylies to instruct the naval commander in the region to break up Vernet's establishment and bring him back to Buenos Aires for trial.[16]

By February, the White House had learned from Slacum that Duncan had sailed for the Falklands. Although unaware of the result, Livingston and Secretary of Navy Woodbury promptly authorized his departure, Livingston declaring Vernet's colony "dangerous to our commerce which it is necessary in self defense that we should break up." Baylies was ordered to defend Duncan's actions, reasserting the need for the Americans to protect themselves against a violation of traditional rights. At the same time, it was naively suggested that the Chargé try to avoid allowing the incident to interfere with his negotiation of a commercial treaty with Buenos Aires. By April 1832 the President had learned of and sanctioned Duncan's reprisals on Vernet's colony. Jackson maintained that Vernet was a pirate who had forcibly seized vessels, imprisoned crews, and forced seamen into his service. His ragged band, comprising "deserters from all nations," deserved to be obliterated.[17]

One American newspaper accurately suggested in May 1832 that "there has been a little rashness on both sides." This rashness did not disappear with the arrival of Baylies in Buenos Aires in June. Even before the Chargé got there, he revealed his prejudices in a letter to Livingston: "Were the government and people of Buenos Ayres like the government and people of other nations, I should apprehend from the language of their official acts that a war was inevitable, but I am inclined to believe that their 'point of honor' may be satisfied by loud talking and their anger may evaporate in bluster."[18]

By the time Baylies arrived in Buenos Aires, the national mood had mellowed and the Chargé was well received. He immediately proceeded to carry out his instructions, discussing the various maritime grievances and the desire for guaranteed fishing rights, but cautiously avoiding negotiation regarding a commercial treaty. The Chargé did not trust the Argentines; he sarcastically suggested that a treaty would be violated on the day that it was signed if the violation were to the Latins' advantage. He did, however, ask for the return of captured property, indemnity, and (without authorization) the restitution of Slacum's consular powers. Foreign Minister Manuel Vicente de Maza treated the exchange as the initial round of diplomatic negotiation and explained that he would investigate the issues. The impatient Chargé, however, demanded answers immediately, especially in terms of fixing responsibility for Vernet's acts. He argued that the Governor's guilt was already established; what mattered now was simply the amount of the indemnity.[19]

De Maza stalled through the summer, refusing to respond to Baylies's inquiries. Finally, on August 8, the Foreign Minister wrote directly to Secretary Livingston, explaining the Argentine position and the Consul's suspension. The latter issue was clearly a stumbling block for the Ministry. Slacum had exceeded his authority, vocally involving himself in a decision-making capacity on the *Lexington* affair. His abrasive, firebrand personality had alienated the Argentine press, public, and Ministry, making it virtually impossible to restore his commercial office or credibility. Baylies, naive and patriotic, did not understand the sensitivity of the issue of Slacum's reinstatement.[20]

In late July the angry Chargé wrote Livingston that he had no hope of successfully resolving the crisis. The Ministry would not openly either support or disavow Vernet but was indirectly sanctioning his "atrocities." Baylies speculated that de Maza was attempting to wait until time had eased the situation, but the American planned to sail for the United States unless the issue was resolved. In a private letter to the Secretary of State, Baylies reiterated his contempt for the Argentines.

The revolutions of these people are seditious—their knowledge chicanery and trick—their patriotism bluster, their liberty a farce—a well regulated tribe of Indians have better notions of national law, popular rights and domestic policy. . . . The best negotiator here would be a naval commander backed by his cannon. . . . None of the South American governments have any idea of justice, but they may have some of national force when they see it.

In a similar letter to his brother-in-law, Baylies suggested that the best the Argentines could hope for was a Tamerlane or Genghis Khan to unite the vast hordes of a despotic empire. By this time the increasingly paranoid Chargé was sleeping with four loaded pistols, a musket, and a sword in his room.[21]

On August 6 the frustrated diplomat drew the line. He told de Maza that the failure to obtain a response to his notes of June 20 and July 10 were an indication that Buenos Aires was rejecting the American position. Two days later de Maza (who had simultaneously written to Secretary of State Livingston) replied but did not emphasize Vernet's actions. Instead, de Maza focused upon Slacum and his collusion with Duncan in destroying Port Louis, "an act of unspeakable inhumanity and perfidy." The consul had exceeded his authority, had been impertinent and conspiratorial. Under no conditions would he be reinstated. In fact, the *Lexington* raid had prompted the Buenos Aires government to file reparations charges against the United States. Until satisfaction of these demands was obtained, negotiations could not proceed. Baylies was astounded. Now on the defensive, he replied that he was not authorized to deal with indemnities, and asked for his passports. Preparing to depart, he advised Livingston, "We have attempted to soothe, and conciliate and coax these wayward and petulant fools long enough. They must be taught a lesson, or the United States will be viewed with contempt throughout Latin America."[22]

De Maza made one final effort to salvage the crumbling relationship. On August 27 he met with Baylies to discuss a lengthy report written by Louis Vernet, which the Minister had submitted for Baylies's consideration and the Chargé had returned unopened. De Maza logically pointed out that the document was valuable information that would clarify the Argentines' right to control the Falklands and the fishing in the area. Duncan had attacked a legitimate outpost of the Buenos Aires government. Baylies could only reply that the Commander had not been specifically ordered to ravage Port Louis; his action was a consequence of the general orders to naval vessels to protect American commerce in the South Atlantic. He repeated that he had not been empowered to negotiate a reparations settlement. De Maza wondered why the Chargé did not have the authority to discuss these issues, or why he did not seek new orders from Washington. But since this had become a quid pro quo, Baylies received his passports on September 3 and sailed for Baltimore with Slacum at the end of the month. Before he departed, he wrote Livingston a final letter in which he reminded the administration that the only alternative was now to "compell" these "mean and malignant" people to respect United States rights.[23]

But even though the Argentines possessed what Baylies referred to as a "burlesque" navy that could be easily eliminated by several American sloops, Jackson did not need further incidents only weeks before the presidential election. Already the opposition press was muttering about the exercise of "summary justice" in the Falklands. While the Democratic papers steadfastly defended Duncan and the President (just as they had rallied behind Downes in Sumatra), hostilities would serve only to disrupt commerce for both nations. Old Hickory advised the House of Representatives, where later there was some talk of war, that relations were not broken with Argentina, only suspended. The Rosas government took no chances, however, on American good faith. In the fall of 1832, the Argentines began to rebuild and reinforce the Falklands' recently destroyed defenses.[24]

While official Washington awaited the arrival of the new minister from Buenos Aires, no American chargé or consul was present in the Argentine to conduct diplomatic or commercial affairs. With the September departure of the impudent Slacum and the proud and tactless Baylies, the forces of reason emerged in the presence of Consul Joshua Bond in Montevideo and Commodore George W. Rodgers of the South Atlantic Squadron. These two men, recognizing the appropriateness of a conciliatory gesture toward the Argentines, decided upon the release of the six prisoners Duncan had seized in the Falklands. (Slacum, ever troublesome, had strenuously opposed the act, chiding and insulting Bond for caving in to the Rosas government.) The Argentines did not reciprocate immediately; in fact, the *Harriet* was ordered sold and the proceeds given to the Buenos Aires government in October. But accommodation was on the way. In December the government appointed a new Minister to Washington to begin direct talks on the issues.[25]

Before that diplomat ever reached the United States, the practical question of the ownership of the Falklands had been resolved. In December 1832, the *Sun*, a sealer out of New London, was warned out of Falklands waters by the Argentine schooner *Sarandi*. The Yankee skipper protested this action to the American navy, who ordered him to return to the disputed area with a promise that the *Sarandi* would be chastised. No action was taken, however, because the American commander received word that the Argentine ship had returned to Buenos Aires. The *Sarandi* had been in the area in conjunction with an attempt to refortify the islands by means of convict labor, but a revolt had erupted in January 1833, demanding the full attention of the ship's captain. The mutineers, led by a black sergeant, murdered the civil and political commandant but were overpowered by the other colonists and the crew from the *Sarandi*. Seven of the rebels had been court-martialed and shot. The Captain had barely restored order when a party from H.M.S. *Clio* landed and demanded that the Argentines leave the island. When the Latin proudly refused, a detachment of Royal Marines hauled down the flag, raised the Union Jack, and forced their departure. Shortly thereafter, the British established a small permanent naval base.[26]

The Argentine government was understandably upset by the *Clio's* action and immediately protested to London. Incredibly, even with the frayed Argentine-American relations at the time, Buenos Aires requested American intervention based upon the Monroe Doctrine. They had asked John Quincy Adams for such assistance in 1826 to help resolve the Brazilian War and had been rejected. This time it was Andrew Jackson who refused: American relations with the British, involving trade and territorial expansion, were not worth jeopardizing over the Falkland Islands.

While the administration had screamed loudly about Argentine claims to sovereignty, it was strangely silent in response to England's maneuvers. Old Hickory spoke in behalf of the Monroe Doctrine, but only when its tenets benefited the United States, perhaps in regard to

Cuba or Mexico. Jackson argued that the Americans could not invoke the doctrine in the Falklands case because the issue was retroactive, involving a dispute that existed prior to Monroe's decree in 1823; the British were simply reasserting a previous occupation. This tact obviously pleased the English, but it severely disappointed the Argentines and contributed little to American leadership in the area. Minister Carlos de Alvear did not reach Washington until 1838, and Jackson, waiting for his promised arrival, never sent another diplomat to Buenos Aires. Rosas had resigned the governorship in December 1832 (he would return in 1835), creating civil war and chaos in Argentina.[27]

Although the President evidenced continued interest in discussing the issues, he did not want to become entangled in the web of Argentine politics. This abdication of continental responsibility blended with the evaporation of American trade in Argentina to doom Washington's influence. As the Americans stepped aside, the British and French eagerly moved in to fill the void. When Consul Eben Dorr finally arrived in Buenos Aires in November, 1834, he faced a thankless task. Continued political instability and a prohibitive tariff against foreign wheat and flour had depressed American imports. The carrying trade declined in 1836 when the Argentines allowed the admission of Spanish ships into their ports. At about the same time, Dorr became involved in what Jackson feared most: meddling in Argentine politics. A controversial letter critical of the Buenos Aires government was published in the local press and attributed to the agent. The mortified Consul was promptly recalled in October 1836 and replaced by Thomas Lumpkin.[28]

Jacksonian diplomacy with Argentina was a tale of inept representatives, differing priorities, and lost opportunities. It was not easy to wend a way through the labyrinths of Argentine politics, but British consul Woodbine Parrish and Minister Henry Fox managed to do so successfully, and Great Britain emerged from the 1830s as the major influence in Buenos Aires—in spite of the Falklands crisis. What had happened to the Americans? Primarily, neither Jackson nor his advisors considered the area critical to American interest. The million-dollar trade in hides might expand marginally, given the chaos and European competition in the region, but in fact, the fishing rights that Jackson was eager to protect were far more important. In defending them, the President risked little; the Argentines certainly could not retaliate.

What Jackson sacrificed was the opportunity to build credibility with the South Americans and reestablish ties with Argentina. His interpretation of the Monroe Doctrine regarding the British claim to the Falklands was pragmatic, if not terribly forthright. His Majesty would not harrass Yankee sealers or whalers about the islands; besides, the Americans were in no position to challenge the world's greatest seapower over a remote outpost in the South Atlantic. Had Old Hickory perceived Argentine-American relations in a more important light, it is unlikely that he would have allowed mediocre diplomats and consuls to bumble their way into a virtual dissolution of those relations.

BRAZIL

American relations with Brazil can be summed up in one word—coffee. As the beverage preference of the United States shifted from tea to coffee after the War of 1812, trade with the world's leading producer of the dark bean took on greater importance to shippers, merchants, and consumers. The importation of coffee into the United States doubled between 1820 and 1830, constituting 90 percent of imports from Brazil by 1834 (sugar was a distant second). Flour made up more than two-thirds of American exports to the eastern coast of South America.

This wheat-for-coffee trade especially benefited the merchants of Baltimore and Richmond. The Jacksonian era found William H. D. C. Wright (of the House of Maxwell, Wright and Company—or, as it was more commonly known, Maxwell House) and New York merchant sea captain Obad Folger as consuls in South America. While American exports to the continent increased from only $4.6 to $5.7 million between 1830 and 1840, imports skyrocketed from $5 million to $8.6 million. Since almost $7 million of that total was in the coffee trade, the Empire of Brazil was easily the major American trading partner on the continent. Eight consuls and a chargé in Rio de Janeiro represented American interests in various Brazilian cities.

The scope of American trade was dwarfed only by that of Great Britain. Since 1810, when the British became involved with the internal affairs of Portugal during the Napoleonic Wars, England had been a controlling influence on the politics and economics of the tiny kingdom and its empire. A hurriedly negotiated treaty granted the British commercial favors they were not eager to surrender. By 1830, English commerce exceeded $30 million, English bankers had lent over six million pounds to the Brazilian government, and English investors had risked millions more on mines. The importance of Brazilian commerce and Anglo-American rivalry in the Empire would dominate relations during the Jackson presidency.[29]

The death of King John VI of Portugal in 1826 muddied the political waters on two continents. In Portugal, John's younger son, Dom Miguel, appeared ready to challenge his older brother, Dom Pedro, for the crown. Dom Pedro, the rightful heir, had in 1822 declared de facto Brazilian independence from Portugal. The question had become whether Dom Pedro still retained a claim to the Portuguese throne. The United States had approached the issue very cautiously, although James Monroe had received Dom Pedro's chargé, José Rebello, in 1824. But when it appeared that Portugal might take action against the upstart son, Monroe refused to apply the principles of his own doctrine. Instead, he told Rebello that this was a quarrel between a mother country and her former colony and therefore did not fall under the guidelines of his 1823 statement.

During the Adams administration the war between Brazil and Argentina placed particular strains upon Brazilian relations. The Emperor's blockade of Buenos Aires led to American charges of violation of neutral rights and impressment of seamen. The American Chargé in Rio, Philadelphia merchant Condy Raguet, was ill equipped to deal with diplomatic crisis and thankfully asked for his passports in 1827. His replacement was the talented William Tudor, formerly consul at Lima, Peru. Tudor was unable to transfer to Rio for a year, leaving Consul William Wright in charge of the legation.

When Tudor arrived in June 1828, events were moving rapidly to alter the course of Brazilian-Portuguese relations. In 1828 Dom Pedro abdicated his Portuguese crown in favor of his daughter, Donna Maria, naming his brother, Dom Miguel, as regent. The ambitious Miguel, however, quickly claimed the throne for himself. As he did so, a junta formed in Oporto in support of Dom Pedro, and civil war threatened. In an effort to achieve recognition before Pedro's forces could act, Dom Miguel dispatched a representative, Torlade d'Azambuja, to Washington in August—the legitimacy of whose appointment was promptly challenged by Chargé Barrozo Pereira, the official representative of the late King John and of Dom Pedro/Dona Maria. President

Adams avoided this hornet's nest, leaving it for Jackson to deal with in 1829.[30]

By September, the President had weighed the evidence regarding the contending factions. Dom Miguel seemed to be in solid control of Portugal, and Jackson simply could not justify recognizing a regime in absentia. The recognition was economically dangerous, however. Because of various tariff regulations, the strong British presence, and the absence of a treaty, American trade with Portugal was inconsiderable. In contrast, not only was commerce with Brazil increasingly valuable, but claims (although small) remained to be settled from the Argentine-Brazilian War. Tudor was sent instructions in September to break the news gently of Jackson's recognition of Dom Miguel. The diplomat did so with finesse, soothing Dom Pedro's wounded ego. In the summer of 1828, Tudor had successfully negotiated a commercial treaty that gave the United States most-favored-nation status, except for Portugal. In spite of the diplomat's failing health, the Jackson administration wished him to stay on in Rio and resolve the claims issue. Given the political turbulence and understandable bitterness of Dom Pedro over the matter of recognition, Tudor's rapid triumph on the claims question was remarkable: within six months he had gotten the Emperor to agree to reparations totaling $250,000. Moreover, when the legislature neglected to appropriate the funds, a special plea from the Chargé resulted in an imperial order for bonds to cover the amount.[31]

William Tudor's death in March 1830 was a serious loss to the American community in Brazil. Although the payment of the claims would remain a gnawing issue for the next several years, Tudor had basically resolved the outstanding issues in Brazilian-American relations before his demise. The difficulty of the post is reflected in the problems encountered by Wright, who once again acted as Chargé until Tudor's successor arrived. Wright's pressures on the method of claims payments, while technically correct and approved by the State Department, agitated the Brazilians, who asked for his replacement.[32]

The new Chargé, Ethan Allen Brown of Ohio, was urged to proceed cautiously. Brown's situation presents an interesting juxtaposition to that of John Murray Forbes in Buenos Aires. When Brown informed his government, after evaluating the milieu, that he must wait to press the claims, the President agreed and gave his agent eighteen months before Livingston instructed him to reopen the issue. Forbes's similar requests for time, in an equally turbulent political climate, were met with chastisement and pleas for greater exertion. Perhaps the Jackson administration feared too hasty exposure for the inexperienced Ohioan. Brown was a former state supreme court judge, governor and United States senator. His Democratic credentials were, of course, impeccable, although he was a diplomatic novice. Brown remained in Rio three years, witnessing seemingly endless social chaos and political turbulence.

Dom Pedro abdicated his Brazilian crown in 1831 in favor of his five-year-old son so that he could sail to Europe and claim the Portuguese throne for his daughter. In Paris, the former monarch conspired with various European powers to place Donna Maria on the throne.

Meanwhile, the Brazilian regency faced internal uprisings from provincial rebels, slaves, and Indians—plus the possibility that the Portuguese government would seize the moment and attempt to reclaim Brazil. The Chevalier de la Rocha, the Brazilian Minister in Paris, presented this interesting possibility to William Rives in December 1831, and inquired whether the American government would view such action as a violation of the Monroe Doctrine. Rives, taken aback by the inquiry, responded that while the United States was supportive of the independence of our "sister states," there was no existing mechanism to make the doctrine operational. While the potential crisis never came to pass, the silence emanating from the State Department on this matter suggests an unwillingness to involve the United States in disputes between mother countries and their former colonies, especially where vital American interests were not at stake.[33]

The regency struggled through the 1830s amidst provincial republican uprisings, slave revolts, and Indian massacres. Fortunately, only one American consul, Isaac Hayes in Rio Grande de Sul, became involved in the rebellions. An ardent republican who wore his politics on his sleeve, he was accused in 1836 of aiding an insurrection. Temporarily imprisoned and then released to return to the United States, Hayes's treatment "excited the most lively sensibility" on the part of the President. Although the Brazilian government later apologized, an investigation by then Chargé William Hunter revealed that he had in fact conspired with revolutionaries. Hunter wisely never pressed the issue with Brazilian officials.[34]

Since a commercial convention and claims settlement had been executed, there was little else for a chargé to do in Rio except press for payment of the claims. Historian Lawrence Hill describes the period after the death of William Tudor as "uneventful." Minor commercial questions, charges of American counterfeiting of Brazilian coins, and the African slave trade were all discussed by various American agents between 1830 and 1837. Clearly, the United States came to view itself in a dual role with Brazil. American trade with the Empire was of obvious significance to each side, and the administration energetically pointed to this factor whenever the status of the United States was threatened. Additionally, the Jacksonians attempted to play the role of kindly Uncle Sam, the disinterested yet concerned neighbor. This theme was emphasized in both Secretary of State Forsyth's and Chargé William Hunter's correspondence. Hunter urged that the United States become Brazil's "tutelary friend"; he was suggesting not a formal alliance or the promise of belligerent aid but rather a recognition of that country's superior position on the southern continent. The Chargé correctly argued that Brazil was special; her land mass, resources, and independence could be nurtured and encouraged by some nation other than Great Britain. Of course, he believed the United States should be that nation.[35]

American influence in Brazil did increase somewhat in the 1830s as the influence of the British leveled off, its decline aided prominently by their eager attempts to force an end to the slave trade. By 1842, American shipping with Rio equaled that of Great Britain, and Washington had raised the rank of its agent there from chargé to minister. This surge did not relate to anything Andrew Jackson or his Cabinet promoted; there was no concerted effort in Washington to suppress British influence and enhance that of the United States. The President viewed Brazil as he did the other South American nations, with a hands-off attitude politically and a promotional attitude commercially. Brazil merited greater concern and patience only because it was the most important American economic link on the continent.[36]

COLOMBIA

United States relations with Colombia in the first Jackson administration were inextricably entwined with the ambitions and goals of the great Latin liberator, Simón Bolívar. Bolívar, a wealthy Venezuelan who had studied in Europe, returned in 1807 to lead the struggle for independence from Spain in the northern half of the continent. Venezuela, freed in 1821, formed an alliance with Colombia and Ecuador named Gran Colombia, with Bolívar as its president.

The Yankees had a warm affection for the Liberator, whose republican principles were welcomed in the Western Hemisphere. In 1824 the Monroe administration negotiated a treaty of amity and commerce with Gran Colombia. The trade, as with most of South America, consisted of flour and coarse cotton fabrics in exchange for coffee, cocoa, and sugar. The British also concluded a treaty with Colombia in 1825, the rivals each averaging a healthy $3 million per year in trade by the mid-1820s. Unfortunately, the political instability that destroyed the aspiring young republic also had a detrimental effect on American commerce and influence in the area.[37]

Simon Bolívar envisioned a grand design for a united South America. Following the establishment of Gran Colombia, he had assisted in the liberation of Bolivia and Peru, hoping to bring them into his Latin American union. But political ambitions, local jealousies, and nationalistic feelings doomed the project. From 1826 to 1828 the Liberator dashed about the continent, attempting to hold his patchwork confederation together. By the time Jackson entered the White House, a desperate Bolívar, dying of tuberculosis, was consulting with the English and French about the possibility of a monarchy in the region as a last-ditch means of preserving his dream after his demise. Although it clashed with Bolívar's long-established principles, a monarchy might be acceptable—if the people through their assemblies agreed. This idea failed, not only because the Latins themselves opposed it but because the British were unwilling to allow either an English or a French prince to assume the prospective throne, and the South Americans reacted strongly against the suggestion of another Spanish Bourbon ruler. The only other option Bolívar could see was a confederation of Latin states—a veritable "league of nations"—under a British protectorate.[38]

Both plans were discussed in 1828 when Henry Clay dispatched William Henry Harrison to Bogotá to investigate the situation. Harrison, a devout republican, reacted swiftly and strongly to the perceived intrigues with England and the betrayal of democratic principles. Clay wanted his agent to use moral suasion to try to defeat the proposed monarchical schemes, an "interventionist" policy sharply criticized by the Jacksonians. Harrison's activities, at least in the minds of the Colombians, far exceeded moral suasion. In 1829, Colombian leaders accused him of aiding General Cordova in fomenting a provincial rebellion, and asked the American to leave the country.[39]

Amidst the embarrassment of the Harrison incident and the pending collapse of Gran Colombia in 1829–30, new Minister Thomas P. Moore of Kentucky arrived in Bogotá. Moore's ministerial rank, the only one assigned by the United States in South America, is indicative of the high regard in which the United States held Bolívar and his confederation. Historian J. F. Rippy accurately refers to Moore as "a Jacksonian spoilsman." Since he had been recommended by the powerful Kentucky Democracy, which included Amos Kendall, William Barry, and Richard M. Johnson, his selection helped cement their loyalty. As for his talents, John Pope, a senator and congressman from Frankfort whom Jackson appointed territorial governor of Arkansas, confided to the President:

Moore is an efficient man of sense and management and although he has not much moral weight and has not done for you one tenth part of what is pretended, yet he has fought the battle with zeal and boldness. He regards neither truth nor principle to carry his point, as a matter of policy I advise you to treat him as well as you can, but don't give him too much influence with you.[40]

Jackson appointed Moore despite this caveat, considering him as well qualified as anyone else who would have accepted the mission. With no diplomatic experience, the Kentuckian had been given a vital post at a critical time. Jackson took an unusual personal interest in Gran Colombia and instructed Moore to assure Bolívar that the new administration would not pursue the policies of the old. To reinforce the point, Van Buren issued an official position on the question of Yankee interference in South American conflicts. American mediation of a potential conflict between Peru and Colombia in 1829 had been requested by both Peru and Chile, but Jackson declared that the United States should not interfere in the internal affairs of other nations, who should be allowed to work out their differences without American aid. The role of mediator "would impose duties and obligations upon the mediating party; the extent or termination of which is impossible to foresee." Old Hickory wanted Moore to be supportive of Bolívar and convince him of American friendship and of the hope that he would not sell out the revolution for "the fleeting and sordid gratification of personal aggrandisement." Since the Minister's instructions ordered him not only to preserve United States treaty rights and gain satisfaction for several minor claims, but also to encourage republican government, it is difficult to discern a real difference between Adams's moral suasion and Jackson's supposed noninterference.[41]

American commerce was almost halved by 1830 as the Gran Colombian union shattered. The Liberator died that year, leaving Jackson more alert to the rumors of proposed European-backed monarchies. Although Moore had earlier erroneously reported that no such conspiracies existed, by 1830 both the Minister and his chief were aware of the possibility that republican government might be temporarily sacrificed for the sake of order. Moore told Van Buren that Americans in Colombia, wearing their constitutions on their sleeves, found themselves caught up in the noble experience of democratic revolution. Such actions, he contended, were not malicious but motivated by patriotism and commitment to native principles.[42]

For Moore, as for many Americans, Latin revolution had centered on Bolívar. With his demise and the splintering of Gran Colombia, the ensuing anarchy caused the Minister to lose much of his respect for the republics. He wrote Van Buren in August 1830, "I have no confidence in the intellectual fitness of this people for free institutions, and still less in the private and public virtue of the majority of public men." His sentiments were echoed by Consul J. G. A. Williamson in LaGuaira, Venezuela, who defined a particular code of Spanish morality: he lamented that bribery was common, money ruled everything, and the legal system was fraudulent and based on extortion. Certainly Jackson, who had experienced the Spanish on the American frontier, agreed with these sentiments.[43]

The troubled Yankees, no doubt disappointed about the crumbling of Gran Colombia, nevertheless rejoiced over the creation of the republics of New Granada (Colombia), Venezuela, and Ecuador. With Bolívar's death, however, and the dream of monarchy dying with him, Great Britain saw separation as a way to maximize her influence. London was prepared to aid the Venezuelan separatists by anchoring His

Majesty's fleet nearby if necessary. The British had likely hoped for a protectorate in Venezuela, but were to be disappointed. Although the crown's political and commercial influence surpassed that of the United States, the English failed to obtain either a monarchy or a protectorate.[44]

The fractionization of Gran Colombia brought new problems to the door of Minister Moore. New Granada quietly negotiated reciprocal treaties with both the Central American Republic and Peru, and by decree applied similar reciprocal provisions to American shipping. But problems arose when these decrees did not fall under the guidelines of several American statutes passed between 1824 and 1828. While the two nations attempted to resolve this uncomfortable, though not serious, problem, the United States learned of the other treaties and demanded reciprocal rights under the most-favored-nation clause of the 1824 United States–Gran Colombia treaty. The Colombians refused, arguing that there was a difference between trade privileges freely given and those reciprocally negotiated: the Americans were not entitled to the same privileges as the Central Americans or Peruvians, since the Yankees had not offered similar concessions.[45]

This interpretation troubled Secretary of State Livingston, who saw frightening possibilities involving the further commercial inroads that Europeans might make into Latin America. Livingston, perceiving violations of the Monroe Doctrine, was surprisingly vocal in chiding the Colombians for such abuse of American rights. In May 1832, under strong pressure from Great Britain, the Colombians rescinded the November 1831 decree granting the United States reciprocal rights, and abrogated the most-favored-nation section of the 1824 agreement. Since United States ports were permitting free access to Colombian coffee and cocoa, while American flour paid heavy duties, Moore was instructed to protest this decree as "unjust and unfriendly."

Livingston's timely assertion of the Monroe Doctrine over commercial rather than political issues, about the same time that the United States refused to invoke the doctrine over the British occupation of the Falklands, is a clear statement of the Jacksonian interpretation. Although Old Hickory would probably have responded to a transatlantic invasion of Latin America, his emphasis was primarily commercial. Concurrent with Edmund Roberts's mission to develop the Asian trade, the President requested Moore to investigate the possibilities of a transisthmian route across Central America. Moore, frustrated by the political and economic chaos of New Granada, asked permission to return home to Kentucky in 1831. The President approved his request, but only for a visit; the Minister was obliged to return and resolve the outstanding claims and commercial problems.[46]

When Moore returned to Colombia early in 1832, the zeal of the first two years of his mission was gone. One factor was certainly the death of Bolívar, a man he had come to admire and esteem as the best political hope for Latin America. The chaos and division that followed, the 1831–32 American–New Granadan dispute over tariffs, and the setback of his own political career incurred by remaining in South America all dampened his enthusiasm. The final year in Bogotá, focusing upon the tariff-treaty issue, was particularly unsatisfactory.[47] Jackson relieved him from his misery by appointing fellow Kentuckian Robert McAfee in March 1833. At the time, the State Department still harbored a faint hope that the Gran Colombian confederation would reunite, which would facilitate American claims and commerce. Washington urged McAfee to use all discreet means to produce this effect, even though such actions would seem to compromise the Jacksonian noninterference policy. The administration admitted the unlikelihood of reunification, however, in the reduction of McAfee's rank to Chargé. Since the trade with Venezuela was more important than that with New Granada or Ecuador, McAfee was empowered to act as the conduit for Consul Williamson in Venezuela. Until the negotiation of new treaties, Washington assumed that all three republics would operate under the 1824 Gran Colombian agreement.[48]

Unfortunately, the economic situation between the United States and Venezuela was deteriorating sharply. By 1832, with no treaty between the two nations and American interests represented only by consuls, the $1.5 million trade was suffering under discriminatory tariffs as high as 50–75 percent. Consul Williamson sailed for Philadelphia and New York to assist in the lobbying effort of merchants and politicians to pressure the administration to recognize the republic. He succeeded admirably, garnering the support of prominent Pennsylvania Democrats William Wilkins and Henry Horn and New Yorkers C. C. Cambreleng and G. C. Verplanck. A North Carolinian, Williamson was also a friend of both Romulus Saunders of the French Claims Commission and Democratic Senator Bedford Brown. In March 1835 he was selected as the first Chargé to Venezuela and empowered to negotiate a commercial treaty.[49]

Williamson's appointment symbolized the abandonment of an official American goal—the reunification of Gran Colombia. But the respective republics had recognized each other, and the ensuing damage to American commerce made action by Washington imperative. The Chargé was urged to get reciprocal provisions based on the 1828 treaty with Brazil rather than the most-favored-nation pact of 1824 with Gran Colombia. Having served as consul for a number of years, Williamson knew the Venezuelans and could thus work quickly and effectively; throughout the negotiations, however, the Chargé was critical of the Venezuelan people, whom he dubbed "provincial and parochial." This condition, he suggested, derived from their Spanish colonial experience and from the character that follows "a general and licensed amalgamation of color." The racial mixing and color lines in Latin America perplexed Williamson, who believed a racial war was inevitable. To him a further problem was the Catholic Church, which, he said, continued to keep the nation in "moral darkness"; only education could redeem it. Despite his marginal evaluation of the Venezuelan character, the commercial treaty talks proved fruitful. By January 1836 the two nations had signed a pact the provisions of which were much like those of the treaty with Brazil.[50]

Williamson's success in completing a treaty with Venezuela in 1836 inspired Secretary of State Forsyth to instruct McAfee to negotiate a similar pact with New Granada. Forsyth hoped that the Ecuadorians would have representation in Bogotá in order that McAfee could include them in the talks. The United States, the Secretary explained, had not been ignoring Ecuador; it was simply more remote and, until recently, too politically unstable. If the third republic did not join in the negotiations, McAfee was to travel to Quito at his earliest opportunity to discuss a treaty with that government. The Chargé failed in both assignments. Commercial pacts would not be concluded until 1839 with Ecuador and 1846 with New Granada.[51]

The record of United States relations with Gran Colombia in the Jackson years is mediocre at best. The administration exhibited an almost paranoid fear in its approach to any involvement in the turbulent political events of the region, especially in determining the fate of the confederation. The British, as in Brazil and Argentina, did not hesitate to go beyond concern to involvement. As Bolívar and the English contemplated New World monarchy, there were no harsh words of warning from Washington concerning possible violations of the Monroe Doctrine; rather, the Americans almost pouted over this flirtation, expressing the disappointment of a scorned suitor. Certainly, American commerce remained strong in the three northern republics. But the wealthy, powerful, and prestigious British were—there as elsewhere—the foreign force to be reckoned with.

PERU AND CHILE

The United States viewed the western coast of South America in the 1820s as an outpost of republicanism in the hemisphere and, secondarily, as a focal point for Yankee sail. The sparsity of the American trade is reflected most poignantly in the absence of United States consuls there. While there was a chargé in Lima, Peru, and another in Santiago, Chile, there was only one consul in Chile and two in Peru. The trade of both the United States and Great Britain with Peru averaged about $500,000 per year, largely an exchange of flour and cottons for minerals. The port of Paita, Peru, did have special significance as a vital rest and resupply stop for the large American whaling fleet, but because of the limited trade along the coast, the Anglo-American rivalry was more lethargic than in other parts of the continent.

The diplomats in Peru generally confined themselves to squabbling about the type of government that would manage the new republic. The Americans became particularly fearful in the 1826–29 period when Bolívar considered the idea of Latin monarchies or British protectorates—views which, of course, conflicted with the Monroe Doctrine and the Yankee preference for Western Hemispheric isolation. Although Bolívar was chosen "President for life" of Peru in 1826, he and his lieutenants were obliged to battle to maintain control of the territory. This placed the British on one side cheering for the preservation of Bolívarian power, and the Americans on the other rooting for the more "democratic" forces.[52]

Ironically, the Americans had little respect for the Peruvians and their capacity for self-government. Consul William Radcliffe in Lima wrote in 1829 that the Peruvians "are ignorant almost universally; indolent, proud and averse to every innovation however desirable and to every improvement however inviting. It will require ages probably to bring them to a level with the people of the United States." As for self-rule, the Consul concluded, "these people are unfit to govern themselves, they are yet unqualified to be free either by knowledge or virtue and can scarcely exist without anarchy or despotism . . . someday . . . they may attain liberty and good order, to which end the example of the United States will essentially contribute." Radcliffe, like Baylies in Buenos Aires, recommended against negotiating a commercial treaty with the Peruvians, since they could not be trusted.[53]

William Tudor had served as consul in Lima before being transferred by Secretary of State Clay to the more critical Brazilian post in 1828. The Jacksonians, responding more to the political than to the economic situation, temporarily shifted Samuel Larned, Chargé in Chile, to Lima. But revolution, British influence, and nationalistic feeling built a foundation of frustration for Larned and his consuls. In an effort to boost their sugar exports, the Peruvians arranged an exchange of sugar for Chilean flour; the tariff on American flour was set at a prohibitive $7.50 per barrel. Then, to protect the country's infant industries, the Lima government passed a tax of 90 percent on the value of coarse cotton imports. This did little damage to English commerce but seriously wounded the American trade.[54]

Into this degenerating economic and political climate, Jackson dispatched Emmanuel J. West in 1829. West was another "true friend of the administration" who was well connected in both political and business circles, having done yeoman service in the Illinois legislature. He possessed the advantages of speaking the Spanish language and being married to a woman of Spanish descent. As Philadelphia merchant Richard Alsop suggested, the latter point was vital in Lima, "where women play no small part in the game." Alsop recounted the old Spanish saying labeling Lima as "the purgatory for men, the heaven for women, and the hell for jackasses." The Peruvian capital was also a very expensive city in which to live.[55] This would be most troublesome for West, a man with a $4,500 salary and six children. Van Buren instructed the new diplomat to negotiate a commercial treaty that would end the discriminatory duties imposed on American cottons and flour by promising an American willingness to admit Peruvian copper without tariff penalty.[56]

Tragically, West never arrived in Lima; he died on the way, in Rio de Janeiro, early in 1830. Larned then received orders to remain in Peru rather than return to his post in Santiago. The unfortunate diplomat spent the next five years in Lima surrounded by civil war and a catatonic economic situation. Emanating a generally antiforeign mood, Peruvian talks with the British on a commercial treaty broke down over several minor points, while Larned's pleas for negotiations were ignored.[57]

In 1835 the Peruvian government, threatened by a new revolution, indicated a sudden willingness to discuss a pact. One was quickly drawn up in February 1835, but the regime of President Luis Obregoso was forced to leave the city before it could be signed, and Larned considered the new government of General Salaverry "too ephemeral" for negotiation. Civil war surged about Lima for the next several months, complete with lawlessness, forced contributions from foreign merchants, and impressment of men and horses. The situation grew particularly tense when Salaverry declared a questionable blockade of Peruvian ports. Commodore Alexander S. Wadsworth of the Pacific Squadron (consisting of the frigate *Brandywine* and sloops *Fairfield* and *Vincennes*) threatened to rescue any American vessel Salaverry might seize. Larned urged moderation in the tense atmosphere of civil war but conceded that the question was moot, since United States ships now avoided Peruvian waters.[58]

As the Salaverry government became more entrenched, Larned decided to correspond with President Andrés Santa Cruz of Bolivia. The Chargé told Forsyth that he realized Bolivia was outside his sphere and he was not empowered to negotiate with Santa Cruz; however, Bolivia had recently completed a treaty with France, and even though the United States did not need a resident agent in LaPaz, Washington should conclude a similar pact. What he neglected to tell the Secretary was that former President Obregozo had escaped to Bolivia and allied himself with Santa Cruz. Larned was hoping to position himself alongside the Bolivian ruler before the oncoming conflict occurred with Salaverry. The Chargé had little time to accomplish his goal, however, since war between Bolivia and Peru began in July 1835.[59]

By the spring of 1836, Santa Cruz had crushed the opposition and

Salaverry had been executed, much to Larned's satisfaction. The Bolivian president proceeded to create a new confederation with Peru, however, that troubled the Chargé: it was "impolitic, unconstitutional," and would probably hurt the chances for a United States–Peru treaty. But Larned's hostility mellowed as the summer progressed, and the new union restored order and granted the Americans more liberal tariff duties. By doing so, however, the confederation dangerously angered the Chileans: the Santa Cruz government abrogated a recently completed Peru–Chile treaty that had been immensely beneficial to the Chileans. But the issues were as much political as economic. Santiago had sympathized with Salaverry over Obregozo, and Lima had given aid and comfort to the losers of an 1829–30 Chilean revolt. The Santa Cruz government added fuel to the fire by encouraging, outfitting, and arming an expedition of exiled Chilean President Ramon Friere in July 1836. Disaster struck quickly: Friere and his 150 men were captured in September.[60]

As war threatened between Chile and the confederation in the fall of 1836, Larned moved rapidly to try to secure a treaty on a most-favored-nation basis. The Chargé had already been chastised and granted a one-year leave by Secretary Forsyth for his excessive energy in attempting to conclude a treaty with Peru on less than most-favored-nation basis and for opening relations with Bolivia without authorization. Now he continued the negotiations with Peru under the guns of the Chilean fleet, and on November 30 the two parties signed the treaty, providing for all the desired advantages except the opportunity to engage in the retail trade.[61]

Larned returned to Rhode Island early in 1837, to be replaced by James Thornton of New Hampshire, a former comptroller in the Treasury Department and friend of cabinet veteran Levi Woodbury. Thornton would have the unenviable task of watching American commerce decline amidst a war that ended in the defeat of Santa Cruz and the dismemberment of the Peru-Bolivia union by Chile in 1839.[62]

The failure of the American relationship with Chile perhaps best symbolized the problems the United States faced in dealing with the emerging Latin American republics and the challenges of the British commercial rivalry. The Monroe administration granted early recognition to Chile, recognizing the republic under the leadership of liberator

Bernardo O'Higgins in 1822. American interest and involvement in the young nation included the participation of Yankees like Samuel Larned in its constitutional convention in 1826. The Chileans initiated the United States form of government with a federal model and extensive local autonomy. While this idealized form was not appropriate to the turbulent Chilean political climate of the decade, the critical point was the extent of the republican bond.

This budding Chilean-American friendship eventually crumbled for two reasons. First, the liberals of the 1820s under Ramon Friere lost power in an 1830 revolution led by Joaquín Prieto, a conservative spokesman for the landowners, the businessmen, and the priesthood. Unlike the Indian and mestizo masses, these men were rich and well educated—and Spanish. In 1833 they implemented a new constitution that incorporated elements of the British parliamentary system, in addition to the American system of checks and balances, and their fondness for things European became readily apparent.

Second, the Americans could offer friendship, advice, and support, but the British could be much more tangible in their assistance. In 1822 two Americans, William Worthington and Jeremiah Robinson, had attempted to promote an investment project in Chile utilizing American capital. When they failed, three British companies promptly moved in and began mining copper in the northern provinces. Seven years later, William Wheelwright of Newburyport, Massachusetts, arrived in Chile from Guayaquil, Ecuador. Wheelwright had a dream of controlling the coastal trade of western South America by establishing a steamship monopoly to Panama, then a short railway across to the Caribbean and Atlantic shipping. He wanted American capital to fund such a venture; unable to find it, he turned to London. By 1840, British bankers and businessmen were backing the formation of his Pacific Steam Navigation Company. The firm sailed British ships under the Union Jack and for a generation was the only line between the western coast of South America and North America or Europe. Wheelwright stayed on to assist in the development of city lighting and water plants and the exploration of coalfields. The Chileans erected a statue in Valparaiso in memory of his contributions. Unfortunately for Washington, Wheelwright's activities reflected the growth and prestige of British maritime interests, not those of the United States.[63]

British banks lent millions of pounds to the Chilean government, and British goods inundated the Chilean market, to the exclusion of those from almost all other countries. English agents married Chilean Catholic women, something the Protestant Americans were reluctant to do. By the time Jackson left office, British trade had reached a healthy $4 million. The Americans exported flour, coarse cottons, and tobacco, but the Chileans had little to offer except copper, so the trade averaged about $2 million per year. Certainly, high Chilean tariffs had something to do with the Anglo-American commercial disparity, but the critical factors involved what each nation could provide for the Chileans. Americans could offer the Monroe Doctrine and its high-minded principles; the British could offer the advantages of the world's most powerful nation. The Chileans, like other Latin American countries, had little difficulty making the choice.[64]

Chilean tariffs, constituting a major source of governmental revenues, became increasingly offensive in the late 1820s. American cotton and flour were taxed at 27 percent and cabinets at 40 percent; whaling vessels paid a $10 anchorage fee. The probable rise in these numbers signaled the need for a commercial treaty, which the Adams administration attempted unsuccessfully to negotiate with Chile in 1827–28.[65]

The Jacksonians made this treaty a priority assignment for their representative. When Samuel Larned, who had been in Chile since 1824, was transferred to Lima in 1829, he was replaced by John Hamm. Hamm was typical of Old Hickory's Latin American appointments. A state senator from Zanesville, Ohio, Hamm had been not only a loyal supporter of the President but a hometown friend of Secretary of War Lewis Cass. Because of his health, a hurricane, and a delayed appointment, the new Chargé did not arrive in Santiago until June 1831.[66] Since Larned had departed in October 1829, the legation had been in the hands of Consul Michael Hogan for over a year and a half. Hogan, his house a garrison most of the time, witnessed the civil war of 1829–30. While regarding Ramon Friere as "being naturally too indolent for everything but cards," the Consul considered him honest and brave, and hoped for the victory of his "constitutional" forces over the "royalists." When Friere's legions were shattered in April 1830, the disappointed Hogan mused that perhaps the popular General lacked both the ability and the brains to win. The final victory of the conservatives in May (followed by Friere's exile to Bolivia) brought stability and order to the Chilean people but did so at the cost of sacrificing their revolutionary goals.[67]

By the time Hamm arrived, the political scene was tranquil, but American trade had declined markedly as gold and silver flowed into British and French coffers. London recognized the Chilean republic in 1831, and Chile's growing closeness not only with Great Britain but with her sister Latin American republics made Hamm's primary task of negotiating a treaty on the basis of reciprocity particularly difficult. The Chargé was empowered to use the most-favored-nation tack (which caused problems with Colombia in 1831–32) only as a last resort because of the uncertain interpretation of trade under it. While Washington was interested in building American commerce with Chile, protecting the Pacific whaling fleet that utilized Chilean ports was also a vital concern.[68]

By May 1832, Hamm had obtained a treaty, but it proved less than satisfactory to the President. The Ohio senator seemed to be out of his league in negotiating with the great South American jurist, Andres Bello. The pact provided for the increasingly undesirable most-favored-nation approach, did not include a provision for the protection of American sealers or whalers, and failed to negotiate several minor ($140,000) merchant claims. As the administration had feared, the most-favored-nation designation did not prohibit the Chileans from granting preferential duties to Peru, Bolivia, or the Argentine, with whom the United States had no treaties. This meant that Peruvian sugar would easily be able to drive the small but growing American sugar trade from the market. Hamm argued that the treaty was the best possible, and that he had succeeded in protecting American commercial vessels from seizure and had made inroads in the granting of neutral rights, such as free ships and free goods. American commercial treaties had been completed with Mexico, Colombia, Brazil, and the Central American federation. In each case their representatives had attempted to negotiate favorable trade exceptions for the sister Latin republics at the expense of any "outsiders," but the Chilean treaty was the first to include this feature. The United States should have needed little further evidence that it was, despite the Monroe Doctrine and the policy of early recognition, not included in the Latin family of nations.[69]

His major assignment completed, John Hamm hoped to come home after one year in Chile. Anti-Catholic (he referred to the Church as a "hydra") and anti-Chilean, Hamm considered the people there indolent and debauched; their only saving grace was their temperance. He was also troubled by the "preponderating influence" of the British, who seemed intent on frustrating American diplomatic and commercial efforts at every turn. They not only dominated the loans, finances, and commerce of Chile but moved to gain the carrying trade as well.[70]

But Hamm spent two more difficult years in Chile futilely attempting to resolve the claims issues and remove from the commercial treaty the exceptional clauses favoring other Latin American nations. Jackson mercifully allowed him to return home in 1834 without accomplishing these goals. In his place the President sent Richard Pollard of Virginia, a perennial appointment seeker (he had earlier sought the posts of naval storekeeper at Pensacola and port collector at Alexandria, Virginia), whose major asset was that he was William Rives's brother-in-law. In his Chilean assignment Pollard was urged to pursue the goals assigned to Hamm, and reminded of the growing importance of the trade. In 1833 the United States had imported only $335,000 worth of goods from the republic, but exported almost $1.5 million to her. The carrying trade between Chile and the Pacific was also a boon to American sail and the use of Chilean ports by whalers a constant necessity. While the $2 million trade with Chile exceeded that of the United States with most other Latin American nations, it was dwarfed by the $6 million in British commerce along the Pacific coast.[71]

Pollard departed from Hampton Roads in November 1834, stopping in Rio de Janiero on his way to Santiago. In Brazil he met with the minister from Bolivia, who convinced him that the United States should not continue to ignore the promise of his country's commerce. The Virginian, demonstrating his lack of preparation for the task ahead, endorsed a Bolivian treaty in a letter to William Rives in which he erroneously commented that Bolivia had ports on both the Atlantic and Pacific Oceans. Although new to the South American continent, Pollard was sensitive to the omnipresence of the British, noting that the Latins viewed them as the greatest nation on earth. He suggested that the United States move eagerly and sincerely to demonstrate that we are "their first and true friends." It was incomprehensible to him that

Duncan's attack upon the Falklands had virtually severed Argentine-American relations, while British trade still continued in spite of their occupation of the islands.[72]

Pollard, who spoke no Spanish, arrived in Valparaiso in early March 1835 and was initially impressed by the country and the government. The wine was robust, the climate pleasant, the people hard-working and attractive. The government he adjudged to be "well constructed and judiciously administered." Only the frequency of earthquakes troubled the young diplomat.[73]

Pollard's tenure began at a most inopportune time. The treaty between Peru and Chile, which would favor Peruvian sugar and Chilean flour at the expense of American commerce, was under negotiation. The Chargé continually bemoaned Hamm's 1832 Chilean treaty, which had permitted "escape clauses" allowing preferential treatment for sister Latin republics. Following the bouncing ball of Pacific coast politics, Pollard endorsed whatever politicians in whichever country seemed to favor American economic interests. He was positive about the "liberal and enlightened" Salaverry regime in Peru, which initially reduced tariffs. But when the General accepted the offensive Peru-Chile treaty, Pollard promptly lost enthusiasm for him. Instead, he embraced the anti-treaty Obregoso–Santa Cruz confederation, likening its future to that of the United States. Short-lived euphoria swept over Pollard in Santiago and Larned in Lima when the confederation abrogated the treaty. Soon, of course, hatred of Santa Cruz and fear of his union would spark a war between Chile and the confederation.[74]

After little more than a year in South America, Pollard was becoming increasingly jaded in outlook. His almost Pollyanna-like optimism had disappeared in contempt for the Catholic Church and the oligarchy that controlled Chile. He told Forsyth that Catholicism was "a religion based upon superstition and ignorance—opposed equally to knowledge and virtue." As for the government, the disillusioned Chargé acknowledged that "the love of power causes those administering the government to turn their sight from the United States and look to European monarchs for political guides." The United States was "too free, her institutions too republican for these lovers of unrestrained power." Diego Portales, the power in Chilean government until his assassination in 1837, strongly opposed the Monroe Doctrine. He reasoned that the United States ultimately planned to conquer all of Latin America, by influence if not by arms. Such views made Pollard's post unenviable, but he remained in Chile another five years, later rejecting entreaties for an alliance with Santiago while at the same time decrying British influence and the fawning imitative practices of the Chilean aristocracy.[75]

Jacksonian foreign policy in South America was only a qualified success, but given the guidelines created, it could have had no other fate. American trade with the continent, so full of promise in the early years of the century, was relegated to Johnny-come-lately status by the economic and military conflicts of the 1806–15 period. The tentative approach of the Monroe and Adams administrations did little to endear Washington to the new republics. Latin leaders were not consulted on the Monroe Doctrine. The opportunities did arise for a positive Yankee role through the mediation of the Argentine-Brazilian War and the Peruvian-Colombian conflicts of the 1820s, and in the implementation of the doctrine in the controversial British occupation of the Falklands in 1833. But the conservative interpretation adopted by the Adams and Jackson administrations revealed the document to be largely a paper tiger. A potential Portuguese invasion of Brazil, British conspiracy with Bolívar, and Royal Navy influence in the Venezuelan separatist movement met with expressions of American concern but produced no concrete action. The Yankees wanted to see republics established and preserved upon American principles but were unwilling to do anything more than serve as a model—unless perhaps immediate territorial goals were threatened. Both Colombia and Chile suggested agreements based upon alliance, but the precepts of George Washington prohibited such commitments. Locked in by a limited interpretation of Washington's Farewell Address and the Monroe Doctrine, the United States allowed the Latin republics under English guidance to drift further in the direction of a European oligarchical model.

Beyond trumpeting republicanism, Jackson restricted his concern to the promotion of commerce. The results were mixed. The President endorsed the negotiation of several new treaties, and trade volume did increase by 50 percent between 1830 and 1840. But Old Hickory used the continent as a dumping ground for political appointees, usually from the western states, who lacked understanding of the culture or sympathy for the religion they would encounter. Many did not speak Spanish. Often ambitious men who hoped to use their diplomatic posts as springboards for political careers, their major goals were generally to enhance their reputations and sometimes their pocketbooks. Moreover, while proclaiming the advantages of Yankee republicanism, they encountered the firm resistance of Great Britain's vast commercial empire. American imports from South America did, in fact, increase sharply—especially from Brazil—but exports rose only slightly more than $1 million as the English maintained their predominance on the continent. American recognition, commercial treaties, and attempts to assist in the reestablishment of positive relations with Spain meant little in competition with British prestige, goods, and gold.

Where the Yankees had failed with South America, however, they might succeed along the Isthmus of Panama. But the goals there went beyond republican models and economic hegemony. The possibility of a canal across Central America and the acquisition of Texas fostered a greater and more immediate interest in the minds of the Jacksonians.

Chapter 8

Mexico and Central America:
Texas and a Transisthmian Canal

Perhaps the greatest similarity in the foreign policies of John Quincy Adams and Andrew Jackson lay in their attitudes toward Mexico and Central America. Adams, the much-lauded architect of the acquisition of Florida and major advisor on the Monroe Doctrine, is considered one of the premier U.S. Secretaries of State and more imaginative Presidents in the area of foreign affairs. Jackson, on the contrary, has been perceived as stumbling, bullish, and insensitive, especially in his relations with Mexico. Yet the two men had similar goals: the renegotiation of the United States-Mexican border, the acquisition of Texas, the completion of commercial treaties with the Central American Republic (Guatemala, Nicaragua, Honduras, Costa Rica, and El Salvador) and Mexico, and the exploration of the advantages and possibilities of a transisthmian route.

Adams had already taken the initial steps to accomplish each of the desired goals before Jackson took office. On the isthmus, for example, the President and Secretary of State Clay had negotiated a treaty with the Central American Republic, attempted to send agents to the Panama Congress, and conducted tentative negotiations for a canal route.[1]

But there were major obstacles to these efforts in the developing nationalism of the newly independent Latin states, the political turmoil that accompanied their emergence, and, of course, Great Britain, who jealously guarded Central America and the Caribbean against a Yankee incursion. England was both primary among the world's leading maritime powers and, unfortunately for expansionist-minded southerners in the United States, antislavery as well. Although the crown had limited territorial ambitions in the region, the British were mindful of the American hegemonic thrust toward Mexico and Cuba. Bent on preserving its investments and commercial advantages, Great Britain functioned as a major barrier to Yankee ambitions.

MEXICO

Adams dispatched Joel Poinsett of South Carolina to Mexico in 1825 to rectify some of his own errors in judgment. Earlier, as Secretary of State, he had concluded the 1819 Adams-Onis (Transcontinental) Treaty with Spain: in essence, the United States received the Floridas in exchange for a western boundary to the Louisiana Purchase. Within the next decade, however, thousands of Americans, responding to a Mexican invitation, began pouring into the province of Texas. As President, Adams first sought to renegotiate the boundary line, pushing it westward from the Sabine River to the Rio Grande. Failing in that objective, he instructed Poinsett in March 1827 to offer the Mexicans $1 million for Texas to the Rio Grande and the territory directly north to the 42nd parallel and out to the Pacific. This would leave the valuable California and New Mexico territories still under Mexican control. But the Mexican government understandably refused and, furthermore, adopted a delaying posture on ratifying the commercial treaty that Poinsett had completed in 1826. A second treaty dealing with the border, concluded in 1828, also languished in the Mexican Congress. Thus by the end of the Adams presidency, although offers had been made and treaties negotiated, neither the boundary issue nor the trade agreement had been resolved.

There were several reasons for Poinsett's failures, not the least of which was the agent himself. Historian J. F. Rippy dubs the South Carolinian "not a happy choice for the position," labeling Poinsett "an imprudent man of good intentions with a propensity for intrigue." Although well traveled and fluent in Spanish, the Minister had a reputation for championing republicanism at the expense of discretion. When he found his influence slipping in Mexico City, he was not beyond organizing a York Rite Masonic order to serve as a base for an opposition political party. Poinsett's efforts bore fruit when the Yorkists were able

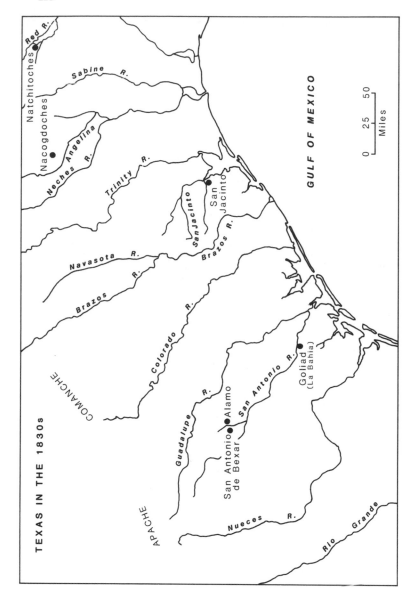

to elect members to Congress, but their internal divisions prevented them from controlling the government. When the British-influenced Scottish Rite Masons seized power in 1828 with Gómez Pedroza as President, Poinsett's star seemed to be fading, but a post-election revolution eliminated Gómez, replacing him with sympathetic Vicente Guerrero.[2]

This game of presidential musical chairs, of course, demonstrated more than Poinsett's power. Since Mexican independence in 1821, particularly after the monarchy of Augustín de Iturbide was overthrown in 1823, the nation had been divided between two major political factions. The conservatives—who were upper class, sympathetic with Spain and the Catholic Church, fearful of the republic and the social, political, and economic instability it had brought—were led by Lucas Alamán and Antonio López de Santa Anna. The liberals—middle and lower class, anti-Spanish and anti-clerical, supportive of the republic and the changes that had come about—were led by Valentín Gómez Farías and José Herrera.

Complicating the Mexican political situation were the republic's internal and external weaknesses. Unlike her sister South American states, Mexico had no Bolívar to lead her through the turbulence of the 1820s. Her broad expanse of territory—from Oregon to the Yucatan—was heavily populated by Indians, mestizos, and incoming Americans, and therefore vulnerable to sectional and secessionist impulse. This basic issue of centralism versus federalism haunted Mexico throughout the decade. A federal system had been established in 1824, but stability had not followed. Instead, developing provincial militias sometimes found themselves battling the regular army for control of a region. The political chaos affected the republic's capability for self-defense and its economic prosperity. In the period 1829–44, fourteen different men occupied the Mexican presidency as the office changed hands twenty times. Although Santa Anna's movement to power in 1834 resulted in the abolition of the federalist system, he failed to achieve the hoped-for stability in the executive office.[3]

British influence and investment in Mexico tried to provide the missing harmony. The English assumed correctly that the Americans wished to take advantage of the situation to obtain Texas and extend their power along the Gulf coast. Talented British Ministers Henry

George Ward (until 1827) and Richard Pakenham worked diligently to build a foundation for the Mexican government under conservative rule (Washington sought to do exactly the same but under liberal control) and stave off American intrusion. Poinsett reported that the impoverished Mexican treasury seemed to survive only on British loans. The Guerrero government borrowed $10 million from English merchants in April 1829, planning to pay it back through duties on liquor and paper.[4]

Ward's ability to finesse Mexican politicos was also apparent in the obtaining of land grants along the Texas border for British subjects, a move designed to hinder Yankee advancement. No doubt the British, troubled by the ascendancy of Guerrero to power in 1829, feared the sale of Texas to the United States. But El Presidente, although a liberal, also realized the lack of wisdom in offending a people who provided his government with multimillion-dollar loans. Poinsett's influence began to decline, and he was attacked in the Mexican legislature for interference in the nation's internal affairs. Foolishly, he responded in a lengthy pamphlet that further exacerbated the situation. Now a liability even to his friends, the Minister's days in the capital were numbered. Unaware of Poinsett's crumbling diplomatic position, Jackson proceeded with his own plans to purchase Texas in the summer of 1829 for $5 million.[5]

Jackson's proposition was almost identical to Adams's except that he had quintupled the amount. The President justified the offer on the basis of mutual advantage: the Americans would secure New Orleans, the Mississippi River, and the western frontier; gain land for Indian removal or perhaps as an area for "free people of color" to settle; and obtain a "natural boundary" with Mexico. The Mexicans would have the boundary, the money, and relief from potential headaches in the form of the troublesome Texans and rebellious Comanche Indians; garrisons to watch over these two groups were costing the Mexicans unaffordable pesos. But to suggest that the Latins needed to sell Texas to dispose of a problem they were incapable of handling was more than offensive to sensitive Spanish pride and honor.[6]

The President had become excited about the idea of acquiring Texas after meeting in mid-August with an old colleague from the Battle of New Orleans, Colonel Anthony Butler. Butler was a South Carolinian who had married into the influential and politically active Kentucky family of John J. Crittenden. After the War of 1812 he moved to Mississippi, became a member of the legislature, and involved himself in speculation in Texas lands. Having known Old Hickory from New Orleans, Butler had access to the President to press his interests, which he did in a lengthy report extolling the virtues of Texas.[7]

Jackson responded energetically to the possibility of annexation. In late August 1829 he dispatched Butler with formal instructions for the purchase of Texas. Soon after the agent had departed, Commodore David Porter, who had spent the previous three years organizing the Mexican navy, arrived in Washington bearing letters and information concerning Poinsett's mounting problems in Mexico City. The Minister must be quickly replaced. In October, Jackson decided to bring him quietly to Washington "for a visit" and leave the legation in Butler's hands as chargé. The President barely had time to act, however, when he received word from Mexico requesting the recall of Poinsett. Although somewhat embarrassing, this simplified matters and allowed Jackson to transfer the responsibilities originally assigned from Poinsett to Butler.[8]

The British were not naive about American intentions. Although Butler's goals were to be kept secret, activity had heated up markedly in London and Washington by the spring of 1830. In lengthy conversations with Foreign Secretary Lord Aberdeen and Mexican Minister Manuel Gorostizo, Louis McLane was obliged to combat the nasty rumors of nefarious American intentions regarding Texas. Both the Mexicans and, consequently, the English were becoming apprehensive over Poinsett's machinations, Butler's known land speculations, the issue of slave expansion, increased American settler movement into Texas, and the activity of the American army along the frontier. McLane branded these suspicions "extravagant and ridiculous" and claimed the United States had only the friendliest of intentions toward Mexico. Land would not be taken by force but might be purchased, if agreeable to both governments.[9]

In Washington, British Minister Charles Vaughan had received secret correspondence from Mexico that detailed the "steady and continuous encroachments" of the Americans. The troubled Minister met in March 1830 with Van Buren, who feigned offense at the thought of

American expansion and assured Vaughan that the United States had no territorial designs upon Mexico. This must have seemed especially incredible to Vaughan, since Mexican newspapers had published the object of Butler's mission—and even the correct price to be offered—in January. Undaunted, Van Buren flatteringly and accurately referred to the ascendancy of British influence in Mexico City and hoped that London would use that power to promote a spirit of harmony and good will between the two neighbors. The experienced Vaughan, who had known about Poinsett's instructions to purchase Texas, was probably not satisfied with Van Buren's assurances.[10]

Butler's arrival in Mexico City in December 1829 coincided almost exactly with the most recent revolution. President Guerrero, who had been in the south leading his army of 3,000, was overthrown in the capital city. Instead of returning to battle his adversaries, El Presidente simply retired to his estate, leaving the government in the hands of the conservative opposition led by General Bustamente. This coup was particularly untimely for the United States. Although Guerrero had not been able to save Poinsett, at least American interests could be heard in Mexico City. Both Jackson and Van Buren respected Guerrero and considered him intelligent. The ascent to power of Bustamente, with Luis Alamán in the Foreign Office, meant the parallel rise of British influence. But conservative government did not bring tranquillity to Mexico. By the spring of 1830 eight states were in revolt, and the confederacy seemed to be collapsing. Many looked to General Santa Anna to bring peace. For a moment, Alamán, providing a fleeting imitation of Bolívar, flirted with Pakenham about the possibility of a monarchy or a British protectorate over Mexico. Neither materialized, in part because the British linked a monarchy to a Spanish Bourbon prince (just as they did in South America), a change the newly liberated Mexicans could not accept.[11]

Political stability had taken on new meaning in the summer of 1829 when a Spanish invasion threatened to destroy the struggling republic. In late July an army of 3,000 Spaniards sailed from Cuba and landed at Tampico. Although they were able to take the city easily, the invaders received little popular support and quickly found themselves isolated and surrounded by Santa Anna and a force of 8,000 men. By all reports the Mexican Army seemed ill prepared, but sheer numbers prompted the capitulation of the Spanish in mid-September. Guerrero reacted rapidly and defensively to the possibility of a second invasion. He ordered a Colonel Basarde to Haiti to speak with President Jean Pierre Boyer about the possibility of inciting a slave insurrection in Cuba to sidetrack the Spanish. Naturally, Jackson was furious about such an attempt and instructed Butler to do all he could to stop it. Butler protested, but the Guerrero government had collapsed. The new regime, while denying any knowledge of the scheme, recalled Basarde and revoked his commission. Meanwhile, Gorostiza in London was querying McLane about whether a Mexican invasion of Cuba prompted by self-defense would incur the wrath of the United States.[12]

Certainly, the Mexicans felt they must do something as soon as possible to remove the dagger pointed at their throats. Cornelius Van Ness, American Minister to Spain, reported 2,000 Spanish troops preparing to depart Cadiz for Havana on chartered American ships in March 1830. Were these troops being sent to defend the island against a Mexican invasion or a slave insurrection, or were they the vanguard of a second attack upon Mexico? The anxiety level in Mexico City rose daily. The British had already moved to mediate to prevent another assault. Attempting to use all the resources at hand, Foreign Secretary Alamán approached Butler about the possibility of United States aid to Mexico in the event of a war with Spain. What type and extent of assistance would the Americans provide? Alamán also suggested that the Cubans might seize the opportunity to ask for the protection of either Great Britain or the United States. How would Washington respond to such a transfer of the island?

In reply, Butler extended the good will of his government but told the Secretary that it was not the role of the United States to come between the two belligerents. For years Washington had attempted to use its influence—without success, Butler pointed out—to get Madrid to recognize the independence of her former colonies. As for Cuba, the Chargé believed that under the tenets of the Monroe Doctrine the United States would not approve the transfer of the island to either England or France. Although the crisis passed and the second invasion did not occur, neither the time nor the government seemed opportune for the resolution of outstanding Mexican-American problems.[13]

Van Buren had glumly told Butler of the increasing hostility of the

Mexicans in recent years; in fact, he confessed to the Chargé, the President could not think of one friendly act toward the United States. Unfortunately for American ambitions, this ill feeling intensified in the following months. As historian Gene Brack has emphasized, the Mexicans came to realize that the United States was not a benevolent ally to aid and protect them from their enemies, but another grasping foreign power that sought to take advantage of their internal problems to enhance its empire. In 1829, General Manuel Mier y Terán had submitted a detailed report of his commission's investigation into the question of Texas. The General elaborated upon the danger of American immigration and the imperative of reducing Yankee influence in the province by curtailing that influx. Texas was vital, he argued, for Mexican security and the foodstuffs it produced. Forts must be built, troops stationed in them, and sovereignty reasserted. Mier y Terán's report dovetailed with the information of José Maria Tornel, Mexican Minister to the United States, regarding the desire of the Jackson administration to acquire Texas. Tornel agreed with the General that measures must be taken immediately to secure the province. Accordingly, in the spring of 1830, Foreign Secretary Alamán successfully moved within the Mexican Congress to implement the recommendations restricting immigration. But Mexico irregularly enforced the 1830 law, and in spite of the military occupation of the province, immigration continued.[14]

Butler ignored the anti-American signals of the Bustamente regime and continued to express hope for a resolution of the Texas issue, optimistically predicting that a settlement could be reached within six months. In spite of recent Mexican legislation to the contrary, no doubt Alamán's cordiality on the issue of American aid in the event of a Spanish invasion, and his agreement to appoint commissioners to discuss a commercial treaty, gave the Chargé unreasonable expectations for a compromise on Texas. Only new April instructions from Van Buren put a halt to Butler's activity regarding Texas, obliging him to concentrate his efforts on the boundary issue and a commercial treaty— with some success: by December, he had concluded a trade agreement with Alamán granting most-favored-nation status to the United States, no discriminatory duties, and neutral rights in time of war. The pact was officially signed in April 1831. At the same time, Butler agreed to sign the long-delayed Poinsett boundary treaty of January 1828, which (also in harmony with the Transcontinental Treaty of 1819) set the Sabine River as the border. Although this was guaranteed not to please the President, and Butler's infrequent correspondence had brought him the admonition of the State Department, his stock rose sharply with the success of the commercial negotiations. Jackson now expected him to proceed with the Texas question.[15]

A new sense of urgency had developed when the President heard the disturbing news that a movement was afoot in the West, led by his old lieutenant from the War of 1812, Sam Houston, to liberate Texas and establish an independent government. Jackson strongly opposed such an effort and instructed Butler in February 1831 to warn the Mexicans about the scheme. Old Hickory pledged to do all he could to stop it, but the Mexicans must realize that he had limited power to act in such matters, especially if the organization occurred west of the Sabine River. But since Americans would be involved in large numbers, the United States would undoubtedly be accused of sanctioning the operation.[16]

In Jackson's mind, the obvious solution was the prompt sale of the province to the United States. Jackson knew the potential difficulty of attempting to annex an independent Texas: open, extended debate in Congress would fuel the fires of antislavery and possibly prevent the acquisition. Indeed, if Texas were added by either purchase or annexation, the antislavery arguments would not evaporate, but the President much preferred the *fait accompli* method used by Jefferson in the purchase of Louisiana in 1803. Jackson's adrenalin flowed even faster with the rumor of pending British encroachment: the White House learned in August that if the United States did not buy Texas, Great Britain would. Solid evidence existed that even if the British did not obtain the province, the strong bond between Texas cotton and English mills would give the crown unacceptable influence in a new Texas republic.[17]

The pressure on Butler increased appreciably. Basking in his recent commercial treaty triumph, he had only lethargically pursued the Texas acquisition, but Jackson's orders produced some movement. The Chargé lamely explained in May that the time had not been right for an exploration of the Texas issue, but he would make the appropriate inquiries. A month later he requested that the President raise the proffered purchase price from $5 million to $7 million. Jackson refused.[18]

In October, Butler cautiously approached Alamán about the transfer of Texas. The Foreign Secretary evasively suggested that it would be unconstitutional for the central government to surrender property that was part of the national confederacy without state approval, but Butler remained optimistic that if he could overcome Alamán's scruples on this point of state sovereignty, the transfer could occur. Jackson disputed the Mexican position, arguing that certainly Alamán's government must be able to deal with the controversial territory. Apparently, the President was not considering the almost simultaneous problems he was having with Maine over the surrender of territory to Great Britain. At this point, however, Butler wisely did not press the issue. Renewed political turbulence combined with Mexican sensitivity to force the Chargé to maintain a lower profile throughout the remainder of the year.[19]

The chief executive exerted renewed pressure in 1832. Jackson, unhappy over the boundary agreement, felt obliged to forward it to the Senate but told Littleton Tazewell, chairman of the Foreign Affairs Committee, that he hoped action on the treaty would be postponed until the next session. If that proved impossible, Jackson wanted the Senate to delay by arguing for an interpretation that would give the United States the west fork of the Sabine, the Neches River. Since the Mexicans were sure to claim that the east fork was meant (the two diverged more than a hundred miles upstream), the subject would again be thrown open to negotiation. To the President's dismay, the Senate approved the treaty in April 1832, making it imperative that Butler push for new talks.

As news of Mexican "oppression" in Texas grew, the President fully expected a revolution within the next six months. He could not allow Texas to slip away. In 1818, Old Hickory had facilitated the United States acquisition of Spanish Florida by his controversial invasion to subdue Indian raiders. He was likely reflecting upon that episode in February 1832 when he told Butler that if the new Texas government were composed of "scoundrels and rogues" who might plunder and murder on the American border, then "this may compel us in self defense to seize that country by force and establish a regular government there over it."[20]

By this time, Butler's zeal to secure Texas was probably exceeded only by his President's. In the summer of 1832, the Chargé toured the northern provinces and returned to find General Santa Anna in command of the government. Talks on the acquisition began in July, and Butler—quickly sizing up the new leader and Mexico's depressed financial state—confided to Jackson that part of the $5 million purchase amount would be used to "facilitate negotiations." This would be handled, of course, through a secret article in the treaty. Butler conferred with Luis Alamán, who had recently resigned his post but still remained highly visible in government circles. The Chargé boasted that the deal would be completed in three months and that he held "the key to unlock his [Alamán's] heart." [21]

Whether Alamán solicited a bribe for himself or for Santa Anna is unclear; Butler's failure to acquire Texas that summer is not. Although not authorizing any bribery attempts, Old Hickory was not shocked by the discussion of personal payment for public service. He had told Butler when he dispatched him to Mexico City, "I scarcely ever knew a Spaniard who was not the slave of avarice, and it is not improbable that this weakness may be worth a great deal to us in this case." [22] Unfortunately for the administration, the ongoing chaos of Mexican politics disrupted all possibilities of negotiations, ethical or not. Butler alternately exulted about his progress and complained about the collapse of the most recent government.

By 1833, Jackson's patience with Butler had worn thin. Communication with Houston told the President that revolution was in the wind. Sensing that he could no longer use the political situation as an excuse, Butler emphasized that a new government would take office in April, and he dramatically pledged, "I will succeed in uniting Texas to our country before I am done with the subject or I will forfeit my head." The possibility existed that Jackson might call for it. Grasping at straws, the Chargé proposed in February a scheme to "mortgage" Texas for $5 million. The state would be transferred to the United States and, of course, the "loan" would not be repaid. This idea met with a resounding lack of enthusiasm in Washington. Secretary of State Livingston informed the Chargé that the plan was unconstitutional. Jackson caustically declared that he hoped he did not die before Butler concluded the talks. The President urged him "to bring the negotiations to a close." [23]

Throughout the remainder of 1833, Butler attempted to wind his way through the Byzantine maze of Mexican politics. Soon he became trapped between the hostile reluctance of the Mexican government to sell Texas and the rising tide of revolution and independence in the province. In correspondence with Jackson in September and October, Butler reported that hundreds of thousands of dollars in bribes had been discussed with various officials in the government. One individual close to Santa Anna had suggested that the sum of $200,000– $300,000 paid to a "very important man," plus an additional several hundred thousand scattered about, would produce the cession of Texas. (Although Butler considered Santa Anna "a vile hypocrite and most unprincipled man," the diplomat, even while entertaining the bribes, somehow saw himself guiltless.) His optimism rapidly fading regarding a legitimate treaty, Butler also requested Jackson to send the army into the Nacogdoches region west of the Sabine. The weak justification for such provocative action was the negative temper toward the United States of the regime in Mexico City and its treatment of American ships and citizens in the midst of the political turbulence.[24]

While not naive about the reported cupidity of Mexican politicians, the President remained stunned by Butler's comments and suggestions, which he had neglected to write in cypher. Old Hickory had told his agent that it was incidental to him whether the Mexicans used the $5 million "for the purchase of men or to pay the public debt"; all he desired was the unencumbered cession of the territory and a permanent boundary west of the Sabine. But Butler was not to use the funds for bribery. Jackson drew a pragmatic line between knowing what certain governmental officials might do with the $5 million after it was delivered, and the prior act of paying bribes to Mexican officials to persuade them to cede the territory. If such activity were revealed in Washington, it would arouse the righteous indignation of an uninformed Congress—and destroy the possibility of annexation.[25]

Amazingly, Butler evidenced no contrition but rather lectured the President on his lack of knowledge of the Mexican character and of the prevalence of corruption in high places. Again he discussed the essential nature of bribery and his impression that it was of no consequence to Jackson how the $5 million was disbursed; again he urged the President to use force to obtain the area west of the Sabine. This time, however, the Chargé—who seemed increasingly to be losing his grip on reality—suggested that he be withdrawn from Mexico City and made the head of the Texas territory.[26]

Jackson finally realized that his diplomat had outlived his usefulness and must be recalled. In a stroke of understatement, he noted "A. Butler: What a scamp" on the Chargé's March 7 letter. Since the President had already ordered Secretary of State McLane to instruct Butler to gain an extension for the commission established by the 1828 treaty to discuss the boundary line, he decided that Butler could bring this extension agreement personally to Washington. If Butler failed to obtain the proviso, he should be recalled anyway.[27]

Butler's removal turned out to be neither as graceful nor as prompt as the President desired. The Chargé rebutted the executive request for a new boundary commission extension by reporting that the Mexican Congress would not meet until January 1835. Could he remain in Mexico the additional six months? New Secretary of State John Forsyth left the matter in Jackson's hands but naively suggested that "probably no evil consequence" would result from Butler's continued presence. From the summer of 1834 into the spring of 1835 the Chargé continued to bombard the President with optimistic reports of negotiations with Santa Anna on a treaty that would give the United States all it could ask.[28]

While such a pact did not materialize, Butler surprisingly did achieve an agreement in April 1835 for a joint commission to survey the disputed territory between the Sabine and the Neches Rivers. He dutifully proceeded to Washington with the treaty and a new proposal for acquiring Texas. In a June 9 meeting with Jackson and Forsyth, Butler urged that the administration provide $500,000 to be "judiciously applied" to Father Ignacio Hernandez, a clerical confidant of Santa Anna, in order to attain the territory. Jackson would not go along with the scheme, explaining that as much as he wanted to alter the boundary, "no means of an equivocal character shall be used to accomplish it." The White House cautioned Butler that "nothing will be countenanced by the Executive to bring this government under the remotest imputation of being engaged in corruption or bribery." Instead of seizing the moment and immediately relieving the Chargé of his commission, however, the President foolishly allowed him to return to Mexico and gave him another six months to resolve the issue.[29]

Even allowing for his modest successes, Anthony Butler remains among the most questionable of Jackson's foreign policy appointments. The President selected him, as he did many other diplomats, because of personal friendship and political loyalty; Butler's timely presentation of ideas on the future of Texas had blended nicely with Jackson's expansionist visions and the diplomatic difficulties of Joel Poinsett. But other contemporaries viewed him with disdain: John Quincy Adams accused him of loose moral principles, political profligacy, vanity, and self-sufficiency; Sam Houston simply stated that Butler was "a much worse man than anyone body else [*sic*]" Houston knew.[30]

Historians unanimously agree. George Rives uses such words as "insolent, scurrilous, vain, ignorant, ill-tempered and corrupt" to describe Butler. Alvin Duckett likewise scorns him, citing John Bassett's evaluation: "His [Butler's] chief object seems to have been to prolong his period of employment and to overcast his failure by deluding the administration with false hopes." Gene Brack denounces him as "an arrogant, vulgar, and calculating person completely devoid of those qualities normally expected in a diplomat." Eugene McCormac contemptuously calls him "conceited, arrogant, boastful and unprincipled, and a disgrace to the nation which he represented." Less emotionally, John Niven points out that Butler "gravely weakened the American position [in Mexico] by his persistent and underhanded schemes to detach Texas." Robert Remini simply dismisses him as "a certifiable scamp."[31]

Several historians, notably Richard Stenberg and more recently Michael Rogin, are critical not only of Butler but also of Jackson. They suggest that the President, far from being an innocent bystander, was a coconspirator in the scheme to bribe and manipulate Mexican officials.[32]

The evidence to indict the President for conspiring with Butler in his bribery schemes appears inconclusive. Jackson's perception of the Latin character did suggest to him that some sort of payoff would occur. Old Hickory believed, however, that if the payment took place among the Mexicans themselves after the cession of Texas, then American integrity would not be sacrificed. He consistently refused to cooperate in his agent's covert plans to provide advance monies, and expressed genuine outrage and sorrow over any of Butler's actions that might have both compromised the administration and affected the acquisition itself.

The question of Jackson's moral culpability and Butler's shady character should also be discussed separately from their goals, given the climate south of the border. Butler had, after all, achieved some success in negotiating both commercial and boundary treaties in a tense environment. Given the political turmoil in Mexico, the growing suspicion of the Yankee colossus, and the intrigues of Great Britain, it is unlikely that any agent could have obtained the territory. Discord had ripped Mexico apart by 1835. Seeking to find fault with others for their problems, Latin editors and politicians began to blame the United States for the difficulties in Texas; the Americans, they argued, had stirred the Texas cauldron, and provoked and abetted dissension in the province. Many Mexicans expressed the concern that once the Yankees overran Texas, Mexico herself would become the next imperial target.

With the Mexican mind in a state of both excitement and paranoia, Jackson made a foolish error in sending Butler back to Mexico City. He did so out of loyalty to his old friend, not because he was optimistic about the possibility of resolution of the Texas issue. If Butler ever possessed credibility, it had vanished by the summer of 1835. Yet the President, perhaps under political pressures from New England fishing interests, instructed the Chargé to offer the Mexicans an additional $500,000 for San Francisco Bay. The timing of the proposition could not have been worse. The Texans rose up in rebellion that autumn, and Mexican officials blamed the Chargé for instigating the revolt. Mexico City asked for his recall in October, but Butler preferred to remain in the capital and attempt to negotiate the interests of his land speculating company.[33]

Finally, however, protesting all the while that just a few more months would lead to a successful conclusion of the Texas question, Butler was replaced in January 1836 by Powhatan Ellis, a former judge and United States senator from Mississippi. Ellis received wise instructions not to press for territorial gains but to counteract Washington's image problem in Mexico City and reassure the government of American good intentions. He was also to argue for the resolution of American claims against the Mexicans, incurred during the various revolutionary outbursts and ultimately totaling about $6.6 million.

Ellis arrived in Mexico City in April 1836—a particularly sensitive time of the Texas revolution. The Alamo and its legendary defenders had fallen in March, but on April 21, Santa Anna had been caught unprepared at San Jacinto, where he was captured and obliged to sign a treaty allowing for Texan independence and the Rio Grande boundary. Since the agreement had been signed under duress and without the authorization of the Mexican government, however, Santa Anna's concessions were repudiated soon after his release.[34]

The United States position with Mexico was severely compromised by the success of the Texas rebellion. Prior to 1836, most Americans had given little thought to Texas, its acquisition, or its independence, but the republic now became a *cause célèbre*. The Americans eagerly provided men, money, and supplies; companies of volunteers formed, and these "emigrants" sailed off for Texas. Jackson, his own feelings hardly neutral, attempted to take the high road for his nation. His response to a desperate plea from Stephen Austin in April 1836 for American aid to throw back Santa Anna was a reassertion of United States neutrality: the President jotted on the appeal letter that the United States had a treaty with Mexico and that the national faith was pledged to it. The Texans, he penned, should have considered this before they engaged in the "rash and premature" act of revolution.[35]

Soon after the war began in October 1835, the Texans sent three commissioners, led by Austin, to seek aid and support in the United States. In New York, as elsewhere, they encountered enthusiastic audiences. One such rally was led by Collector of the Port Samuel Swartwout, a well-known Jacksonian. Levi Woodbury received a pro-Texas broadside from Swartwout, prompting presidential criticism and an admonishment to avoid breaching the official neutrality of the United States. Although the administration attempted to assure Gorostizo and the Mexican government that the United States viewed the revolution as a domestic affair and would assure absolute neutrality, such logic evaporated when the Mexicans observed the rallies, parades, recruiting, and supplying done by Americans for the revolution. All this was quite within the law, of course, but the Mexicans could not really comprehend that such activities could be conducted without the approval of the government.

The President's course therefore was to abide by the treaty and do nothing overt to offend the Mexicans. He definitely blundered in the spring of 1836, however, by dispatching General Edmund P. Gaines to the Sabine with an army to protect that area from depredations by Texans, Mexicans, or marauding Indians. Gaines arrived on the Louisiana border about the same time that Santa Anna moved his army toward San Jacinto. Understandably, this preventive strategy made Mexican Minister Gorostiza more than uncomfortable. The situation collapsed in July when Gaines, even though the Mexican Army had retreated south of the Rio Grande, ordered troops into the region west of the Sabine, ostensibly in pursuit of the Caddo Indians. Jackson quickly realized that the rumor of a red menace was fabricated, probably in New Orleans, by vested interests and accordingly put Gaines on a short leash, granting him discretionary power to move into Texas and take "speedy and decisive action" only if it was imperative and in accord with strict neutrality.

Gorostiza, of course, protested vehemently, interpreting this order as a subterfuge to guarantee Texan independence. His complaints fell on deaf ears in Washington, as neither Forsyth nor Jackson felt apologetic. The Secretary told Gorostiza that under the 1832 treaty the Americans had the right to penetrate into Mexico itself if the security of the border warranted it. Gaines's troops remained in the Nacogdoches area on the flimsiest of evidence, a constant irritant to the helpless Mexican government. Even though the General exercised questionable judgment, Jackson was not going to apologize to Gorostiza for the invasion or occupation. The frustrated Mexican diplomat—angered at the curt responses to his protests, the seemingly unneutral stance of the Jackson administration, and the unnecessary violation of the sovereignty of Mexican territory—asked for his passports and returned to Mexico City by the end of the year.[36]

At the same time, south of the border, Ellis harvested the fruits of Mexican anger at the United States. His primary responsibility had been shifted to the resolution of the claims question, an issue of importance to the President. The Mexicans had grudgingly acknowledged responsibility in a few cases over the years but reversed this policy in the spring of 1836 on the grounds that the Americans, through their support of the Texas revolution, had forfeited any right to the claims. The Mexican government would no longer discuss them. By July, Jackson's patience vanished, and he ordered Ellis to return to Washington if no progress was made. Ellis did so in December, closing the legation.[37]

The crumbling of relations between the United States and Mexico in 1836 could only be exacerbated by the burning question of the recognition of Texan independence. The matter was far from easy to resolve. Agents of the Republic of Texas were very active, and there was heavy political pressure applied to the chief executive to view recognition favorably. By the summer of 1836, petitions from around the nation had poured into the Democratic Congress, where opinions seemed divided between the supportive Senate and the more reluctant House of Representatives. The debates revealed that many of the House reservations were founded on the idea that the proposal to recognize Texas was part of a slave expansion conspiracy. A majority in Congress leaned toward recognition, but a formal deadlock between the two chambers resulted in failure to take join action before the July 4 adjournment.

This placed the matter squarely on the President's shoulders. Jackson had already decided to send a special agent, Henry Morfit, to Texas to determine the fitness of the infant republic for independence. Morfit was to ascertain the political, civil, and military situation and the feeling of Texans regarding annexation to the United States. The mission was not secretive, and Morfit was given letters of introduction to leading Texas politicos. He proved to be one of Jackson's more capable agents. In the six weeks he spent in Texas, he met with the most important figures in the republic, and his reports to the President were frequent, informative, and impartial.[38]

Morfit was clearly impressed with the energy and ability of the Texas leadership: provisional President David G. Burnet, Secretary of War Mirabeau Lamar, and Generals Sam Houston and T. J. Rusk. The army, comprising 2,000 actives and 3,000 reserves, was well equipped and combat-ready. While the early battles for the republic had been fought by Texans of some years in residence, the forces now included recent volunteers from the United States. The navy, consisting of three 9-gun vessels, was likewise small but tough. Morfit's communiqués emphasized that further military action was expected: the Texans proposed one expedition against Matamoras and another, in league with the Comanches, against Chihuahua.

The major political issue, Morfit reported, was deciding the fate of Santa Anna; the "extremists" wanted him executed, while the "moderates" would exchange him for bargaining leverage in the treaty negotiations. Morfit spoke with the General, who assured him that upon returning to Mexico City he would use his good offices to deal favorably with the independence issue. Santa Anna opined that Jackson would be a good choice to resolve the dilemma. The President replied to this suggestion in September, noting that as a prisoner, the General no longer represented his government; therefore, Jackson must remain neutral until Mexico City asked for his intervention. As for the boundary, after some earlier discussion of extending it to reach California, the Texans resolved to ask only for the Rio Grande. The new republic's finances appeared solid, its debt was small, and public land sales would yield millions in revenues. Morfit perceptively noted, however, that the republic's position was tenuous and that its longevity could hinge on the outcome of a single battle. Its fate depended more on the weakness of Mexico than on the strength of Texas.

Fortunately for the Texans, Mexico was struggling with internal problems. In Santa Anna's absence, political factionalism was rife in the capital city, and the treasury was bare. It would be difficult to raise another army to cross the Rio Grande. But Mexico had eight million people; once her situation stabilized, the Texans, only 50,000 strong, would have problems resisting without foreign aid. Morfit's chalkboard, then, revealed numerous pros and cons: the huge, struggling young republic was rich in potential but could be felled by a glancing blow. He adjudged that most Texans desired annexation to the United States; they had voted overwhelmingly for it on September 5 and had, thus far, made no overtures to any other foreign powers. In the final analysis, even if annexation were not forthcoming, the agent decided, Texas did have the capability of surviving.[39]

Morfit's reports reached Washington by October 1836, concurrent with the inauguration of the new permanent Texas government under Sam Houston. William F. Wharton, a close friend of Stephen Austin, was given the vital post of Minister to the United States. Wharton met with both Jackson and Forsyth in December and was disappointed to find them still noncommittal. In fact, the information about the Texas vote for annexation had placed them in an embarrassing situation. Jackson personally felt that Texas met the prerequisites for recognition but, sensitive to charges that the United States had interfered in the domestic affairs of Mexico, spoke very cautiously in his annual message to Congress. In effect, the President left the matter to that body to decide without his recommendation.

His hesitancy to urge recognition may have been based upon the conservative advice of incoming President Van Buren and Secretary of State Forsyth, or perhaps upon the physical problems that sapped his energy and affected his attitude. The years had begun to take their toll on Jackson's delicate constitution. At the age of sixty-nine, his six-foot, 140-pound frame was ravaged by old wounds and new diseases. A bullet remained in his body from a long-ago contest. Lung ailments, abdominal pains, and headaches contributed to the deteriorating state of the General's health. Deadly concoctions such as "sugar of lead" were among the "remedies" he ingested. In 1833 the President had almost died following a tour of New England. Now, as he once again began to fail, he rallied for the final struggle of his political career.[40]

Andrew Jackson, in the twilight of his presidency, did not want to create an appearance of collusion between the executive and the Texas revolutionaries by a too rapid recognition of that republic. The sensibilities of both the Europeans and the Mexicans must be soothed. In addition, Santa Anna was about to visit Washington, and the President was hopeful that some agreement might be reached that would make the recognition process unnecessary. This hope vanished when Santa Anna appeared in January and was ignored by the Mexican Chargé, a sure sign that the General did not represent his government. Political considerations also played a role, since Jackson did not wish to embarrass the newly elected Van Buren administration by taking an executive course incompatible with the sentiments of a Congress containing a vocal antislave element and one apprehensive of war with Mexico. Forsyth, who had never been a policymaker, opposed both recognition and annexation on political and diplomatic grounds (considering the United States treaty with Mexico). By denying Wharton's diplomatic delegation a formal hearing, the Secretary had scrupulously avoided legitimizing the Texas position.

In any case the legislators were surprised by the lack of vigor in the often impetuous Old Warrior's address to Congress. Wharton and his colleagues angrily viewed the President's course as "cold-blooded and ungenerous." But one perceptive Texas booster, Fairfax Catlatt, while noting his disappointment, suggested that the message was motivated by expediency and the desire to placate the Mexicans and Europeans. The Texas delegation had only to regroup and work with greater zeal in 1837. Wharton remained optimistic: he wrote Austin that he was "certain" of ultimate Texas recognition but warned his compatriot that annexation was unlikely, given the omnipresent issue of slavery, which divided and threatened the nation.[41]

The first months of 1837, and the revitalization of Old Hickory's fragile health, brought new revelations from the White House. Jackson, having assumed a nonaggressive posture for international and domestic consumption in his December 21 message, was now prepared to launch a more typical assault in support of recognition. Meeting with William Wharton on February 9, the President explained that while he favored the immediate recognition of Texas, he could not send another message to Congress on the issue. If a congressional majority recommended recognition, then Jackson committed himself to a favorable response. But, he emphasized, Texas should stake a claim for California if it hoped to paralyze the northeastern opposition, a group that would perhaps compromise its antislavery position to gain the valuable fishing and trading port of San Francisco.[42]

Jackson was motivated by more than the fear that Texas recognition would be lost because of antislavery sentiment. Rumors of English military involvement in the Texas-Mexican War had surfaced in the summer of 1836. Such involvement, it was feared, might eventually result in British control of Mexico and domination of the Gulf, a position incompatible with American commercial and territorial interests. Minister Powhatan Ellis reported that the Mexicans planned to utilize the ruse of antislavery to involve Great Britain; their ploy would be to solicit British aid to restrain the extension of slavery. Since the revolutionary Texans violated the Mexican constitution by owning slaves, English assistance might be required to put down the rebellion and halt the spread of the institution. Secretary Forsyth, implementing the Monroe Doctrine without specifically referring to the document, instructed Andrew Stevenson in London to inform Lord Palmerston that the United States would not tolerate the interference of any European power in Texas, and that such intervention would oblige Washington to take defensive action to prevent it. Forsyth contended, erroneously, that it mattered little to Americans whether Texas approved or forbade slavery, but the Jackson administration would not tolerate the dictation of Texas domestic policy by a foreign power.[43]

When Palmerston and Stevenson discussed the issue frankly in October 1836, the Foreign Secretary admitted that he had conferred upon the subject with the Mexicans. Although individual Americans had been nonneutral in the conflict, Palmerston believed that the President had striven to keep his government above the fray; consequently, he had declined the Mexican request for intervention. Palmerston was surely not intimidated by the threats of American interposition, but he had a record of cordiality toward the Jackson administration, and a Mexican civil war was not sufficient cause to destroy that positive relationship.[44]

Another factor, and one of increased concern to Old Hickory in January 1837, was the dominant role that Great Britain might play in a new Texas Republic. An independent Texas between the United States and Mexico would provide a buffer to American expansion. Meanwhile, British penetration of the Texas cotton economy through loans and purchases could place London in a position of overriding influence. Stephen Austin threatened as much in a letter to the President, declaring that if American recognition were not promptly forthcoming, the Texans would negotiate a pact with Great Britain, offering her exclusive commercial privileges. Jackson did not respond well to such threats, but the message was clear: the longer the United States delayed recognition, the more it furthered the opportunities of the English.

But the wheels of democracy turned slowly. By the end of January 1837, Congress had still not taken up the Texas issue. Such other matters as the admission of the Michigan territory, antislavery petitions, and public land sales had captured the attention of the cautious legislators. Senator Robert John Walker of Mississippi introduced a Texas recognition resolution in mid-January but attached no immediacy to its consideration. Consequently, the measure languished into the next month. When it was called up, the bill met opposition from some of the leading Jacksonians, who sensed the explosive nature of the slavery issue. The vote resulted in postponement until March. When the debate began, Walker and Calhoun led the South and West in supporting recognition; Clay and Buchanan championed the Northeast in opposition. A deadlock, 24 to 24, told the pro-Texas cadre that the measure was definitely in trouble in the Senate. Meanwhile, the House Committee on Foreign Affairs, chaired by Waddy Thompson of South Carolina, on February 18 reported favorably on recognition, but the full House voted 98 to 86 to table the matter.

Congress escaped the political quagmire by throwing the issue back to the President: the members decided during the first week of March to grant Jackson the power to appoint a representative to Texas whenever he had reason to believe that it had become "an independent power." Since Morfit's mission had already convinced Old Hickory of that point, the President was prepared to move immediately. On March 3 he named Alcee LaBranche of Louisiana as Chargé to Texas. By the following week Jackson was gone from the White House, but Congress approved the selection without opposition. Forsyth and Van Buren had their reservations, but the Old Man would have his last hurrah. During the summer of 1837, the agents of the two republics formally took their places.[45]

Jackson's relations with Mexico were part of a continuum, picking up the pieces of the Adams administration's goals of gaining a commercial treaty, extending the boundary, and adding Texas to the Union. He added one issue—the claims of American merchants for losses during the revolutions—which was a constant unresolved irritant. Jackson wished to purchase Texas and to do so quietly, without drawing the attention of the American people or Congress to this potentially dangerous subject. He succeeded in maintaining the low profile of his negotiations, even through the indiscretions of the unstable and self-seeking Butler. When the Texas Revolution began, it spelled the doom of the President's dream of annexation.

Jackson had been steadfastly opposed to the rebellion, and those who argue that he conspired with Sam Houston to launch such a movement are incorrect. He knew that a revolution in Texas would compromise Butler's mission and draw international attention to North America, and that the United States government would receive the blame for fomenting or aiding any insurrection. Jackson attempted to maintain the facade of official neutrality in a nation that generally viewed the Texas struggle as a noble crusade. The President himself could not wish for the failure of the revolution; his unneutral dispatch of Gaines and accompanying unsympathetic attitude toward Gorostiza's protests demonstrate a reluctant acceptance of a rebellion he initially opposed. The General had hoped to purchase Texas and expand the borders of the United States perhaps to San Francisco Bay; he was reluctantly obliged to settle for the recognition of the Lone Star Republic, an unstable nation ripe for British intrigue, whose annexation the anti-slavery forces rendered unlikely. Only four months before his death in June 1845 did Jackson's imperial dream become a reality, when Congress approved the admission of Texas to the Union.

The Texas issue, primary as it became in the 1830s, combined with the claims and boundary issues to destroy Mexican-American relations during the decade. Before Old Hickory left the White House, he informed Congress that Mexico had provided just cause for war through her insults, attitude, and recalcitrance in negotiating the claims. The President urged Congress to take reprisals if the posture of the Mexican government did not promptly change.

Historian Herman Von Holst had depicted Jackson's policy on the claims as "an unworthy comedy," designed to provoke a war with Mexico and facilitate Texas annexation. John Quincy Adams had earlier argued the point in the House of Representatives. But the Tennesseean was leaving office, and a less than bellicose Congress agreed to the reappointment of Powhatan Ellis and a second chance for negotiated settlement. The claims issue would, in fact, be settled to the satisfaction of most Americans by an international commission in 1842. But the missions of Poinsett and Butler and the attitude of the Jackson administration had been much too abrasive on the disruptive questions of the day, leaving a legacy of bitterness and suspicion that would reach its unhappy fruition in the Mexican-American War of 1846.[46]

THE ISTHMUS

For a brief time in the mid-1820s, American attention focused upon Central America. Not only did the United States negotiate a commercial treaty with the new Central American Republic (C.A.R.) in 1825, but the Panama Congress became the subject of heated debate in the Congress and press. American participation in the inter-American gathering was, of course, doomed by internal political bickering, while an English representative anxiously observed the proceedings. The unwillingness of the United States to involve itself in the affairs of the isthmus through the decade facilitated British influence in the young Central American Republic. The House of Barclay had lent over 1.5 million pounds to the Guatemala-based confederation, and British-controlled Belize acted as a funnel for the indigo trade, the republic's major export. The United States, once again, had no capital to lend to developing nations and showed little active interest in developing trade along the isthmus.

By 1829 no real Anglo-American rivalry existed in the area, because there was virtually no Yankee presence except for two consuls stationed at Guatemala City and Truxillo, Honduras. Occasionally, these agents would complain about the English presence in Belize, or denounce the English occupation of the Bay Islands off Honduras as a territorial incursion on the C.A.R. Since the British had been there prior to 1823, it was debatable whether this constituted a violation of the Monroe Doctrine. No American chargé stayed long enough at the capital to protest formally. In 1827, John Quincy Adams had dispatched William Rochester, who returned to New York without ever reaching Guatemala, and Jackson considered the post so insignificant that he pleaded with Van Buren to run interference for him with those eager merchants promoting the appointment. The Secretary told them the government simply did not have the $4,500 available for the salary.[47]

The lack of interest and abdication of influence in Central America disappeared quickly in 1831 when Jackson learned of a treaty between the Dutch government and the C.A.R. for a canal across the isthmus. According to the agreement, a private Dutch firm would construct and operate the canal, which would be neutral territory. While not even the Dutch government would receive most-favored-nation status in the treaty, the firm would profit handsomely from the duties collected. The canal would remain under C.A.R. sovereignty, but the foreign company would control the operations until it recovered its investment.[48]

The United States itself had expressed an interest in a canal project during the Adams presidency. The C.A.R.'s minister in Washington had spoken with Secretary of State Henry Clay about a waterway, and both were enthusiastic about such a project. Adams and Clay accordingly pushed to have the subject of a canal placed on the agenda of the ill-fated Panama Congress. American representatives Richard Anderson and John Sergeant were both enthusiastic and idealistic in their approach to the new route: "The benefit of it not ought [*sic*] to be exclusively appropriated to any one nation, but should be extended to all parts of the Globe." While nothing came of their recommendation— anything the unpopular Adams administration urged fell upon deaf ears—the idea of an Atlantic-to-Pacific canal remained alive in the minds of North Americans, Latins, and Europeans alike.[49]

Domestic problems with the Belgian revolution doomed the Dutch project, but a nerve had been touched in Washington. Secretary of State Livingston responded promptly to word of the treaty. He wanted to be certain that no nation received better treatment than the United States in interoceanic tariffs, and that this accord would not negatively affect the emerging East Indian, Philippine, and China trade. President Jackson, who was particularly interested in the canal and the impact it would have on American commerce, received a lengthy letter from a New York correspondent detailing the advantages and costs of a trans-isthmian route. Although skeptical of a canal because of geography and cost, the writer believed a combined railroad and steam navigation link feasible and urged an active American role to guarantee the neutrality of the passage.[50]

Accordingly, the President named William Jeffers of New Jersey as Chargé in July 1831, with instructions stressing that "a ship canal would render a good understanding between the United States and that republic an object of primary importance to us." Livingston was more concerned about insuring the American position than about the proposal to carve a canal through Nicaragua. But, he advised Jeffers, "should the grant not be completed, you will endeavor to procure for the citizens of the United States, or for the government itself, if Congress should deem the measure constitutional and proper, the right of subscribing to the stock (should it be issued later)." The Secretary wanted all available information on the feasibility of the project and on the geography and trade of the area.[51]

Jeffers reached Pensacola by August 1831, where a letter caught up with him from the Secretary relieving him of his post. It seems that Jeffers had been indicted for forgery of a collateral bond in Cincinnati in 1810; he had posted a $50 bond but never appeared for adjudication. A grand jury had followed up this proceeding, and an indictment was yet pending. The much-embarrassed administration replaced Jeffers with James Shannon of Lexington, Kentucky, in February 1832. Unfortunately, Shannon died that summer on his way to Guatemala. His successor was Charles De Witt of New York, a two-term Democratic Congressman who had recently lost a reelection bid. De Witt's nomination prompted a letter from Van Buren complaining to the President that the appointment had been badly received in the Empire State. The Red Fox conceded that De Witt was a "well disposed man, but vastly inferior in the general estimation of the people to a station like the one in question." In a rare sardonic moment with his trusted friend, the President responded, "I would remark that the Secretary of State [Livingston] and many of your friends in New York were the cause of the selection of Mr. De Witt."[52]

De Witt proved to be a disappointing choice. First his health prevented him from departing immediately for Guatemala; then he requested permission to travel around Cape Horn and up the Pacific Coast to his post. The President, anxious that no further time be lost, denied the request, but by September De Witt was still dallying in New York. Only Livingston's threat that the appointment would be canceled on October 1 hastened his departure. The rumor of a recently negotiated French treaty with the C.A.R. daily increased fears in Washington, but the New Chargé's presence in Guatemala did little to strengthen the American position. He wrote the State Department infrequently and by the spring of 1835 had failed to comply with his orders to forward the much-desired information on the proposed canal project. An angry Jackson demanded that this material be sent immediately.[53]

Although the Dutch project in Nicaragua had foundered, the government of New Granada created additional interest in May 1834 when it issued a decree throwing open construction through its Panamanian province for international bids. An 1829 study commissioned by Bolívar and conducted by British engineer John Lloyd had verified the possibility of a canal or road across Panama. The builders would receive 100,000 acres of land and revenue for ten to fifty years. Proposals had to arrive in Bogotá by January 15, 1835, when bids would be opened and the best contract recommended to the legislature.[54]

Both Old Hickory and Foreign Relations Committee Chairman Henry Clay realized the project's importance to American trade and security. Aware of British influence in Mexico, the C.A.R., and the former Gran Colombian confederation, the President sought to forestall additional European inroads in an area so sensitive to American interests. Clay agreed, and his committee recommended that the executive appoint a commissioner to travel to the Central American Republic and New Granada and investigate the possibility of a canal. The Senate concurred with this suggestion on March 3, 1835.

The importance of a transisthmian route and the unique position of Central America in Jacksonian foreign policy at this point was mirrored in two specific actions taken by the administration. In the summer of 1831, Jackson learned from the President of the C.A.R. that dissident residents of his republic had been promoting friction between the C.A.R. and Mexico in the hope of inciting a war. The Latin leader wished Old Hickory to use the influence of his office to assure the Mexicans that these words or actions were not representative of the government of the C.A.R. Jackson promptly instructed his minister in Mexico City, Anthony Butler, to provide such assurances from the United States "as a common friend interested in reestablishing harmony or preventing misunderstanding between members of the great family of American Republics." On several occasions, the President had had the opportunity to provide his good offices in South America but refused. Obviously, the C.A.R. and especially Mexico were nations whose stability was of greater importance to the United States than that of previous petitioners.[55]

American good will could have made inroads in Guatemala, where relations with Great Britain became increasingly strained in the 1830s. The C.A.R. wearied of the economic control of the British crown and sought help both in Washington and European capitals. In 1834 the republic dispatched an Irishman named John Galindo to seek volunteers to aid in the recovery of disputed lands from Great Britain. He hoped to persuade Secretary of State Forsyth that the English settlements were in violation of the Monroe Doctrine and merited American censure. Equally important was his assignment to obtain funds from the American government or private investors for a canal project. But Galindo did not arrive in Washington until June 1835, by which time the ever-alert British Minister Charles Vaughan had spoken with Forsyth about the impropriety of American intervention in the matter. The Secretary of State met with Galindo and reaffirmed American interest in a transisthmian route (especially since a canal would juxtapose nicely with the trade goals of the second Roberts mission to Asia), but Forsyth would not interfere in the land dispute. The Monroe Doctrine remained a defensive political statement; Jackson would not endanger critical Anglo-American relations over the cutting of Belize hardwood.[56]

The President's decision not to involve the United States in the Central American–English imbroglio did not compromise his commitment to foster the goal of a canal, and he proceeded rapidly to identify a candidate for the difficult mission. The task became more difficult because of De Witt's inexcusably lethargic information gathering in Guatemala City; it was questionable how much assistance he would be to the new agent. Conversely, Robert McAfee in Bogotá had proven himself a capable if undistinguished chargé; after two years in New Granada, he was expected to assist in selecting a possible Panamanian route.

The President no doubt surprised many people with the choice of Charles Biddle for the Central American mission. The younger brother of Jackson's antagonist, banker Nicholas Biddle, Charles was a widower with seven children, and a former Philadelphia merchant whose business had failed in 1826. Following this misfortune he had moved to Nashville, where he was admitted to the bar. As for his character, his financial errors had led his father to disinherit him (although he did provide for Charles's children), and his brother Richard regarded his temper as one of "utter recklessness of feeling and conduct," while Nicholas wrote confidentially of "my unfortunate brother Charles whose conduct has been for some years the source of great unhappiness to all our family." But Charles had shown political judgment in working for Jackson's election. In 1832 he established a semiweekly paper, the *Tennessee Reporter*, to support the General's candidacy for a second term. It was at this time that Jackson nominated him to be a district judge in the Florida territory, but the Senate rejected the nomination. Over the next several years Biddle persevered in his attempts to gain political favor, receiving serious consideration for appointment as territorial governor of Michigan. Finally, in 1835, his persistence was rewarded.[57]

Preparing hurriedly for his voyage, the Philadelphian departed for Cuba after making the necessary business contacts in his hometown and New York. Now forty-seven, a slight five feet eight inches, with gray eyes, light hair and complexion, a large nose, round chin, and oval face, the inexperienced Biddle looked perhaps more the part of a Latin teacher than of a presidential commissioner.[58]

His instructions from Forsyth suggested but did not insist that he proceed first to Port St. John, Nicaragua, traverse the St. John River to Lake Nicaragua, and then proceed overland to the Pacific Ocean—in other words, that he follow the possible canal route most widely discussed in contemporary writings. He was then to travel to Guatemala City and obtain all available documents on the legalities of incorporation in the republic and ascertain the involvement of foreign powers in the area. After completing that assignment, the agent was to repeat the procedure in Panama and Bogotá. Forsyth emphasized that this itinerary was not obligatory, and Biddle need not feel tied to it if it hindered the accomplishment of his objective. The Secretary also encouraged him to keep a comprehensive journal and report to the President. For his service, Biddle would receive $6.00 a day plus traveling expenses.[59]

By November 1835, Biddle and his companion, a Dr. Gibbons, had sailed only as far as Kingston, Jamaica. Bad luck and worse information on the scheduled departure of ships had kept them in Santiago de Cuba for five weeks, where Biddle made in-depth observations and reported on the politics and culture of the island. Finally, late in the month, he arrived at the Chagres River (Panama), the only Atlantic port on the isthmus.

While this varied from Forsyth's suggested route, Biddle decided, after discussing the matter with knowledgeable North Americans and Latins, that "the opening of a canal for vessels of heavy tonnage is a chimera and that a canal for vessels of lighter draught cannot be accomplished north of Panama." This "universal and decisive" view seemed to obviate a Nicaraguan crossing. Within a week after his arrival, Biddle was making some startling, naive, but occasionally profound statements about Latin America and a transisthmian route. His estimates of the situation were based in part upon lengthy conversations with a group of Panamanian businessmen and politicians who euphemistically called themselves the "Society of the Friends of Peace."[60] Biddle opined that revolution was likely, perhaps within the year, and Panama would become independent. Already a group of influential men had sought to have the isthmus placed under British protection (an observation guaranteed to agitate Washington), but London refused because it did not wish to offend the United States.

To confuse matters further, in May 1835 the government of New

Granada had granted the transisthmian contract to an Englishman, Charles Thierry. Thierry, a colorful ne'er-do-well who claimed French royal blood and called himself "Baron," succeeded in obtaining the grant apparently because of his supposed connections with British capitalists. After examining the terrain, however, the Baron decided the land was too soft for construction of a railroad and that all the iron for such a project would have to be imported at tremendous cost. A canal seemed the logical alternative, but Thierry could not get the necessary capital for such a venture. He decided to abandon the Panamanian project and accept a government post in recently independent New Zealand.

The Baron's departure cleared the way for United States involvement, but Biddle advised caution. With revolution in the wind and the British reticent to become involved, American interests would be best served by watching and waiting.[61] In the meantime, the commissioner urged the President to fortify the U.S. presence in the region through a greater naval display. This would impress the natives, build confidence in the consuls, and create respect for the United States. Biddle rightly feared that without additional naval protection, the American merchant marine—which controlled 60 percent of the entire tonnage in the Pacific Ocean—would be endangered in a war.[62]

Biddle remained in Panama through December, traversing the isthmus via the Chagres River and four days by muleback to the city of Panama, gathering information but keeping both the politicians in Washington and his so-far-unidentified business associates in Philadelphia and New York generally in the dark about his activities. Biddle's ties with the Society of the Friends of Peace (to which the American consul in Panama, John B. Ferraud, and the Panamanian representative to the Colombian Congress, Don José Obaldia, belonged) became increasingly close over the months. The society wanted not only independence for Panama but also an interoceanic link, which presumably would bring prosperity to the isthmus. After examining the alternative means, the society agreed with Thierry that the heavy cost of shoring up the ground for a railroad was prohibitive, and that a canal would be possible but costly. The best idea was a road connecting with the steamboat route on the Chagres River.[63]

Accompanied by the Panamanian delegation to the Congress of

New Granada, the travel-weary Biddle arrived in Bogotá in March 1836. By this time he was convinced of the viability of a transisthmian road. A ship canal "must be reserved for the patriotic exertions of a future generation"; no well-advised capitalist would invest money in a project that would collapse in "utter ruin." Moreover, a railroad would cost at least $2 million, whereas a comparatively inexpensive road, in combination with steamboats, would carry goods across the isthmus in only twelve hours. Besides, Biddle still feared the expected revolution, as the government had resigned over a treaty dispute and the nation was deeply in debt. All these factors weighed against the heavy investment necessary to build a canal.[64]

In the midst of the governmental crisis in Bogotá, Biddle resolutely, or perhaps naively, pressed his attempt to get the New Granadan Congress, with Panamanian sponsorship, to approve a contract for a road. He requested fifty-year exclusive rights for his private corporation, the Atlantic and Pacific Transportation Company, to steam-navigate seventeen miles of the Chagres and to build and operate forty miles of road from the junction with the Trinidad River to Panama City. The company would receive one league of land on each side of the road tax free; private property in the path of the road would be purchased. The government would also surrender thirty square leagues of public land for fuel and landing places, and two hundred leagues "for purposes of encouraging agriculture and domestic industry." There would be no government inspection, molestation, or duties charged on goods imported or conveyed by the firm. The government of New Granada could transport its men and supplies at half the regular duty. In return, Biddle pledged to place two steamboats on the Chagres by July 1838, and to commence operations on the road by the same date.[65]

Headily, he continued to blend his public duties with his private goals by assuring the members of the Congress of New Granada that the United States was not interested in territorial annexation of the isthmus. The United States had "more than enough territory" already and respected the rights of other nations with "a most religious integrity." By May 1836, after thirty-eight days of debate, the Congress approved the Atlantic-to-Pacific road. The ebullient Biddle then moved quickly to convince Secretary of Foreign Affairs Luis de Pombo and President Francisco de Paula Santander of its necessity. At this point his diplomatic inexperience revealed itself in a series of protocol blunders, from which he attempted to extricate himself by lengthy apologies. It is difficult to estimate the damage done by these faux pas, but in any case President Santander vetoed the bill. Biddle felt betrayed because Santander had previously assured him of his hearty support of the road.[66]

There were good reasons for the veto. The government, having been scarred by the Thierry experience, preferred that the project be conducted by local capitalists. A movement launched by a New Granadan company resulted in a petition that offered better terms than Biddle's. Santander may also have possessed a healthy skepticism as to whether the American had the funds for such a venture, and probably frowned upon his association with Panamanian dissidents.

To counter the President's surprise move, Biddle assured Secretary Pombo that he would post a $1 million bond with a New Granadan agent upon his return to the United States. Chargé Robert McAfee lent support by adding that "there was no doubt of his [Biddle's] ability and intention to carry this important work into immediate operation." Their words made no impact.[67]

A bitter Biddle railed against those who opposed the road. President Santander's action, he claimed, gave credibility to the European press reports that frequently scoffed at South American leaders and emphasized their instability. The foreign trade of Panama in 1835 amounted to only $500,000 worth of goods (largely pearls, gold, and silver), far below its potential. This depressed economic situation would remain, Biddle predicted, because of the shortsightedness of certain "adventurers and stockjobbers." He vowed to go to Guatemala (which he had been initially instructed to do but had cavalierly disregarded) and secure a right of passage through the Central American Republic. There would be a road across Nicaragua "many years" before one dollar was spent by Americans in Panama. Biddle told the Panamanians he could "not omit an expression of my feelings of intense disgust. . . . my personal friends shall never participate in the scheme [in Panama] and if my government is guided by my advice it will be many years before its interest in the affairs of the isthmus will be revived." To make certain that the New Granadan company planning to construct the road would not be granted credit in the United States, Biddle wrote a caustic, destructive letter to leading American businessmen and commercial newspapers in Boston, New York, Philadelphia, and Baltimore. If the Atlantic and Pacific Transportation Company could not build the road, no United States firm would. Significantly, in this brouhaha, Biddle relegated his role as government agent to a secondary position, concerning himself primarily with the advocacy of his partnership.[68]

The Philadelphian's petulant behavior ultimately had a positive effect, as he worked furiously behind the scenes to promote a union between the Atlantic and Pacific Company and the New Granadan organization. Within the month Santander reversed his decision, withdrew the veto, and approved the road by executive decree. Biddle and fourteen citizens of New Granada received the final grant, but the Americans controlled the company. A joyous McAfee believed that the road would have immense importance for the commerce of the United States and, as "the highway of nations," would eventually give new directions to world trade. The Chargé pledged that he would work diligently in Bogotá to facilitate its completion.[69]

Thus, amidst toasts that pledged inter-American unity regardless of color, language, or religion, Biddle reached his moment of triumph. The government grant had only slightly altered his former petition. His company received 140,000 acres outright and 750,000 acres at 50 cents per acre. The contract stipulated that the work begin by April 1838 and be completed within three years. Although the government of New Granada would decide controversies in the road zone, management of the highway and the property surrounding it would be the company's prerogative for fifty years, after which it would revert to the state.[70]

Charles Biddle returned to the United States in September 1836, eager to pursue his project. He reaffirmed his business ties in Philadelphia and then sped to Washington, hoping to obtain a diplomatic appointment; how convenient if Robert McAfee were to leave Bogotá and Biddle were to be named in his stead. Jackson, however, was piqued with his agent. Biddle had traveled to the Quaker City rather than report first to the President. In fact, the State Department had not heard from the commissioner in four months, a lapse that brought strong chastisement from Forsyth. One can only imagine Jackson's reaction when he read about the Biddle contract in a Washington newspaper. He had partially vented his frustrations by instructing McAfee to "disassociate" the government from the Biddle mission. Jackson would certainly not have appointed the controversial commissioner to another post, but the point became moot when Biddle died unexpectedly on December 21. Nicholas Biddle's family loyally marked the event by wearing black crepe on their hats.[71]

On January 10, 1837, Jackson (deliberately ignoring Biddle's road) advised the Senate that the possibility of a canal or railroad in Central America was remote and that it was "not expedient to open negotiations with any foreign government upon the subject." The irate President obviously viewed Biddle's actions as taken in a private rather than a public capacity. He was also probably convinced at this point that there was no imminent danger of British involvement in the isthmus. Chargé Williamson in Venezuela reported in January 1837 that the Biddle contract had awakened "British cupidity" and that Palmerston was planning to take the isthmus by force before it fell to American influence, but even had this rumor reached Jackson before he left the White House, it is unlikely that he would have acted. The British Foreign Secretary had proved supportive of positive relations with the Americans. Before jeopardizing Anglo-American harmony, a compact (perhaps similar to the Clayton-Bulwer Treaty of 1850, which provided for joint construction of a possible canal) would have been negotiated.[72]

While Biddle's company could have proceeded with the road with neither help nor hindrance from the United States government, Biddle's death, followed by the Panic of 1837, destroyed any hope for an American venture across the isthmus in the 1830s. When economic recovery dawned in 1839, President Van Buren considered the report of an agent, John Stephens, whom he had sent to the area. Stephens had completed the Biddle mission and argued favorably for a Nicaraguan canal route that he estimated at $25 million. The economy continued to doom any progress, but the Mexican War, the annexation of California (which Jackson had championed), and the Gold Rush were all to emphasize anew the need for a transisthmian route. By the decade of the 1850s, under the well-financed leadership of Charles Morgan and Cornelius Vanderbilt, United States businessmen made genuine progress in planning Central American transit, and the American government completed negotiations with New Granada and Nicaragua for canal rights.

Of what significance then was the Biddle mission? The commissioner had not proved to be an exceptional diplomat or governmental representative. He had provoked Jackson by not following instructions, by staying too long in some places and ignoring others altogether. While his lengthy, detailed report on Cuba had been submitted promptly to the President, almost a year passed until his final message in November 1836. Absence of information on Nicaragua meant that Old Hickory knew precious little about the alternative routes, and prompted a strong and sarcastic rebuke from Secretary Forsyth in December. In addition, Biddle had shown little sensitivity in New Granada. He had fraternized with Panamanian separatists and agitated important leaders in Bogotá. What is perhaps most surprising is that he actually succeeded in obtaining a contract. At some point, probably from the outset of the mission, Biddle confused his public trust with his private role, disregarding the President's instructions and directing his energies toward furthering his company's interests.

The President and Congress recognized the importance of a transisthmian route. Jackson had pressed for an American commercial presence on the west coast of Latin America through treaties with Mexico (California), Chile, and the Peru-Bolivia Confederation. He was fully aware of the importance of the whaling fleets in the Pacific, the elusive trade potential of the Far East, and the alluring California ports. Jackson also knew the extent of the British presence in the region and the commercial rivalry that existed.

For the United States, therefore, the Biddle mission did serve several purposes. For one, it advanced the idea of United States strategic concern for Latin America in a very real sense and was the first tangible American involvement in the area in a decade. For another, it suggested bipartisan involvement in Central America: the administration manifested interest in a transisthmian route as early as the 1831 Dutch threat and responded accordingly; Congress joined in when New Granada enlarged the stakes and Clay assumed a power role on the Senate Foreign Relations Committee.

Although Biddle never built his road, his mission was not a total failure. It demonstrated a vital link between American governmental and business interests. As such, it was the most important diplomatic expression of United States concern for the region between the Panama Congress of 1826 and James K. Polk's treaty for a transisthmian route in 1846.[73]

Postscript

Jacksonian Diplomacy in Retrospect

The tale is apocryphal but fits the Jackson legend. A cynical eastern journalist covering the General's funeral, it is said, spotted Old Hickory's long-time slave-servant at the bier. "Well," cracked the reporter in a tone half joking, half serious, "do you think your master will go to heaven?" The elderly servant paused a moment and then replied, "He will, if he wants to."

Jackson was an indomitable figure, a man who has received high presidential marks from historians for his hard-hitting and forceful domestic policy. Not without flaws in thought or personality, Jackson utilized his advisors, Congress, the Democratic Party, the press, and the people both to further his goals and to temper his views. Historians have been reluctant to see that this "iron will" was also applied to foreign affairs in a calculated and often successful fashion.

Andrew Jackson was the Hero in the White House. He brought scant national political or diplomatic experience to the office—only brief tenures as United States congressman and senator. His military and frontier baggage did not include diplomatic training in The Hague or St. Petersburg, as did that of John Quincy Adams, but Jackson never allowed the lack of experience to deter him. With a locket containing a portrait of his beloved departed wife Rachael firmly clasped on a chain about his neck for spiritual support, an abiding faith in the justice of his acts, and the cheers of the people providing political sustenance, Old Hickory proceeded with a vigor that bordered on the precipitous. His foreign programs often presented a mirror image of his domestic policies. In each he appears headstrong, impetuous, brash, and uncompromising. Yet this same man possessed tact, patience, and finesse. His moods were mercurial. Jackson was an emotional but intelligent man. Sometimes the outbursts were simply fusillades fired for effect, sometimes not. The tirades against the Bank of the United States and the South Carolina nullifiers rivaled those targeted for the French Chamber of Deputies and various Mexican generals. His compromises on the tariff and federal funding for internal improvements were balanced by his wisdom and forbearance in dealing with the Neapolitans and the Vietnamese.

A republican of the old school, but free of a binding ideology, Jackson operated pragmatically in a flexible world of changing Cabinet members and their more rapidly changing tactics. The ultimate goals were not altered, but the strategy varied. Edward Pessen suggests that Jackson had foreign "policies." He is correct. Jackson developed old ideas, entertained new ones, and was willing to experiment with both.

Fundamentally, Old Hickory never left the frontier; he was forever a Tennessee planter and speculator, a businessman and a capitalist who had attained riches and status through land acquisition. Like his fellow Americans—90 percent of whom lived in nonurban (under 2,500 persons) areas—Jackson believed in the necessity of the growth of the cotton, tobacco, and grain markets. He could neither politically nor economically ignore the iron manufacturer of Pennsylvania or the textile weaver of New England, but his focus remained upon the yeoman farmer and the planter. The impulses of Jackson's foreign policy derived from an imperative of the American system: this nation of twelve million people had proved its inability to absorb its own industrial and agricultural largesse.

Jackson was also a warrior. On numerous occasions the sound of the drum had called him away from the Hermitage to do battle with the Indians, English, or Spanish, and his successes doubtless contributed to his belief in the proper use of military force to accomplish a particular goal. As President, Jackson never built a mighty army, yet he recognized the need for increased naval strength to foster, facilitate, and protect both American markets and the merchant marine around the world. To him, economics and diplomacy were symbiotic. A prosperous United States required a strong executive who would assert the rights of the nation, settle outstanding claims with other countries (thus salvaging both money and honor), and judiciously implement naval force when doing so was prudent and necessary to accomplish those goals.

Jacksonian foreign policy, then, was a meld of republican virtue and self-righteousness with entrepreneurial spirit and practical diplomacy. It was energetic, sometimes imaginative, and often fruitful. The General leaned heavily upon the neutrality and nonentanglement maxims of George Washington and the hemispheric defensiveness of James Monroe, imbuing them with his own particular brand of conservatism. Neither stirrings of democracy in a Greek revolution nor tenuous pleas for assistance from struggling young Latin American nations moved the President. Brazil, Mexico, Argentina, and the Central American Republic were among the nations frustrated by Jackson's unwillingness to intercede in halting inter-American warfare or possible European invasion. Arbitration between squabbling Latin American nations or between those republics and their former mother countries was not under the American purview. Jackson strictly defined his neutrality; the Monroe Doctrine received a narrow interpretation. His perception of the 1823 message was limited without being myopic. A strong British presence in Mexico or interference in Texas, the possible transfer of Cuba, or exclusive European control and use of a transisthmian canal: these issues touched the very fabric of United States commerce and security and thus fell under the scrutiny of the doctrine.

Jacksonian diplomacy was a vital part of the American diplomatic continuum rather than a departure from it. The goals of the Jackson administration differed little from those of John Quincy Adams; for both men, expanding commerce and settling claims remained the highest priorities. Yet Jackson succeeded where Adams failed. Old Hickory's task was generally made easier by a supportive Congress, at least through 1834. The anti-Jacksonians put forth a valiant effort to politicize foreign policy on several occasions, including the *Friendship* affair in Sumatra and, most notably, the French claims crisis. While they faltered in their election-year attempt (1832) to embarrass the President over Quallah Battoo, the Whigs had more success in 1834–35. By then they controlled the Senate and were able to censure Jackson for his removal of the Bank deposits and stifle his efforts to prepare the nation for a possible conflict with France.

Jacksonian diplomacy was personal—it had the markings of the President, not of his Cabinet or even his secretaries of state. Old Hickory believed that the chief executive held the constitutional reins in determining policy; he should receive suggestions from his ministers, advice and consent from the Congress, and support from the people, but even friendship did not guarantee decision-making authority. Consider the case of Edward Livingston: he was a long-time associate of the President but a man rarely involved in policy formation. Martin Van Buren, the most powerful of the State Department heads, maintained his influence with Jackson because of a commonly held philosophy, a close personal relationship, and an uncanny ability to know when to press "the Old Man" and when to withdraw.

Jackson both reformed and politicized the State Department. The General took an active interest in the reorganization of the department, which McLane and Forsyth efficiently handled. He also supported improvements in the consular and diplomatic service, several times recommending needed changes to the Congress (which, while agreeing to modest reform, refused to endorse the broader-based alterations in salary structure urged by the secretaries to attract and maintain quality personnel in the foreign service). At the same time, however, Jackson used the diplomatic branch for political reward. He kept a close watch upon appointments of ministers, chargés, consuls, and special agents; they might be politicians, businessmen, editors, or naval officers, but he nearly always chose party loyalists. The founder of the Democracy might occasionally maintain a previously assigned National Republican or Whig, but he rarely appointed one.

Some of Jackson's selections performed brilliantly; others proved self-seeking and a few incompetent. Europe, the President's highest priority, received the best and the brightest, including Louis McLane, William Rives, James Buchanan, and Henry Wheaton. Latin America frequently inherited the residue of Jackson's penchant for funneling the faithful into the diplomatic corps or consular service. Men of suspect abilities or compromised national commitment such as Andrew Butler, Charles De Witt, Charles Biddle, and Francis Baylies were thrust upon unwary South American leaders. Often the diplomats spoke little Spanish, expressed contempt for the native population, and accorded Latin officials just slightly more esteem than bandits. Sometimes motivated by self-aggrandizement, by a desire to resuscitate a dying political career or build a commercial base for themselves, too many of these men made poor or ineffective representatives for their nation.

The combination of Jacksonian style and diplomatic talent produced almost predictable results. The United States enjoyed positive commercial and political relations with most of Europe. A warm bond existed with Great Britain, sealed by the West Indian trade treaty of 1830. The failure to arrive at an elusive northeastern boundary settlement rested more with Maine or Capitol Hill than with the White House or Whitehall. But Jacksonian patience, so evident in dealing with the Russians or the Portuguese, evaporated with the French by 1834.

The French struck a match to the kindling of Jackson's patriot temper. After Rives's triumph in reaching the claims accord in 1831, Jackson waited three years for the French to pay their debts. Their failure to do so and the cavalier manner with which they treated the question prompted the Tennesseean to reach for his dueling pistols. Both his and the nation's honor were being challenged. Still, though his instincts may have pushed him in a rash direction, sweet reason and the sage counsel of his advisors kept him on a moderate path of urging limited reprisals. And even though these recommendations caused as much concern in Washington as in Paris, they produced the desired effect. The payment was made, and trade could flourish unimpaired with the nation's most lucrative Continental partner. Jackson told the French they would get "neither an apology or explanation" from him on the issue—and he did not apologize but coyly offered the olive branch, which the French eagerly grasped.

Jackson's mixed success with Spain was due partially to the chaotic political climate in the country. The President recognized Madrid's weakened economic position and demonstrated a willingness to compromise on acknowledged claims debts. But he became infuriated by the continued insistence of the Ministry on hampering the very profitable United States trade with Cuba and Puerto Rico. By 1834 he suggested to Congress a trade war with Spain unless the duties charged American goods and vessels were lowered. The unsuccessful resolution of this issue resulted largely from the political and economic needs of the Spanish to control what remained of their empire. Likely nothing less than military force would have altered Spain's position, and Jackson understandably hesitated to make such a commitment.

In addition to those with France and Spain, the Jacksonians negotiated claims treaties totaling millions of dollars—long sought by several administrations—with Naples, Portugal, and Denmark. The United

States also signed commercial pacts with Great Britain, Russia, and Turkey. Old Hickory's diplomatic arsenal included flattery, intimidation, patience, and bluster—all weapons that were generally used with effectiveness in Europe.

The pathway to Latin America proved rough and thorny for the United States. Jackson viewed the Western Hemisphere paternally and (like Monroe) hoped for the establishment of democratic governments that would provide the blessings of liberty and tranquillity. He suffered disappointment. Latin America was convulsed in revolution and turmoil throughout the decade. This chaos and political instability created power vacuums that the Jackson administration, hamstrung by a philosophy preaching nonintervention and neutrality, felt helpless to fill. The British, wealthy and powerful, lacked such reservations and eagerly moved to strengthen their positions both commercially and territorially. The Jacksonians, unwilling to alienate Great Britain, muttered and grumbled but acquiesed to the Union Jack. The Yankees tried but simply could not compete in capital investments, technology, naval or merchant marine tonnage. Though politically tentative and economically frustrated, the United States did conclude commercial treaties with Mexico, Chile, Venezuela, and Peru-Bolivia. Trade grew, but never reached anticipated levels.

The United States also offered aspiring Latin nations attractive democratic and republican ideology, preached too frequently by ill-advised or self-righteous diplomats. The South Americans soon realized that for all their appeal, ideas produced no revenues for depleted treasuries.

The greatest Jacksonian failure in Latin America was in Mexico. The President earnestly hoped for a mutually beneficial trade agreement and a boundary settlement, but these two areas were complicated by the tumultuous Mexican political situation and Jackson's desire for Texas. Probably no Mexican president who wished to remain in office could have sold Texas to the United States. When revolution broke out north of the Rio Grande, the Mexicans logically attributed it to Washington's imperial designs. The responsibility for the ensuing collapse in Mexican-American relations rests on both sides of the Rio Grande. The Mexicans, who harbored suspicion and mistrust about Jackson's designs on Texas, failed to perceive his basic opposition to the

Texas Revolution and his desire for peaceful annexation. And Jackson, who had little respect for the Mexicans, treated their representatives and national feelings with a minimum of sensitivity.

Jackson set the goals and policies for his administration and the United States. Frequently, they were met; occasionally—in Texas, for example—they were unfulfilled. In every case, the Tennesseean pursued a course designed to enhance the size, prestige, and wealth of his country. An ardent nationalist, he fought to promote American interests around the globe. Yet while the President argued and threatened in a brinksmanlike manner, the nation involved itself in no foreign wars during his two terms. Sometimes he chafed against a system—involving senators, Cabinet members and advisors—that threatened to limit his efforts toward a rich and powerful America. If such a threat arose, the President exercised the option of appointing a special agent: an Edmund Roberts to explore the commercial opportunities of Japan, Muscat, Siam, and Cochin China; a Charles Biddle to chart the possibilities of a Central American canal or road that would link the Far East and the west coasts of North and South America with the United States.

Andrew Jackson formulated and exercised the most expansive and aggressive foreign policy between the presidencies of Thomas Jefferson and James K. Polk. In so doing, he developed the power of the chief executive beyond the horizon of domestic affairs for which he is usually credited, and helped to lay the foundations for the more dynamic diplomatic actions of the modern presidency.

Appendix A

American Diplomats, 1829–37

ARGENTINA
John M. Forbes, Chargé, March 1825–June 1831
Francis Baylies, Chargé, January 1832–September 26, 1832

BELGIUM
Hugh S. Legaré, Chargé, April 1832–June 1836

BRAZIL
William Tudor, Chargé, June 1827–March 1830
Ethan A. Brown, Chargé, May 1830–April 1834
William Hunter, Chargé, June 1834–

CHILE
Samuel Larned, Chargé, February 1828–December 1829
John Hamm, Chargé, May 1830–December 1833
Richard Pollard, Chargé, June 1834–

COLOMBIA
William H. Harrison, Minister, May 1828–September 1829
Thomas P. Moore, Minister, March 1829–April 1833

Robert B. McAfee, Chargé, February 1833–June 1837

DENMARK
Henry Wheaton, Chargé, March 1827–May 1835
Jonathan Woodside, Chargé, March 1835–

FRANCE
William C. Rives, Minister, April 1829–September 1833
Levett Harris, Chargé, March 1833–September 1833
Edward Livingston, Minister, May 1833–April 1835
Lewis Cass, Minister, October 1836–

GERMANY (PRUSSIA)
Henry Wheaton, Chargé, March 1835–

GREAT BRITAIN
Louis McLane, Minister, April 1829–June 1831
Martin Van Buren, Minister, August 1831–March 1832 (not confirmed)
Aaron Vail, Chargé, July 1832–July 1836

Andrew Stevenson, Minister, March
1836–

GUATEMALA (CENTRAL
AMERICAN REPUBLIC)
William N. Jeffers, Chargé, June 1831
(did not proceed)
James Shannon, Chargé, February
1832 (died en route)
Charles DeWitt, Chargé, January
1833–

MEXICO
Joel Poinsett, Minister, March
1825–November 1829
Anthony Butler, Chargé, November
1829–November 1835
Powhatan Ellis, Chargé, January
1836–December 1836

NAPLES (TWO SICILIES)
John Nelson, Chargé, November
1831–November 1832

NETHERLANDS
Christopher Hughes, Chargé,
March 1825–January 1830
William A. Preble, Minister, June
1829–May 1831
Auguste Davezac, Chargé, November 1831–

PERU
Samuel Larned, Chargé, December
1828, May 1830–March 1837
Emmanuel West, Chargé, November
1829 (died en route)
James Thornton, Chargé, June 1836

PORTUGAL
Thomas L. L. Brent, Chargé, March

1825–November 1834
Edward Kavanagh, Chargé, March
1835

RUSSIA
John Randolph, Minister, May
1830–September 1830
James Buchanan, Minister, January
1832–August 1833
William Wilkins, Minister, June
1834–December 1835
John Randolph Clay, Chargé, June
1836

SPAIN
Cornelius P. Van Ness, Minister,
June 1829–December 1836
William T. Barry, Minister, April
1835 (died en route)
John Eaton, Minister, March 1836

SWEDEN
John J. Appleton, Chargé, May
1826–August 1830
Christopher Hughes, Chargé,
March 1830

TURKEY
David Porter, Chargé, April 1831

VENEZUELA
John G. A. Williamson, Chargé,
March 1835

SOURCE: Richardson Dougall and
Mary Patricia Chapman, eds.,
United States Chiefs of Mission,
1778–1973 (Washington, D.C.: Historical Office, Bureau of Public Affairs, Department of State, 1973).

Appendix B

American Consuls and Commercial Agents, 1829–37

ARGENTINA
George Slacum, Buenos Aires, 1829
Eben Dorr, Buenos Aires, 1835
Alred Slade, Buenos Aires, 1837

AUSTRIAN EMPIRE,
TUSCANY, SARDINIA
John G. Schwarz, Vienna, 1829
Thomas Appleton, Leghorn, 1829
James Ombrosi, Florence, 1829
Robert Campbell, Genoa, 1829
Victor Sasserno, Nice, 1829
George Moore, Trieste, 1829
Charles Barnet, Venice, 1831
Albert Dabadie, Venice, 1837

BARBARY STATES
Henry Lee, Algiers, 1829
George Brown, Algiers, 1831
Samuel Heap, Tunis, 1829
Charles D. Coxe, Tripoli, 1829
Daniel S. McCauley, Tripoli, 1831
John Mulloway, Tangiers, 1829
James Leib, Tangiers, 1831, 1835
Samuel Carr, Tangiers, 1833

BRAZIL, URUGUAY
William H. D. C. Wright, Rio de
Janeiro, 1829

John M. Baker, Rio de Janeiro, 1831
George Slacum, Rio de Janeiro, 1837
Woodbridge Odlin, San Salvador,
1829
John T. Mansfield, Pernambuco, 1829
Joseph Ray, Pernambuco, 1837
José dos Santos Monteiro, Maran-
hão, 1829
Charles B. Allen, Para, 1829
Abraham R. Smith, Para, 1831
Charles J. Smith, Para, 1835
Joshua Bond, Montevideo, 1829
John Patrick, Montevideo, 1837
Leonard Corning, Maranhão, 1829
Charles B. Allen, Maranhão, 1831
Isaac Hayes, Rio Grande, 1829
George Black, Santos, 1831
Lemuel Wells, St. Catherines, 1831

CENTRAL AMERICA
Charles Savage, Guatemala, 1829
G. Coursault, Truxillo, 1831

CHILE
Michael Hogan, Valparaiso, 1829
Thomas Russell, Valparaiso, 1831
George Hobson, Valparaiso, 1835
Daniel Wynne, Santiago, 1829
Thomas T. Smith, Coquimbo, 1835

CHINA

John H. Grosvenor, Canton, 1829

Peter Snow, Canton, 1835

COLOMBIA, VENEZUELA, ECUADOR

J. C. Pickett (Secretary of Legation), Bogotá, 1830

John McPherson, Carthagena, 1829

John G. A. Williamson, La Guaira, 1829

Benjamin Renshaw, LaGuaira, 1835

William Seaver, Santa Marta, 1829

Alexander Danouille, Santa Marta/ Guayaquil, 1831

Seth Sweetser, Guayaquil, 1835

Abraham P. Nones, Maracaibo, 1829

Alfred Laussat, Maracaibo, 1831

William Dubbs, Maracaibo, 1835

Franklin Litchfield, Porto Cabello, 1829

Silas K. Everett, Panama, 1829

Gilbert Dennison, Panama, 1831

J. B. Feraud, Panama, 1835

Thomas Knox, Angostura, 1831

Thomas B. Nalle, Angostura, 1835

DENMARK

John Raynals, Copenhagen, 1829

Charles Hambro, Copenhagen, 1835

Thomas Barker, Elsinore, 1835

Edmund Raynals, Elsinore, 1837

Nathan Levy, St. Thomas, 1829

Joseph Ridgway, St. Croix, 1829

David Rogers, St. Croix, 1837

FRANCE

Nathaniel Niles (Secretary of Legation), Paris, 1829

Thomas P. Barton (Secretary of Legation), Paris, 1835

Charles Anderson (Secretary of Legation), Paris, 1837

Isaac Coxe Barnett, Paris, 1829

Daniel Brent, Paris, 1835

Daniel Stroebel, Bordeaux, 1829

George Strobel, Bordeaux, 1831

Daniel Croxall, Marseilles, 1829

Francis Fenwick, Nantes, 1829

Edward Church, L'Orient, 1829

Reuben Beasley, Le Havre, 1829

Cornelius Bradford, Lyon, 1829

Samuel Allinson, Lyon, 1831

T. W. Oldfield, Lyon, 1837

Dominick Lynch, Bayonne, 1835

Theodore Privat, Cette, 1829

James DeBesse, La Rochelle, 1829

Henry Van Bibber, La Rochelle, 1837

Francis Faures, Guadaloupe, 1829

Peter Suau, Guadaloupe, 1831

John Meircken, Martinique, 1829

Robert Chase, Martinique, 1835

Charles Garavini, Algiers, 1837

GERMANIC STATES

Theodore S. Fay (Secretary of Legation), Berlin, 1837

Frederick Kahl, Darmstadt, 1829

William T. Simons, Elberfield, 1829

Frederick Schillow, Leipzig, 1829

C. F. Goehring, Leipzig, 1831

Frederich List, Leipzig, 1835

Frederick Schillow, Stettin, 1831

John Cuthbert, Hamburg, 1829

Frederic Wilchelhausen, Bremen, 1829

Joshua Dodge, Bremen, 1831

Joseph Clark, Lubec, 1829

Ernest Schwendler, Frankfort, 1829

Frederich List, Baden, 1831

Robert de Ruedorffer, Munich, 1835
Charles Graebe, Hesse/Cassel, 1835
Edward Rivinus, Dresden, 1837
C. F. Schultz, Rostock, 1837

GREAT BRITAIN
England
Aaron Vail (Secretary of Legation),
London, 1829
Thomas Aspinwall, London, 1829
Francis B. Ogden, Liverpool, 1829
Herman Visger, Bristol, 1829
Thomas Dennison, Bristol, 1835
Robert Fox, Falmouth, 1829
Thomas W. Fox, Plymouth, 1829
Albert Davy, Kingston (Hull), 1829
Robert Hunter, Isle of Wight, 1829

Scotland
Joel Hart, Leith (Edinburgh), 1829
Robert Grieve, Leith, 1835
David Walker, Glasgow, 1829–31,
1833–35
Alexander Thompson, Glasgow,
1831–33, 1835–37
Edward Baxter, Dundee, 1835

Ireland
Thomas Wilson, Dublin, 1829
Reuben Harvey, Cork, 1829
John Murphy, Cork, 1837
Samuel Luke, Belfast, 1829
Thomas W. Gilpin, Belfast, 1831
Thomas Persse, Galway, 1831
James Corscaden, Londonderry, 1835

EUROPE AND AFRICA
Bernard Henry, Gibraltar, 1829
Horatio Sprague, Gibraltar, 1831
Paul Froberville, Mauritius, 1831
John Pulis, Malta, 1829

Paul Eynaud, Malta, 1831
William Andrews, Malta, 1835
William Carroll, St. Helena, 1831
Isaac Chase, Capetown, 1835

AMERICAS
William Higinbotham, Bermuda,
1829
W. T. Tucker, Bermuda, 1831
John Storr, Nassau, 1829
George Huyler, Nassau, 1835
Ralph Higinbotham, Antigua, 1829
Thomas Wynns, Turk's Island, 1829
John Arthur, Turk's Island, 1835
Edmund Roberts, British Guiana,
1829
Moses Benjamin, British Guiana,
1831
Peter Lanman, Kingston, Jamaica
1829
Robert M. Harrison, Kingston, Ja-
maica 1831
Charles Bartlett, Trinidad, 1829
John M. Kankey, Barbados, 1829
John Haley, Barbados, 1831
John Morrow, Halifax, 1831
Thomas Leavitt, St. Johns, 1835

ASIA AND AUSTRALIA
James Williams, Sidney, 1837
Joseph Balcstier, Singapore, 1837

GREECE
James Wilkin, Isle of Syra, 1835
G. A. Perdicaris, Athens, 1837

HAITI
Francis Dimond, Port au Prince,
1829
Joshua Webb, Aux Cayes, 1829

William Miles, Aux Cayes, 1835
Samuel Israel, Cape Haytien, 1829
George Howe, Cape Haytien, 1837
Daniel Carney, Santo Domingo,
  1837

HAWAII, TAHITI
John C. Jones, Oahu, 1829
T. A. Moerenhout, Society Islands,
  1835
S. R. Blackler, Society Islands, 1837

ITALY (KINGDOM OF TWO
SICILIES, ROMAN STATES)
Felix Cicognani, Rome, 1829
George W. Greene, Rome, 1837
Alexander Hammet, Naples, 1829
Benjamin Gardner, Palermo, 1829
John Payson, Messina, 1829

MEXICO
Charles Ellis (Secretary of Lega-
  tion), Mexico City, 1837
James Smith Wilcocks, Mexico City,
  1829
William S. Parrot, Mexico City, 1835
William D. Jones, Mexico City, 1837
George Robertson, Tampico, 1829
Thomas Reiley, Aguatulco, 1829
Harvey Gregg, Acapulco, 1829
William Taylor, Vera Cruz, 1829
James James, Vera Cruz, 1831
John Cameron, Vera Cruz, 1833
Marmaduke Burrough, Vera Cruz,
  1835
Daniel Smith, Matamoras, 1829
John Ward, Sante Fe, 1829
James Davis, Sante Fe, 1831
Ceran St. Vrain, Sante Fe, 1835
John Langham, Chihuahua, 1831
James McGoffin, Saltillo, 1829

Henry Perrine, Campeche (Yuca-
  tan), 1829
Samuel Haight, Campeche (Yuca-
  tan), 1835
James L. Kennedy, Mazatlan, 1829
Chauncey Bush, Mazatlan, 1837
Joseph Wallace, San Antonio, 1829
David Barnet, San Antonio/Galves-
  ton, 1831
Francis Slaughter, Galveston, 1835
William Keath, Guaymas, 1831
Charles Davis, Guaymas, 1835
Daniel Pope, Tabasco, 1831
Robert S. Hicks, Tabasco, 1835
Henry Coleman, Tabasco, 1837
John Langdon, Laguna, 1831
John Parker, Brazoria (Texas), 1835
John Stryker, Matagorda, 1835
John McCall, Tampico, 1837
William Gilliam, Monterey, 1837
Jose Maria Castanos, San Blas, 1837

MUSCAT
R. P. Waters, Zanzibar, 1837

NETHERLANDS, BELGIUM
John W. Parker, Amsterdam, 1829
Emanuel Wambersie, Rotterdam,
  1829
William D. Patterson, Antwerp, 1829
Thomas Barker, Antwerp, 1837
Thomas Trask, Surinam, 1829
Louis Paimboeuf, Curaçao, 1829
John Shillaber, Batavia, 1829
Owen Roberts, Batavia, 1835
Louis Mark, Ostend, 1829
Jehu Hollingsworth, St. Eustacia,
  1829
Joseph Balestier, Straits of Malacca,
  1835

PERU

Asa Worthington, Lima, 1829
Edwin Bartlett, Lima, 1837
William F. Taylor, Arica/Quilca, 1829
Obadiah Folger, Paita, 1831
James Girdon, Jr., Paita, 1835

PORTUGAL

Israel Hutchinson, Lisbon/Oporto, 1829
John Marsh, Isle de Madeira, 1829
C. W. Dabney, Fayal (Azores), 1829
William G. Merrill, Cape Verde Islands, 1829
Ferdinand Gardner, Cape Verde Islands, 1837
William Vesey, St. Ubes, 1835

RUSSIA

John R. Clay (Secretary of Legation), St. Petersburg, 1831
William W. Chew (Secretary of Legation), St. Petersburg, 1837
Abraham Gibson, St. Petersburg, 1829
Charles Rhind, Odessa, 1829
John Ralli, Odessa, 1831
Henry Schielin, Tagranrog, 1831
Edmund Brandt, Archangel, 1831
Alexander Schwartz, Riga, 1835

SPAIN

Arthur Middleton (Secretary of Legation), Madrid, 1831
Alexander Burton, Cadiz, 1829
William Stirling, Barcelona, 1829
Joseph Borras, Barcelona, 1835
Obadiah Rich, Valencia, 1829
George G. Barrell, Malaga, 1829
George B. Adams, Alicante, 1829
Francisco de Ealo, Bilbao, 1829

Máximo de Aguirre, Bilboa, 1831
George W. Hubbell, Manila, 1829
Alfred Edwards, Manila, 1831
Payton Gay, Canary Islands, 1829
Joseph Cullen, Canary Islands, 1835
George T. Ladico, Balearic Islands, 1829
Obadiah Rich, Balearic Islands, 1835

Spanish Caribbean

William Shaler, Havana, Cuba, 1829
Nicholas Trist, Havana, Cuba, 1833
Robert Stewart, Trinidad de Cuba, 1829
E. C. Watmough, Trinidad de Cuba, 1835
Thomas Backus, Santiago de Cuba, 1829
John Leonard, Santiago de Cuba, 1831
Michael Mahon, Santiago de Cuba, 1835
Lewis Shoemaker, Matanzas, 1829
John Owen, Puerto del Principe, Cuba, 1829
Sidney Mason, San Juan, Puerto Rico, 1829
G. W. Montgomery, San Juan, Puerto Rico, 1835
Thomas Davidson, Ponce, Puerto Rico, 1829
Hopeful Toler, Ponce, Puerto Rico, 1831
James Gallaher, Ponce, Puerto Rico, 1837
William Tracy, Guyama, Puerto Rico, 1829
Sampson Russell, Mayaguez, Puerto Rico, 1829
George Latimer, Mayaguez, Puerto Rico, 1835

Henry Stearns, Barascoa, Puerto
   Rico, 1829–32

SWEDEN, NORWAY
David Erskine, Stockholm, 1829
C. D. Arfwedson, Stockholm, 1837
C. A. Murray, Gothenburg, 1829
Henry Janson, Christiansand
   (Bergen), 1829
Robert Harrison, St. Bartholo-
   mews, 1829
George Crump, St. Bartholomews,
   1831

SWITZERLAND
John Booker, Basel, 1831

TURKEY, EGYPT
George Porter, Constantinople, 1837

David Offley, Smyrna, 1829
Nicholas Perick, Brousa, 1835
B. W. Llewellen, Salonica, 1835
Dalmas D'Avenant, Isle of Stanco,
   1835
Marino de Mattey, Isle of Cyprus,
   1835
Chevalier Durighello, Aleppo, 1835
Jasper Chasseaud, Beruit/Damascus,
   1835
John Gliddon, Alexandria, 1835
Vincent Rosa, Candia, 1835
D. Bonnal, Canea, 1835

SOURCE: U.S. Department of State,
*The Biennial Register of All Officers
and Agents in the Service of the
United States* (Washington, D.C.:
Blair and Rives, 1829–37).

Appendix C

Cabinet Members in Jackson's Administrations

SECRETARY OF STATE
Martin Van Buren (New York),
  1829–31
Edward Livingston (Louisiana),
  1831–33
Louis McLane (Delaware), 1833–34
John Forsyth (Georgia), 1834–37

SECRETARY OF THE TREASURY
Samuel D. Ingham (Pennsylvania),
  1829–31
Louis McLane (Delaware), 1831–33
William Duane (Pennsylvania), 1833
Roger B. Taney (Maryland), 1833–34
Levi Woodbury (New Hampshire),
  1834–37

ATTORNEY-GENERAL
John Berrien (Georgia), 1829–31
Roger B. Taney (Maryland), 1831–33

Benjamin F. Butler (New York),
  1833–37

SECRETARY OF WAR
John Eaton (Tennessee), 1829–31
Lewis Cass (Michigan), 1831–36
Benjamin F. Butler (New York),
  1836–37

SECRETARY OF THE NAVY
John Branch (North Carolina),
  1829–31
Levi Woodbury (New Hampshire),
  1831–34
Mahlon Dickerson (New Jersey),
  1834–37

POSTMASTER-GENERAL
William Barry (Kentucky), 1829–35
Amos Kendall (Kentucky), 1835–37

Appendix D

Composition of Congress in Jackson's Administrations

HOUSE OF REPRESENTATIVES	Democrats	Opposition	Other
21st Congress (1829–31)	139	74 (Nat. Rep.)	—
22nd Congress (1831–33)	141	58 (Nat. Rep.)	14
23rd Congress (1833–35)	147	53 (Anti-Masonic)	60
24th Congress (1835–37)	145	98 (Whig)	—

SENATE			
21st Congress (1829–31)	26	22	—
22nd Congress (1831–33)	25	21	2
23rd Congress (1833–35)	20	20	8
24th Congress (1835–37)	27	25	—

Notes

INTRODUCTION

1 Daniel Cheever and H. F. Haviland, Jr., *American Foreign Policy and the Separation of Powers* (Cambridge, Mass.: Harvard University Press, 1952), 39–40; James C. Curtis, *Andrew Jackson and the Search for Vindication* (Boston: Little, Brown, 1976), 170–71; preface remarks by J. Franklin Jameson in John Spencer Bassett, ed., *The Correspondence of Andrew Jackson* (Washington, D.C.: Carnegie Institute, 1926–35), 4:v, 5:vi. For works that reflect a more activist approach in foreign affairs by Old Hickory, see the fine synthesis by Edward Pessen, *Jacksonian America: Personality and Politics* (Homewood, Ill.: Dorsey Press, 1968; rev. ed. 1978), and the impressive and flattering portraits of Jackson drawn in Robert Remini's trilogy, *Andrew Jackson and the Course of American Empire* (New York: Harper and Row, 1977), *Andrew Jackson and the Course of American Freedom* (New York: Harper and Row, 1981), 280–90, and *Andrew Jackson and the Course of American Democracy* (New York: Harper and Row, 1984). Remini is one of the few scholars to deal with Jackson's foreign policy and signal the need for a more extensive study of the topic. He contends that "Jackson's record in foreign affairs in his first administration was nothing less than outstanding" (*Jackson and the Course of Freedom*, 290).

2 Statistical information for the introduction was gathered from E. R. Johnson, et. al., *The History of Domestic and Foreign Commerce of the United States*, vol. 2 (Washington, D.C.: Carnegie Institute, 1915), and Chester Jones, *The Consular Service of the United States* (Philadelphia: University of Pennsylvania Press, 1906).

3 Andrew Jackson to Congress, December 1829, James Richardson, ed., *Messages and Papers of the Presidents of the United States, 1789–1902* (Washington, D.C.: Bureau of National Literature and Art, 1904), 2:443.

4 Ibid., 2:437, 592.

5 Ibid., 2:443.

6 Ibid., 2:552.

7 Ibid., 2:437–38.

8 Ibid., 2:20–22, 3:106–07.

CHAPTER ONE

1 Douglas Astolfi, "Foundations of Destiny: A Foreign Policy of the Jacksonians, 1824–1837," Ph.D. diss. Northern Illinois University, 1972, vi–viii. Astolfi examines the Adams-Jackson differences and the Jacksonian desire for Oregon and Texas quite thoroughly. Since the Adams administration reached a further accommodation with the British on the joint occupation of the Oregon country and the issue was not renewed by Old Hickory, the subject will not be discussed in the following chapters. It should be noted, too, that Indian affairs have sometimes been considered "foreign policy" but will not be treated as such for the purposes of this study (Remini, *Jackson and the Course of Empire*, 91–112; Curtis, *Andrew Jackson*, 29–31).

2 Merrill Jensen, *The New Nation* (New York: Knopf, 1965), 173.

3 Remini, *Jackson and the Course of Empire*, 91–112. Jackson, angry over Washington's foreign policy—especially the Jay Treaty with Great Britain—was one of a handful of congressmen who voted nay on a congressional resolution of gratitude to the Virginian as he prepared to leave office.

4 For fine accounts of the politics of the period, see Robert Remini's durable *The Election of Andrew Jackson* (Philadelphia: Lippincott, 1963) and John Niven's new and more complex *Martin Van Buren: The Romantic Age of American Politics* (New York: Oxford University Press, 1983).

5 Astolfi, "Foundation of Destiny," 2–6; Paul Varg, *United States Foreign Relations, 1820–1860* (East Lansing: Michigan State University Press, 1979), 50–51; Ernest May, *The Making of the Monroe Doctrine* (Cambridge, Mass.: Harvard University Press, 1975).

6 Remini, *Election of Jackson*, 39–44; Astolfi, "Foundations of Destiny," 6–29; Remini, *Jackson and the Course of Freedom*, 67; Samuel F. Bemis, ed., *American Secretaries of State and Their Diplomacy*, (New York: Knopf, 1927–29), 3:137–55.

7 Remini, *Jackson and the Course of Freedom*, 111–12.

8 Ibid., 217–19; G. R. Rives, *The United States and Mexico, 1821–1848* (New York: Scribner, 1913), 155–81; Astolfi, "Foundations of Destiny," 33–37.

9 Bemis, *American Secretaries of State*, 3:124–30. Varg, *United States Foreign Relations*, 61–73, is an excellent chapter on Anglo-American rivalry.

CHAPTER TWO

1 Leading exponents of the "Whig school" in the nineteenth century included James Parton, whose brilliant three-volume biography *The Life of Andrew Jackson* (New York: Mason Brothers, 1861) still must be considered; Herman Von Holst, *The Constitutional and Political History of the United States*, 8 vols. (Chicago: 1876–92); William Graham Sumner, *Andrew Jackson as Public Man* (Boston, 1882); and in the early twentieth century, James Schouler, *A History of the United States of America* (New York, 1913). Sumner attacked Jackson as a "barbarian"; Holst saw him as coarse and arrogant; Schouler labeled him "illiterate." These patricians all resented the intrusion of "the people" on the process of government—the democratization of American politics.

2 Holmes Alexander, *The American Talleyrand: The Career and Contemporaries of Martin Van Buren* (New York: Harper, 1935), 247; John Fitzpatrick, ed., *The Autobiography of Martin Van Buren* (Washington, D.C.: Carnegie Institute, 1920), 230–31 (Van Buren's major concern in the winter of 1828–29 was jockeying for political position within the new administration, not envisioning foreign policy changes. Both the State and Treasury Departments appealed to the New Yorker and his supporters, the former for its eminence and potential for building a reputation, the latter for its patronage powers and less politically exposed situation); S. Wright to Van Buren, Dec. 9, 1828; Martin Van Buren Papers, Library of Congress, Washington, D.C.; Van Buren to unknown, Dec. 17, 1828, ibid.; James Hamilton, Jr., to Van Buren, Jan. 23, Feb. 13, 1829, ibid.; E. Kane to Van Buren and McLane to Van Buren, Feb. 19, 1829, ibid. (McLane refers to newly appointed Navy Secretary John Branch as "a miserable old woman"); Ritchie to Van Buren, March 27, 1829, ibid. Jackson defended his cabinet selections by emphasizing that greats Washington and Jefferson had personal friends Hamilton and Madison as high-ranking cabinet officials. Only Eaton, the General claimed, was his friend, and "if my personal friends are qualified and patriotic why should I not be permitted to bestow a few offices on them" (Jackson to Van Buren, March 31, 1829, Basett, *Correspondence of Andrew Jackson* [hereafter cited as *Jackson Correspondence*], 4:19; Richard Latner, "A New Look at Jacksonian Politics," *Journal of American History* 61:977).

3 Richard P. Longaker, "Was Jackson's Kitchen Cabinet a Cabinet?" *Mississippi Valley Historical Review* 44:95; Fitzpatrick, *Autobiography of Van Buren*, 251, 262. The *cause célèbre* was the scandal involving Eaton's wife, Peggy, a former barmaid who was rejected by polite Washington society—including many Cabinet members. Jackson defended Peggy, and the social explosion that followed soon took on political dimensions (Curtis, *Andrew Jackson*, 94–101).

4 Aware that his Vice-President and his Secretary of State both hoped to succeed

him, the President moved to placate the rivals by awarding patronage within the Cabinet to the South Carolinian and within the diplomatic corps to the New Yorker. Since neither secretaries nor diplomats would determine policy, Jackson was not overly concerned whether he personally knew them—just so they were loyal Democrats. Most of the initial Cabinet members and ministers were qualified and did have judicial or legislative experience. Jackson quickly became impressed with Van Buren's political and social skills and equally disillusioned with Calhoun's. See Jackson to John Overton, Dec. 31, 1829, *Jackson Correspondence*, 4:108–09; Longaker, "Kitchen Cabinet," 95–96; William Stickney, ed., *The Autobiography of Amos Kendall* (Boston: Lee and Shepard, 1872), 635.

5 Longaker, "Kitchen Cabinet," 96–100; Latner, "Jacksonian Politics," 944, 962. See also Latner's excellent *Presidency of Andrew Jackson: White House Politics, 1829–1837* (Athens: University of Georgia Press, 1979), and E. B. Smith's *Francis Preston Blair* (New York: Free Press, 1980), 45–89. Donelson had a post in the land office, and Kendall was an auditor in the Treasury Department. The general rule was that dissenting advisors were not discharged or exiled; they were simply not consulted further on the question at issue (Longaker, "Kitchen Cabinet," 101, 107–08). The more traditional view of Van Buren as chief advisor is argued by John Spencer Bassett, "Martin Van Buren," in Bemis, *American Secretaries of State*, 4:179. He states that the entire Kitchen Cabinet stood in awe of Jackson. Van Buren, never certain what ideas the President would have, proceeded with caution, but in some cases the Fox was successful and notably modified Old Hickory's political course.

6 Eugene McCormac, "John Forsyth," in Bemis, *American Secretaries of State*, 4:323; William B. Lewis to James A. Hamilton, Dec. 12, 1828, Van Buren Papers (Lewis, a Van Buren supporter, told Hamilton that Jackson was going to the capital to work, and he expected those around him to work, too: "He wants no idlers about him"); Albert Somit, "Andrew Jackson as Administrator," *Public Administration Review* 8 (1948): 188–96 (Somit sees Jackson as an administrator with acumen, tact, and the ability to achieve his ends); Van Buren to Jackson, Nov. 28, 1829, Van Buren Papers.

7 Bassett, "Martin Van Buren," 161–68, 203; Fitzpatrick, *Autobiography of Van Buren*, 258–60 (Van Buren was likely not troubled by the Moore appointment, since they were friends); G. Ver Planck to Van Buren, Dec. 6, 1828, Van Buren Papers; William Rives to T. P. Moore, March 18, 1829, ibid.; Wright to Van Buren, Dec. 9, 1828, ibid.; Littleton Tazewell to Jackson, March 30, 1829, *Jackson Correspondence*, 4:15–16; Niven, *Van Buren*, 274.

8 Fitzpatrick, *Autobiography of Van Buren*, 251–57; Jackson to Van Buren, April 9, 1829, Van Buren Papers. McLane at the age of forty-three and Rives at thirty-six were much younger than Tazewell and Livingston.

9 Fitzpatrick, *Autobiography of Van Buren*, 251–60; Livingston to Jackson, May 3, Van Buren Papers; Woodbury to Van Buren, April 27, ibid.; Van Buren to Van Ness, May 3, ibid.; Van Buren to Rives, May 5, 1829, ibid.; John Munroe, *Louis McLane: Federalist and Jacksonian* (New Brunswick, N.J.: Rutgers University Press, 1973), 253–56.

10 Gerald Johnson, *Randolph of Roanoke: A Political Fantastic* (New York: Minton, Balch, 1929), 251–59; Jackson to Randolph, Sept. 16, 1829, *Jackson Correspondence*, 4:75; Fitzpatrick, *Autobiography of Van Buren*, 418–21.

11 Niven, *Van Buren*, 287.

12 Bassett, "Martin Van Buren," 183–90; Jackson to Van Buren, July 30, 1830, Van Buren Papers; Jackson to Van Buren, Sept. 5, 1831, *Jackson Correspondence*, 4:348; Benjamin F. Butler to Van Buren, April 22, 1831, Van Buren Papers; Van Buren to Jackson, April 11, 1831, ibid.,; Fitzpatrick, *Autobiography of Van Buren*, 274–75.

13 Fitzpatrick, *Autobiography of Van Buren*, 593, 704–05; Colonel Robert Butler to Jackson, June 9, 1831, *Jackson Correspondence*, 4:294; Jackson to Van Buren, Dec. 17, 1831, ibid., 385; Alfred Balch to Nicholas Trist, Sept. 1831, Nicholas Trist Papers, Library of Congress, Washington, D.C.; J. Coolidge to Trist, Aug. 3, 1831, ibid.; Francis Rawle, "Edward Livingston," in Bemis, *American Secretaries of State*, 4:207–10.

14 William Hatcher, *Edward Livingston: Jeffersonian Republican and Jacksonian Democrat* (University, La.: Louisiana State University Press, 1940), 395–96, 400, 416; Rawle, "Edward Livingston," 207, 221, 225–56.

15 Munroe, *McLane*, 395–400; Fitzpatrick, *Autobiography of Van Buren*, 588, 593–94; Eugene McCormac, "Louis McLane," in Bemis, *American Secretaries of State*, 4:267–98. Samuel Smith was a forty-year veteran of Congress. Nominally a Jacksonian, he pursued an independent course on several issues such as the Bank recharter, which may have cost him a Cabinet seat (Smith to Van Buren, Dec. 23, 1832, Van Buren Papers).

16 Alvin Duckett, *John Forsyth: Political Tactician* (Athens: University of Georgia Press, 1962), 167–69, 191–93; clippings, 1834–35, Levi Woodbury Papers, Library of Congress, Washington, D.C. Forsyth did aspire to the vice-presidency but was pushed aside for Richard Johnson, a westerner, in 1836 (McCormac, "John Forsyth," 304–28).

17 Jackson to Congress, December, 1829, in Richardson, *Messages and Papers*, 2:461; Gaillard Hunt, *The Department of State of the United States* (New Haven, Conn.: Yale University Press, 1914), 201, 210–11. The eight European posts were Great Britain, France, Spain, the Netherlands, Portugal, Denmark, Sweden, and Russia. The seven in Latin America were Argentina, Brazil, Colombia, Chile, Mexico, Central America, and Peru (William Barnes and John H. Morgan, *The Foreign Service of the United States: Origins, Development and Functions* [Washington,

D.C.: Historical Office of the Department of State, 1961], 69–70, 73, 88–89, 349–50). While patronage was clearly a factor in his appointment policy, there was little immediate turnover among State Department personnel with Van Buren at the helm. Substantial change had occurred by 1837, but that was more likely due to factors other than partisan politics (Graham H. Stuart, *The Department of State: A History of Its Organization, Procedures and Personnel* [New York: Macmillan, 1949], 71). Diplomatic and consular appointments (1829–41) show twenty removals (eleven between 1829 anbd 1833) and forty-four new consular appointments (Barnes and Morgan, *Foreign Service*, 90).

18 Barnes and Morgan, *Foreign Service*, 83–85; Graham Stuart, *American Diplomatic and Consular Practice* (New York: Appleton-Century-Crofts, 1952), 168–70. Livingston wanted to pay the thirty consuls $2,000 per year and the 126 vice consuls $1,000 per year, a total cost of $186,000 (*Message from the President of the United States to Congress in Relation to the Consular Establishment of the United States* (Washington, D.C.: F. P. Blair, 1833], 1–11).

19 Stuart, *Diplomatic and Consular Practice*, 170–71; Barnes and Morgan, *Foreign Service*, 70, 77, 88.

20 Stuart, *Department of State*, 78–81; Hunt, *Department of State*, 203–07.

21 Stuart, *Department of State*, 82–83; Hunt, *Department of State*, 207–09, 211–19. Extra clerks could be and were hired by the department as the need arose.

22 Glyndon Van Deusen, *The Life of Henry Clay* (Boston: Little, Brown, 1937), 297; E. M. Carroll, *The Origins of the Whig Party* (Durham, N.C.: Duke University Press, 1925), 178–80; Stickney, *Autobiography of Kendall*, 297.

23 Carroll, *Whig Party*, 181–84.

24 Clinton Rossiter, *The American Presidency* (New York: Harcourt, Brace, 1956), 63–64, 72; Stickney, *Autobiography of Kendall*, 417 (the opposition *National Intelligencer* felt that Jackson's remarks on foreign affairs in his first message to Congress in December 1829 "sound for a Republican President rather too imperially"); Carroll, *Whig Party*, 178; Jackson to John Coffee, April 6, 1834, *Jackson Correspondence*, 5:260; Jackson to Andrew Jackson, Jr., April 15, 1834, ibid., 261.

25 Patrick Macaulary to Trist, March 30, 1833; Trist Papers; C. P. Curtis to Trist, Dec. 16, 1832, ibid.; Payton Gay to Trist, Aug. 10, 1832, ibid.; Silas Burrows to Van Buren, Jan. 24, 1830, Van Buren Papers; William J. Quincy to Woodbury, Nov. 1, 1834, Woodbury Papers.

26 Jackson to Van Buren, Oct. 31, 1829, Oct. 23, 1830, Van Buren Papers; Van Buren to Jackson, July 16, 1831, ibid.; Van Buren to George M. Dallas, May 11, 1836, ibid. Van Buren understated his influence with Jackson in writing to Dallas. As a leader of the Pennsylvania Democracy, Dallas's relations with the New Yorker had been strained for some years.

27 Hatcher, *Livingston*, 416–18; Jackson to Livingston, Aug. 7, 1831, *Jackson Correspondence*, 4:327–28.

28 Munroe, *McLane*, 413; Woodbury to Russell Jarvis, March 14, 1836, Woodbury Papers. Jackson interfered even with such appointments as a draftsman to the General Land Office and the Navy Agent at Gibraltar (Jackson to Woodbury, July 13, 1835; J. C. Pickett to Woodbury, May 27, 1835, Woodbury Papers). The Navy Agency was a $7,000-per-year plum, and the President used political aplomb in offering it to the brother of Calhounite South Carolina Senator Robert Y. Hayne. Jackson postulated that "in four years, if one knows the mercantile world, one could make an ample fortune" (Jackson to Colonel A. P. Hayne, *Jackson Correspondence*, 4 : 135–36).

29 *Register of Debates in Congress, 1825–1837*, 21st Cong. 1st sess., Report of the Secretary of the Treasury, Dec. 1829, 65; Report of the Secretary of the Navy, ibid., 36–37.

30 23rd Cong., 2d sess., ibid., 15; 24th Cong., 2d sess., ibid., 7; 25th Cong., 2d sess., ibid., 8–9.

31 Jackson to Congress, March 4, 1837, Richardson, *Messages and Papers*, 3 : 307.

32 24th Cong., 2d sess., vol. 13, 1836. The size of the naval manpower had also increased from 4,000 men in 1831 to 6,000 in 1834, not including the marines.

33 Charles O. Clapp to Van Buren, April 9, 1829, Van Buren Papers; Samuel Smith to Van Buren, May 11, May 14, May 20, 1829, ibid.; Van Buren to Smith, Oct. 15, 1830, ibid.; Jackson to Van Buren, Oct. 23, Nov. 15, 1830, ibid. Total American tonnage approached 1.5 million, of which Massachusetts registered 400,000, New York 320,000, and Maine 200,000—over 50 percent of the total: Clippings, 1833–34, Woodbury Papers; Asa Clapp to Woodbury, July 31, 1826, Asa Clapp estate, Jan. 1, 1836, ibid.; Richard A. McLemore, *Franco-American Diplomatic Relations, 1816–1836* (Baton Rouge: Louisiana State University Press, 1941), 48–49.

34 James A. Hamilton to William Rives, April 19, 1830, William Rives Papers, Library of Congress, Washington, D.C.; Samuel Smith to Van Buren, March 20, 1831, Van Buren Papers.

35 Van Buren to Preserved Fish, June 4, 1829, Domestic Correspondence, Department of State; Van Buren to David Winchester, June 4, 1829, ibid.; Van Buren to Robert Oliver, April 7, 1830, ibid.; Van Buren to A. J. Schwartz, April 7, 1830, ibid.; Robert Oliver to Van Buren, March 31, 1830, ibid.; Daniel Brent to John Connell, June 18, Nov. 22, 1830, ibid.; Daniel Brent to Robert Oliver, May 3, 1832, ibid.

36 J. Moriarty to Levi Woodbury, Dec. 10, 1832, Woodbury Papers; Samuel Smith to William Rives, Oct. 5, 1831, Rives Papers.

37 Livingston to McKim, March 19, 1833, Domestic Correspondence, Department of State; Clippings on Naval Affairs, Woodbury Papers; James Phillips, *Salem and the Indies* (Boston: Houghton Mifflin, 1947), 209; Nathaniel West to Woodbury, March 25, 1835, *Letters of Claimants, Neapolitan Indemnity*, U.S. Treasury Department, 2 vols. (1835–36). Also see U.S. Treasury Department, *Register of*

Neapolitan Indemnity, 1835–36, and *Register of Certificates Issued in Payment of the French Indemnity,* 3 vols., 1836, National Archives. A close relationship existed between the McKims and the premier merchant house of Alexander Brown (Frank R. Kent, *The Story of Alexander Brown and Sons* [Baltimore, 1925], 107).

38 Van Buren to George Winchester, March 12, 1831, Domestic Correspondence, Department of State; McLane to Neapolitan Commissioners, Sept. 18, 1833, ibid.; Personal Political Clippings, 1834–40, Woodbury Papers; Joseph Cabot to Woodbury, Dec. 9, 1833, and Woodbury to Cabot, Dec. 16, 1833, ibid.; Washington, D.C. Committee to Woodbury, March 11, 1835, ibid. Van Buren unsuccessfully requested the President to award one of the Neapolitan commission slots to Democratic Senator John Forsyth's brother-in-law (Van Buren to Jackson, Feb. 6, 1833, Van Buren Papers).

39 Daniel Brent to John Connell, Aug. 22, 1832, Domestic Correspondence, Department of State; Livingston to Romulus Saunders, May 4, 1833, ibid.; McLane to the French commissioners, Nov. 18, 1833, ibid.; Fitzpatrick, *Autobiography of Van Buren,* 599–600; Statement of Andrew Jackson Donelson, Nov. 13, 1830, *Jackson Correspondence,* 4:203. The Spanish claims, settled by treaty in February 1834, amounted to $600,000. Since relatively few ships were involved, the President appointed one commissioner, Lewis Henry, to make the awards.

40 Remini, *Jackson and the Course of Democracy,* 290.

41 Rives to Trist, March 19, 1829, Trist Papers; Trist to A. J. Donelson, May 20, 1829, ibid.; Livingston to Trist, April 24, 1833, ibid.; Thomas Bulfinch to Trist, May 2, 1833, ibid. Trist was originally appointed to a clerkship by Secretary of State Henry Clay.

42 John Mumford to Trist, May 4, 1833, ibid.; Hefferman to Trist, May 5, 1833, ibid.; Petition on Behalf of John Hefferman to Edward Livingston, April 18, 1833, ibid.; Trist to Hefferman, May 8, 1833, ibid.

43 C. P. Curtis to Trist, May 12, 1833, ibid.; H. D. Gilpin to Trist, Sept. 25, 1833, ibid.; Thomas Bulfinch to Trist, May 6, 1833, ibid.; Donelson to Trist, Dec. 28, 1833, ibid.

44 Cleveland to Trist, May 28, July 31, 1833, ibid.; Trist to Cleveland, June 28, 1833, ibid. American vessels were charged an average of $4.00 as a "ship deposit fee." Of this sum, the consul received $1.00.

45 Trist to McLane, Aug. 9, 1833, ibid.; L. B. Randolph to Trist, May 17, 1834, ibid.; Louis Johnson to Trist, Oct. 30, 1834, ibid.; William B. Randolph to Trist, Sept. 7, 1834, ibid. Two men from Massachusetts, Hezekiah Bradford and Thomas Smith, established the Cuba Mining Company in 1836 to mine and smelt copper. They incorporated at a capital stock issue of $500,000 (Agreement between John Baker and Nicholas Trist, Dec. 23, 1836, ibid.).

46 *U.S. Register* (1829), 12ff.; ibid. (1837), 4ff. Also see Jonathan Elliot, *The American Diplomatic Code* (New York, 1834), 22–24.

47 Committee to Jackson, March 5, 1829, Rives Papers; Moore to Riggs, Jan. 14,

Feb. 25, April 21, July 7, Oct. 13, 1830, Moore Correspondence, Riggs Family Papers, Library of Congress, Washington, D.C.; Holding to Moore, March 25, 1830, ibid.; Moore to Holding, April 24, 1830, ibid.

48 Riggs to Moore, Feb. 19, 1831, Jan. 12, Feb. 4, 1832, Domestic-Foreign Letterbook, ibid.; Moore to Riggs, May 7, June 28, July 27, 1831, ibid.; Holding to Moore, July 12, and Moore to Holding, July 14, 1831, ibid.; Moore to Riggs, Feb. 24, 1832, Jan. 14, Feb. 28, Sept. 29, Nov. 1, 1833, ibid.; Rafel A. Taylor to Moore, April 4, 1833, ibid.

49 McAfee to Riggs, Sept. 1, 1833, Jan. 20, Feb. 14, 1834, Jan. 23, 1835, March 21, Oct. 14, 1836, ibid.; Riggs to McAfee, Oct. 13, 1834, ibid. The Gran Colombian federation had collapsed by 1833, leaving Colombia (New Granada), Venezuela, and Ecuador squabbling with each other. Jackson accordingly reduced the rank of the mission to Bogotá from $9,000-per-year minister to $4,500-per-year chargé. Moore, although from slaveholding Kentucky, held Taylor in special esteem. "No man possesses more incorruptible integrity," Moore noted. "He [Taylor] was never made for a servant . . . and here his color does not materially injure him" (Moore to Riggs, July 27, 1831, ibid.).

50 Henry Wriston, *Executive Agents in American Foreign Relations* (Baltimore, 1929), 236–57.

CHAPTER THREE

1 David B. Davis, "Some Themes of Counter Subversion: An Analysis of Anti-Masonic, Anti-Catholic and Anti-Mormon Literature," *Mississippi Valley Historical Review* 47:205–24; U.S. Bureau of the Census, *Historical Statistics of the United States* (Washington, D.C.: GPO, 1960), 245–51.

2 Globally, the United States imported $74 million worth of goods in 1829 and exported $72 million. By 1836 the imports had skyrocketed to $190 million and the domestic exports to $107 million (Remini, *Jackson and the Course of Freedom*, 290).

3 Michael P. Rogin, *Fathers and Children: Andrew Jackson and the Subjugation of the American Indian* (New York: Knopf, 1975), 141–42. For an in-depth discussion of the events surrounding the Falklands crisis of 1831–32 between the United States and Argentina, see ch. 7, "South America"; Kenneth Bourne, *Britain and the Balance of Power In North America, 1815–1908* (Berkeley: University of California Press, 1967), 68–69.

4 Munroe, *McLane*, 262–66; F. Lee Benns, *The American Struggle for the British West Indies Carrying Trade, 1815–1830* (Bloomington: University of Indiana, 1923), 154–62; Van Buren to McLane, July 20, Dec. 26, 1829, U.S. Department of State, Instructions, Great Britain (such diplomatic correspondence is hereafter cited as

Instructions, Dispatches, or Consular Dispatches, with the appropriate nation or city: e.g., "Instructions, Great Britain"); Remini, *Jackson and the Course of Freedom*, 282–85.

5 McLane to his wife, April 29, 1829, Louis McLane Papers, Library of Congress, Washington, D.C.; McLane to Van Buren, Sept. 22, Oct. 14, Oct. 17, 1829, Dispatches, Great Britain; Munroe, *McLane*, 272–79.

6 McLane to Van Buren, Nov. 14, Nov. 28, Dec. 14, 1829, Dispatches, Great Britain; Benns, *West Indian Trade*, 162–70; Jackson to Congress, Dec. 8, 1829, Richardson, *Messages and Papers*, 2:443.

7 McLane to Van Buren, Jan. 14, April 14, 1830, Dispatches, Great Britain; Munroe, *McLane*, 274–79; Jackson to Van Buren, April 10, 1830, *Jackson Correspondence*, 4:133.

8 McLane to Cambreleng, March 30, 1830, Van Buren Papers; John Pancake, *Samuel Smith and the Politics of Business, 1752–1839* (University: University of Alabama Press, 1972), 190–91; Frank Cassell, *Merchant Congressman in the New Republic: Samuel Smith of Maryland, 1752–1839* (Madison: University of Wisconsin Press, 1971), 239–40; Benns, *West Indian Trade*, 170–74; Jackson to Congress, May 26, 1830, Richardson, *Messages and Papers*, 2:480–81. Cambreleng had a vested interest—the port of New York—in reviving the direct trade and had engaged in lengthy correspondence with Van Buren over possible means to restore the tie: see Cambreleng to Van Buren, July 24, 1829, April 9, April 11, 1830, Van Buren Papers; Van Buren to Cambreleng, July 27, 1829, ibid.

9 McLane to Van Buren, July 6, Aug. 20, Nov. 22, Dec. 22, 1830, Dispatches, Great Britain; McLane to Aberdeen July 12, ibid.; Aberdeen to McLane, Aug. 17, 1830, ibid.; Munroe, *McLane*, 277–79; McLane to Henry Ridgely, Dover, Delaware, Aug. 19, 1830, McLane Papers; McLane to Woodbury, Aug. 30, 1830, Woodbury Papers. Prior to 1826 the average yearly export of the British West Indies to the United States was valued at approximately $4 million, while American exports to the colonial ports were about $2 million (Clippings on Political Affairs, 1832–33, ibid.; Pancake, *Smith*, 191; Benns, *West Indian Trade*, 156, 185–88).

10 Jackson to A. Butler, Oct. 6, 1830, *Jackson Correspondence*, 4:182; Jackson to John Overton, Sept. 30, 1830, ibid., 181; Robert Y. Hayne to Van Buren, Oct. 23, 1830, Van Buren Papers; Thomas Ritchie to Van Buren, Nov. 2, 1830, ibid.

11 C. C. Cambreleng to Van Buren, Oct. 11, 1830, Van Buren Papers; Munroe, *McLane*, 279; Fitzpatrick, *Autobiography of Van Buren*, 523–27; Benns, *West Indian Trade*, 174–75, 180–84.

12 Jackson to McLane, March 8, 1831, *Jackson Correspondence*, 4:246–47; James Callahan, *American Foreign Policy in Canadian Relations* (New York, 1937), 148–49; Samuel F. Bemis, *John Quincy Adams and the Foundations of American Foreign Policy* (New York: Knopf, 1949), 469–81. The dispute also involved the

claims of the parent state of Massachusetts and, to a lesser extent, those of Vermont and New Hampshire. Bemis believes that both Gallatin and Webster represented the interests of their nation poorly in their respective dealings with Great Britain.

13 Notes on conversation with Vaughan, April 8, 1829, Van Buren Papers; Van Ness to Van Buren, Jan. 3, 1829, ibid.

14 Van Buren to Preble, Nov. 2, 1829, Jan. 4, 1830, Instructions, All Countries; Preble to Van Buren, Feb. 14, Nov. 26, 1830, Van Buren Papers; Preble to Jackson, Dec. 25, 1830, ibid.; Preble to Stephen Thatcher, Lubec, Maine, June 1, 1830, William Preble Papers, Library of Congress, Washington, D.C.

15 Preble to Rives, Jan. 17, 1831, Rives Papers; Callahan, *Canadian Relations*, 148–49.

16 Davezac to Jackson and Davezac to Van Buren, Jan. 15, 1831, Van Buren Papers; Preble to Van Buren, Jan. 17, 1831, ibid.; Van Ness to Van Buren, Feb. 6, 1831, ibid. The London Conference of the major powers met at this time to insure Belgian independence and neutrality. It was ultimately necessary to dispatch a French force to quiet the Dutch, who were attempting to reconquer the seceded provinces.

17 McLane to Preble, Feb. 15, 1831, Preble Papers; Rives to Preble, April 24, 1831, ibid.; James A. Hamilton to Van Buren, March 12, 1831, Van Buren Papers; Van Ness to Van Buren, Feb. 6, 1831, ibid.

18 Jackson to Van Buren, March 6, 1831, Van Buren Papers; Van Buren to Governor Samuel Smith, March 9, March 18, 1831, Domestic Correspondence, Department of State.

19 Livingston to Van Buren, Aug. 1, 1831, Instructions, All Countries; Jackson to Van Buren, Aug. 10, 1831, Van Buren Papers.

20 Van Buren to Jackson, Sept. 28, Oct. 14, 1831, Van Buren Papers; Van Buren to Livingston, Nov. 5, 1831, *Jackson Correspondence*, 4:373–74; Livingston to Van Buren, Nov. 13, 1831, ibid.; Jackson to Van Buren, Nov. 14, 1831, ibid.

21 Callahan, *Canadian Relations*, 151–52; Hatcher, *Livingston*, 398–400.

22 Callahan, *Canadian Relations*, 152–53; Memorandum of Livingston, Feb. 15, 1832, Instructions, Special Missions; Livingston to Preble, March 9, April 25, 1832, ibid.; Livingston to Jackson, March 29, 1832, ibid.; Livingston to Governor Smith, April 17, 1832, ibid.; Maine continued to push for the free navigation of the St. Johns River and instructed its representatives to incorporate this proviso in the Senate's demands.

23 Samuel Smith to Preble, March 6, 1832, and Preble to Maine correspondent, 1832, Preble Papers; Protocol memorandum of Maine Commissioners, June 1832, Instructions, Special Missions. Van Buren had first suggested the idea of compensation to Livingston and the President in the fall of 1831.

24 Callahan, *Canadian Relations*, 153–54; Fitzpatrick, *Autobiography of Van Buren*,

454; Livingston to Bankhead, July 20, 1832, Instructions, Special Missions; Jackson to J. Campbell, Feb. 9, 1832, Van Buren Papers; Jackson to Van Buren, Feb. 12, 1832, ibid.

25 Callahan, *Canadian Relations*, 155–56; Vail to Livingston, July 12, Aug. 14, Aug. 21, Oct. 13, Oct. 16, Oct. 30, 1832, Dispatches, Great Britain, Vail to Van Buren, Aug. 22, 1832, Van Buren Papers.

26 Livingston to Vail, Feb. 26, 1833, and Livingston to Stevenson, March 15, 1833, Instructions, Great Britain; John A. Doyle, ed., "The Papers of Sir Charles Vaughan," *American Historical Review* 7 : 500–503.

27 Trist Memorandum on Jackson, May 4, 1833, Trist Papers.

28 Doyle, "Papers of Charles Vaughan," 500–503.

29 Munroe, *McLane*, 411–12; Henry Burrage, *Maine in the Northeastern Boundary Controversy* (Portland, Maine: Marks Printing House, 1919), 215–21; Duckett, *Forsyth*, 203–04; Callahan, *Canadian Relations*, 157–58.

30 Forsyth to Bankhead, Feb. 29, March 5, 1836, W. R. Manning, ed., *Diplomatic Correspondence of the United States (Canadian Relations), 1784–1860* (Washington, D.C.: Carnegie Endowment, 1940–45), 3 : 4–7.

31 Francis Wayland, *Andrew Stevenson: Democrat and Diplomat* (Philadelphia: University of Pennsylvania Press, 1949), 103–11, 140–43. Stevenson was favorably viewed by the Maine congressional delegation; five of the seven lobbied the President in support of his nomination.

32 Forsyth to Stevenson, Dec. 30, 1836, April 7, 1837, Instructions, Great Britain; Stevenson to Forsyth, Feb. 6, Feb. 22, 1837, Dispatches, Great Britain.

33 Wayland, *Stevenson*, 115–23. Jackson eagerly but unsuccessfully pursued a treaty to end impressment, an issue that had little practical significance in the 1830s but haunted the General from the War of 1812: Jackson to Van Buren, Dec. 17, Dec. 19, 1831, Van Buren Papers; Van Buren to Jackson, March 10, 1832, ibid.; Vaughan to Palmerston, Aug. 22, Sept. 4, Sept. 20, 1833, PRO (London), FO 84/143.

34 Fitzpatrick, *Autobiography of Van Buren*, 450–51; McLane to Woodbury, Jan. 4, 1830, Woodbury Papers; McLane to Rives, Jan. 2, 1830, Rives Papers.

35 Vail to Van Buren, July 18, 1835, Van Buren Papers; Herbert C. F. Bell, *Lord Palmerston* (London: Longmans, Green, 1936), 243–45. See also C. K. Webster, "British Mediation between France and the United States, 1834–36," *English Historical Review*, 42 : 58–78, and Kenneth Bourne, *Palmerston: The Early Years, 1784–1841* (New York: Free Press, 1982).

36 *Digest of Commercial Regulations of Foreign Countries with the United States* (Washington: Blair and Rives, 1836), 1 : 276, 430–31; *Historical Statistics of the U.S.*, 218; Lester Langley, *The Cuban Policy of the United States: A Brief History* (New York: Wiley, 1968), 14–23.

37 Woodbury had gone so far as to draft a letter of resignation from the Senate in

order to accept the Spanish post. Because of Democratic infighting in New Hampshire, he lost his Senate seat in 1830 to Isaac Hill. Jackson thereafter appointed him Secretary of the Navy: Woodbury draft letter, May 1829, and Van Buren to Woodbury, April 29, 1829, Woodbury Papers.

38 Van Buren to Van Ness, Oct. 2, 1829, OLct. 13, 1830, April 25, 1831, Instructions, All Countries; Van Ness to Van Buren, July 11, 1829, Van Buren Papers. American vessels paid an exorbitant duty of $2.50 per ton in Cuba and $1.00 per ton in Puerto Rico. Langley reports $1.50 for American vessels and 62 cents for Spanish vessels (*Cuban Policy*, 21–23).

39 Van Ness to Van Buren, Aug. 14, Sept. 1, Oct 9, 1830, Dispatches, Spain. The politically moderate Ferdinand had recently decreed that females could ascend the throne. Since his wife was pregnant, the birth would in any case exclude his ambitious brother Don Carlos from immediate succession. Ferdinand's death would also open the possibility of war between the conservative followers of Don Carlos and the liberals who would receive support from revolutionary France.

40 Jackson to Congress, Dec. 6, 1830, Richardson, *Messages and Papers*, 2:507; Van Ness to Van Buren, Jan. 31, Feb. 6, 1831, Van Buren Papers.

41 Van Buren to Van Ness, April 25, 1831, Instructions, All Countries; Jackson to Van Buren, Sept. 18, 1831, *Jackson Correspondence*, 4:350; Jackson to Livingston, Sept. 3, 1831, ibid. 345; Jackson to Congress, Richardson, *Messages and Papers*, 2:549.

42 Forsyth to John Smith, Oct. 27, 1835, Domestic Correspondence, Department of State; Van Ness to Van Buren, Feb. 23, March 19, 1832, Van Buren Papers; Van Ness to Rives, May 19, 1832, Rives Papers; Jackson to Congress, Dec. 4, 1832, Richardson, *Messages and Papers*, 2:593.

43 Livingston to Van Ness, March 24, April 12, 1833, Instructions, Spain; McLane to Van Ness, Aug. 27, Aug. 28, 1833, ibid.

44 Van Ness to Don Francisco Zea Bermudez, Dec. 19, 1832, Dispatches, Spain; Bermudez to Van Ness, May 18, June 8, 1833, ibid.; Van Ness to Bermudez, May 24, June 10, 1833, ibid.; Van Ness to Livingston, Feb. 11, June 12, 1833, ibid.; Van Ness to McLane, Nov. 28, Dec. 21, 1833, Feb. 18, 1834, ibid. For all relevant correspondence, see *Register of Debates*, 23rd Cong., 2d sess., Appendix 231–71.

45 Jackson to Congress, Dec. 3, 1833, Richardson, *Messages and Papers*, 3:23–24.

46 McLane to Van Ness, May 30, 1834, Instructions, Spain; Forsyth to Van Ness, July 28, Aug. 29, 1834, ibid.

47 Forsyth to Van Ness, May 16, 1835, Jan. 20, 1836, Instructions, Spain; Forsyth to Eaton, April 27, 1836, March 14, 1837, ibid.; Duckett, *Forsyth*, 189–91. Van Ness blasted Barry "as a wretched object" who knew virtually nothing about Spain and "who, besides, had already one foot in the grave"; he also criticized Eaton for extended socializing in Cadiz, where he passed out 1,000 cards with his name

and the title "Chargé d'Affaires" (Van Ness to Jackson, Feb. 10, 1837, Van Buren Papers).

48 William L. Lucey, *Edward Kavanagh: Catholic Statesman Diplomat from Maine, 1795–1844* (Francestown, N.H.: Marshall Jones, 1946), 122–27.

49 Van Buren to T. L. L. Brent, April 4, Oct. 5, 1829, Aug. 5, 1831, Instructions, All Countries; Hatcher, *Livingston*, 411–12; Forsyth to Edward Kavanagh, March 27, 1835, Instructions, Portugal.

50 Van Buren to Livingston, March 12, 1832, Van Buren Papers; Lucey, *Kavanagh*, 127–29; Woodbury to John Randolph, April 11, 1832, Woodbury Papers.

51 Lucey, *Kavanagh*, 116–21, 130–42.

52 Major commercial problems with the treaty included the granting of special status to Portuguese wines in America and allowing Brazil (an American competitor in some goods) special status in the Portuguese market: Kavanagh to Woodbury, Sept. 7, 1835, March 28, 1836, Woodbury Papers; Forsyth to Kavanagh, March 27, 1835, Jan. 7, May 30, 1836, Instructions, Portugal.

53 Randolph to Jackson, March 28, 1832, *Jackson Correspondence*, 4 : 426; James A. Hamilton to Van Buren, Jan. 18, 1830, Van Buren Papers; Joseph O. Baylen, "James Buchanan's 'Calm of Despotism,'" *Pennsylvania Magazine of History and Biography* 77 : 294; Johnson, *Randolph*, 258–59. Van Buren anticipated that Randolph would return to the United States as soon as he negotiated the treaty (Fitzpatrick, *Autobiography of Van Buren*, 419).

54 Johnson, *Randolph*, 259–61 (Randolph's collection of his salary and expenses for his aborted mission drew heavy partisan fire from Henry Clay and John Quincy Adams in Congress); Benjamin P. Thomas, *Russo-American Relations, 1815–1867* (Baltimore: Johns Hopkins University Press, 1930), 70–72, 81–88. The United States engaged heavily in the carrying trade with Russia, particularly in raw materials such as sugar from the West Indies. In 1830, American exports to Russia amounted to only $350,000 and imports a significantly higher $1.6 million.

55 John R. Clay to William Rives, March 21, 1832, Rives Papers; Thomas, *Russo-American Relations*, 70–72; Baylen, "Buchanan," 295–97; Simon Pleasanton to Buchanan, Nov. 25, 1830, Buchanan-Johnston Papers, Library of Congress, Washington, D.C. Buchanan hoped to use the Russian mission as a springboard to the vice-presidency in 1832 (George Plitt to Buchanan, July 3, 1831, ibid.).

56 Philip S. Klein, *President James Buchanan* (University Park: Pennsylvania State University Press, 1962), 78–81, 86; Buchanan to Rives, Jan. 19, 1833, Rives Papers; Baylen, "Buchanan," 297–301.

57 Baylen, "Buchanan," 295–301; Klein, *Buchanan*, 83–86; Buchanan to Rives, Aug. 13, 1832, Jan. 19, 1833, Rives Papers.

58 Baylen, "Buchanan," 297–305; Klein, *Buchanan*, 87–90.

59 Klein, *Buchanan*, 87–90; Thomas, *Russo-American Relations*, 88–91.

60 Thomas, *Russo-American Relations*, 88–98; Jackson to Van Buren, Aug. 16, 1833, Van Buren Papers; Forsyth to Wilkins, July 30, 1835, Instructions, Russia.

CHAPTER FOUR

1 *Digest of Commercial Regulations* (France), 2:8–9. More historical literature has appeared on Franco-American relations than any other diplomatic topic in the Jackson presidency, beginning with Richard McLemore's *Franco-American Relations*, supported by an earlier article, "The French Spoliations Claims, 1816–36: A Study in Jacksonian Diplomacy," *Tennessee Historical Magazine* 2:234–54. More recently, the issue has been updated by Henry B. Cox, "To the Victor: A History of the French Spoliations Claims Controversy, 1793–1955," Ph.D. diss., George Washington University, 1967. Also valuable are Robert C. Thomas, "Andrew Jackson versus France: American Policy toward France, 1834–36," *Tennessee Historical Quarterly* 35:51–64, and his "Partisan Politics and Foreign Policy: The French Chamber of Deputies, 1834–35," *Maryland Historian* 5:98–103. Remini's *Jackson and the Course of Democracy*, 211–36, 274–92, includes a detailed account of the 1834–36 crisis. William Rives deserves a published biography, but thus far none has appeared. Informative are Ann Liston, "William C. Rives, Diplomat and Politician, 1829–1853," Ph.D. diss., Ohio State University, 1972, and Deborah Ignatz, "The Political and Diplomatic Career of William Cabell Rives," M.A. thesis, University of South Florida, 1981. For earlier negotiations and commercial intercourse, see McLemore, *Franco-American Relations*, 1–42, and Willis H. Walker, *Franco-American Commercial Relations* (Fort Hays, Kan., 1928), 64ff.

2 Liston, "Rives," 74–76; Hatcher, *Livingston*, 410–18.

3 Liston, "Rives," 76–80; McLemore, *Franco-American Relations*, 41–46.

4 Crawford to Van Buren, Sept. 9, 1829, Van Buren Papers; Van Buren to Rives, May 5, 1829, Rives Papers; Liston, "Rives," 83–90; Van Buren to Rives, July 20, 1829, Instructions, France.

5 A. Curcier, Philadelphia, to Rives, July 20, 1829, Rives Papers; Rives to Van Buren, Aug. 12, 1829, Dispatches, France; McLemore, *Franco-American Relations*, 47–50.

6 Liston, "Rives," 94–99; Rives to Van Buren, Sept. 12, Sept. 27, 1829, Dispatches, France.

7 Rives to Van Buren, Oct. 17, 1829, Van Buren Papers; Rives to Van Buren, Nov. 7, 1829, Dispatches, France.

8 Rives to Van Buren, Dec. 17, 1829, Jan. 16, 1830, Dispatches, France; Rives to Polignac, Jan. 13, 1830, Rives Papers; Rives to Van Buren, Jan. 13, 1830, ibid.

9 Rives to Van Buren, Jan. 28, Feb. 16, Feb. 25, 1830, Dispatches, France; Lafayette to Rives, Jan. 28, 1830, Rives Papers; Liston, "Rives," 102–17.

10 Rives to Van Buren, March 3, March 19, March 21, April 6, 1830, Dispatches, France; Rives to Polignac, March 26, 1830, ibid.

11 J. Randolph to Van Buren, Aug. 3, 1830, Van Buren Papers. The best general study of the subject is contained in the reliable but uninspired Soren Fogdall, *Danish-American Diplomacy, 1776–1920* (Iowa City: University of Iowa Press, 1922), 44–50. Also important is Elizabeth F. Baker, *Henry Wheaton, 1785–1848* (Philadelphia: University of Pennsylvania Press, 1937), 94–96.

12 Baker, *Wheaton*, 97–99; Fogdall, *Danish-American Relations*, 50–52.

13 Baker, *Wheaton*, 99–101.

14 Ibid., 102–103; Fogdall, *Danish-American Relations*, 53–54; Van Buren to Wheaton, April 3, May 2, 1829, Jan. 13, 1830, Instructions, All Countries; John Connell to William Rives, Oct. 29, 1829, Rives Papers; Wheaton to Rives, Nov. 10, 1829, Jan. 10, 1830, ibid.

15 Baker, *Wheaton*, 102–05; Fogdall, *Danish-American Relations*, 54–56; Wheaton to Rives, March 27, April 10, 1830, Rives Papers; Remini, *Jackson and the Course of Freedom*, 286.

16 Liston, "Rives," 127–34; A. Curcier to Rives, July 20, 1829, Rives Papers.

17 Van Buren to Rives, April 6, 1830, Rives Papers; Hamilton to Rives, April 19, 1830, ibid.; Van Buren to Rives, April 3, 1830, Instructions, France; Samuel Smith to Van Buren, March 20, 1831 (?), Van Buren Papers; Robert Oliver to Van Buren, March 31, April 7, 1830, Domestic Correspondence, Department of State; Van Buren to A. J. Schwartz, April 7, 1830, ibid.; Daniel Brent to J. Connell, June 18, Nov. 22, 1830, ibid.; Rives to Van Buren, May 29, 1830, Dispatches, France. Rives was also getting pressure from public figures such as Louis McLane for special considerations; see McLane to Rives, April 20, 1830, Rives Papers.

18 Van Buren to Rives, April 20, 1830, Instructions, France. The administration was being flexible; Rives was told to abandon any claim from before 1803 if necessary. As for French claims under the supposed violation of Article 8 of the Louisiana Treaty, American estimates placed the total amount the French might claim at about $100,000 (Rives to Van Buren, May 20, May 29, 1830, Dispatches, France; Rives to Polignac, June 2, 1830, ibid.; Jackson to Van Buren, April 10, 1830, *Jackson Correspondence*, 4:133).

19 Rives to Van Buren, June 8, 1830, Dispatches, France.

20 Rives to Van Buren, June 18, June 29, ibid.

21 Rives to Van Buren, July 17, July 30, Aug. 8, 1830, ibid.; Liston, "Rives," 127–34; McLemore, *Franco-American Relations*, 51–69.

22 Liston, "Rives," 134–67; Rives to Van Buren, July 30, 1830, Dispatches, France.

23 Liston, "Rives," 141–42; Rives to Van Buren, Aug. 18, Aug. 19, 1830, Dispatches, France.

24 Rives to Van Buren, Sept. 8, Sept. 18, Sept. 29, Oct. 19, Oct. 20, 1830, Dispatches,

France; Liston, "Rives," 151–57. An ongoing problem was the several-month delay in communication between Paris and Washington. Polignac had proposed a reciprocal "wines-for-cotton" reduction in the summer. The President in turn had submitted the proposal to Samuel Smith for his consideration and recommendation. By the time a response arrived in December, the French ministry had changed several times (Van Buren to Samuel Smith, Oct. 15, 1830, Van Buren Papers; Jackson to Van Buren, Oct. 23, 1830, ibid.).

25 Van Buren to Rives, Oct. 16, Nov. 8, Dec. 22, 1830, Instructions, France; Rives to Van Buren, Nov. 8, Nov. 18, 1830, Dispatches, France.

26 Rives to Van Buren, Dec. 30, 1830, Feb. 14, 1831, Van Buren Papers.

27 Liston, "Rives," 167–77; Lafayette to Rives, Feb. 8, April 18, May 7, May 29, 1831, Rives Papers; Rives to Van Buren, March 10, April 14, 1831, Dispatches, France; Rives to Preble, April 24, 1831, Preble Papers; McLemore, *Franco-American Relations*, 71–81.

28 Rives to Van Buren, April 28, May 7, 1831, Dispatches, France.

29 Rives to Van Buren, June 14, 1831, Dispatches, France; Rives to Van Buren, May 30, 1831, Van Buren Papers; Lafayette to Rives, June 3, 1831, Rives Papers; General S. Bernard to Rives, June 12, 1831, ibid. Bottled wine was reduced from 30 cents to 22 cents per gallon, white wine in casks from 15 cents to 10 cents, red wine in casks from 10 cents to 6 cents; long-staple cotton was cut from 40 francs to 20 francs per hundred kilos (Rives to Livingston, June 29, 1831, Dispatches, France; McLemore, *Franco-American Relations*, 81–88).

30 Rives to Livingston, July 8, 1831, Dispatches, France.

31 Livingston to Rives, Sept. 26, 1831, Instructions, France; Jackson to Coffee, Sept. 7, 1831, *Jackson Correspondence*, 4:350; Van Buren to Jackson, Aug. 14, Oct. 11, ibid., 334–35, 354–58; Jackson to Van Buren, Sept. 5, 1831, Van Buren Papers; Livingston to Rives, Oct. 20, 1831, Rives Papers.

32 Rives to Van Buren, Sept. 29, Oct. 25, 1831, Rives Papers; Van Buren to Jackson, Oct. 29, 1831, ibid.; Rives to Livingston, Oct. 9, Oct. 29, 1831, Dispatches, France; Van Buren to Rives, Jan. 25, 1832, Rives Papers.

33 Liston, "Rives," 188–97; Smith to Rives, Jan. 3, Jan. 27, 1832, Rives Papers.

34 Beasely to Rives, July 6, 1831, Rives Papers; Van Buren to Rives, Jan. 25, 1832, ibid.; McLemore, *Franco-American Relations*, 93–94.

35 McLemore, *Franco-American Relations*, 97; Liston, "Rives," 181–87; Livingston to Rives, April 25, 1832, Rives Papers; Rives to Livingston, March 8, 1832, ibid.; Rives to Van Buren, Feb. 20, 1832, ibid. Before Rives departed, he achieved a final diplomatic victory on the issue of the tobacco monopoly. He had naturally opposed a measure that could have cost Virginia planters an anticipated $200,000 annually. With added resistance from United States consuls such as Beasely and prominent politicos like Lafayette, the old system was restored in

1832: Liston, "Rives," 198–99; Rives to Van Buren, Aug. 18, Aug. 19, 1830, Dispatches, France.

36 Niles to Livingston, Oct. 30, 1832, Dispatches, France; Harris to Livingston, March 15, March 23, March 26, April 13, April 20, April 29, May 14, June 6, 1833, ibid.; McLemore, *Franco-American Relations*, 99–106.

37 Livingston to Rives, April 30, 1833, Rives Papers; Jackson to Van Buren, April 25, July 30, 1833, Van Buren Papers; McLane to Livingston, June 3, July 25, 1833, Instructions, France.

38 Harris to Livingston, June 14, June 22, June 28, Dispatches, France; Lafayette to the Chamber of Deputies, June 13, 1833, ibid.; McLemore, *Franco-American Relations*, 106–07.

39 Harris to McLane, Sept. 22, 1833, Dispatches, France; Livingston to McLane, July 28, July 30, Sept. 22, 1833, ibid. Niles waged a two-year battle, with the support of Rives and other administration figures, to receive a diplomatic appointment, but his selection was doomed by rumor of his "bad moral character" in Boston plus his unauthorized borrowing of funds in Paris and, most important, his importing antiadministration newspapers into France (Rives to Niles, June 9, 1835, Nathaniel Niles Papers, Library of Congress, Washington, D.C.).

40 Livingston to McLane, Sept. 29, Oct. 4, Oct. 13, Oct. 22, Nov. 22, 1833, Dispatches, France.

41 Livingston to McLane, Nov. 22, Dec. 30, 1833, Jan. 6, 1834, Dispatches, France; McLane to Livingston, Dec. 11, 1833, Instructions, France.

42 Livingston to McLane, Feb. 6, March 7, March 12, April 3, April 8, April 13, 1834, Dispatches, France; Munroe, *McLane*, 415–20.

43 Gibbes to Rives, April 2, 1834, Van Buren Papers; Niles to Woodbury, April 20, 1834, Niles Papers; Rives to Van Buren, May 15, 1834, Van Buren Papers; Rives to Jackson, May 17, 1834, Rives Papers; Woodbury to Niles, May 14, 1834, Woodbury Papers; McLane to Livingston, May 17, 1834, Instructions, France.

44 Fitzpatrick, *Autobiography of Van Buren*, 612–13; Munroe, *McLane*, 420–27; McLane to Livingston, June 27, 1834, Instructions, France; Jackson to Livingston, June 27, 1834, *Jackson Correspondence*, 5:272.

45 Livingston to Jackson, June 23, 1834, Jackson Correspondence, 5:270–71; Livingston to McLane, June 22, June 28, July 6, 1834, Dispatches, France; Livingston to Forsyth, July 26, Aug. 4, Aug. 10, 1834, ibid.; Duckett, *Forsyth*, 170.

46 Niles to Rives, Jan. 22, 1834, Rives Papers; Beasely to Rives, Sept. 8, Sept. 24, 1834, ibid.

47 Rives to Van Buren, Oct. 14, Nov. 15, 1834, Van Buren Papers; Jackson to Van Buren, Oct. 5, 1834, ibid.; Van Buren to Jackson, Oct. 13, 1834, ibid.; Van Buren to Rives, Oct. 23, 1834, Rives Papers; Woodbury to Niles, Oct. 10, 1834, Woodbury Papers; Jackson to Van Buren, Oct. 27, 1834, *Jackson Correspondence*, 5:303.

48 Forsyth to Livingston, Nov. 6, 1834, Instructions, France; Livingston to Forsyth,

Nov. 12, Nov. 14, 1834, Dispatches, France; McLemore, *Franco-American Relations*, 127–28.

49 Duckett, *Forsyth*, 171–72; McLemore, *Franco-American Relations*, 128–29; Hatcher, *Livingston*, 216–25; Thomas, "Jackson versus France," 55.

50 Duckett, *Forsyth*, 172; Van Buren to Rives, Dec. 3, 1834, Rives Papers; Van Buren to Mrs. Rives, Dec. 12, 1834, ibid.; J. Welles, Paris, to Woodbury, Dec. 15, 1834, Woodbury Papers; Hatcher, *Livingston*, 432–35; Jackson, Annual Message to Congress, Dec. 1, 1834, Richardson, *Messages and Papers*, 3:1325; McLemore, *Franco-American Relations*, 133–34; *National Intelligencer*, Dec. 4, 1834; *Niles Register*, Dec. 20, 1834.

51 Thomas, "Jackson versus France," 57–59; McLemore, *Franco-American Relations*, 137–38; Van Deusen, *Clay*, 294; Hatcher, *Livingston*, 339–40; Washington *Globe*, Dec. 17, 1834.

52 Tallmadge to Rives, Dec. 21, 1834, Rives Papers; King to Rives, Jan. 1, Jan. 12, 1835, ibid.

53 C. C. Cambreleng to Rives, Feb. 1, 1835, Rives Papers; *Register of Debates*, 23rd Cong., 2d sess., 104–05.

54 Thomas, "Jackson versus France," 60–61; Van Buren to Rives, Jan. 25, 1835, Rives Papers; Washington Irving to Van Buren, Dec. 15, 1834, Van Buren Papers.

55 Welles to Woodbury, Jan. 16, 1835, Woodbury Papers; Livingston to Forsyth, Dec. 22, 1834, Jan. 11, Jan. 14, 1835, Dispatches, France; McLemore, *Franco-American Relations*, 143.

56 Livingston to Jackson, Jan. 15, Jan. 31, 1835, *Jackson Correspondence*, 5:318–19, 323–24; Beasely to Rives, Jan. 16, Jan. 17, 1835, Rives Papers; McLemore, *Franco-American Relations*, 144–48; P. T. Guestier to Beasely, Jan. 15, Jan. 16, Jan. 17, 1835, Rives Papers.

57 Gibbes to Rives, Feb. 6, 1835, Rives Papers; Beasely to Rives, Jan. 22, 1835, ibid.; Livingston to Forsyth, Feb. 3, Feb. 24, March 15, Dispatches, France.

58 Forsyth to Livingston, Feb. 24, 1835, Instructions, France; McLemore, *Franco-American Relations*, 154–60.

59 Van Deusen, *Clay*, 289–93; *Register of Debates*, 23rd Cong., 2d sess., 730–44; Edwin Whipple, ed., *The Great Speeches and Orations of Daniel Webster* (Boston: Little, Brown, 1899), 412, 420–21.

60 *National Intelligencer*, March 9, 1835; *Niles Register*, March 7, March 14, 1835.

61 Gibbes to Rives, Feb. 6, 1835, Rives Papers; Jackson to Livingston, March 10, 1835, *Jackson Correspondence*, 5:329–30; John M. Belohlavek, "Let the Eagle Soar: Democratic Constraints upon the Foreign Policy of Andrew Jackson," *Presidential Studies Quarterly* 10:44; McLemore, *Franco-American Relations*, 158–60; Hatcher, *Livingston*, 444–47. For a good contemporary account see Thomas Hart Benton, *Thirty Years' View* (New York, 1854–56), 1:554ff, 588ff.

62 Livingston to Forsyth, April 19, April 23, 1835, Dispatches, France; Livingston to

de Rigny, Jan. 29, 1835, ibid.; Gibbes to Rives, March 19, 1835, Rives Papers; Beasely to Rives, April 24, 1835, ibid.; Hatcher, *Livingston*, 445–54.

63 Barton to Forsyth, May 7, June 15, Aug. 15, Aug. 31, Sept. 7, 1835, Dispatches, France; Welles to Woodbury, June 29, 1835, Woodbury Papers; N. M. Rothschild to Niles, May 15, Aug. 7, 1835, Niles Papers; Baron de Rothschild to Rives, April 23, 1835, Rives Papers; Rives to Van Buren, June 2, 1835, ibid.; Lewis to Rives, July 6, 1835, ibid.; Beasely to Rives, July 1, 1835, ibid.; Woodbury to Cass, June 12, 1835, Woodbury Papers; Jackson to Kendall, July 19, 1835, *Jackson Correspondence*, 5:357. Surprisingly, trade did not suffer markedly in this period: almost 200 ships annually sailed to Le Havre from 1831 to 1836 (Beasely to Secretary of State, semi-annual reports, Consular Dispatches, Le Havre).

64 Duckett, *Forsyth*, 172–74; Jackson to Forsyth, Sept. 6, 1835, *Jackson Correspondence*, 5:363; Jackson to Kendall, Oct. 31, 1835, ibid., 374–75.

65 Forsyth to Barton, Sept. 14, 1835, Instructions, France; Barton to Forsyth, Sept. 22, Nov. 7, Dispatches, France; Barton to de Broglie, Oct. 24, ibid.; de Broglie to Barton, Oct. 26, 1835, ibid.

66 Annual Message to Congress, Dec. 7, 1835, Richardson, *Messages and Papers*, 3:152–60; Notes for Annual Message, *Jackson Correspondence*, 5:377–79; McLemore, *Franco-American Relations*, 171–73.

67 A. Vail to Trist, Nov. 21, 1835, Trist Papers; Lee to Van Buren, Nov. 14, 1835, Van Buren Papers; Beasely to Rives, Nov. 29, 1835, Rives Papers; C. W. Gooch to Woodbury, Nov. 23, 1835, Woodbury Papers.

68 Vail to Forsyth, Nov. 6, Nov. 21, Dec. 14, Dec. 30, 1835, Jan. 5, Jan. 6, Jan. 14, 1836, Dispatches, Great Britain; Webster, "British Mediation," 50–78.

69 Niles *Register*, Feb. 6, 1836; I. McKim to Rives, Dec. 26, 1835, Rives Papers; Duckett, *Forsyth*, 177–79; McLemore, *Franco-American Relations*, 192–98.

70 Hatcher, *Livingston*, 455–56; Vail to Forsyth, Feb. 13, 1836, Dispatches, Great Britain; Jackson to Congress, Jan. 15, 1836, Richardson, *Messages and Papers*, 3:188–213 (includes relevant diplomatic correspondence); Parton, *Andrew Jackson*, 3:574–76 (for the French imbroglio see pp. 561–79); Vincent Carosso and Lawrence Leder, eds., "Edward Livingston and Jacksonian Diplomacy," *Louisiana History* 7:247–48; McLemore, *Franco-American Relations*, 197–200.

71 Vail to Forsyth, Feb. 13, Feb. 27, March 22, 1836, Dispatches, Great Britain; Forsyth to Vail, Feb. 20, 1836, Instructions, Great Britain; Duckett, *Forsyth*, 179–81.

72 Rush to Jackson, Jan. 11, 1836, Andrew Jackson Papers, Library of Congress, Washington, D.C.; Rush to Woodbury, Feb. 18, 1836, Woodbury Papers; H. M. Hatch to Rives, Feb. 2, 1836, Rives Papers. The Whig/National Republican Party had offered sectional candidates for the presidency in 1836, including Daniel Webster in New England, H. L. White in the West, and Willie P. Mangum in the South. William Henry Harrison was the well-received Anti-Masonic Party candidate.

73 McLemore, "French Spoliations Claims," 254; McLemore, *Franco-American Relations*, 211; Thomas, "Jackson versus France," 64; Belohlavek, "Let the Eagle Soar," 44. It should be mentioned that the growing crisis of the Texas Revolution diverted Jackson's attention from France in the fall of 1835.

CHAPTER FIVE

1 James A. Field, Jr., *America and the Mediterranean World, 1776–1882* (Princeton, N.J.: Princeton University Press, 1969), 142–43.

2 L. C. Wright, *United States Policy towards Egypt, 1830–1914* (New York: Exposition Press, 1969), 27–29.

3 Field, *Mediterranean*, 198; Van Buren to Biddle, Offley, and Rhind, Sept. 12, 1829, Instructions, Turkey; Jackson to John Branch, Secretary of the Navy, Sept. 12, 1829, ibid.; Fitzpatrick, *Autobiography of Van Buren*, 269–70.

4 Thomas Bryson, *American Diplomatic Relations with the Middle East, 1784–1975* (Metuchen, N.J.: Scarecrow Press, 1977), 18–19; Thomas Bryson, *An American Consular Officer in the Middle East in the Jacksonian Era: A Biography of William Brown Hodgson, 1801–1871* (Atlanta: Resurgens Publications, 1979), 41–43; Charles O. Paullin, *The Diplomatic Negotiations of American Naval Officers, 1778–1883* (Baltimore, Md.: Johns Hopkins University Press, 1912), 143–53. U.S. District Attorney for New York James Hamilton questioned Rhind's appointment. Hamilton, a son of the great Federalist Alexander Hamilton, was a political confidant of Van Buren and friend of the President. He advised Old Kinderhook that Rhind was not sufficiently well informed and had neither "the address or character" to accomplish the goals of the Turkish mission (Hamilton to Van Buren, Aug. 23, 1829, Van Buren Papers).

5 Bryson, *Hodgson*, 43–45; Fitzpatrick, *Autobiography of Van Buren*, 756; A. G. Davis to N. Trist, March 28, 1831, Trist Papers.

6 Jackson to Congress, Feb. 22, 1831, *Jackson Correspondence*, 4:245; Rhind to Van Buren, Feb. 21, 1831, Dispatches, Turkey; James A. Hamilton to Van Buren, April 21, 1831, Van Buren Papers. Jackson ordered federal marshalls to sell the horses at auction in New York City. The sale netted about $2,000—not enough to pay for their transportation and keep.

7 Van Buren to George Erving, March 3, 1831, Instructions, Turkey; Erving to Van Buren, March 7, 1831, Van Buren Papers.

8 Bryson, *Hodgson*, 49–52; David F. Long, *Nothing Too Daring: A Biography of Commodore David Porter, 1780–1843* (Annapolis, Md.: U.S. Naval Institute, 1970), 284–86.

9 Van Buren to Porter, April 15, Instructions, Turkey; Van Buren to Hodgson, April 15, 1831, ibid.

10 Livingston to Porter, April 3, 1832, ibid.; Bryson, *Hodgson*, 53–58.

11 Field, *Mediterranean*, 16–170; Bryson, *Hodgson*, 76–78; Long, *Porter*, 290–93.

12 Long, *Porter*, 308–11; Livingston to Porter, March 23, April 3, 1832, April 1, 1833, Instructions, Turkey; McLane to Porter, Oct. 10, 1833, ibid.; Bryson, *Hodgson*, 62–82.

13 Wright, *Egypt*, 21–23; Field, *Mediterranean*, 167; Bryson, *Hodgson*, 85–98.

14 Leiber to Woodbury, Feb. 12, 1833, July 8, Oct. 2, 1834, Woodbury Papers; Woodbury to Leiber, March 12, 1833, ibid.

15 Bryson, *Hodgson*, 30–31, 85–98; McLane to Hodgson, Oct. 10, 1833, Instructions, Special Missions; Field, *Mediterranean*, 194–96.

16 Gliddon to Forsyth, Aug. 28, 1835, Consular Dispatches, Alexandria. Hodgson remained in good standing with the administration in spite of his conflict with Porter; soon after his return from Egypt, Forsyth asked him to return to Morocco to exchange the ratified treaties: Forsyth to Hodgson, Aug. 8, 1835, Instructions, Barbary States; A. Durighello, Aleppo, to Forsyth, Aug. 25, 1835, Consular Dispatches, Aleppo, Syria; J. Chaussaud, Beruit, to Forsyth, March 25, 1836, ibid., Beruit; N. de Mattey, Cyprus, Dec. 23, 1835, ibid., Cyprus; Bryson, *Hodgson*, 85–98.

17 Bryson, *Middle East*, 18–19; Field, *Mediterranean*, 195–96.

18 Memorandum, Oct. 15, 1836, Trist Papers; Field, *Mediterranean*, 195–96.

19 Field, *Mediterranean*, 186–88; I. McKim to Van Buren, July 1, 1830, Van Buren Papers; William Churchill, Constantinople, six-month report to Livingston, June 1833, Consular Dispatches, Constantinople; William Llewellyn, Salonica, Oct. 14, 1835, to Porter, ibid.

20 Field, *Mediterranean*, 207; D. Brent to Samuel Carr, Aug. 19, Instructions, Turkey; Brent to Daniel MacCauley, Aug. 23, 1831, ibid.

21 Carr to Trist, July 15, Sept. 12, 1831, March 21, 1832, Trist Papers; Carr to Rives, April 4, 1832, Rives Papers; Livingston to Carr, Feb. 24, June 13, 1832, Instructions, Turkey.

22 Field, *Mediterranean*, 207; Carr to Trist, Oct. 8, Nov. 1, 1832, Trist Papers.

23 Livingston to James Leib, Jan. 16, Feb. 19, April 25, 1833, Instructions, Turkey; McLane to Leib, May 20, 1834, ibid.

24 Forsyth to Captain James Riley, Nov. 4, 1834, Domestic Correspondence, Department of State; Forsyth to Swartwout, Nov. 15, Nov. 22, 1834, Feb. 5, Feb. 14, 1835, ibid.; Forsyth to Directors of Asylums, Feb. 14, 1835, ibid.; Asbury Dickens to Henry Meigs, May 7, 1835, ibid.; Forsyth to Leib, Jan. 30, 1837, Instructions, Barbary States. American gifts to the Emperor included field guns, powder and balls, cloth, and luxury items totaling $20,000.

25 Livingston to John Nelson, Oct. 27, 1831, Instructions, All Countries; Paul C. Perrotta, *The Claims of the United States against the Kingdom of Naples* (Washing-

ton, D.C.: Catholic University Press, 1926), 18–26; Howard R. Marraro, "John Nelson's Mission to the Kingdom of the Two Sicilies," *Maryland Historical Magazine* 44:149–53.

26 Jackson to Van Buren, Sept. 18, 1831, *Jackson Correspondence*, 4:351.

27 Leiber to Woodbury, Oct. 19, 1831, Woodbury Papers; Cooper to Rives, Nov. 1, 1830, Rives Papers; Alexander Hammett to Van Buren, Nov. 1, 1830, Consular Dispatches, Naples.

28 Caleb Cushing to Nathaniel Niles, Oct. 3, 1831, Caleb Cushing Papers, Library of Congress, Washington, D.C., Box 7; Fitzpatrick, *Autobiography of Van Buren*, 574–75; Nelson to Van Buren, Feb. 7, 1829, Van Buren Papers; Rives to Van Buren, Sept. 8, 1830, ibid.

29 Livingston to Nelson, Oct. 27, 1831, Instructions, All Countries; Perrotta, *Naples*, 52–55; Marraro, "Nelson," 153–60; Hatcher, *Livingston*, 412–13.

30 Nelson to Livingston, March 12, 1832, Dispatches, Naples. All correspondence between the Secretaries of State and American diplomats in Naples has been printed in Howard R. Marraro, ed., *The Diplomatic Relations between the United States and the Kingdom of the Two Sicilies (Instructions, and Dispatches), 1816–1861*, 2 vols. (New York: S.F. Vanni, 1951); for Nelson's dispatches, Oct. 1831–Jan. 1833, see 1:201–337. Also see *Documents Relating to the Convention with Sicily*, S. Doc. 70, 22d Cong., 2d sess., for significant correspondence.

31 Perrotta, *Naples*, 56–60; Marraro, "Nelson," 160–65; Livingston to Nelson, June 11, 1832, Instructions, All Countries; Hatcher, *Livingston*, 412–13.

32 Perrotta, *Naples*, 65–66; Clippings on Naval Affairs, 1832, Woodbury Papers. The New York and Washington newspapers engaged in heated speculation about the intent of the President regarding the navy and the Neapolitans in the fall of 1832.

33 London *Globe*, Clippings on Political Affairs, 1832–33, Woodbury Papers; Vail to Livingston, Aug. 6, 1832, Dispatches, Great Britain.

34 Niles to Livingston, Oct. 31, 1832, Dispatches, France.

35 Nelson to Livingston, Oct. 2, Oct. 15, 1832, Dispatches, Naples; Perrotta, *Naples*, 66–76; Marraro, "Nelson," 165–66. The larger claimants included Adams's supporter Israel Thorndike ($230,000) and Jacksonian Nathaniel West ($157,000). Total claims reached slightly over $2 million (Perrotta, *Naples*, 26).

36 Perrotta, *Naples*, 77–78.

37 Livingston to Nelson, Jan. 17, 1833, Instructions, All Countries.

38 Livingston to Davezac, Jan. 29, March 13, 1833, Instructions, The Netherlands (Davezac's major problems in the Netherlands involved the negotiation of a commercial treaty and the settlement of American claims from the damage done to American vessels in Antwerp during the Revolution in 1830); Perrotta, *Naples*, 79; Hatcher, *Livingston*, 213; Howard Marraro, "Auguste Davezac's Mission to the Kingdom of the Two Sicilies, 1833–34," *Louisiana Historical Quarterly*, 32:

791. Davezac's correspondence of Jan. 1833–Feb. 1834 can be found in Marraro, *Two Sicilies*, 338–71.

39 Perrotta, *Naples*, 79–83; Livingston to Davezac, March 1, 1833, Instructions, All Countries; Marraro, "Davezac," 791–99.

40 Davezac to Livingston, Paris, Oct. 12, 1833, Dispatches, France; Livingston to Davezac, Oct. 27, 1833; ibid.; Livingston to McLane, Nov. 22, 1833, ibid.; Marraro, "Davezac," 800–808.

41 McLane to Davezac, Dec. 26, 1833, Instructions, The Netherlands (McLane also chastised his agent for not having communicated with the Department since August); Hammett to Forsyth, June 30, 1835, Feb. 20, 1836, Consular Dispatches, Naples; Marraro, "Davezac," 800–808.

CHAPTER SIX

1 Tyler Dennett, *Americans in Eastern Asia* (New York: Macmillan, 1922), 30.

2 Jacques Downs, "American Merchants and the China Opium Trade, 1800–1840," *Business History Review* 42 : 419–31; Jacques Downs, "Fair Game: Exploitative Role Myths and the American Opium Trade," *Pacific Historical Review* 41 : 143, 146–48; Stuart C. Miller, "The American Traders' Image of China, 1785–1840," *Pacific Historical Review* 36 : 381 (both Downs and Miller stress the friendly rivalry that existed between the Americans and British in China; they considered themselves civilized men operating in a world of barbarians and heathens, which enabled most traders to sell opium to the Chinese with little moral uncertainty or remorse); Clippings on Naval Affairs, 1832–33, Woodbury Papers.

3 G. Bhagat, *Americans in India, 1784–1860* (New York: New York University Press, 1970), viii, 106–09; Dennett, *Eastern Asia*, 27–28.

4 David F. Long, "Martial Thunder: The First Official American Armed Intervention in Asia," *Pacific Historical Review* 42 : 144–47, is an excellent article on the *Friendship* affair at Quallah Battoo.

5 *American State Papers, Naval Affairs*, No. 485, Report of Captain Endicott, 154–55; Pessen, *Jacksonian America*, 342–43; Long, "Martial Thunder," 147–50; Dennett, *Eastern Asia*, 31. The approximate population of the Quallah Battoo area was 4,000–5,000.

6 Clippings, Box 30, Woodbury Papers.

7 Woodbury to Nathaniel Silsbee, et. al, July 25, 1831, *Naval Affairs*, No. 485, 152.

8 Long, "Martial Thunder," 147–50; Woodbury to Downes, Aug. 9, 1831, *Naval Affairs*, No. 485, 153.

9 Downes to Woodbury, Feb. 17, 1832, *Naval Affairs*, No. 485, 156; Lt. I. Shubrick to Downes, Feb. 6, 1832, ibid., 157–58.

10 Article from the *Essex Register* (Salem, Massachusetts) as reported in the Wash-

ington *Globe*, Oct. 2, 1832; article from the New York *Evening Post* as reported in the *National Intelligencer*, July 10, 1832; Clippings on Naval Affairs, Box 30, Woodbury Papers.

11 Richardson, *Messages and Papers*, 2:551.

12 *National Intelligencer*, July 10, 1832.

13 Washington *Globe*, July 11, 1832; article from the New York *Evening Post* as reported in the *National Intelligencer*, July 10, 1832; Salem *Gazette* in Clippings on Naval Affairs, Box 30, Woodbury Papers.

14 *National Intelligencer*, July 13, 1832; Clippings on Naval Affairs, Box 30, Woodbury Papers.

15 New York *Commercial Advertiser* in Clippings on Naval Affairs, Box 30, Woodbury Papers; various newspaper clippings, ibid.

16 Baltimore *American*, July 16, 1832; Woodbury to Downes, Aug. 9, 1831, *Naval Affairs*, No. 485, 153; Downes to Woodbury, Feb. 17, 1832, ibid., 156; Jackson to Speaker of the House, July 12, 1832, ibid., 150; Long, "Martial Thunder," 155–59. Reports of Malayan casualties ranged generally from 100 to 200 injured; Lieutenant Shubrick, who commanded the expedition, suggested 150 killed and many more wounded.

17 Washington *Globe*, July 16, 1832.

18 *Debates in Congress*, vol. 8, pt. 3, July 14, 1832, 3914.

19 Washington *Globe*, July 16, 1832.

20 Washington *Globe*, July 19, 1832; *National Intelligencer*, July 18, 1832.

21 Washington *Globe*, July 25, 1832.

22 *Naval Affairs*, No. 485; Richardson, *Messages and Papers*, 2:442. Downes's actions and fate can be contrasted with those of Commodore George C. Read, who was obliged to deal with a similar incident along the Sumatran coast in 1838: in a model exercise, Read negotiated before he attacked, and only one casualty (a Sumatran) resulted; Read was rewarded with the command of the African Squadron (Long, "Martial Thunder," 160–61). See also John M. Belohlavek, "Andrew Jackson and the Malaysian Pirates: A Question of Diplomacy and Politics," *Tennessee Historical Quarterly* 36:19–29.

23 Roberts to Woodbury, Jan. 5, Dec. 19, Dec. 26, 1828, Edmund Roberts Papers, Library of Congress, Washington, D.C.; Woodbury to Roberts, Dec. 22, 1828, ibid. The trade with the Sultan, as Roberts described it, consisted of Western cotton goods and firearms in exchange for ivory, spices, hides, coffee, and sugar.

24 Roberts biographical sketch, undated ms, Roberts to his wife, Jan. 2, 1830, ibid. Roberts married Katharine, the daughter of Judge Woodbury Langdon and niece of Governor John Langdon. John was the first Jeffersonian senator from New Hampshire and was considered for the vice-presidential slot on the ticket with James Madison in 1812.

25 Woodbury to Livingston, Dec. 7, 1831, Woodbury Papers; Livingston to Woodbury, Jan. 3, 1832, ibid.; Roberts to Woodbury, Dec. 20, 1831, ibid.; Woodbury to Roberts, Jan. 3, 1832, ibid.; Woodbury to Roberts, Dec. 14, 1831, Roberts Papers; Roberts to M. Woolsey, Jan. 22, 1834, ibid.

26 Roberts to his daughter Harriet, Feb. 1, Feb. 4, 1832, Roberts Papers. Traveling to Washington in January, Roberts met with the President regarding his mission and held "daily intercourse" with Livingston during his visit: Roberts to his children, Jan. 27, 1832, ibid.; Livingston to Roberts, Jan. 27, 1832, Instructions, Special Missions.

27 Roberts to Livingston, Jan. 24, 1832, Instructions, Special Missions; Livingston to Roberts, July 23, Oct. 21, 1832, ibid. Before Roberts departed, the cautious seafarer gave his power-of-attorney to Fish, Grinnell to prosecute his spoliations claim under the recently signed French Treaty; the balance of his account with Grinnell, Minton in New York City was $4,000 (Roberts to Fish, Grinnell, March 3, 1832, and Roberts account sheet, 1833, Roberts Papers).

28 Roberts to Woodbury, March 1, June 23, 1832, Woodbury Papers. Roberts left Boston without the presents on board; they were to be purchased and sent on the sloop *Boxer* to the rendezvous point of Batavia, Sumatra, in September.

29 Roberts to his children, June 23, Sept. 10, 1832, Roberts Papers.

30 Livingston to Roberts, July 23, 1832, ibid.

31 Seward W. Livermore, "Early Commercial and Consular Relations with the East Indies," *Pacific Historical Review*, 15: 45–53.

32 Livingston to Roberts, Oct. 28, 1832, Instructions, Special Missions; Livermore, "East Indies," 45–53. The government first became seriously aware of Japanese trade potential when Secretary of State Henry Clay requested and received reports on the subject from Consul John Shellaber at Batavia. Shellaber suggested that (in addition to profits from Siam and Cochin China) Japanese trade might reach $300,000 within three or four years. Shellaber's recommendations brought no response from the State Department, so he returned to the United States in 1827 to press his case—to no avail (Dennett, *Eastern Asia*, 244–46).

33 Roberts to Livingston, Dec. 1, Dec. 20, 1832, Roberts Papers.

34 Rev. R. Morrison to Roberts, 1832, ibid.; Clippings on Naval Affairs, 1833–34, Woodbury Papers.

35 Roberts Cochin China Journal, Dec. 29, 1832–Feb. 9, 1833, Roberts Papers; Roberts to his children, June 7, 1833, ibid.

36 Roberts Cochin China Journal, Feb. 18–April 3, 1832, ibid.; Dennett, *Eastern Asia*, 128–34; Roberts to his children, June 7, 1833, Roberts Papers; Donald C. Lord, "Missionaries, Thai and Diplomats," *Pacific Historical Review* 35: 415–16. The failure to incorporate the opium provision in the treaty was a sharp blow to the Captain. Except for cotton goods, the drug constituted the major trade item with Siam.

37 Roberts to Livingston, May 10, June 22, 1833, Roberts Papers; Dennett, *Eastern Asia*, 244–46. The Secretary of State had extended the option to his agent to visit Burma, not designated on the original list. He cautioned Roberts, however, that Rangoon—the commercial center—was far from the capital and that the Burmese had a habit of procrastination in conducting business and diplomacy. Roberts needed no additional information to convince him to sail on without stopping. (Livingston to Roberts, July 23, 1832, Instructions, Special Missions). Roberts did visit the bustling port of Singapore. A British colony, the city had quickly emerged to dominate trade in Southeast Asia, functioning as a center for the exchange of agricultural produce, woolen and cotton goods, and the ever-present opium (Clippings on Naval Affairs, 1831–32, Woodbury Papers).

38 Roberts Cochin China Journal, Aug. 1833–April 1834, Roberts Papers; Roberts to McLane, Jan. 17, May 14, 1834, ibid.

39 Roberts to McLane, May 14, 1834, ibid.; report on the Sultan's navy, 1833, ibid.

40 Roberts to his daughter Harriet, May 10, 1834, ibid.

41 Roberts to McLane, Jan. 10, 1834, ibid.; Roberts to Samuel Bell, Nov. 8, 1834, ibid.; Roberts to Henry Hubbard, Nov. 10, 1834, ibid.; Roberts to Isaac Hill, Nov. 20, 1834, ibid.; Roberts to Amasa J. Parker, Feb. 3, 1835, ibid. Roberts's supporters had introduced a bill to grant him an additional $7,300. Although he had the backing of such leading New Hampshire Democrats as Hill in the Senate and Hubbard in the House, the Senate Foreign Relations Committee was controlled by Clay and the Whigs, whom Roberts knew would oppose his claim.

42 Roberts to McLane, May 12, 1834, ibid.; Forsyth to Roberts, Aug. 5, Aug. 21, 1834, Instructions, Special Missions; Dennett, *Eastern Asia*, 244–46.

43 John Latimer to Roberts, Oct. 30, 1834, Feb. 13, 1835, Roberts Papers.

44 Forsyth to Roberts, Aug. 5, Aug. 21, 1834, ibid.; Roberts to Forsyth, Aug. 12, 1834, ibid.; Roberts to Amasa J. Parker, April 22, 1835, ibid. Roberts had rivals for the honor of publishing an account of the cruise of the *Peacock*: Woodbury and Forsyth received correspondence from J. N. Reynolds of New York, who wished to examine Roberts's journals (which were the property of the State Department) to assist in writing a "short and spirited . . . delicately done" view of our relations with the East (Reynolds to Forsyth, July 28, Aug. 16, 1834, Woodbury Papers).

45 Forsyth to Roberts, March 16, March 17, March 20, 1835, Roberts Papers.

46 Ibid.; Forsyth to Roberts, Sept. 18, Sept. 26, Oct. 9, 1834, March 26, March 31, 1835, April 10, 1835, Instructions, Special Missions; Asbury Dickins to Roberts, Feb. 19, 1835, Roberts Papers.

47 Roberts to his children, April 2, 1835, ibid.

48 Mahlon Dickerson to Captain E. P. Kennedy, April 2, April 7, 1835, Roberts Papers.

49 Roberts to his daughter Harriet, April 23, 1835, ibid.; Roberts to his children,

Sept. 9, Sept. 28, 1835, ibid.; Roberts Cochin China Journal, 1835–36, ibid.; R. Waldron, purser of the *Enterprise*, to Woodbury, Sept. 20, 1835, Woodbury Papers. The *Enterprise* did not sail to Muscat with the *Peacock*; it remained at Zanzibar and then proceeded directly to Bombay.

50 Roberts to his children, Oct. 22, 1835. Roberts Papers; William R. Taylor to Edmund Roberts, undated, ibid.

51 Roberts to his children, Dec. 24, 1835, ibid..

52 Roberts noted that the major articles involved in the Japanese trade included copper and camphor from the island in exchange for sugar and oils: Roberts's Notes on Japan, ca. 1835, ibid.; Roberts to Woodbury, Jan. 17, 1836, Woodbury Papers.

53 Roberts to Forsyth, Oct. 10, 1835, Feb. 16, April 18, 1836, Roberts Papers; Roberts to William Price, Jan. 24, 1836, ibid.; R. Waldron, Feb. 6, April 20, 1836, to Woodbury, Woodbury Papers.

54 W. Ruschenberger to Woodbury, June 18, 1836, Roberts Papers; Roberts to his children, June 4, 1836, ibid.; R. Morrison to Roberts, June 2, 1836, ibid.; R. R. Waldron to Roberts, June 4, 1836, ibid.; A. P. Peabody to Amasa Parker, Dec. 19, 1836, ibid. (the cholera swept through the American contingent in 1836, claiming the lives of many sailors, including Captain Archibald Campbell of the *Enterprise*); Charles Burroughs to Amasa J. Parker, Nov. 17, 1836, ibid. A collaborative effort between Parker, Roberts's son-in-law, and the eager author Reynolds led to the publication of an edited version of Roberts's adventures, *Embassy to the Eastern Courts of Cochin China, Siam and Muscat during the Years 1832–1834*, published by Harper in 1838: Reynolds to Parker, Sept. 4, 1836, ibid.; Grinnell, Minturn and Co. to Parker, March 22, 1837, ibid.; Harper to Parker, Oct. 21, 1837, ibid.; Reynolds to Woodbury, Sept. 30, 1836, Woodbury Papers; Amasa Parker to Woodbury, March 24, 1836, ibid.

Roberts died having achieved his goal of modest wealth. His banking firm informed his heirs that he held over $10,000 on account with them, plus another draft for $5,500 in Canton. The government also settled his spoliations claim for approximately $5,000, and in 1839 Congress added another $7,000 in compensation for the first voyage (Grinnell, Minturn and Co. to Amasa Parker, Jan. 10, 1837, Roberts Papers; V. Maxey to Woodbury, undated, ibid.).

55 Lord, "Missionaries," 415–16. The first consul to Zanzibar, Richard Waters, was appointed by Jackson in April 1836. When he arrived one year later, the first order of business was to get permission from the Sultan to sell gunpowder to his subjects (Waters to Forsyth, April 1837, Consular Dispatches, Zanzibar).

Although the British allowed the Americans to trade with India, they were reluctant to open the newly acquired colonial port of Singapore to American vessels. The question of accessibility was left hanging by the 1830 treaty, but the

British were not eager to resolve the issue and allow their archrivals into the carrying trade with the region (Van Buren to Charles Vaughan, 1830, Van Buren Papers; Joseph Balestier, consul at Singapore, to J. H. Groninor, Canton, May 22, 1834, Consular Dispatches, Singapore; Balestier to Forsyth, Aug. 29, 1836, ibid.).

The treaty with Siam met with mixed reactions in the American press. Because of the antiforeign and isolationist policies pursued by later rulers of the kingdom, and especially the overpricing of goods due to tariffs and royal monopolies, virtually no American ships visited for the next twenty years (Livermore, "East Indies," 45–53; clippings on naval affairs, 1833–34, Woodbury Papers).

CHAPTER SEVEN

1 J. F. Rippy, *Rivalry of the United States and Great Britain over Latin America, 1808–1830* (Baltimore, Md.: Johns Hopkins University Press, 1929), ix–x, 107–09, 303–09. Major British investments were in mines, which generally did not produce the anticipated amount or quality of ore; see J. F. Rippy, *British Investments in Latin America, 1822–1949* (Minneapolis: University of Minnesota Press, 1959).

2 Harold F. Peterson, *Argentina and the United States, 1810–1960* (New York: State University of New York Press, 1964), 80–87. Peterson presents an excellent recent account of relations in the period, utilizing both American and Spanish sources. American trade in 1825 was about $1 million; that of Great Britain almost $6 million. By 1830, American trade had doubled to $2 million, but English commerce had also increased to $8 million annually: Forbes to Secretary of State, Feb. 20, March 25, 1829, Dispatches, Buenos Aires.

3 H. S. Ferns, *Britain and Argentina in the Nineteenth Century* (London: Oxford University Press, 1960), 195–217; Peterson, *Argentina and the United States*, 92–96; Forbes to Van Buren, May 29, July 1, July 28, 1829, Dispatches, Buenos Aires.

4 Van Buren to Forbes, April 29, 1830, Jan. 28, Feb. 10, Feb. 28, 1831, Instructions, Buenos Aires; Forbes to Van Buren, Nov. 12, Dec. 9, 1829, May 10, Nov. 29, 1830, Dispatches, Buenos Aires; Livingston to Forbes, July 29, 1831, Instructions, Buenos Aires.

5 Van Buren to Forbes, Feb. 10, 1831, Instructions, Buenos Aires. There were approximately 15,000–20,000 wild cattle on the islands, a legacy from the days of the Spanish settlers (Ferns, *Britain and Argentina*, 226–27).

6 Ferns, *Britain and Argentina*, 224–28; Peterson, *Argentina and the United States*, 101–04. The British exhibited renewed interest in the Falklands at the time for

use as a shipping station. See also Julius Goebel, *The Struggle for the Falkland Islands: A Study in Legal and Diplomatic History* (New Haven, Conn.: Yale University Press, 1927). For a fine recent account, see Craig Evan Klafter, "United States Involvement in the Falkland Islands Crisis of 1831–33," *Journal of the Early Republic* (forthcoming).

7 Peterson, *Argentina and the United States*, 104–06; Ferns, *Britain and Argentina*, 228.

8 Slacum to Livingston, Nov. 23, 1831, Dispatches, Buenos Aires; Slacum to Minister of Foreign Affairs Nicholas Anchorena, Nov. 21, Nov. 26, 1831, ibid.

9 Duncan to Slacum, Nov. 29, Dec. 1, 1831, Dispatches, Buenos Aires; Slacum to Duncan, Nov. 30, 1831, ibid.; Peterson, *Argentina and the United States*, 104–06.

10 Slacum to Anchorena, Dec. 6, 1831, Dispatches, Buenos Aires; Anchorena to Slacum, Dec. 9, 1831, ibid.; Slacum to Livingston, Dec. 20, 1831, ibid.

11 Slacum to Livingston, Dec. 9, Dec. 20, 1831, ibid.

12 Ferns, *Britain and Argentina*, 229–30; Peterson, *Argentina and the United States*, 106–08; Clippings on Naval Affairs, 1832, Woodbury Papers.

13 Peterson, *Argentina and the United States*, 106–08.

14 Clippings on Naval Affairs, 1832, Woodbury Papers. Jackson could not yet have had official word of the seizures, because Slacum's first dispatch on the question was dated November 23. Van Buren first learned of Vernet's decree when it was protested by Noyes Barber, a Jacksonian congressman from Connecticut (Van Buren to Forbes, Feb. 10, 1831, Instructions, Buenos Aires). The American Atlantic Squadron that arrived off Montevideo in April 1832, under Commodore Rogers, consisted of the sloops *Lexington* and *Warren* and the schooner *Enterprise* (Clippings on Naval Affairs, 1832, Woodbury Papers).

15 Miscellaneous papers, Box 5, Francis Baylies Papers, Library of Congress, Washington, D.C.; Baylies to unknown, June 16, 1831, ibid.; Peterson, *Argentina and the United States*, 108–09; Charles F. Adams, ed., *Memoirs of John Quincy Adams* (Philadelphia: Lippincott, 1874–77), 9:446–47.

16 Livingston to Baylies, Jan. 6, Jan. 26, 1832, Instructions, Buenos Aires. By the time of Baylies's arrival, the commercial potential of the Argentine had increased in Jackson's mind, and he urged his Chargé to push for a treaty. Uncertain of legitimate claims to the islands, Livingston instructed Rives in Paris and Van Buren in London to investigate (Livingston to Rives, Feb. 4, 1832, Instructions, France; Rives to Livingston, May 18, 1832, Dispatches, France; Van Buren to Livingston, Feb. 28, 1832, Dispatches, Great Britain). Palmerston told Van Buren that Great Britain did have a claim to ownership of the Falklands. American rights in the area were based upon the Anglo-American treaty of 1782 and Anglo-Spanish treaty of 1790 (Peterson, *Argentina and the United States*, 108–09).

17 Livingston to Baylies, Feb. 14, April 3, 1832, Instructions, Buenos Aires; Peterson, *Argentina and the United States*, 109–11.

18 Clippings on Naval Affairs, 1832, Woodbury Papers; Baylies, Rio de Janeiro, to Livingston, May 18, 1832, William R. Manning, ed., *The Diplomatic Correspondence of the United States (Inter-American Affairs), 1831–1860* (Washington, D.C.: Carnegie Endowment, 1932–39), 1:98–99. In July, Baylies got reassurance from British Minister Henry Fox that His Majesty did maintain a claim and that the Crown had protested the 1829 decree (Fox to Baylies, July 4, 1832, ibid., 109; Baylies to John Wool, May 16, 1832, Samuel Rezneck, ed., "An American Diplomat Writes about Latin America in 1832," *The Americas* 28:206–09).

19 Baylies to Manuel Vicente de Maza, Acting Foreign Minister, June 20, June 26, July 10, 1832, Manning, *Inter-American Affairs*, 1:99–128; de Maza to Baylies, June 25, July 10, 1832, ibid.

20 Peterson, *Argentina and the United States*, 109–11.

21 Baylies to Livingston, July 24, 1832, Manning, *Inter-American Affairs*, 1:127–36; Baylies to Wool, Rezneck, "Diplomat," 209–11.

22 Baylies to de Maza, Aug. 6, Aug. 18, 1832, Manning, *Inter-American Affairs*, 1:138–39, 152; de Maza to Baylies, Aug. 8, Aug. 14, ibid., 141–52; Baylies to Livingston, Aug. 6, Aug. 19, 1832, ibid., 139, 152; Peterson, *Argentina and the United States*, 111–12.

23 Minutes of the de Maza-Baylies meeting, Aug. 27, 1832, Manning, *Inter-American Affairs*, 1:155–65; de Maza to Baylies, Sept. 3, ibid.; Baylies to Livingston, Sept. 26, 1832, ibid.; Peterson, *Argentina and the United States*, 112–13.

24 New York *Journal of Commerce*, Sept. 21, 1832; Clippings on Miscellaneous Political Affairs, 1831–32, Woodbury Papers; Philadelphia *Gazette*, Sept. 13, 1832; Michael Hoffman, House of Representatives, to Van Buren, Dec. 19, 1832, Van Buren Papers; Peterson, *Argentina and the United States*, 112–13.

25 Bond to Livingston, Oct. 6, 1832, Consular Dispatches, Montevideo (The United States did not have a diplomatic agent in Montevideo; although it had a million-dollar trade with the port, Washington restricted its representation to a consular office); Bond to McLane, Feb. 24, 1834, ibid.

26 J. D. Mendenhall to George Slacum, Jan. 16, 1833, Consular Dispatches, Buenos Aires; New York *Journal of Commerce*, Political Clippings, 1833, Woodbury Papers; Ferns, *Britain and Argentina*, 230–32.

27 Peterson, *Argentina and the United States*, 113–24; Hatcher, *Livingston*, 407–08; Forsyth to Minister of Foreign Affairs Manuel de Irigoyen, July 29, 1834, Dispatches, Buenos Aires (amazingly, the administration considered reappointing Slacum, who fortunately declined); Irigoyen to Forsyth, Dec. 10, 1834, ibid.

28 Dorr to Forsyth, Jan. 11, Jan. 16, Feb. 22, Oct. 15, 1836, Consular Dispatches, Buenos Aires. When the flour market collapsed in 1835, so did American trade with the region.

29 F. R. Rutter, *South American Trade of Baltimore* (Baltimore, Md.: Johns Hopkins University Press, 1897), 16, 27–28; Robert Martin, *British Relations with the Chi-*

nese Empire in 1832: A Comparative Statement of the English and American Trade with India and Canton (London: Parbury Allen, 1832), 32–34. Folger pressed for an appointment, then declined in 1833, citing personal reasons; perhaps a post in distant Peru was not to his liking (Folger to Livingston, June 4, 1833, Consular Dispatches, Paita, Peru; Rippy, *Rivalry*, 128–36). Other major coffee producers included Cuba, Java, Santo Domingo, and Arabia (Lawrence F. Hill, *Diplomatic Relations between the United States and Brazil* [Durham, N.C.: Duke University Press, 1932], 90n).

30 Hill, *United States and Brazil*, 27–40, 57–58.

31 Van Buren to Tudor, April 22, Sept. 4, 1829, Instructions, Brazil; Hill, *United States and Brazil*, 62–64, 70–73.

32 Van Buren to Brown, Oct. 20, 1830, June 16, 1831, Instructions, Brazil; Van Buren to Wright, Sept. 10, 1829, Nov. 3, 1831, William Wright Papers, Maryland Historical Society, Baltimore, Md. Brown served until 1834, when he returned home to become Commissioner General of the Land Office.

33 Rives to Livingston, Jan. 8, 1832, Dispatches, France. In 1833 Brazil's population included three million free people and two million slaves: Roberts Papers; Brown to Van Buren, March 14, April 7, 1831, Manning, *Inter-American Affairs*, 2 : 187–88.

34 Hunter to Forsyth, July 26, Aug. 29, Oct. 18, 1836, Dispatches, Brazil; Forsyth to Hunter, Nov. 16, 1836, April 14, 1837, Instructions, Brazil; Livingston to Brown, June 16, 1831, Jan. 15, 1833, ibid. Hunter was a former United States Senator from Rhode Island and supporter of conservative Georgian William Crawford for the presidency in 1824. This loyalty helped him considerably within certain elements of the Jackson party—especially Van Buren: James Hamilton, Jr., to Van Buren, March 5, 1829, Van Buren Papers; Hill, *United States and Brazil*, 74–79.

35 Hill, *United States and Brazil*, 74–77; Forsyth to Hunter, Nov. 29, 1836, Instructions, Brazil; Hunter to Forsyth, Feb. 10, 1837, Manning, *Inter-American Affairs*, 2 : 215–16.

36 Alan Manchester, *British Preeminence in Brazil* (Chapel Hill: University of North Carolina Press, 1933), 221, 333.

37 Rippy, *Rivalry*, 176–77.

38 Ibid., 207–08; J. G. A. Williamson to H. Clay, March 21, 1828, Consular Dispatches, LaGuaira, Venezuela.

39 Rippy, *Rivalry*, 192–94, 212–16; Van Buren to Moore, Dec. 1830, Van Buren Papers; Jackson to Van Buren, May 23, 1829, June 25, 1830, ibid.

40 Pope to Jackson, Feb. 19, 1829, *Jackson Correspondence*, 4 : 8; Jackson to Van Buren, March 31, 1829, ibid., 19–20; Rippy, *Rivalry*, 194ff.; James A. Hamilton to Van Buren, Feb. 27, 1829, Van Buren Papers. Moore planned on remaining in Colombia only eighteen months before returning to Kentucky to run for governor.

41 Van Buren to Moore, April 7, June 9, Aug. 17, 1829, Instructions, Colombia.

Moore had originally been chosen for the Rio mission, but his assignment was changed at the last moment (Van Buren to Larned, Aug. 17, 1829, ibid.).

42 E. T. Parks, *Colombia and the United States, 1765–1934* (Durham, N.C.: Duke University Press, 1935), 153–58; Van Buren to Moore, Dec. 12, 1829, Instructions, Colombia; Moore to Van Buren, March 27, May 7, 1830, Dispatches, Colombia; Rippy, *Rivalry*, 198–99, 212–16.

43 Moore to Van Buren, Aug. 28, 1830, Dispatches, Colombia; Rippy, *Rivalry*, 198–99; Williamson to Clay, Jan. 1, 1828, Consular Dispatches, LaGuaira, Venezuela.

44 Williamson to Van Buren, Oct. 31, Nov. 12, Nov. 26, 1829, April 29, 1830, Consular Dispatches, LaGuaira, Venezuela; Rippy, *Rivalry*, 192–94.

45 Hatcher, *Livingston*, 405–06.

46 Ibid.; Livingston to Moore, June 9, 1831, Feb. 16, Oct. 31, 1832, Instructions, Colombia; Parks, *Colombia and the United States*, 165–77.

47 Moore to William Rives, March (?), 1830, March 7, 1831, Rives Papers; Livingston to Moore, Oct. 31, 1832, March 30, 1833, Instructions, New Granada.

48 Livingston to McAfee, March 30, 1833, Instructions, New Granada.

49 Williamson to Livingston, Sept. 1, June 13 (Philadelphia) and May 8 (New York), 1832, Petitions of Merchants to Jackson, Consular Dispatches, La Guaira, Venezuela. Total Venezuelan trade was about $6 million in 1832; the American trade, mostly in coffee and cocoa, amounted to about $1.8 million—slightly more than the British and slightly less than the Danish (Foster to Livingston, July 1, 1833, ibid.).

50 Forsyth to Williamson, March 18, April 15, 1835, Instructions, Venezuela; Williamson to Forsyth, Jan. 30, Oct. 8, 1836, June 25, 1837, Dispatches, Venezuela.

51 Forsyth to McAfee, Nov. 11, 1835, April 21, July 8, 1836, ibid. American trade with Guayaquil, Ecuador's major port, was erratic through the 1830s. It generally ranged between $500,000 and $1 million annually, evenly divided between the usual assorted goods for export and cocoa and specie for import (Consular Dispatches, Guayaquil, Ecuador, 1830–37).

52 Rippy, *Rivalry*, 150–59.

53 Radcliffe to Secretary of State, April 27, July 18, 1829, Consular Dispatches, Lima, Peru. The New England whaling fleet exceeded four hundred vessels in 1833 (Forsyth to Pollard, Sept. 5, 1834, Instructions, Chile).

54 Rippy, *Rivalry*, 168–69, 173–74; Radcliffe to Secretary of State, April 27, 1829, Consular Dispatches, Lima, Peru; Tudor to Clay, Aug. 9, 1827, ibid.; Samuel Harrison, Truxillo, to Tudor, June 28, 1827, ibid.; S. Prevost to Clay, April 26, 1828, ibid.

55 Merchants of New York Petition to Jackson, April 7, 1829, *Letters of Application and Recommendation during the Administration of Andrew Jackson, 1829–37*, National Archives; Richard Alsop to Van Buren, Dec. 19, 1829, ibid.; Citizens of

Illinois Petition to Jackson, March 6, 1829, ibid.; T. H. Benton to Van Buren, March 14, 1829, ibid..

56 Van Buren to West, Oct. 26, Oct. 29, 1829, Instructions, Peru. The importation of both flour and cotton had earlier been prohibited, and by 1829 they were still severely limited.

57 Van Buren to Larned, Oct. 26, 1829, May 4, June 2, 1830, Instructions, Chile; Taylor to Van Buren, April 1, 1831, Oct. 1, 1834, Consular Dispatches, Arequipa, Peru; Larned to Forsyth, Jan. 12, Jan. 28, 1835, Dispatches, Lima.

58 Larned to Forsyth, March 20, March 26, May 8, 1835, Dispatches, Peru.

59 Larned to Forsyth, June 28, July 25, 1835, ibid.

60 Larned to Forsyth, March 1, March 9, June 13, July 6, Aug. 20, Sept. 3, 1836, ibid.

61 Larned to Mariano Sierra, Minister of Foreign Relations, May 23, 1836, ibid.; Larned to Forsyth, April 13, Sept. 5, Nov. 19, 1836, ibid.; Forsyth to Larned, Aug. 26, 1835, Instructions, Peru.

62 Thornton to Forsyth, June 18, 1836, Dispatches, Peru.

63 H. C. Evans, *Chile and Its Relations with the United States* (Durham, N.C.: Duke University Press, 1927), 31–36, 42–49, 56–59; Simon Collier, *Ideas and Politics of Chilean Independence, 1808–1833* (Cambridge: Cambridge University Press, 1967), 323–60.

64 Pollard to Forsyth, March 25, 1835, Dispatches, Chile; Rutter, *Trade of Baltimore*, 36; Rippy, *Rivalry*, 124–25.

65 Larned to Clay, July 17, 1828, Jan. 23, 1829, Dispatches, Chile.

66 Van Buren to Hamm, May 28, Oct. 15, 1830, Instructions, Chile; Zanesville Democrats to Jackson, June 30, 1829, *Letters of Application and Recommendation*.

67 Hogan to Van Buren, Dec. 26, 1829, Jan. 31, March 6, April 4, May 10, May 20, May 31, 1830, Consular Dispatches, Valparaiso, Chile.

68 Van Buren to Hamm, Oct. 15, 1830, Instructions, Chile; Livingston to Hamm, April 19, 1833, ibid.

69 Hamm to Livingston, May 25, May 28, 1832, Dispatches, Chile; Evans, *Chile and the United States*, 42–53.

70 Hamm to E. Hayward, May 30, 1832, Dispatches, Chile; Hamm to Livingston, Oct. 5, Oct. 6, 1832, July 28, July 29, Nov. 23, 1833, ibid.; Hamm to Jackson, May 25, 1832, ibid. Hamm was so critical of the Chilean government in his diplomatic correspondence that the Secretary of State urged him to cypher his messages (McLane to Hamm, Dec. 26, 1834, Instructions, Chile).

71 Forsyth to Pollard, Sept. 5, 1834, Instructions, Chile; Commercial Returns, Jan.–June 1834, Consular Dispatches, Valparaiso, Chile; Pollard to Rives, June 13, 1829, Rives Papers.

72 Pollard to Rives, Jan. 12, 1835, Rives Papers; Pollard to Forsyth, Jan. 14, 1835, Dispatches, Chile.

73 Pollard to Rives, May 7, 1835, Rives Papers.

74 Pollard to Forsyth, March 4, March 18, April 3, July (?), Aug. 13, 1835, June 11, July 3, 1836, Dispatches, Chile; Forsyth to Pollard, July 9, 1835, Instructions, Chile.

75 Pollard to Forsyth, Aug. 5, Dec. 30, 1836, Dispatches, Chile; Evans, *Chile and the United States*, 60–65; Arthur P. Whitaker, *The United States and the Southern Cone: Argentina, Uruguay, and Chile* (Cambridge, Mass.: Harvard University Press, 1976), 60.

CHAPTER EIGHT

1 Rives, *United States and Mexico*, 1:234–35; Rippy, *Rivalry*, 71.

2 Rippy, *Rivalry*, 91–97, 253–302. Two studies of Poinsett's Mexican missions are J. F. Rippy, *Joel R. Poinsett: Versatile American* (Durham, N.C.: Duke University Press, 1935), 104–33, which is sympathetic with its subject's motives and critical of his behavior. A weaker effort is Dorothy Parton, *The Diplomatic Career of Joel Robert Poinsett* (Washington, D.C.: Catholic University Press, 1934).

3 Harold Davis, John Finan, and F. T. Peck, *Latin American Diplomatic History: An Introduction* (Baton Rouge: Louisiana State University Press, 1977), 93–94; Gene Brack, *Mexico Views Manifest Destiny, 1821–1846* (Albuquerque: University of New Mexico Press, 1975), 53–54.

4 Rippy, *Rivalry*, 103–06; Poinsett to Van Buren, March 10, April 3, April 15, 1829, Dispatches, Mexico.

5 Poinsett to Van Buren, Aug. 7, 1829, Dispatches, Mexico; Van Buren to Poinsett, Aug. 25, 1829, Instructions, Special Missions; Rippy, *Rivalry*, 91–97.

6 Rives, *United States and Mexico*, 236–39; Adams, *Memoirs of John Quincy Adams*, 11:359; Butler to Van Buren, Aug. 11, 1829, Van Buren Papers; Jackson to Van Buren, Aug. 15, 1829, ibid.; Jackson to Van Buren, Aug. 12, 1829, *Jackson Correspondence*, 4:57; Notes on Poinsett Instructions, Aug. 13, 1829, ibid., 58–59; Jackson to Butler, Oct. 19, 1829, March 23, 1830, ibid., 82, 129.

7 Rives, *United States and Mexico*, 234–36; Jackson to Van Buren, Aug. 13, 1829, Van Buren Papers.

8 Van Buren to Butler, Oct. 12, 1829, Instructions, Special Missions; Jackson to Butler, Oct. 10, 1829, *Jackson Correspondence*, 4:79; Van Buren to Poinsett, Oct. 17, 1829, Van Buren Papers. There were twelve consuls stationed in Mexico by 1829, indicating the level of American interest, if not the value of trade at the time. Butler's appointment as Chargé rather than Minister to Mexico was a constant source of irritation to him (Rives, *United States and Mexico*, 241–44).

9 McLane to Van Buren, May 21, May 29, 1830, Dispatches, Great Britain; Butler to Van Buren, Jan. 10, 1830, Dispatches, Mexico.

10 Unknown correspondent to C. Vaughan, Feb. 18, 1830, Doyle, "Papers of Charles Vaughan," 308–09; Rippy, *Rivalry*, 105–06.

11 Ibid., 302; Butler to Van Buren, Dec. 31, 1829, Jan. 5, March 9, 1830, Dispatches, Mexico; Van Buren to Butler, Oct. 16, 1829, Instructions, Mexico.

12 Poinsett to Butler, Aug. 19, Aug. 22, Sept. 2, Sept. 22, 1829, Dispatches, Mexico; McLane to Van Buren, Dec. 22, 1829, Dispatches, Great Britain; Van Buren to Butler, Nov. 30, 1829, Instructions, Mexico; Butler to Van Buren, Feb. 19, 1830, Dispatches, Mexico.

A pervasive fear existed in the United States that Boyer would launch a Haitian army to convert Cuba or Puerto Rico into black republics. This imperial concern combined with racism to more than offset the strong commercial bond between the two nations (American trade with Haiti averaged well over $1 million per year, surpassing that of many European and Latin American states). Various east coast merchants urged Jackson to send a representative to Boyer's government, and the Haitian leader himself asked Commodore Jesse Elliott of the Home Squadron to offer Old Hickory a reduction of duties in exchange for recognition, but Jackson refused. As American commercial agent William Miles accurately observed, "The sore spot was color." The Lincoln administration finally recognized Haiti during the American Civil War. See Rayford Logan, *The Diplomatic Relations of the United States and Haiti, 1776–1891* (Chapel Hill: University of North Carolina Press, 1941), 201–02, 233; Ludwell L. Montague, *Haiti and the United States, 1714–1938* (New York: Russell and Russell, 1966), 54–55; Charles C. Tansill, *The United States and Santo Domingo, 1798–1873* (Baltimore, Md.: Johns Hopkins University Press, 1938), 122–23.

13 Butler to Van Buren, April 10, 1830, Dispatches, Mexico; Butler to Van Buren, April 7, 1830, Van Buren Papers; Van Ness to Van Buren, March 17, 1830, ibid. Butler wrote to Van Buren in cypher that he believed Mexican agents had infiltrated Cuba for the purpose of sparking revolt and separating the island from Spain (Butler to Van Buren, April 10, 1830, Dispatches, Mexico).

14 Brack, *Manifest Destiny*, 57–67; Van Buren to Butler, Oct. 10, 1829, Instructions, Mexico; Butler to Van Buren, Feb. 19, March 9, 1830, Dispatches, Mexico; Rives, *United States and Mexico*, 244–45.

15 Butler to Van Buren, April 15, May 19, 1830, Dispatches, Mexico; Butler to Van Buren, April 7, Dec. 22, 1830, Van Buren Papers; Van Buren to Butler, April 1, Dec. 10, Dec. 14, 1830, Instructions, Mexico; Jackson to Butler, Feb. 15, 1831, *Jackson Correspondence*, 4:243–44. Butler blamed the boundary treaty on Poinsett and urged Jackson not to submit it to the Senate (Butler to Jackson, Jan. 2, 1832, Jackson Papers).

16 Jackson to William Fulton, Dec. 10, 1830, *Jackson Correspondence*, 4:212–14; Jackson to Butler, Feb. 15, 1831, ibid., 243–44.

17 Jackson to Butler, Aug. 24, 1831, ibid.; Livingston to Butler, Feb. 27, 1832, Instructions, Mexico.

18 Butler to Jackson, May 25, June 23, 1831, Jackson Papers; Jackson to Butler, Aug. 17, 1831, ibid.; Rives, *United States and Mexico*, 241–49.

19 Butler to Jackson, Oct. 6, 1831, *Jackson Correspondence*, 4:354; Jackson to Butler, Dec. 9, 1831, ibid., 380.

20 Jackson to Butler, Feb. 25, March 6, April 19, 1832, ibid., 408–09, 413, 435.

21 Rives, *United States and Mexico*, 249–51; Butler to Jackson, June 21, July 18, Aug. 12, Aug. 30, Oct. 10, 1832, *Jackson Correspondence*, 4:450, 463–64, 465–66, 471–72, 479–80.

22 Jackson to Butler, Oct. 10, 1829, *Jackson Correspondence*, 4:79.

23 Rives, *United States and Mexico*, 249–51; Butler to Jackson, Jan. 2, 1833, *Jackson Correspondence*, 4:2; Butler to Jackson, Feb. 10, 1833, Dispatches, Mexico; Hatcher, *Livingston*, 404–05; Livingston to Butler, March 20, 1833, Instructions, Mexico. There was pressure for replacing Butler in 1833 with someone of ministerial rank. Jackson, willing to give his agent more time, refused on the basis of cost and Mexican political instability. See Jackson to Van Buren, Dec. 23, 1832, Van Buren Papers; Joe Gibson, "A. Butler: What a Scamp!" *Journal of the West* 11: 244–47.

24 Rives, *United States and Mexico*, 252–54; Butler to Jackson, Sept. 26, Oct. 2, Oct. 28, 1833, *Jackson Correspondence*, 5:209–11, 214–15, 219–20.

25 Jackson to Butler, Oct. 1, Oct. 30, Nov. 27, 1833, *Jackson Correspondence*, 5:213, 221–22, 228–29.

26 Butler to Jackson, Feb. 6, March 7, 1834, *Jackson Correspondence*, 5:244–45, 249–53.

27 Rives, *United States and Mexico*, 254–55; McLane to Butler, Jan. 13, 1834, Instructions, Mexico.

28 Rives, *United States and Mexico*, 255–59; Butler to Jackson, Oct. 20, Nov. 21, 1834, *Jackson Correspondence*, 5:299–300, 311–12.

29 Butler to Forsyth, June 17, 1835, Dispatches, Mexico; Forsyth to Butler, July 2, 1835, Instructions, Mexico; Duckett, *Forsyth*, 194–96; Rives, *United States and Mexico*, 255–59.

30 Rives, *United States and Mexico*, 236.

31 Duckett, *Forsyth*, 195; Brack, *Manifest Destiny*, 67; McCormac, "John Forsyth," 318, Niven, *Van Buren*, 281; Remini, *Jackson and the Course of Freedom*, 289.

32 Rogin, *Fathers and Children*, 303; Richard Stenberg, "Jackson, Anthony Butler and Texas," *Southwest Social Science Quarterly* 13:264–87, and "President Jackson and Anthony Butler," *Southwest Review* 22:391–404.

33 Brack, *Manifest Destiny*, 67–71; Forsyth to Butler, Aug. 6, 1835, Instructions, Mexico; Rives, *United States and Mexico*, 259–60; Butler to Jackson, Nov. (?), Dec. 19, 1835, *Jackson Correspondence*, 5:375–77, 381.

34 McCormac, "John Forsyth," 318–42; Forsyth to Ellis, Jan. 29, 1836, Instructions, Mexico; Brack, *Manifest Destiny*, 71–76.

35 Jackson to Newton Cannon, Aug. 3, 1836, *Jackson Correspondence*, 5:415–16; Jackson to Kendall, Aug. 12, 1836, ibid., 420–21; Jackson to Gaines, Sept. 4, 1836, ibid., 423–24; Austin to Jackson, April 15, 1836, ibid., 397–98; Rives, *United States and Mexico*, 362–82.

36 Brack, *Manifest Destiny*, 71–76; Woodbury to Swartwout, May 2, 1836, Woodbury Papers.

37 Forsyth to Ellis, July 20, Dec. 10, 1836, Instructions, Mexico; Gibson, "Butler," 241.

38 Rives, *United States and Mexico*, 386–91; Forsyth to Morfit, June 23, 1836, Instructions, Special Missions.

39 Morfit to Forsyth, Aug. 13, Aug. 23, Aug. 27, Sept. 4, Sept. 6, Sept. 9, Sept. 10, Sept. 12, 1836, Dispatches, Texas; Jackson to Santa Anna, Sept. 4, 1836, *Jackson Correspondence*, 5:425–26. The revolutionary state of Texas had first sent commissioners to the United States in October 1835, soon after the conflict had erupted. The agents were replaced several times over the next eighteen months.

40 Rives, *United States and Mexico*, 391–96, 401–05; Jackson to Van Buren, Nov. 1836, Van Buren Papers; Van Buren to John Van Buren, Dec. 22, 1836, ibid.; William Wharton to Stephen F. Austin, Dec. 25, 1836, Jan. 6, 1837, George F. Garrison, ed., *The Diplomatic Correspondence of the Republic of Texas* (Washington, D.C.: Government Printing Office, 1911), 1:158–59, 170–71.

41 Duckett, *Forsyth*, 198–201; Jackson to Kendall, Dec. 8, 1836, *Jackson Correspondence*, 5:441. Stevenson in London was miffed by Jackson's December message, which, he reported "produced quite a sensation" (Stevenson to Van Buren, Jan. 30, 1837, Van Buren Papers).

42 Wharton to Austin, Jan. 6, and Wharton to Rusk, Feb. 19, Feb. 20, 1837, Garrison, *Correspondence of Texas*, 1:170–71, 193. The Texas state constitution of 1827 and a presidential decree two years later had abolished slavery in all Mexico, but under heavy pressure in 1829 from provincial officials, Guerrero had excepted Texas from the fiat.

43 J. Catron to Jackson, June 8, 1836, *Jackson Correspondence*, 5:402; Forsyth to Stevenson, Sept. 14, 1836, Instructions, Great Britain; Ellis to Forsyth, Aug. 3, 1836, Dispatches, Mexico; James Callahan, *American Foreign Policy in Mexican Relations* (New York, 1932), 91–99 (Callahan discusses the international joint commission that awarded the Americans over $2 million in 1842).

44 Stevenson to Forsyth, Oct. 29, 1836, Dispatches, Great Britain.

45 Jackson to Benjamin Howard, Feb. 2, 1837, *Jackson Correspondence*, 5:456–57; Rives, *United States and Mexico*, 396–401, 417–18; Justin Smith, *The Annexation of Texas* (New York: AMS Press, 1911), 59–62; Richard Stenberg, "The Texas Schemes of Jackson and Houston," *Southwest Social Science Quarterly* 15:229–50; Eugene Barker, "President Jackson and the Texas Revolution," *American Historical Review* 12:797–803, and "The United States and Mexico, 1835–1837," *Missis-*

sippi Valley Historical Review 1:3–30. See also Curtis R. Reynolds, "The Deterioration of Mexican-American Diplomatic Relations, 1833–1845," *Journal of the West* 11:213–24. K. J. Brauer, "The United States Navy and Texas Independence: A Study in Jacksonian Integrity," *Military Affairs* 34:44–48, notes that Jackson supported the navy's efforts to enforce the 1818 neutrality law in the Gulf of Mexico.

46 Reeves, *American Diplomacy*, 84–86.

47 Mario Rodriguez, *A Palmerstonian Diplomat in Central America: Frederick Chatfield* (Tucson: University of Arizona Press, 1964), 53–58, 114–15; Mary W. Williams, *Anglo-American Isthmian Diplomacy, 1815–1915* (New York: Russell and Russell, 1914), 29–30; Rippy, *Rivalry*, 225–26, 237–40; Jackson to Van Buren, Oct. 6, 1829, Van Buren Papers.

48 Charles Savage, Guatemala, to Van Buren, Aug. 29, Sept. 3, Dec. 3, 1830, Aug. 10, 1831, Dispatches, American States.

49 Anderson and Sargeant to Clay, May 8, 1826, ibid.

50 Livingston to Jeffers, June 14, 1831, Instructions, American States; W. R. to Jackson, Aug. 1831, Van Buren Papers ("W. R." was likely William Radcliffe, a New York merchant and former counsel to Lima who had been interested in a canal project since 1826).

51 Livingston to Jeffers, July 20, 1831, Instructions, American States.

52 Clippings on Naval Affairs, 1831, Woodbury Papers; Livingston to Jeffers, Aug. 15, 1831, Instructions, American States; Livingston to James Shannon, Feb. 10, 1832, ibid.; De Witt to Woodbury, July 18, 1831, Dec. 17, 1832, Woodbury Papers; Van Buren to Jackson, Jan. 9, 1833, Van Buren Papers; Jackson to Van Buren, Jan. 13, 1833, ibid.

53 Livingston to De Witt, April 20, 1833, Instructions, American States; McLane to De Witt, June 29, Sept. 9, Nov. 5, 1833, ibid.; Forsyth to De Witt, April 30, 1835, ibid.

54 Decree of the Congress of New Granada, May 25, 1834, Charles Biddle Papers, New York Historical Society, New York, New York.

55 Livingston to Butler, June 21, 1831, Instructions, Mexico; Rodriguez, *Chatfield*, 53–58; Williams, *Anglo-American Diplomacy*, 33–34.

56 Forsyth to Galindo, June 10, June 24, June 27, Aug. 4, 1835, Manning, *Inter-American Affairs*, 3:19–21; Rodriguez, *Chatfield*, 81, 106–07.

57 J. Eaton to Jackson, March 13, 1832, *Jackson Correspondence*, 4:417; Jackson to F. P. Blair, Aug. 7, 1834, ibid., 5:281; Biddle to Jackson, Jan. 11, 1832, Jackson Papers; Biddle to W. B. Shephard, Jan. 26, 1835, ibid.; Biddle to R. E. W. Earle, Jan. 27, 1835, ibid.; Wilfred Jordan, ed., *The Colonial and Revolutionaries Families of Pennsylvania* (New York: Lewis Historical Publishing, 1935), 6:215–16; Washington *Globe*, Feb. 4, 1832. Biddle family data on Charles Biddle have been courteously provided by Nicholas B. Wainwright of the Historical Society of Pennsylvania.

58 Notes of J. N. Barker, June 5, 1835, Philadelphia Customs House Papers, Historical Society of Pennsylvania. For the best secondary account of the Biddle mission, see Parks, *Colombia and the United States*, 178–89.

59 Forsyth to Biddle, May 1, 1835, Jan. 18, 1836, Instructions, Special Missions.

60 Biddle to Forsyth, Dec. 8, 1835, Biddle Papers; undated Biddle dispatch (probably Nov. 1835), ibid.; Biddle to Society of Friends of Peace, Dec. 7, 1835, ibid.

61 Biddle to Forsyth, Dec. 7, Dec. 29, 1835, ibid.; A. Signette, Secretary for Baron Thierry, to Congress of New Granada, undated, ibid. Panama, with a population of 72,633, contained a potential male labor force of 9,000 between the ages of sixteen to fifty. The isthmus also had preserved the institution of slavery.

62 Biddle to Jackson, Dec. 8, 1835, ibid.

63 Biddle to Forsyth, Dec. 16, Dec. 20, 1835, ibid.; Society of Friends of Peace to Biddle, Jan. 10, 1836, ibid.

64 Biddle to McAfee, March 3, 1836, ibid.; Biddle to Forsyth, March 24, 1836, ibid.

65 Biddle to Congress of New Granada, undated (March), 1836, ibid.

66 Biddle to Jose de Obaldia, May 4, 1836, ibid.; Biddle to Dr. Pedro Gual, May 9, 1836, ibid.; Biddle to Lorenzo Lleras, Chief Clerk of Foreign Affairs, May 19, May 23, 1836, ibid.; Biddle to Members of Congress from Panama, May 21, 1836, ibid. Santander, a "liberal" and former lieutenant of Bolivar, had been President of New Granada since 1832; see David Bushnell, *The Santander Regime in Gran Colombia* (Newark: University of Delaware Press, 1954).

67 Biddle to Pombo, May 23, 1836, Biddle Papers; Robert McAfee to Pombo, May 24, 1836, ibid.

68 Biddle to Members of Congress from Panama, May 21, 1836, ibid.; Lleras to Biddle, May 19, 1836, ibid.

69 McAfee to Biddle, June 24, 1836, ibid.; Biddle to Forsyth, undated (November 1836), ibid.

70 *National Intelligencer*, undated, 1836.

71 Biddle to J. C. Pickett, Nov. 7, 1836, Biddle Papers; Pickett to Jackson, Nov. 8, 1836, ibid.; Forsyth to Biddle, July 19, Sept. 26, 1836, Instructions, Special Missions.

72 Williamson to Forsyth, Jan. 20, Feb. 13, 1837, Dispatches, Venezuela; Jackson to the Senate, Jan. 9, Jan. 10, 1837, Richardson, *Messages and Papers*, 3 : 272–73.

73 Biddle to Forsyth, Sept. 25, 1836, Dispatches, Special Missions; Forsyth to Biddle, Dec. 5, 1836, Instructions, Special Missions; Lawrence O. Ealy, *Yanqui Politics and the Isthmian Canal* (University Park: Pennsylvania State University Press, 1971), 13–14.

Bibliography

PRIMARY SOURCES

Manuscripts

Baylies, Francis. Papers. Library of Congress, Washington, D.C.
Biddle, Charles. Papers. New York Historical Society, New York, New York.
Buchanan-Johnston. Papers. Library of Congress, Washington, D.C.
Cushing, Caleb, Papers. Library of Congress, Washington, D.C.
Jackson, Andrew. Papers. Library of Congress, Washington, D.C.
McLane, Louis. Papers. Library of Congress, Washington, D.C.
Niles, Nathaniel. Papers. Library of Congress, Washington, D.C.
Preble, William. Papers. Library of Congress, Washington, D.C.
Riggs Family. Papers. Library of Congress, Washington, D.C.
Rives, William. Papers. Library of Congress, Washington, D.C.
Roberts, Edmund. Papers. Library of Congress, Washington, D.C.
Trist, Nicholas. Papers. Library of Congress, Washington, D.C.
Van Buren, Martin. Papers (on microfilm). Library of Congress, Washington, D.C.
Woodbury, Levi. Papers. Library of Congress, Washington, D.C.
Wright, William. Papers. Maryland Historical Society, Baltimore, Maryland.

Published Collections

Adams, Charles F., ed. *Memoirs of John Quincy Adams.* 12 vols. Philadelphia: Lippincott, 1874–77.
Bassett, John Spencer, ed. *The Correspondence of Andrew Jackson.* 6 vols. Washington, D.C.: Carnegie Institute, 1926–35.
Benton, Thomas Hart. *Thirty Years' View.* 2 vols. New York, 1854–56.

Doyle, John A., ed. "The Papers of Sir Charles Vaughan." *American Historical Review* 7 (1902): 304–29, 500–533.

Fitzpatrick, John, ed. *The Autobiography of Martin Van Buren*. American Historical Association Annual Report for 1918, II. Washington, D.C.: Carnegie Institute, 1920.

Garrison, George P., ed. *The Diplomatic Correspondence of the Republic of Texas*. 3 vols. American Historical Association Annual Report for 1907–08. Washington, D.C.: Government Printing Office, 1911.

Hamilton, James A. *Reminiscences*. Washington, D.C., 1874.

Hasse, A. R., ed., *Index to Documents Relating to United States Foreign Affairs*. 3 vols. Washington, D.C., 1921.

Legaré, Hugh S. *Writings*. 2 vols. Charleston, S.C.: Burges and James, 1846.

Manning, William R., ed. *The Diplomatic Correspondence of the United States (Canadian Relations), 1784–1860*. 4 vols. Washington, D.C.: Carnegie Endowment, 1940–45.

———. *The Diplomatic Correspondence of the United States (Inter-American Affairs), 1831–1860*. 12 vols. Washington, D.C.: Carnegie Endowment, 1932–39.

Marraro, Howard R., ed., *The Diplomatic Relations between the United States and the Kingdom of the Two Sicilies (Instructions and Dispatches), 1816–1861*. 2 vols. New York: S. F. Vanni, 1951.

Miller, Hunter, ed. *Treaties and Other International Acts of the United States of America, 1776–1863*. 8 vols. Washington, D.C., 1931–48.

Rezneck, Samuel, ed. "An American Diplomat Writes about Latin America in 1832." *The Americas* 28 (Oct. 1971): 206–11.

Richardson, James, ed. *Messages and Papers of the Presidents of the United States, 1789–1902*. 10 vols. Washington, D.C.: Bureau of National Literature and Art, 1904.

Roberts, Edmund. *Embassy to the Eastern Courts of Cochin China, Siam and Muscat during the Years 1832–1834*. New York: Harper, 1838.

Stickney, William, ed. *The Autobiography of Amos Kendall*. Boston: Lee and Shepard, 1872.

Whipple, Edwin P. *The Great Speeches and Orations of Daniel Webster*. Boston: Little, Brown, 1899.

Government Documents

Customs House Reports, Philadelphia, 1835. Historical Society of Pennsylvania.

Great Britain. *Foreign Office #5 (United States); #84 (Slave Trade)*. Microfilm, Public Record Office, London.

Message from the President of the United States to Congress in Relation to the Consular Establishment of the United States. Washington, D.C.: F. P. Blair, 1833.

United States *American State Papers, Naval Affairs, 1831–36.*

————. Bureau of Customs. *French Spoliation Claims.* R636, National Archives.

————. Court of Claims. *French Spoliations Awards.* National Archives.

————. *Register,* 1829–37. National Archives.

————. *Register of Debates in Congress, 1825–1837.* 29 vols. Washington, D.C., 1825–37.

————. *Congressional Globe,* 1833–73. 109 vols.

————. *Documents Relating to the Convention with Sicily.* S. Doc. 70, 22d Cong., 2d sess.

————. *Digest of Commercial Regulations of Foreign Countries with the United States.* 2 vols. (Washington, D.C.: Blair and Rives, 1836).

————. *Bureau of the Census. Historical Statistics of the United States, Colonial Times to 1957* (Washington, D.C.: GPO, 1960).

————. *Letters of Application and Recommendation during the Administration of Andrew Jackson, 1829–1837.* National Archives.

————. Treasury Department, *Register of Certificates Issued in Payment of the French Indemnity, 1836.* 3 vols. National Archives.

————. Treasury Department. *Register of Neapolitan Indemnity, 1835–36.* National Archives.

————. Treasury Department. *Letters of Claimants, Neapolitan Indemnity, 1835–36.* 2 vols. National Archives.

————. State Department. Domestic Correspondence. National Archives.

————. State Department. Instructions and Dispatches (1828–37): All Countries (1829–33), American States (1829–33), Barbary States, Brazil, Buenos Ayres, Central American States, Chile, Colombia, Denmark, France, Great Britain, Italian States, Mexico, The Netherlands, New Granada, Peru, Portugal, Russia, Spain, Special Missions, Texas, Turkey, Venezuela. National Archives.

————. State Department. Consular Dispatches (1828–37): Aleppo (Syria), Arequipa (Peru), Buenoa Aires, Constantinople, Cyprus, Guayaquil (Ecuador), LaGuaira (Venezuela), Le Havre, Lima, Montevideo, Naples, Paita (Peru), Singapore, Valparaiso, Zanzibar.

Newspapers

Baltimore *American*
National Intelligencer (Washington, D.C.)
New York *Journal of Commerce*
Niles *Register*
Philadelphia *Gazette*
Washington *Globe*

SECONDARY WORKS

Books

Alexander, Holmes. *The American Talleyrand: The Career and Contemporaries of Martin Van Buren*. New York: Harper, 1935.

Baker, Elizabeth. *Henry Wheaton, 1785–1848*. Philadelphia: University of Pennsylvania Press, 1937.

Barnes, William, and John H. Morgan. *The Foreign Service of the United States: Origins, Development and Functions*. Washington, D.C.: Historical Office of the Department of State, 1961.

Barrett, Walter. *The Old Merchants of New York*. 5 vols. New York: Greenwood, 1862.

Bell, Herbert C. F. *Lord Palmerston*. London: Longmans, Green, 1936.

Bemis, Samuel F., ed. *American Secretaries of State and Their Diplomacy*. 10 vols. New York: Knopf, 1927–29.

———. *John Quincy Adams and the Foundations of American Foreign Policy*. New York: Knopf, 1949.

Benns, F. Lee. *The American Struggle for the British West Indies Carrying Trade, 1815–1830*, Bloomington: University of Indiana Press, 1923.

Bhagat, G. *Americans in India, 1784–1860*. New York: New York University Press, 1970.

Bourne, Kenneth, *Britain and the Balance of Power in North America, 1815–1908*. Berkeley: University of California Press, 1967.

———. *Palmerston: The Early Years, 1784–1841*. New York: Free Press, 1982.

Brack, Gene. *Mexico Views Manifest Destiny, 1821–1846*. Albuquerque: University of New Mexico Press, 1975.

Bryson, Thomas. *American Diplomatic Relations with the Middle East, 1784–1975*. Metuchen, N.J.: Scarecrow Press, 1977.

———. *An American Consular Officer in the Middle East in the Jacksonian Era: A Biography of William Brown Hodgson, 1801–1871*. Atlanta: Resurgens Publications, 1979.

Burrage, Henry. *Maine in the Northeastern Boundary Controversy*. Portland, Maine: Marks Printing House, 1919.

Bushnell, David. *The Santander Regime in Gran Colombia*. Newark: University of Delaware Press, 1954.

Callahan, James M. *American Foreign Policy in Canadian Relations*. New York, 1937.

———. *American Foreign Policy in Mexican Relations*. New York, 1932.

Carroll, E. M. *The Origins of the Whig Party*. Durham, N.C.: Duke University Press, 1925.

Cassell, Frank. *Merchant Congressman in the New Republic: Samuel Smith of Maryland, 1752–1839*. Madison: University of Wisconsin Press, 1971.

Cheever, Daniel, and H. F. Haviland. *American Foreign Policy and the Separation of Powers*. Cambridge, Mass.: Harvard University Press, 1952.

Collier, Simon. *Ideas and Politics of Chilean Independence, 1808–1833*. Cambridge: Cambridge University Press, 1967.

Curtis, James C. *Andrew Jackson and the Search for Vindication*. Boston: Little, Brown, 1976.

Davis, Harold; John Finan; and F. T. Peck. *Latin American Diplomatic History: An Introduction*. Baton Rouge: Louisiana State University Press, 1977.

Dennett, Tyler. *Americans in Eastern Asia*. New York: Macmillan, 1922.

Duckett, Alvin. *John Forsyth: Political Tactician*. Athens: University of Georgia Press, 1962.

Ealy, Lawrence O. *Yanqui Politics and the Isthmian Canal*. University Park: Pennsylvania State University Press, 1971.

Elliott, Jonathan. *The American Diplomatic Code*. New York, 1834.

Evans, Henry C. *Chile and Its Relations with the United States*. Durham, N.C.: Duke University Press, 1927.

Ferns, H. S. *Britain and Argentina in the Nineteenth Century*. London: Oxford University Press, 1960.

Field, James A., Jr. *America and the Mediterranean World, 1776–1882*. Princeton, N.J.: Princeton University Press, 1969.

Fogdall, Soren. *Danish-American Diplomacy, 1776–1920*. Iowa City: University of Iowa Press, 1922.

Goebel, Julius. *The Struggle for the Falkland Islands: A Study in Legal and Diplomatic History*. New Haven, Conn.: Yale University Press, 1927.

Gregory, Frances. *Nathan Appleton: Merchant and Entrepreneur, 1779–1861*. Charlottesville: University of Virginia Press, 1975.

Hatcher, William. *Edward Livingston: Jeffersonian Republican and Jacksonian Democrat*. University, La.: Louisiana State University Press, 1940.

Hidy, Muriel. *George Peabody: Merchant and Financier, 1829–1854*. New York: Arno Press, 1978.

Hill, Lawrence. *Diplomatic Relations between the United States and Brazil*. Durham, N.C.: Duke University Press, 1932.

Hunt, Freeman. *The Lives of American Merchants*. 2 vols. New York, 1857.

Hunt, Gaillard. *The Department of State of the United States*. New Haven, Conn.: Yale University Press, 1914.

Jensen, Merrill. *The New Nation*. New York: Knopf, 1965.

Johnson, E. R., et al. *The History of the Domestic and Foreign Commerce of the United States*. 2 vols. Washington, D.C.: Carnegie Institute, 1915.

Johnson, Gerald. *Randolph of Roanoke: A Political Fantastic*. New York: Minton, Balch, 1929.

Jones, Chester. *The Consular Service of the United States*. Philadelphia: University of Pennsylvania Press, 1906.

Jordan, Weymouth. *George Washington Campbell of Tennessee: Western Statesman*. Tallahassee: Florida State University Press, 1955.

Jordan, Wilfred, ed. *The Colonial and Revolutionary Families of Pennsylvania*. New York: Lewis Historical Publishing, 1935.

Kent, Frank R. *The Story of Alexander Brown and Sons*. Baltimore, 1925.

Klein, Philip. *President James Buchanan*. University Park: Pennsylvania State University Press, 1962.

Langley, Lester. *The Cuban Policy of the United States*. New York: Wiley, 1968.

Latner, Richard. *The Presidency of Andrew Jackson: White House Politics, 1829–1837*. Athens: University of Georgia Press, 1979.

Levi, Leone. *History of British Commerce, 1763–1870*. London: John Murray, 1872.

Logan, Rayford. *The Diplomatic Relations of the United States and Haiti, 1776–1891*. Chapel Hill: University of North Carolina Press, 1941.

Long, David F. *Nothing Too Daring: A Biography of Commodore David Porter, 1780–1843*. Annapolis, Md.: U.S. Naval Institute, 1970.

Lucey, William. *Edward Kavanagh: Catholic Statesman Diplomat from Maine, 1795–1844*. Francestown, N.H.: Marshall Jones, 1946.

McLemore, Richard. *Franco-American Diplomatic Relations, 1816–1836*. Baton Rouge: Louisiana State University Press, 1941.

Manchester, Alan. *British Preeminence in Brazil*. Chapel Hill: University of North Carolina Press, 1933.

Martin, Robert. *British Relations with the Chinese Empire in 1832: A Comparative Statement of the English and American Trade with India and Canton*. London: Parbury, Allen, 1832.

May, Ernest. *The Making of the Monroe Doctrine*. Cambridge, Mass.: Harvard University Press, 1975.

Montague, Ludwell. *Haiti and the United States, 1714–1938*. New York: Russell and Russell, 1966.

Munroe, John A. *Louis McLane: Federalist and Jacksonian*. New Brunswick, N.J.: Rutgers University Press, 1973.

Niven, John. *Martin Van Buren: The Romantic Age of American Politics*. New York: Oxford University Press, 1983.

Pancake, John. *Samuel Smith and the Politics of Business, 1752–1839*. University: University of Alabama Press, 1972.

Parks, E. T. *Colombia and the United States*. Durham, N.C.: Duke University Press, 1935.

Parton, Dorothy. *The Diplomatic Career of Joel Robert Poinsett*. Washington, D.C.: Catholic University Press, 1934.

Parton, James. *The Life of Andrew Jackson*. 3 vols. New York: Mason Brothers, 1861.

Paullin, Charles O. *The Diplomatic Negotiations of American Naval Officers, 1778–1883*. Baltimore, Md.: Johns Hopkins University Press, 1912.

Perrotta, Paul C. *The Claims of the United States against the Kingdom of the Naples*. Washington, D.C.: Catholic University Press, 1926.

Pessen, Edward. *Jacksonian America: Personality and Politics*. Homewood, Ill.: Dorsey Press, 1968; rev. ed., 1978.

Peterson, Harold F. *Argentina and the United States, 1810–1960*. New York: State University of New York Press, 1964.

Phillips, James. *Salem and the Indies*. Boston: Houghton Mifflin, 1947.

Reeves, Jesse S. *American Diplomacy under Tyler and Polk*. Baltimore, Md.: Johns Hopkins University Press, 1907.

Remini, Robert. *Andrew Jackson and the Course of American Empire*. New York: Harper and Row, 1977.

———. *Andrew Jackson and the Course of American Freedom*. New York: Harper and Row, 1981.

———. *Andrew Jackson and the Course of American Democracy*. New York: Harper and Row, 1984.

———. *The Election of Andrew Jackson*. Philadelphia: Lippincott, 1963.

Rippy, J. Fred. *British Investments in Latin America, 1822–1949*. Minneapolis: University of Minnesota Press, 1959.

———. *Joel R. Poinsett: Versatile American*. Durham, N.C.: Duke University Press, 1935.

———. *Rivalry of the United States and Great Britain over Latin America, 1808–1830*. Baltimore, Md.: Johns Hopkins University Press, 1929.

Ritter, Abraham. *Philadelphia and Her Merchants*. Philadelphia: 1860.

Rives, George. *The United States and Mexico, 1821–1848*. New York: Scribner, 1913.

Rodriguez, Mario. *A Palmerstonian Diplomat in Central America: Frederick Chatfield*. Tucson: University of Arizona Press, 1964.

Rogin, Michael. *Fathers and Children: Andrew Jackson and the Subjugation of the American Indian*. New York: Knopf, 1975.

Rossiter, Clinton. *The American Presidency*. New York: Harcourt, Brace, 1956.

Rutter, Frank. *South American Trade of Baltimore*. Baltimore, Md.: Johns Hopkins University Press, 1897.

Scharf, James T. *History of Baltimore*. 2 vols. Philadelphia: 1881.

Scharf, James T., and T. Westcott. *History of Philadelphia*. 3 vols. Philadelphia, 1884.

Schouler, James. *A History of the United States of America*. New York, 1913.

Seaburg, Carl, and Stanley Paterson. *Merchant Prince of Boston: Colonel T. H. Perkins, 1764–1854*. Cambridge, Mass.: Harvard University Press, 1971.

Smith, E. B. *Francis Preston Blair*. New York: Free Press, 1980.

Smith, Justin. *The Annexation of Texas*. Reprint. New York: AMS Press, 1911.

Soulsby, Hugh. *The Right of Search and the Slave Trade in Anglo-American Relations, 1814–1862*. Johns Hopkins University Studies, ser. 11, no. 2. Baltimore, Md.: Johns Hopkins University, 1933.

Stuart, Graham. *American Diplomatic and Consular Practice*. New York: Appleton-Century-Crofts, 1952.

———. *The Department of State: A History of Its Organization, Procedures and Personnel*. New York: Macmillan, 1949.

Sumner, William G. *Andrew Jackson*. Boston, 1882.

Tansill, Charles C. *The United States and Santo Domingo, 1798–1873*. Baltimore, Md.: Johns Hopkins University Press, 1938.

Thomas, Benjamin P. *Russo-American Relations, 1815–1867*. Baltimore: Johns Hopkins University Press, 1930.

Van Deusen, Glyndon. *The Life of Henry Clay*. Boston: Little, Brown, 1937.

Varg, Paul. *United States Foreign Relations, 1820–1860*. East Lansing: Michigan State University Press, 1979.

Von Holst, Herman. *The Constitutional and Political History of the United States*. 8 vols. Chicago, 1876–92.

Walker, Willis. *Franco-American Commercial Relations*. Fort Hays, Kan., 1928.

Wayland, Francis. *Andrew Stevenson: Democrat and Diplomat*. Philadelphia: University of Pennsylvania Press, 1949.

Whitaker, Arthur P. *The United States and the Southern Cone: Argentina, Uruguay and Chile*. Cambridge, Mass.: Harvard University Press, 1976.

Wildes, H. E. *Lonely Midas: The Story of Stephen Girard*. New York, 1943.

Williams, Mary W. *Anglo-American Isthmian Diplomacy, 1815–1915*. New York: Russell and Russell, 1914.

Willson, Beckles. *America's Ambassadors to England (1785–1929)*. New York: Frederick Stokes, 1929.

Wright, L. C. *United States Policy Towards Egypt, 1830–1914*. New York: Exposition Press, 1969.

Wriston, Henry. *Executive Agents in American Foreign Relations*. Baltimore, Md., 1929.

Articles

Barker, E. C. "President Jackson and the Texas Revolution." *American Historical Review* 12 (1907): 788–809.

———. "The United States and Mexico, 1835–1837." *Mississippi Valley Historical Review* 1 (1914): 3–30.

Bauer, Kinley J. "The United States Navy and Texas Independence: A Study in Jacksonian Integrity." *Military Affairs* 34 (1970): 44–48.

Baylen, Joseph. "James Buchanan's 'Calm of Despotism.'" *Pennsylvania Magazine of History and Biography* 77 (1953): 294–310.

Belohlavek, John M. "Andrew Jackson and the Malaysian Pirates: A Question of Diplomacy and Politics." *Tennessee Historical Quarterly* 36 (1977): 19–29.

———. "Let the Eagle Soar!: Democratic Constraints upon the Foreign Policy of Andrew Jackson." *Presidential Studies Quarterly* 10 (1980): 36–50.

———. "The Philadelphian and the Canal: The Charles Biddle Mission to Panama, 1835–1836." *Pennsylvania Magazine of History and Biography* 104 (1980): 450–61.

Carosso, V., and L. Leder, eds. "Edward Livingston and Jacksonian Diplomacy." *Louisiana History* 7 (1966): 241–48.

Davis, David B. "Some Themes of Counter Subversion: An Analysis of Anti-Masonic, Anti-Catholic and Anti-Mormon Literature." *Mississippi Valley Historical Review* 47 (1960): 205–24.

Downs, Jacques. "American Merchants and the China Opium Trade, 1800–1840." *Business History Review* 42 (1968): 418–42.

———. "Fair Game: Exploitative Role Myths and the American Opium Trade." *Pacific Historical Review* 41 (1972): 133–49.

Garrison, George. "The First Stage of the Movement for the Annexation of Texas." *American Historical Review* 10 (1904): 72–96.

Gibson, Joe. "A. Butler: What a Scamp!" *Journal of the West* 11 (1972): 235–47.

Klafter, Craig Evan. "United States Involvement in the Falklands Islands Crisis of 1831–33," *Journal of the Early Republic* (Winter, 1984).

Latner, Richard B. "A New Look at Jacksonian Politics." *Journal of American History* 61 (1975): 943–70.

Livermore, Seward W. "Early Commercial and Consular Relations with the East Indies." *Pacific Historical Review* 15 (1946): 31–58.

Long, David. "Martial Thunder: The First Official American Armed Intervention in Asia." *Pacific Historical Review* 42 (1973): 143–63.

Longaker, Richard P. "Was Jackson's Kitchen Cabinet a Cabinet?" *Mississippi Valley Historical Review* 44 (1957): 94–108.

Lord, Donald C. "Missionaries, Thai and Diplomats." *Pacific Historical Review* 35 (1966): 413–32.

McLemore, Richard C. "The French Spoliations Claims, 1816–36: A Study in Jacksonian Diplomacy." *Tennessee Historical Magazine* 2 (1932): 234–54.

McNiell, Sarah. "Andrew Jackson and Texas Affairs, 1819–36." *East Tennessee Historical Society Publications* 28 (1956): 86–101.

Marraro, Howard R. "Auguste Davezac's Mission to the Kingdom of the Two Sicilies, 1833–34." *Louisiana Historical Quarterly* 32 (1949): 791–808.

———. "John Nelson's Mission to the Kingdom of the Two Sicilies, 1831–32." *Maryland Historical Magazine* 44 (1949): 149–76.

Miller, Stuart C. "The American Traders' Image of China, 1785–1840." *Pacific Historical Review* 36 (1967): 375–97.

Reynolds, Curtis. "The Deterioration of Mexican-American Diplomatic Relations, 1833–1845." *Journal of the West* 11 (1972): 213–24.

Somit, Albert. "Andrew Jackson as Administrator." *Public Administration Review* 8 (1948): 188–96.

Stenberg, Richard. "Jackson, Anthony Butler and Texas." *Southwest Social Science Quarterly* 13 (1932): 264–87.

———. "The Texas Schemes of Jackson and Houston." *Southwest Social Science Quarterly* 15 (1934): 229–50.

———. "President Jackson and Anthony Butler." *Southwest Review* 22 (1937): 391–404.

Thomas, Robert C. "Andrew Jackson versus France: American Policy toward France, 1834–36." *Tennessee Historical Quarterly* 35 (1976): 51–64.

———. "Partisan Politics and Foreign Policy: The French Chamber of Deputies, 1834–35." *Maryland Historian* 5 (1974): 98–103.

Webster, C. K. "British Mediation between France and the United States, 1834–36." *English Historical Review* 42 (1927): 58–78.

Winston, James. "The Attitude of Newspapers of the United States towards Texas Independence." *Mississippi Valley Historical Proceedings* 8 (1914–15): 160–75.

Dissertations and Theses

Astolfi, Douglas. "Foundations of Destiny: A Foreign Policy of the Jacksonians, 1824–1837." Ph.D. dissertation, Northern Illinois University, 1972.

Cox, Henry B. "To the Victor: A History of the French Spoliations Controversy, 1793–1955." Ph.D. dissertation, George Washington University, 1967.

Dunham, Chester. "The Diplomatic Career of Christopher Hughes." Ph.D. dissertation, Ohio State University, 1968.

Ignatz, Deborah. "The Political and Diplomatic Career of William Cabell Rives." M.A. thesis, University of South Florida, 1981.

Liston, Ann. "W. C. Rives: Diplomat and Politician, 1829–1853." Ph.D. dissertation, Ohio State University, 1972.

Index